Lament

LAMENT

Studies in the Ancient Mediterranean and Beyond

Edited by
ANN SUTER

OXFORD
UNIVERSITY PRESS

2008

OXFORD
UNIVERSITY PRESS

Oxford University Press, Inc., publishes works that further
Oxford University's objective of excellence
in research, scholarship, and education.

Oxford New York
Auckland Cape Town Dar es Salaam Hong Kong Karachi
Kuala Lumpur Madrid Melbourne Mexico City Nairobi
New Delhi Shanghai Taipei Toronto

With offices in
Argentina Austria Brazil Chile Czech Republic France Greece
Guatemala Hungary Italy Japan Poland Portugal Singapore
South Korea Switzerland Thailand Turkey Ukraine Vietnam

Published by Oxford University Press, Inc.
198 Madison Avenue, New York, New York 10016

www.oup.com

Oxford is a registered trademark of Oxford University Press

Library of Congress Cataloging-in-Publication Data
Lament : studies in the ancient Mediterranean and beyond / edited by Ann Suter.
p. cm.
ISBN 978-0-19-533692-4
1. Laments—History and criticism. I. Suter, Ann, 1938–
PN1389.L36 2008
809'.93353—dc22   2007023159

1 3 5 7 9 8 6 4 2
Printed in the United States of America
on acid-free paper

For
Fenn
Gwynnevere
and
Halvor
and to the memory of the twins

ACKNOWLEDGMENTS

It is a pleasure to record here my gratitude to all of the contributors to this volume. They have been truly collegial in helping to bring this project to completion. Through them and their work I have learned so much, not only about the subjects of their chapters but also about ways of framing questions, of thinking through puzzling data, of weighing perspectives to discover possible approaches to apparent contradictions. They have made this book for me far greater than the sum of its parts. I thank them all.

Two other people also have my gratitude. First, Iñaki Pérez-Ibáñez, who has been a model of patience with my computer inexpertise and of ingenuity in putting together a very disparate manuscript. And second, Melissa Henneberry, who typed and proofed the Bibliography and the index with wonderful accuracy and cheerfulness. Many, many thanks to them both.

CONTENTS

CONTRIBUTORS

MARY R. BACHVAROVA, Assistant Professor of Classics, Classical Studies Program, Willamette University

BRENDAN BURKE, Assistant Professor of Classical Archaeology, Department of Greek and Roman Studies, University of Victoria

DOROTA DUTSCH, Assistant Professor of Classics, Department of Classics, University of California at Santa Barbara

ANDROMACHE KARANIKA, Assistant Professor of Classics, Department of Classics, University of California at Irvine

ALISON KEITH, Professor of Classics and Women's Studies, Victoria College, University of Toronto

OLGA LEVANIOUK, Assistant Professor of Classics, Department of Classics, University of Washington

RICHARD P. MARTIN, Professor of Classics, Department of Classics, Stanford University

CHRISTINE PERKELL, Associate Professor of Classics, Department of Classics, Emory University

IAN RUTHERFORD, Professor of Greek, Reading University

KAREN STEARS, Lecturer, Department of Classics, University of Edinburgh

ANN SUTER, Professor of Classical Studies, Department of Languages, University of Rhode Island

Lament

1

INTRODUCTION

A N N S U T E R

T he subject of lamentation has enjoyed considerable scholarly attention in the past two or three decades.[1] Feminists in particular have
found the subject a rewarding study, in that ritual lament was a prominent
activity for women in ancient societies. It seems to have been the one
medium in which they might have expressed themselves and their concerns
publicly and thereby have influenced a community's affairs. These studies have had several focuses: using literary and iconographic evidence,
scholars have reconstructed the likely order of funeral rituals of different
societies and the part lamentation played in them. They have analyzed the
appearances of represented lament and attitudes toward it in different
literary genres (epic, tragedy, lyric, elegy) and endeavored to understand
the social meaning of its forms and performance in these genres and if or
how that meaning might have reflected ritual lament in real life.

Most scholarly work on lament in both ancient Greek and Roman
society has used Margaret Alexiou's seminal 1974 study (rev. 2002) as the
source for basic vocabulary for discussing lamentation and for the various
forms and structures that laments took. The problems of classification of
ancient lament that she has outlined are with us still, chiefly because, as she
puts it, "the differing kinds of sources available" suggest a variety of
possibilities.[2] Still, her division of ritual lament into types based on who
or what is being lamented—the human dead, cities, and gods and heroes—
remains basic, as do our principal sources of information from which this
classification derives: literary and iconographical depictions and ethnographic comparanda, especially fieldwork in modern Greek lament.[3]

3

We have a good idea of what the ritual lament and its funeral context were, thanks to Alexiou: " 'to honour and appease the dead [and to] give expression to a wide range of conflicting emotions.' It seeks to mend the fabric which had been torn by loss, and to reconcile those close to the dead to their loss. Reconciliation may require various things, depending on the circumstances of the death: acceptance, forgiveness, vengeance."[4] We have examples from the ancient world; the several from Sumer and the Hittite Kingdom that are the subject of later chapters in this volume are for gods and heroes, however, not the human dead.[5] But we have none from Greece and Rome. Hence scholars, in building on Alexiou's work, have looked to the manifestations of ritual lament (almost always for the human dead) in iconography and literature (chiefly epic and tragedy); that is, they have studied represented lament and have used modern ethnographical and anthropological findings to interpret it. These studies have been able to reconstruct many details of the funeral ritual and the division of roles between men and women in it and to speculate profitably on the attitudes that informed the ritual.[6] Those focusing on represented laments in trage-dy have seen political events and attitudes in Athens reflected in them. For example, the several laws attempting to restrict lamentation, beginning in the sixth century B.C.E., in Athens and elsewhere in Greece, have been noted and interpreted as efforts to control women's public activity or to curb the power of aristocratic families in the developing democracy in the *polis*. The represented laments and their dramatic contexts have been seen to complement and explicate the contemporary social attitudes behind those laws, showing the close interactions between tragic drama and the *polis* on this and other issues.[7] Studies of represented lament in epic have investigated lamentation's relation with the heroic ethos of the Homeric warrior. They have sharpened our perception of social relationships among the lamenters and the dead and of the hierarchies of the society depicted in the epics.[8]

Roman ritual lament has usually been discussed as part of specifically Roman funerary practice, when it has been discussed at all.[9] Oddly, though, lament is often overlooked entirely in studies of the Roman funeral.[10] Investigations of represented lament in Roman literature and iconography, on the other hand, have assumed the universality of lament practices, using Greek sources as comparanda for Vergil and Lucan, for example.[11] And rightly so: even though the role and function of ritual lament in Roman funerals differed from those in Greek funerals, the treatment and attitudes toward represented lament in Latin literature seem to derive from representations of the Greek realities.

The conclusions of this scholarship have several things in common: that lamentation was a female-gendered activity and that men were not supposed to lament, either in literature or in real life. A lamenting woman was a powerful figure and was seen as a potential threat to the orderly functioning of the male public sphere and as undermining the heroic male code of military glory. It is argued further that in ancient Greece, efforts to control female lamentation existed in real life and grew more stringent through the fifth century B.C.E. and that the intensification of these efforts is reflected in tragedy. All these conclusions are based on the examination of representations of lamentation in literature and of attitudes toward the expression of grief generally, as seen in tragedy and a range of other texts (philosophers, orators). They have been accepted as basic to the phenomenon of lament and are now rarely challenged.

It seems time to revisit these issues, to bring together a number of essays that represent new work on lamentation, and to suggest its continued potential for fruitful study.[12] This collection seeks to do so in several ways: it reexamines what kinds of functions the term *lament* can include and expands the study of lament to other genres of literature, other cultures, and other periods in the ancient world. The studies included here reflect the variety of critical issues raised over the past twenty-five years in lament studies and, as such, provide an overview of the history of critical thinking on the subject.

The chapters in this collection fall roughly into three groups, which follow two simultaneous progressions: from more ancient to more recent and from east to west. The first group comprises two studies, one on the laments of Sumerian male *gala* priests in the women's dialect *emesal*, and the other on the role of the *taptara*-women's laments in the Hittite funeral ritual for deceased royalty. The second group covers Greek materials; one chapter discusses the Bronze Age Aegean iconographic representations of lamentation, and two others examine the final laments in the *Iliad*. Three chapters cover the Greek Classical period: one on sixth- and fifth-century B.C.E. iconographic depictions, one on the role of male lament in Greek tragedy, and one on comedy's parody of lament. A study of how the lament in Erinna's *Distaff* combines with wedding song completes the Greek materials. Last, two chapters are devoted to Roman lament: one analyzes represented lament in Lucan's *Bellum Ciuile*; the other reconstructs the role of the *nenia* and of the *praeficae* in Roman funeral ritual.

In chapter 2, Bachvarova offers a close look at the role of the *gala* priests in Sumerian ritual lament and the kind of songs they sang. *Galas* were cross-dressing priests who lamented in a woman's dialect of Sumerian, *emesal*. The function of these ritual laments went beyond the simple mourning of the human dead; they were also used to "focus the attention of the gods on human suffering and persuade them to relieve it," thereby encouraging the general prosperity of the land and its inhabitants. Other laments were apopotraic and sought to avert divine anger before it occurred. As such, both the *gala* and their laments performed a critical service to the state. Bachvarova looks at the origins of the *gala* and why feminized men were thought to be especially "effective at turning aside the gods' wrath and raising the dead." The *galas*' "transgendered behavior...enabled the breaching of the other natural barrier, that between the living and the dead" and produced a more efficacious appeal to the gods. Bachvarova compares their function with that of men who dressed as women and lamented in the tragedies of the Festival of Dionysos in Athens. She examines the themes of *gala* city laments and of ritual laments, in particular the mourning goddess/dying god motif, and compares them with several choral odes from fifth-century tragedy. She is able to trace a possible route of influence from the Sumerian evidence through the Anatolian material (Dumuzi, Cybele's *galloi*, Attis, Adonis) to Dionysiac ritual and fifth-century B.C.E. represented lament in tragedy, thus suggesting that the similarities between the Sumerian and Greek data are "more than typological."

Rutherford examines the Hittite death ritual for royalty, the *sallis wastais*, in chapter 3. He first surveys the ritual as a whole: *sallis wastais* is translated as "[i]f a great loss [or 'fault'] occurs . . . [the king] or queen becomes a god—everyone . . . begins to wail." The death of royalty was conceived as a great fault (perhaps in the cosmic structure); the rectification of this was the concomitant deification of the royal personage. A series of subrituals assured a pleasant afterlife for them. Rutherford then focuses on the episodes of ritual lamentation during the fourteen-day proceedings, with special attention to the performances of the *taptara*-women. They were specialized wailers, with at least a degree of institutional organization. Whereas sometimes individuals lamented, apart from the communal wailing at the beginning of the ritual, all group lamentation seems to have been done by the *taptara*. Sometimes their performance accompanied ritual action by others; more commonly it was in antiphonal response to lamentation by an individual (the Cup Bearer, the Old Woman), which was prompted by the destruction of a ritual object. Only one text has been preserved that can be interpreted with any confidence: on the night before the last day of the rites, the *taptara* would wail: "[W]hen you go to the meadow/do not pull the cord/May your will be done." Rutherford suggests that "pulling the cord" signifies the final separation from this world for the deceased, and "May your will be done" is an effort to mollify the dead by assuring them that their wishes will continue to be respected. In offering this communication to the dead, the *taptara* may have been acting as scapegoats, absorbing the anger of the deceased and deflecting it from the community as a whole.

Next, Burke offers an overview of iconographic representations of lamentation and burial customs in the Bronze Age Aegean. He points out that most scholarship on this subject "look[s] back at the Aegean Bronze Age through a philological lens" and interprets the evidence "based on [an] understanding of later Greek practice." He questions the accuracy of this approach and chooses instead to focus on what the contemporary evidence itself tells us. He examines in particular the Cycladic folded-arm figurines from the Early Bronze Age (ca. 2500 B.C.E.), the Tanagra larnakes from Boeotia (ca. 1200 B.C.E.), the painted sarcophagus from Ayia Triada on Crete (1370–1360 B.C.E.), and the so-called Warrior Vase from Mycenae (1150 B.C.E.). The Cycladic figurines are the earliest Greek representation of lament that we have, exhibiting painted details with "red and blue pigment, possible indicating . . . tears" or perhaps blood from scratches. Burke discusses the artistic relationship between the Tanagra larnakes and the funerary art of the Minoans and highlights the iconographic differences in Minoan and Mycenaean funerary art. The Tanagra material shows lamenting women in procession with arms raised and women preparing the *prothesis*. Males appear in hunting scenes, which Burke argues is part of the burial ritual. He then moves to the Ayia Triada sarcophagus and examines the gestures and activities of its figures, which he finds "perhaps comparable to those described in the contemporary Hittite . . . [r]itual." Once again, both males and females are in procession. He sees the women as lamenting, but with "controlled dignity" and without the raised-arm pose or wild gestures that became common in later times. The Warrior Vase from Mycenae, long argued to represent a woman waving good-bye to a group of soldiers marching to battle, is reinterpreted as a scene of lamentation. Burke bases this contention on the depositional context of the vase in a Mycenaean cemetery. The woman mourns, the men engage in funeral games, and both the mourning and the games are "controlled ritual actions associated with burial."

Perkell, in chapter 5, reads the three laments of *Iliad* 24 as they function poetically to shape the *Iliad*'s closure, both formally and ideologically. She notes that many features of these laments give them exceptional textual authority. Among these are their emphatic—because they are closural—position, their ritual status, their collocation, and their exceptional length. Through these features, the poet gives the laments great importance—greater than that of other laments in the poem, which are not for the whole people (internal audience) and not so emphatically placed (for the external audience). Thus the external audience is invited to reflect on the poet's purposes in so structuring the poem as to conclude with these particular laments, specifically, for Hektor. In the first instance, then, these laments for Hektor contribute to creating the affirmative closure for which the *Iliad* is known. On the other hand, close reading of the laments—the final memory of Hektor in the *Iliad*—reveals a suggestive disparity between Hektor's own wishes for heroic memorialization and the women's words in praise of him. Perkell argues that this disparity functions to put into question the value of heroic death for which Hektor gave his life. Thus, whereas other scholars have argued that the *Iliad* puts heroic ideology into question through the utterances and actions of Achilles, Perkell argues that these particular laments, too, in their voicing of moral values alternative to Hektor's heroic ambitions, participate importantly in the poem's pervasive if quiet challenge to epic's conventional values. The poet has combined the emotive power and moral authority of ritual lament with the poetic importance of closure to pose a subtle challenge to the dominant ideology of heroic epic. Thus Perkell, comparing other epic closures that use lamentation (Lucan's *Bellum Civile* [see Keith, this volume], and *Beowulf*), hypothesizes that the ultimate function of laments within any given epic poem may be seen to reflect not only an essential nature of lament but also, above all, the poet's choices.

In chapter 6 Martin also studies Helen's lament in the *Iliad*, using an anthropological approach rather than Perkell's strictly literary one; their results are compatible, even overlapping. Rather than fitting her lamentation into the context of the represented laments in the *Iliad*, Martin puts Helen's into the context of all her speeches in the poem. He finds that, although they are not specifically designated as *goos* or *thrênos*, they often "contain the strategies and phrases of that genre," to the point where an ancient audience would have recognized her as a mourner from her diction even before she begins her lament for Hektor. She is, in short, the prototypical lament figure.[13] Martin adduces carefully chosen comparanda from the living tradition of lament in modern Greece to explicate several of Helen's speeches that have long puzzled commentators. These explications depend on two arguments: first, that Homeric lament is a basically choral form and that in Helen's use of the genre's poetic devices, she performs as both soloist and chorus; and second, that Homeric diction characterizes her as a "metonym" for lament, "the original authorizing [figure] that lies behind *all* poetry of commemoration." This in turn suggests a reason for Helen's performance as the climactic one of the *Iliad*: "[S]he is the female Muse who counterbalances the Muse invoked at the poem's beginning.... [S]he is the true inspiration for the Trojan War—and thus also for the stories told about it." Martin uses these insights to clarify passages in medieval and modern Irish poetry. Admitting the basically choral nature of lament, we can see "traces of a dramatized, interlocutory style in Irish lament," usually thought to be performed by individuals as individuals. He suggests, for instance, that a detail of the *Scéla Muicce Meic Dathó* (ca. 800 C.E.) indicates the establishment of a continuing choral institution with the verbal resonances of lament, commemorating a victory won over the chorus' people. In turn, the non-Homeric myths of Helen—that her *eidolon* only went to Troy, while she herself was in Egypt—may be better understood "by reference to Irish folklore on lamenters," which tells of visions of lamenters at the site of coming deaths.

Stears's essay, reproduced here as chapter 7, was first published in 1998. It is worth reprinting, not only for basic facts of the role of ritual lament in Greek death rites but also for its iconographic evidence, often underused by philologists. Stears presents a detailed summary of the Archaic/Classical Athenian funeral ritual and describes the activities performed by women at the time of death, at the funeral, and throughout the mourning period. She argues against accounts that see women's polluted condition in death ritual as reinforcement of a perceived low social status. Rather, the containment of ritual pollution served as a means for the construction and display of female power in both the domestic and the political arenas. She considers the roles of men and women in funeral rituals, within both the *oikos* and the *polis*, noting the reification and restatement of the ideology of male/public, female/private. This ideology was not a social reality, she argues, and the boundary between the two spheres, while important, was fluid. She then considers the cross-cultural reality that women are perceived as more emotional and lacking in self-control than men. In Athens, women may have felt obliged to express their emotion (and men obligated to restrain theirs). But the expression of grief in a ritual lament was the "correct" behavior for women and was ritually necessary irrespective of the personal feelings or personality of the lamenter. It was as well an essential factor in constructing the public face of the household, the power of the family of the deceased, and the right to claim a part of the estate of the deceased. As such, it empowered the women within their *oikos* and, to an extent, with the *polis* also.

In my chapter I undertake to "redress the imbalance in the focus of current scholarship" on the gendering of represented lament in fifth-century B.C.E. Greek tragedy, where the pervasive assumption has been that because ritual lament was a female activity in real life, it was a female activity in tragedy. Using guidelines developed from a careful analysis of meters and stylistic features of represented lament passages in tragedy, I show that, if we had only the evidence of tragedy to inform us, we would not see lament as a particularly gendered genre. I discuss represented lament in numerous plays, arguing that earlier claims—of criticism of male lamentation or of the feminization of males because they lament—are rarely justified. Rather, most males lament freely, and legitimately, and in so doing often achieve for themselves a restoration of moral authority lost earlier in the drama and a reintegration into their society. Finally, I discuss what it may be that legitimizes a male lamenting in tragedy—not the male in woman's dress lamenting in the character of a female but a male lamenting in a male role. Using psychological and religious discussions of this issue, I suggest that male lament has been an integral part of tragedy from its origins (partly) in Dionysiac ritual and hero cult, which included male lamentation for the god or the dead hero. My arguments complement those of Bachvarova on the origins and function of the gendering of lament. I suggest that it may be that the scorn felt for a lamenting male in real life began developing only in the fifth century. But even Plato, closely read, seems not to be talking about *ritual* lamentation in his warning against enjoying emotion in drama but, rather, is only expressing his personal dislike of "unmasculine" expressions of grief.

In chapter 9, Karanika considers a hitherto unexamined use of lament in classical drama: its parody in fifth-century B.C.E. comedy. Focusing on Aristophanes' *Thesmophoriazusae*, she shows how he uses the forms of ritual lament as part of his parodies of the *Telephus*, the *Helen*, and the *Andromeda*. These parodies are part of what has become known as the competition between comedy and tragedy. Karanika shows how the use of lament, a frequent and telling tool for complaint and criticism in tragedy, fits into this competition and functions in comedy too as political commentary in a play sometimes described as "the least politically engaged of all extant comedies." She traces the presence of lament in the myth and rites of the Thesmophoria itself and their formative influence on the action of the play, putting the action into a (now) doubly ritual context. The parodies of lament in the play renegotiate the boundaries both of comedy's license and of tragedy's politics and thus the boundary between comedy and tragedy themselves.

Levaniouk argues in chapter 10 that Erinna's *Distaff*, long recognized as a (represented) lament, is not only that but also a poem that is "so distinctly full of wedding diction as to constitute a wedding song for the dead Baukis." The genre of the *Distaff* is thus double. Baukis herself, and perhaps Erinna too, is an "embodiment both of this genre" and of the occasion on which it was sung, a wedding usurped by death. Levaniouk shows how wedding diction informs the poem, even those parts (the description of the "torty-tortoise" game) that seem to be no more than recollections of everyday life. Comparisons of the poem's scenes, diction, and imagery with the Nausikaa episode from *Odyssey* 6 and with Iphigeneia's arrival in Aulis as the (supposed) bride of Achilles in Euripides' play help to clarify and confirm the situation in the *Distaff* as a prenuptial one. Levaniouk ends her discussion with an analysis of song and dialect in the *Distaff*. The poem emerges as a "stylized representation of a wedding song for the untimely dead," which uses elements from both epic and popular song. Its dialect is a mixture of Doric with some Aeolic (specifically Lesbian) forms and a few Ionic forms taken from epic (not from any Ionic vernacular). Levaniouk traces antecedents to this dialect in choral lyric in Doric/Aeolic, and in non-epic hexameter poetry. The mixture is typical of "the [poetry] of small occasional genres," such as *hymeneia* and *thrênoi*. Erinna seems to be imitating this kind of hexameter poetry in her wedding lament.

Then, Keith turns her attention to the represented lament in Lucan's *Bellum Ciuile*. She considers its thematic functions in the poem, intertextual relationships with lament as depicted in Vergil's *Aeneid* and other epic, the extent to which lament is characterized as a gendered or class-marked genre, and how Lucan's represented lament reflects Roman attitudes. She finds "that Lucan plays on his audience's expectation of lamentation as a female genre, and, more specifically, a wifely obligation," but notes also that there is an equal obligation "owed the *patronus* by his social inferiors" of both sexes. She examines the interplay of the functions of public and private lament in the poem: public and private lamentation is confounded in the people's initial reactions to the beginning of the civil war. The focus of the narrative shifts, and Cornelia's early speeches rehearse her later full lament for Pompey, whose death will signal the death of the Republic, and the laments for whom will once again combine private and public. The actual funeral rites for Pompey are conducted by his quaestor Cordus, who buries and laments his commanding officer; they are repeated later by Cornelia. Both mourn the dead Pompey in "spontaneous private lamentation." This is then sharply contrasted by Lucan with Cato's eulogy, which follows Cornelia's performance. Keith finds this is a conventional public *laudatio*, with the added call to Pompey's soldiers to pursue the war against Caesar. When the soldiers initially rebel at this, Cato appropriates Cornelia's revenge themes into his address. He "confers political legitimacy on the personal pleas for vengeance" she has expressed, thus making the private public. In Keith's interpretation, Lucan "affirms the power of women's lamentation in ancient Rome."

Finally, in chapter 12 Dutsch sets as her goal the assembling of the scattered secondary evidence regarding the Roman *nenia* and the reconstruction of the rules of the genre as well as its cultural connotations. In the earliest times for which we have evidence ("before the Punic War"), the *nenia* seems to have been an incantation of mourning following a eulogy to the deceased. It was performed by *praeficae*, professional female mourners, who took part in the funeral procession, performing the chant and directing the onlookers in the particulars of mourning. The *praeficae* marched directly in front of the coffin with the impersonators of the dead members of the deceased's clan, urging the deceased (who were imagined to hear the dirge) to accept their new status and proceed quietly to their new position among the ancestors. *Praeficae* and their *neniae* were thus associated spatially in the procession with the afterlife (the living relatives of the deceased walked behind the bier); their shrieks and self-mutilation produced blood and milk, which were thought of as nourishment for the dead. Dutsch then reconstructs the form of the *nenia*, based on the represented lament for Claudius in Seneca's *Apocolocyntosis* and Catullus's mock dirge for Lesbia's *passer*. Although they are parodies, the "structural and stylistic features of the two poems fit the ritual function and the performance context" Dutsch has elaborated for a ritual *nenia*. Her investigation of the *nenia*'s cultural meanings shows it to be a discourse used in several kinds of social performance in addition to the funeral context: healing, snake charming, and children's games, all concerned with boundary crossing and easing transitions.

Many of the essays in this collection, building on previous scholarship, bring new evidence to bear on the old questions of the gendering of ritual and reenacted lament, both Greek and Roman, and offer a welcome nuancing of our understanding of the gendered roles in lament, which are more complex than previously described. Men lament as much as women in tragedy, for example (Suter); it is sometimes a person's social or political position rather than gender that prescribes what behavior or attitude toward lamentation he or she takes (Keith), or his or her place within the family group. There is also evidence that men lamented in real life in the Mycenaean Age (Burke) and in the Archaic Age (Stears, Suter). Recognizing and maintaining the distinction between ritual lament and reenacted lament, on the one hand, and the general "expression of grief," on the other (see n. 1), is perhaps the key to understanding this male behavior (Suter, Stears). The suggestion that men took over female lament in Greek tragedy finds a cross-cultural comparandum in Bachvarova's essay, where it is shown how the *gala* priests of Sumer took over ritual lament there, often using the female language *emesal*. The efficacy of the ritual lament was felt to be enhanced by a male performer, but the use of the female *emesal* was deemed necessary. In Athenian tragedy also, men dressed as females and lamented. They also lamented in the character of males, and evidence exists to suggest that part of the origin of male lament in Greek tragedy was in male lament in real life (Suter).

Other essays make clear the various functions of lamentation in literary contexts. Some authors make use of modern Greek ethnographic studies, which provide useful comparanda for understanding ancient (especially Greek) lament (Martin, Suter, Karanika, Levaniouk). Others have chosen to treat ancient literary laments predominantly as literature; they study lament as a literary device, integral to the structure and purpose of the literary work (Perkell, Levaniouk, Keith). In so doing, they all expand and deepen our understanding of the different functions and applications that lamentation seems to have had in the ancient world, presumably in ritual lament as well as in its reflection in literature: as confessional (Suter), as productive of civic order (Bachvarova, Rutherford, Suter), as propitiatory to the gods (Bachvarova, Rutherford), for example, or in relation to other social contexts such as marriage (Levaniouk) or to social and literary criticism (Perkell, Karanika). This way of distinguishing among types of lament is not based on who or what is lamented but, rather, on the various functions of the lament. This in effect offers an additional way of categorizing lamentation that reckons its connection to various social contexts rather than its strictly religious function in the funeral ritual. These new lamentation types come principally from the identification of represented laments in different genres of poetic literature. One literary genre, underrepresented in the present collection, in which the study of lament could profitably be pursued is that of lyric poetry. Levaniouk's essay focuses on the Hellenistic period, but earlier lyric also offers rich possibilities. For example, Lardinois has touched on the wedding lament in Sappho's poetry, but more can surely be done here.[14]

The collection also enlarges the study of lamentation to cultures outside the world of Greece and Rome. It seems to have been universal in the ancient world, and as such, it is an excellent touchstone for the comparative study of attitudes toward death and the afterlife, human relations to the divine, views of the cosmos, and the constitution of the fabric of society in different times and places. This collection includes studies of lamentation in iconography from the Aegean Bronze Age as well as from Greece in the fifth and sixth centuries B.C.E. It goes back to the Sumerians and the Hittites, through the Greeks, and ends with the Romans, to see how different cultures organized the ritual expression of grief at the loss of life. These cross-cultural comparanda offer interesting views on what is culture specific and what is shared in the phenomenon of lament. Attitudes toward the gods differed markedly; for example, Rutherford shows how the Hittite *sallis wastais* ritual for dead royalty was in part a means of deification of the dead.[15] The Sumerian city laments discussed by Bachvarova are formulated as hymns to the god of the destroyed city that lament the god's abandonment of the city's population and beg his return.

Compare the city lament for Troy in Euripides' *Trojan Women* (1272–1332), where Hekabe, in two (only) brief remarks, is angry at the gods for their abandonment of her city. Or contrast the characterization of the professional mourners in Roman funerals as babblers of insincere praise and feelings, in part perhaps because they did not feel the real pain of loss (Dutsch), with the attitude toward the professional singers of *thrênoi* in Greek ritual, who seem to have been (and still are; see Martin) highly respected. Several chapters (Bachvarova, Rutherford, Stears, Dutsch) note the distinction between lament types performed by professionals and those sung by members of the deceased's family. An interesting line of investigation would be why, on what basis, this distinction was made: Are the words of lamentation more or less effective for being sung by professionals or family members, and why?[16]

Women's prominent role in ritual lamentation seems, on the other hand, to be a constant, whether as a mysterious power to be co-opted by men (Bachvarova, Suter) or as an unquestioned part of funeral ritual (Rutherford, Martin, Stears, Perkell, Dutsch), with noteworthy cross-cultural parallels (e.g., between the Hittite *taptara* and the Roman *praeficae*). The chapters on pre-Classical lament suggest the background and development of some aspects of later Greek and Roman practices (Burke): how men came to dress as women to lament in Greek drama, for example, or the function of lamentation in calming the anger of the deceased. Both Hittite (Rutherford) and Roman (Dutsch) ritual conceived of the lamenters as nurses, indicating a shared view of death as a kind of rebirth. The Greek cry *ololugê*, sounded at the birth of a child and at the discovery of a death, suggests a similar equivalence. Burke notes aspects of funeral practices in the Aegean Bronze Age that seem not to have survived into the Archaic and Classical periods. These early chapters also make clear that the current techniques for identifying occurrences of represented lament in epic and tragedy, though useful for laments for the human dead, are constrained in ways that ignore the inherited influence of lament forms from earlier Aegean Bronze Age and Near Eastern societies. Knowing the Near Eastern background enables us to understand aspects of Greek (especially) epic and tragedy as lamentation; we are now able to see city laments and laments for gods and heroes as well in tragic drama and in Greek prayer in general (Bachvarova). Both Martin and Perkell seem to feel in the *Iliad*'s represented laments the presence of inherited traditions that Homer is manipulating but to which we have no access. Bachvarova and Rutherford offer possible entries into these traditions; the *Iliad* is, after all, in part the tale of the destruction of a city, abandoned by its gods. This is not immediately obvious, perhaps, for our poet tells the story mostly from the perspective of the destroyers. But from the perspective of the population of the destroyed city, with whose laments the poem ends, we can look toward the East and its traditions for possible antecedents.

Studies of ancient lament until now have typically seen it as a political and social phenomenon; very seldom has its religious nature been investigated since Alexiou's basic study. Neither is it often (if ever) discussed at any length in studies of the role of women in ancient Greek ritual practice, although it was clearly a part of funeral ritual and therefore a religious act.[17] It is not studied as a ritual act—at least in scholarship on Greek lament—perhaps because it consists of more than the simple repetition of fixed words and actions. Rather, it permits—even requires—ad hoc invention on the part of the lamenter. The religio-magical nature of lament, while not the focus, is at least part of some of the essays in this collection (Bachvarova, Rutherford, Dutsch). Still, modern comparanda, which discuss lament's "similarities with spirit possession," suggest that more work could be done in this area.[18]

Another interesting way to build on the findings of this collection would be to pursue the cross-cultural study of lament. Bachvarova and Martin offer excellent examples of the fruitfulness of this approach. The similarities noted between the Hittite and the Roman rituals are tantalizing and beg for further investigation. Burke's suggestion that some depictions of rituals on Mycenaean larnakes panels seem almost like illustrations of the *sallis wastais* funeral ritual for Hittite royalty is also provocative. Work on other Near Eastern lament traditions could be brought into relation with the Greek and Roman materials. One way to do this has already been suggested: the usefulness of Near Eastern lament models for understanding what Homer is doing in the laments in the *Iliad*. Bachvarova shows that some of the literary genre classifications developed by Plato and Aristotle are not necessarily traditional to Greek practice. Further work in this direction would clarify the evolution of Greek efforts to communicate with the divine. Her essay and mine suggest also that more work on city laments in tragedy might prove fruitful, both in itself and for what it might imply retrospectively about the lack of (proleptic) city lament in the *Iliad*.

Last, the peculiarity of represented lament in Roman literature following Greek models is another question begging attention. Dutsch's suggestion that Roman ritual lament may have been considered "unworthy of portrayal in epic"[19] is startling and thought provoking. Stears's and Dutsch's essays, although this is not the point of their investigations, show the dissimilarities in the actual funeral ritual and the part lament played in it for the Greeks and Romans.[20] This too would be useful to set out explicitly. In the meantime, we hope that these essays will provoke interest and further investigation in this remarkable pancultural phenomenon.

NOTES

1. In an effort to be as precise as possible in terminology, I distinguish the following concepts: (1) "ritual lament" specifically from funeral ritual in general; (2) the ritual expression of grief (whether for the human dead, cities, or gods and heroes) in a "ritual lament" from the expression of grief because someone is sad and

gives way to emotion; and (3) how "ritual lament" is *re-presented* iconographically or *reenacted* in literature (= "represented lament") from how it is *described*, that is, with what vocabulary and imagery. All of these are distinguished from generalized, nonritual grief. When the simple term *lamentation* is used it refers to the general activity, whether in literature, iconography, or real life. Unfortunately, it was not feasible to follow this terminology in all the chapters, but the distinctions are maintained and I hope are clear in context.

2. Alexiou [1974] 2002, 3 and chs. 4–6.

3. Ibid., 128.

4. Suter 2003, 11, quoting Alexiou [1974] 2002, 55. Alexiou disclaims any intention of "reconstruct[ing]...from the laments of ancient tragedy how ordinary people lamented their dead in classical Athens." Rather, she "indicate[s] those features which belong to a common tradition" ([1974] 2002, xii). Nonetheless, she has given us our basic understanding of it.

5. In point of fact, the Hittite *sallis wastais* ritual was for the death of royalty, who were deified as a result of the ritual.

6. Based on Alexiou [1974] 2002, ch. 1. One of the best of those utilizing iconographic evidence is Stears 1998 (reprinted in this volume); see Stears, this volume, for bibliography.

7. See Foley 2001; Holst-Warhaft 1992; McClure 1999; Suter 2003; Zeitlin 1996.

8. See Derderian 2001; Dué 2002; Holst-Warhaft 1992; Monsacré 1984; Murnaghan 1999; Pantelia 2002.

9. See Corbeill 2004; Kierdorf 1980; Latte 1960; Pagán 2000; Toynbee 1971. Richlin 2001 is a welcome exception.

10. Ochs (1993) does not mention lament, and Flower (1996), although she offers a thorough discussion of the *laudatio*, again, says nothing about lament.

11. See Dietrich 1999; Fantham 1999; Lovatt 1999; Nugent 1992; Perkell 1997; Wiltshire 1989.

12. The collection includes two reprints: one (Stears 1998) provides iconographic background on sixth- and fifth-century B.C.E. ritual lament; the other (Martin 2003) is a cross-cultural study that may not be known to most classicists.

13. Martin's conclusions on the Iliadic Helen are cited in Ebbott 1999. Here are the full arguments.

14. Lardinois 2001, 80–88.

15. This would be comparable to the Greek laments for heroes; see Alexiou [1974] 2002, 61–62.

16. There are interesting comparanda in modern Greek attitudes: "[T]here were never paid mourners in Inner Mani.... *Tears shed without a common history of reciprocity* [between mourner and mourned] *are matter out of place*" (Seremetakis 1991, 216; emphasis in original). Elsewhere in modern Greece, the "pain" that makes a piece of poetry a "true lament" can be felt by kin or non-kin (Caraveli 1986, 172, passim). See also Alexiou [1974] 2002, 10, 40–41.

17. In a recent comprehensive work on women in Greek religion by Barbara Goff (2004, 31–35), for example, it gets five pages, with the usual political focus.

18. Caraveli 1986, 177.

19. Personal communication with the author.

20. See also Richlin 2001 for some examples of the differences.

16

BIBLIOGRAPHY

Alexiou, Margaret. [1974] 2002. *The Ritual Lament in Greek Tradition*. Rev. D. Yatromanolakis and P. Roilos. Cambridge. (Originally published in Lanham, Md.)

Caraveli, Anna. 1986. The Bitter Wounding: The Lament as Social Protest in Rural Greece. In *Gender and Power in Rural Greece*, ed. Jill Dubisch, 169–194. Princeton, N.J.

Corbeill, Anthony. 2004. *Nature Embodied: Gesture in Ancient Rome*. Princeton, N.J.

Derderian, Katharine. 2001. *Leaving Words to Remember: Greek Mourning and the Advent of Literacy*. Leiden.

Dietrich, J. S. 1999. *Thebaid*'s Feminine Ending. *Ramus* 28: 40–52.

Dué, Casey. 2002. *Homeric Variations on a Lament by Briseis*. Lanham, Md.

Ebbott, Mary. 1999. The Wrath of Helen: Self-Blame and Nemesis in the *Iliad*. In *Nine Essays on Homer*, ed. M. Carlisle and O. Levaniouk, 3–20. Lanham, Md.

Fantham, R. E. 1999. The Role of Lament in the Growth and Eclipse of Roman Epic. In *Epic Traditions in the Contemporary World*, ed. M. Beissinger, J. Tylus, and S. Wofford, 221–235. Berkeley.

Flower, H. I. 1996. *Ancestor Masks and Aristocratic Power in Roman Culture*. Oxford.

Foley, Helene P. 2001. *Female Acts in Greek Tragedy*. Princeton, N.J.

Goff, Barbara. 2004. *Citizen Bacchae: Women's Ritual Practice in Ancient Greece*. Berkeley.

Greene, E. 1995. The Catullan Ego: Fragmentation and the Erotic Self. *American Journal of Philology* 116: 77–93.

Holst-Warhaft, Gail. 1992. *Dangerous Voices: Women's Laments and Greek Literature*. London.

Kierdorf, W. 1980. Laudatio funebris: *Interpretationen und Untersuchungen zur Entwicklung der römischen Leichenrede*. Meisenheim am Glan, Germany.

Lardinois, André. 2001. Keening Sappho: Female Speech Genres in Sappho's Poetry. In *Making Silence Speak: Women's Voices in Greek Literature and Society*, ed. André Lardinois and Laura McClure, 75–92. Princeton, N.J.

Latte, Kurt. 1960. *Römische Religionsgeschichte*. Munich.

Lovatt, H. 1999. Competing Endings: Re-Reading the End of the *Thebaid* Through Lucan. *Ramus* 28: 126–151.

Martin, Richard P. Forthcoming. Myth, Performance, Poetics—The Gaze from Classics. In *Ethnographica Moralia: Experiments in Interpretive Anthropology*, ed. George Marcus and Neni Panougiá. New York.

McClure, Laura. 1999. *Spoken Like a Women: Speech and Gender in Athenian Drama*. Princeton.

Monsacré, Hélène. 1984. *Les larmes d'Achille: Le héros, la femme, et la souffrance dans la poésie d'Homère*. Paris.

Murnaghan, Sheila. 1999. The Poetics of Loss in Greek Epic. In *Epic Traditions in the Contemporary World: The Poetics of Community*, ed. M. Beissinger, J. Tylus, and S. Wofford, 203–220. Berkeley.

Nugent, S. G. 1992. Vergil's "Voice of the Women" in *Aeneid* V. *Arethusa* 25: 255–292.

Ochs, D. J. 1993. *Consolatory Rhetoric: Grief, Symbol, and Ritual in the Greco-Roman Era*. Columbia, S.C.

Pagán, V. E. 2000. The Mourning After: Statius' *Thebaid* 12. *American Journal of Philology* 121: 423–452.

Pantelia, M. 2002. Helen and the Last Song for Hector. *Transactions of the American Philological Association* 132: 21–27.

Perkell, Christine. 1997. The Lament of Juturna: Pathos and Interpretation in the *Aeneid. Transactions of the American Philological Association* 127: 257–286.

Richlin, Amy. 2001. Emotional Work: Lamenting the Roman Dead. In *Essays in Honor of Gordon Williams: Twenty-five Years at Yale*, ed. Elizabeth Tywalsky and Charles Weiss, 229–248. New Haven, Conn.

Segal, Charles. 1993. Female Death and Male Tears. In *Euripides and the Poetics of Sorrow: Art, Gender and Commemoration in* "Alcestis," "Hippolytus," *and* "Hecuba." Durham, N.C.: 142–158.

Seremetakis, C. Nadia. 1991. *The Last Word: Women, Death, and Divination in Inner Mani.* Chicago.

Stears, Karen. 1998. Death Becomes Her: Gender and Athenian Death Ritual. In *The Sacred and the Feminine in Ancient Greece*, ed. Sue Blundell and Margaret Williamson, 113–127. London.

Suter, Ann. 2003. Lament in Euripides' *Trojan Women. Mnemosyne* 56 (1): 1–27.

Toynbee, J. M. C. 1971. *Death and Burial in the Roman World.* Ithaca, N.Y.

Wiltshire, S. F. 1989. *Private and Public in Virgil's* Aeneid. Amherst, Mass.

Zeitlin, Froma I. 1996. *Playing the Other: Gender and Society in Classical Greek Literature.* Chicago.

2

SUMERIAN *GALA*
PRIESTS AND EASTERN
MEDITERRANEAN
RETURNING GODS

Tragic Lamentation in Cross-Cultural
Perspective

MARY R. BACHVAROVA

In the tragic dramas of fifth-century B.C.E. Athens, men dressed up as
women and sang laments put into the mouths of legendary heroines
and female choruses. Why did Athenian men engage in such behavior?
Although ethnographic studies of modern folk lament have been instrumental in advancing our understanding of ancient Greek lament, it is also
important to set the practices of first-millennium B.C.E. Greece in the
larger context of the ancient Mediterranean world and the preceding
second millennium.[1] In this chapter I use material from the second-
millennium Near East to argue that because lamentation was used not
only to mourn the dead and to appease them but also to focus the
attention of the gods on human suffering and persuade them to relieve
it, lamentation was considered useful in encouraging the fertility of the
land and the prosperity of humans. For this reason, lament was used to
effect the return of disappeared vegetation gods, and tragic lamentation
was necessary to the state. The practice of male transvestism and men
taking on other aspects of female behavior was not only a carnivalesque
overturning of norms; it was essential to the efficacy of tragic performances,

18

because transgendered behavior allowed men to tap into the conciliatory powers of women and enabled the breaching of the other natural barrier, that between living and dead. The comparative data from the Near East in fact allow us to rethink the prehistory of tragedy.

I will look in detail at the characteristics of the Mesopotamian *gala* priest, who performed laments in the so-called women's dialect of Sumerian, *emesal*. These priests have been well studied by Assyriologists and scholars of the history of transsexuality and homosexuality, and they have been compared with Cybele's *galloi*, the effeminate eunuch priests who performed frenzied laments for the goddess and her mortal consort. Yet their role within the Mesopotamian state has not yet been compared with that of tragedy in Athens, nor have the themes of their laments been compared with those of tragedy. After examining the origins of the Sumerian *gala* priest and the uses to which his lamentations were put, I will look at the use of the mourning goddess and dying god motifs, which help to explain how men could make use of a women's genre, and why the Mesopotamians thought feminized men were particularly effective at turning aside the gods' wrath and raising the dead. Furthermore, by taking into account how the ancient Near Easterners, not only Mesopotamians but also Anatolians, delimited the genre of lament and used "feminine" performances to invoke and propitiate disappeared gods, I will offer a new understanding of the connection between Dionysiac cult and Greek tragedy. The material from first- and second-millennium Anatolia provides a way to link the two sets of data, Greek and Mesopotamian, and shows that the similarities between the two could be more than typological ("that's how people think"). Rather, Athenian tragedy is a particular manifestation of a set of cult practices found throughout the East Mediterranean area.

The comparative material from the Near East sheds light on possible uses of lamentation beyond songs for the dead or for a human catastrophe, meant to manipulate human feelings and the human dead. Though such oral performances must have taken place in Mesopotamia, they are lost to us. Because the written Sumerian texts were the province of the elite, the temple, those in power, we only see the transferred use of lament applied to the worship of dying gods, the return of disappeared gods, and the propitiation of potentially angry deities. In the Greek material, on the other hand, we have relatively abundant reflections of the use of lament for the human dead, especially in tragedy, although it is transferred to a world in a time long past or far away. However, the use of lament to worship Cybele, dying gods (such as Attis, Hyacinth, or Adonis), or heroes such as Achilles is known primarily through allusions rather than examples of actual texts, either literary imitations or recordings of folk performances.[2] Euripides' *Bacchae* does provide an unparalleled glimpse into the use of lament/complaint in the worship of a disappeared god that will be discussed here, for among the patterns Dionysiac myth shares with both Mesopotamian and Anatolian myths of dying or disappeared gods is the idea that human lament or tearful complaint is efficacious in restoring the god to his desired state.

The Sumerian *gala*s were only one particularly prominent category of a variety of professionals, both male and female, who were employed in a number of kinds of ritual displays of grief in the service of temples and were called to perform at high-status funerals.[3] *Gala*s are typically grouped with singers and musicians in lexical lists and temple accounts.[4] They played a range of drums and stringed instruments and are so portrayed in the lament literature.[5] In the earliest attestations, *gala*s can appear in large groups, as many as 176 at once. They can belong to a wide range of economic classes, from slave to prince, and they are associated with a variety of temples dedicated to a variety of gods in a variety of towns.[6] From their earliest appearance, *gala*s are grouped with female mourners, and some early references indicate that in the second millennium women could occasionally hold the office of *gala*.[7]

We know from a lexical list that *gala* priests were associated early on with the *emesal* dialect.[8] I have argued that *eme-sal*, "tongue (of a) woman," was in fact a regional dialect of Sumerian and that it became associated with lamentation when a particularly proficient group of women from this region (perhaps in the north of Mesopotamia, where Sumerian died out first) developed a supraregional reputation for their lament performances.[9] Women are never attested using this dialect outside of literary texts. That is, quotes from women in law cases or letters are not in *emesal*.[10] All recitations known to belong to the *gala* priests are in *emesal*, and frequently modern scholars assign texts to *gala* priests only on the basis of the use of *emesal*.

On the one hand, the *gala*s were in charge of lamentation, but on the other, they were grouped with other categories of people of an "irregular sexual nature," including the *assinnu*, the *kurgarrú*, and temple prostitutes.[11] Although they were mocked as catamites, and willingly assuming the passive role in sexual relations was considered to be transgressing the boundaries of accepted masculine behavior, it seems unlikely that they were always homosexual or (primarily) eunuchs in the modern sense of the word.[12] Transsexuals and transvestites were the province of Inanna, who could change men into women and women into men, and the goddess herself exhibited traits of both sexes; furthermore, as we will see, myths about Inanna connect the transgression of gender boundaries to the ability to mourn and raise the dead.[13]

The *gala*'s repertoire of laments and hymns composed in *emesal* is attested in materials dating from Old Babylonian times (1900 B.C.E.) until 500 B.C.E.[14] The material becomes more abundant by the first millennium, and more information is provided concerning their ritual context in this time period, but our earliest reference to *gala* priests singing laments (in a graveyard) goes back to the time of Gudea of Lagash (2140 B.C.E., Statue B v 1 ff.). The lament material that was the province of the *gala* priests was only one of many manifestations of Near Eastern lament as a literary genre, and the literary phenomenon surely had its roots in a nonliterary tradition of lament. The Old Testament Book of Lamentations in particular, which shares topoi with the various types of Sumerian literary laments, makes use of a female voice that is best assumed to be drawn from the nonliterary performance of laments.[15]

The genre of lament in the eastern Mediterranean is best represented by city laments, a subgenre with a long history encompassing not only Old Babylonian Sumerian city laments and the biblical Book of Lamentations but also laments in ancient and premodern Greece.[16] The second-millennium Sumerian city laments were not part of the *gala*'s repertoire but sometimes included passages in *emesal*.[17] The city laments, apparently composed to commemorate actual historical events, were preserved as part of the Old Babylonian scribal curriculum. Five in total are attested, preserved in Old Babylonian copies.[18] Three city laments were composed in the standard dialect of Sumerian (*emegir*): the "Uruk Lament," the "Eridu Lament" (except for a single cry), and the "Lament over the Destruction of Sumer and Ur" (except for a single line). The two others, the "Nippur Lament" and the "Lament over Ur," include passages in *emesal*, especially those put into the mouths of goddesses or the city itself but also narrative passages. Apparently, the link between "women's language" and lamentation was felt but not rigidly maintained in writing for this particular manifestation of the lament tradition. However, the logographic writing system did not necessarily reflect dialectal variation in the pronunciation of words.[19] As far as we know these city laments belonged to the (male) Old Babylonian scribal curriculum only and were separated from whatever living oral tradition existed. Yet there are internal references to the king performing lamentation as a pleasing offering to the gods in each city lament, which may explain why the city laments were composed in the first place.[20]

The *emesal* laments belonging to the repertoire of the *gala* priest shared themes and phraseology with the city laments. Three types are attested in the Old Babylonian period and were maintained until Neo-Assyrian times: *balags*, *ershemmas*, and *ershahungas*, all of which draw on common themes, phrases, and passages. *Balags* were named after the *balag* lyre.[21] These tend to be long, repetitive compositions focusing on the destructive power of the gods and the suffering they inflict on cities and their inhabitants. The *ershemma*—"wail of the *shem* drum"—shares the themes and phrases of the *balags*, but *ershemmas* are shorter and more compact, although they became more protracted by Neo-Assyrian times. While some are clearly laments in the sense followed by modern scholars, that is, displays of grief put in the mouth of a goddess or the singer, in others praise of a god predominates, although his or her destructive power is the key theme; the Old Babylonian examples tend to include narratives about dead or disappeared gods or goddesses. Many of the themes and tropes of *emesal* laments will be familiar to a classical scholar or ethnographer of modern Balkan lament traditions. The *ershahunga*—"wail that pacifies the heart"—is a personal appeal to a god, apparently performed by the priest on behalf of a client as part of an apotropaic ritual. The other two types of *emesal* song discussed here, the *balag* and *ershemma*, also have an apotropaic function. There is some evidence that they could be performed at funerals, but typically they are imbedded in the temple liturgy, performed in a yearly cycle "as a constant vigil to prevent the anger of the gods over acts unknowingly committed by the city or king."[22] They could be performed for particular occasions as well, such as setting out on a journey, at an eclipse, or when a building or instrument underwent repair or construction—whenever in fact a belonging of a god was destroyed or damaged and thus there was a danger that the god might be offended.[23]

The use of *emesal* laments to mourn a specific grievous occasion in order to soothe the angry god who caused it is already one step removed from the function assigned to what modern scholars label laments. The performance of *emesal* laments by *gala* priests in service of the state even if no specific calamity had occurred moves lament one more step away from its "original" function and has puzzled Near Eastern scholars. Cohen puts it thus: "Since the function of the lament is to assuage divine anger, a seemingly secondary use of the lament developed for other occasions when the priest or king needed to placate the passions of the gods, lest misfortune befall the nation."[24] And Black writes about *balag* laments: "Among other ritual adaptations in the first millennium, the appropriateness of the material to, for example, rituals attending the demolition of a buckling temple wall prior to its rebuilding, was evidently perceived, but must be seen as a more or less incidental use of a body of poetry rich in allusions and complex resonances."[25]

In fact, this type of adaptation is central to the development of the literary genre in Mesopotamia and to understanding the role of its performers. While classicists, using comparative material from modern traditional Greece, have focused on the use of lament to express a woman's grievances and foment revenge and on men's concomitant desire to control and limit the public performance of this powerful genre, Near Eastern scholars such as Frymer-Kensky and Harris have focused on the role of women, especially mothers, as intercessors between generations and between their natal family and their in-laws, arguing that the power of women to assuage anger and soften hearts was put to use in interactions with the gods.[26] Men were attempting to harness the powers of a well-established type of female verbal art to conciliate the gods, just as they were known to be proficient in conciliating humans, and they turned it to new purposes, as they did with tragic lament in Athens. By co-opting women's powers to meet the needs of the larger community beyond the family, *galas* promoted the continuity of the larger social unit, politically rather than biologically defined. Thus, *gala* priests' performances present a particularly apposite comparandum to the performance of fifth-century Athenian tragedy.

Such an analysis for the function of the women's genre of lament works particularly well for the dochmiac ode accompanying the death of Oedipus in Sophocles' *Oedipus at Colonus* (1556–1578), an otherwise anomalous use of the dochmiac meter that is characteristic of laments, so long as we expect laments to be cries for justice and revenge, bewailing one's suffering or the death of another.[27] The chorus, a group of old men, intercedes on Oedipus's behalf with the god Aidoneus:

If it is proper for me to reverence with prayers the unseen god
and you, nocturnal lord, Aidoneus, Aidoneus, I beseech you
that the stranger arrive by his death at the plain of corpses below,
which conceals all, and the Stygian abode not with difficulty and
to loud cries. (1556–1564)

The chorus begs the god of the dead for a safe and untroubled journey for
Oedipus, not back from the Underworld as would be expected for a hero
or dying god but, rather, to the Underworld. In this case the old men in
the story draw on the powers of women to mediate a natural transition,
not a supernatural one that overcomes the finality of death.[28]

In the hopes of better understanding other songs in Greek tragedy,
some of which have proved difficult to classify, I turn now to the content of
two representative *ershemma*s in order to demonstrate some of the interesting similarities between the repertoire of the *gala* and the songs of tragedy.
The following themes will be analyzed: mimesis and self-reference to the
efficacy of the performance, vivid description of the destruction of cities, the
fear and joy that anticipation of the advent of the god produces, and the use
of song to soothe and call back an angry or disappeared god or dead human,
particularly with reference to Dumuzi, Inanna, and Ishkur in the Mesopotamian sphere, which will be related to the use of lament/complaint with
reference to Orestes and Dionysus in the Greek sphere. Hittite *mukessar*s,
complaints to recall the disappeared vegetation god Telipinu, provide a key
link between the Mesopotamian material and the worship of Dionysus.

I begin with an Old Babylonian *ershemma* in which the poet enters
into the story as an effective mourner who enables Inanna, here called by
the epiclesis Ningirgilu, to return from the underworld. The presentation
of the story thus approaches the mimesis of tragedy. This is only one of
many versions of this famous and widely told Mesopotamian story and the
first of several versions I will examine in this chapter:

[A]mong the shoots I shed tears.
My clever one, the princess Ningirgilu!
The devastatrix of the mountain, the hierodule, Inanna! (1–3)
. . .
While(?) sitting . . . among the shoots,
. . . among the shoots in the clear sky,
. . . among the shoots on the earth,
upon the place where I stay silent, (I shed tears).

Passerby, speak to my mother! When will she release her?
Speak to Ningirgilu! When will she release her?
Speak to the messenger of the house, the lady, the beautiful woman!
When will she release her!
From the marshlands speak to Nanna![29] "When will she release her?"
From the wide marshlands of holy An[30] speak to my father!
"When will she release her, (my) silver (which) she heaped up?
    When will she release her?" (7–16)

...

"Before her(?) very eyes, my house of the ešda-barrel has been destroyed!
Before her(?) very eyes, my city of the ešda-barrel has been destroyed!(20–21)
...

Before her(?) very eyes, (oh) my father, (my) [precious stones] have been
    plundered!"

At the lament of the reposing one [...] sheds tears,
At the lament of the reposing one Ningirgilu sheds tears. (23–25)
...

My mother, while shedding sorrowful tears, (says) "I [shall ...]!"
I shall go to Enlil![31] "Oh [my] men!" [shall I say].
"Oh my destroyed city!" I shall go to him! "Oh [my] men!" [shall I say].
"My destroyed house and city!" faithfu[lly. ...]

Her hands *have become heavy.*[32] ... She cries bitter tears.
She destroys her breasts (as if beating) a drum. She cries bitter tears.
She pulls out her hair (like) reeds. She cries bitter tears.
On the very day when that word was heard
The ... Ereškigal, caused her sister to go about (freely).
My clever one, the princess Ningirgilu, came out from the netherworld.
(29–38)

An eršemma of Ningirgilu[33]

As is typical of these laments the disappearance of a divinity allows for the
destruction of his or her city, and a goddess plays the motherly role of intercessor, although there is slippage here between the role Inanna's own mother
should play by begging for her freedom and that of Inanna protecting her city.[34]
Civic concerns are thus fitted into a framework of personal grief, a key element
in the adaptation of a female genre meant to benefit and affect members of a
woman's family by men who wished to use its powers for the benefit of the city-
state.[35] Inanna, by being trapped in the Underworld or steppe, which was
conceived of as the province of death and the dead, cannot intercede with Enlil
on behalf of her city. From line 15 on the narrator apparently quotes the words
of Inanna in the first person, lamenting the suffering of her city because of her
absence, although he seems to be having some trouble keeping his pronominal
referents straight. Is he quoting her words directly or paraphrasing them? Is he
bewailing the disappearance of his goddess whom he metaphorizes as silver and
gems, or does he quote her mourning the destruction of her city and its
storehouses? Beginning at 29 does he quote her mother or Inanna herself
taking her decision to seek the aid of Enlil? Her sister Ereshkigal, the queen of
the Underworld, eventually responds to the cries and allows her out of the
Underworld to pay a visit to her city. However the roles of Inanna and her
mother are conceived of in the narrative, the singer himself, by articulating
aloud the story, makes an effective appeal to Ereshkigal, the queen of the
Underworld, who, as soon as she hears the lamentation, frees Inanna.[36]

Despite the differences between the function of this lament and of ancient Greek laments for the human dead as assumed by modern scholars, we can recognize the convention of appealing to passersby to remember the dead, found everywhere from roadside grave monuments to modern Greek laments, a convention that gives context to Electra's wanderings outside of the palace in the opening of Sophocles' *Electra*, making known her grief to all who can hear. While the chorus of Mycenaean women insists, "But indeed you will not raise up your father out of the marsh common to all of Hades, neither with groans, nor with prayers" (137–138), Mesopotamians seem to have been more sanguine about the effectiveness of unceasing lament to raise the dead, for in the "*Ershemma* of Ningirgilu," when the lament is heard by the correct ears, Inanna is released.[37] And, as we will see, relentless lament with appeals to a series of potential intercessors is a topos of Mesopotamian stories concerning the dying gods Dumuzi and Inanna. The use of lament as a tool to galvanize others to action creates the ambiguity of voice, for the priest laments to galvanize the goddess into action, relating a historiola that provides the exemplum according to which he wishes the goddess to act, and in the myth the goddess herself laments to rouse her own mother, and her mother does so in turn (?) to rouse Enlil.

Even more relevant to the plots of tragedies such as Sophocles' *Electra* and *Antigone* are the laments put in the mouth of Geshtinanna, Dumuzi's sister, which may be compared with Greek songs of mourning for a brother by a sister, whether Antigone for Polyneices, killed attacking his own city, or Electra for Orestes, whom she supposes to have died in exile. In an Old Babylonian *ershemma* both Dumuzi's mother and sister are depicted mourning for Dumuzi, the shepherd consort of Inanna:

The captured young man! How horrible!
The captured Dumuzi! How horrible! (1–2)

. . .

In tears his mother . . . for him.
In tears and sighs she . . . for him.
I walk—I shed bitter tears.
I sit down—*I stretch(?) (my) hand to(?) (my) heart.*
I cry—those tears are bitter.
I sing—that song is bitter. (14–19)

. . .

He, along with the galla-demons, went down the road.
The "murderer" knew the road.
The "binder-of-hands" *causes him to be afraid.* (26–28)

. . .

The [. . .] of Dumuzi does not consider the words his sister had spoken.

(Still) she screams out; (still) she calls out to him.
"I shall go out with[. . .]! I shall *bring a garment* for you!" (45–46)

. . .

"[. . .] return to my mother! Let them . . . for my mother.
My mother will call out 'My five breads!' (48–49)
. . .

[. . .] my [. . .]; I am being sought.
May she scratch out her eyes for me! May she scratch her nose for me! (52–53)
. . .

May she [go] to the house (of) her personal god for me!
May she [go] for me, (that) I, the young man, can stay away from the
    galla-demon!" (56–57)

An eršemma of Dumuzi and Ṣirtur[38]

   The lament slides between first person and third person, and the first
person referent can be either the *gala* priest performing the lament or a
character within the story. It is thus partially mimetic and partially breaks
the frame of the story it tells, allowing the male performer to assume a
female role, enacting the ritual gestures of grief proper to the lamenting
woman.[39] The offer by his sister to bring a garment for Dumuzi may
allude to preparing him for burial and would therefore match the obligation felt by Antigone toward her dead brother in Sophocles' tragedy,
despite the express prohibition by her uncle of any funerary honors for
Polyneices, which Antigone violates to her own doom. Although it does
not seem that Dumuzi is restored to life within this lament, the narrative
probably assumes the story's stock ending, a successful intercession.
   The parallels between this Mesopotamian plot of brother and sister separated only to be reunited and the reunion of Electra and Orestes in Sophocles'
Electra are illuminating, although one obvious difference between this lament
and the scenario portrayed in *Electra* is the joint mourning of mother and
sister for Dumuzi, whereas Electra mourns in defiance of her mother, Clytemnestra, and without the support of her sister Chrysothemis. The earlier Mesopotamian examples suggest that Sophocles was perhaps working in
counterpoint to a traditional topos of mother and daughter or a pair of sisters
united in mourning for a son/brother.[40] As with Orestes, who, Electra laments, "died away from home and an exile in another land, evilly, separated from
your sister" (1136–1137), the very distance between the captured Dumuzi
and his sister symbolizes his death.[41] As with Dumuzi, Orestes does return,
because he in fact did not die, not because the lament itself caused the return.
Yet the recognition scene between Electra and Orestes plays with the topoi
proper to the return of a dying god.[42] Furthermore, the link between effective
lament and returning the dead is maintained by the use of the dochmiac.[43]
   I turn now to an Old Babylonian *ershemma* in praise of Ishkur, the
Sumerian Storm God, which describes his advent and the destruction it
brings to Sumer. On the one hand, this song expands our repertoire of
themes common to both Sumerian laments and tragic laments; on the

other, it shows how we may need to expand our definition of lament in order to understand fully how this genre was defined and used by the ancients:

The lord has watered the hills with soaking water.
The lord, father Iškur, has watered the hills with soaking water. (1–2)
. . .
Where the ḫalappu-trees abound and the mesu-trees sprout forth,
[where] the sun rises and (where) the sun sets
(has) . . . Iškur, oh Luḫi! Luḫi!
. . . who sprinkles the trees with health-giving waters,
. . . who plants . . . at the side of a canal, (7–11)
. . .
"Oh Iškur!" commands his father Enlil:
"My [young man], harness (the storms)! (13–14)
. . .
Bring a storm against him who does not obey Enlil! . . . " (19)

The warrior gave heed to the words of his father begetter.
When the great warrior goes out from (his) house, indeed he is a fierce lion.
When father Iškur walks upon the earth, indeed the earth rumbles.
When my lord walks in the marshes, indeed he is a roaring(?) storm. (24–27)
. . .
proceeding(?), a devastating flood, rising high, he is majestic.
My most mighty one rushes forward with the . . . of a storm.
The lightening bolt, (his) weapon, proceeds like the wind; *he holds firmly
    onto its base.*

He destroys the rebellious land like the wind. He makes it barren like the
    ašagu-plant.
He who chases out the . . . from the rebellious land. . . . (30–34)
. . .
Though the elder . . . , he bows low.

Though the children are not piles of grain, the daylight dries them out.
Its old woman . . . beer and butter.
Though its young girl is not an *apkallu*-priest, she lets her hair hang loosely.
Its young man lies prone, an overturned vessel among vessels.

My king, if only your titanic strength were known!
Like the lion, like the muscle man were you but known! . . .
Were your *stalking* known like that of the lion!
Were your deadliness known like that of a dragon!
Your greatness goes out to the nation, your praise being uttered. (39–49)[44]

The *ershemma* relies on the description of the suffering of the devastated city to activate the sympathy of the gods, as is typical of *ershemma*s and de rigueur in *balag*s. Such a function can be found in the city lament proleptically sung by the female chorus of *Seven Against Thebes* (321–368). This *ershemma* and the *balags* in general are also comparable to the opening of Sophocles' *Oedipus the King*, in which Oedipus emerges from his palace and asks the boys who are seated at his doorstep with suppliant branches in hand why they are there and why Thebes is full of "incense, and at the same time paeans and groans" (4–5), a description indicating that males and females are separately engaged in their characteristic propitiatory performances.[45] In response to Oedipus's question, the priest who accompanies them uses the flood imagery ubiquitous in Mesopotamian laments to describe the suffering of Thebes:

> The city, as you yourself see, is now too much tossed and is
> no longer able to keep its head above the depths and the
> deadly swell, perishing with its flowers within which are the
> fruits of the earth, perishing with the grazing bovine herds,
> and the birthings of women rendered childless; and the
> fire-bearing god, falling upon the city, drives it, a most terrible
> plague by which the Kadmeion house is being emptied. (22–29)

Their conversation is interrupted by the arrival of a message from the Delphic oracle, which states that the murderer of the previous king, Laius, must be found and driven out of the city. After Oedipus leaves to set a search in motion, the chorus of Theban elders sings a kletic prayer addressed to the divine pantheon describing the suffering of the Thebans and the supplicatory mourning of their women for their dead:

> [U]nable to count the number of which the city dies; without pity its
> offspring lies on the ground, bearing death, unmourned; in it wives
> and grey-haired mothers as well, each at a different place groan aloud
> from grievous toils as suppliants by the altar's edge. The paean shines
> and moaning voices chime in; for the sake of which things, oh golden
> daughter of Zeus, send protection beautiful to see. (179–189)

The typical response of modern scholars is to note the unharmonious juxtaposition of paean and lament in the parodos, and this may have been the impression made on the original Athenian audience as well, yet I contend that this prayer evokes archaic practices that parallel those found in the Mesopotamian laments.[46]

The city lament is a genre in which public and private interests intersect, as the doom of a city spells doom for the individuals residing in it. Thus, the death of a city has an analogous significance for all its citizens as the death of her *kyrios* does for a woman. And it is appropriate for men—such as the Theban elders in *Oedipus the King*—as well as women to lament both after the destruction of the city and before, seeking sympathy and protection from the gods, or for men to send their womenfolk, as the most vulnerable and the most skilled at lamenting of the inhabitants, to supplicate the gods with a show of grief and fear.[47] Yet it seems that in Greece such a display became less and less acceptable. The opening scenes of *Seven against Thebes* present a complex commentary on the use of apotropaic city lament, which is viewed by Eteocles as an unacceptable form of *dysphemia*. The chorus, which makes a point of describing itself as made up of maidens and therefore particularly adept at supplicating (110–111, 171–172), emphatically tries to attract the attention of the gods, describing in vivid detail the fearful sights and sounds of the surrounding army in the parodos (78–157) and then turning in the first stasimon to what Thebes will be like when the enemy runs amok sacking it (321–368).[48] Eteocles' criticism of the chorus's prayers comes across as extreme in its misogyny (esp. 187–190), yet the audience must have agreed with him at least in part when he warns that voicing aloud what they fear can actually make the events they dread so much come to pass.[49] This is the very power they make use of when cursing six of the opposing warriors at the Theban gates (417–630), bringing to a crescendo the theme of the magical power of words to make things happen. This theme must have been an important leitmotif running throughout the trilogy of which *Seven Against Thebes* is the final play, given the fateful prophecy that Oedipus would kill his father and sleep with his mother, which must have been featured in *Laius*, and Oedipus's curse against his two sons, which must have appeared in *Oedipus* and is finally realized during the course of the final tragedy.[50]

Synchronic irregularities such as the nonseparation of hymn and lament can be the key that opens up a view to an earlier stage in the evolution of Greek prayer. The emphasis on keeping laments separate from paeans, curses from prayers, chthonic from heavenly, which is such a concern in tragedy, was part of a drive to categorize, compartmentalize, and purify the range of human activities in Classical Greek thought, which is reflected by the delineation of "better" and "worse" literary genres by Aristotle in his *Poetics* and by Plato's concern at the inappropriate mixing of genres, which he considers a characteristic of his modern degenerate age (*Laws* 700).[51] Though modern scholars have found the categories and oppositions good to think with for many generations, these carefully defined classifications did not necessarily descend from time primeval, as indicated by the fact that chthonic and heavenly gods were not in fact consistently worshiped by the types of sacrifices considered appropriate to them and that the rhythms that were most associated with paeans on the one hand, the cretic-paeonic, and laments on the other, the dochmiac, show striking similarities that are best explained by a common origin.[52]

Besides city lament imagery the *ershemma*s also draw on motifs of myths concerning disappearing gods. By paying close attention to the data here we again may be able to shed some more light on the prehistory of ancient Greek song. Although not all their elements correspond to themes commonly defined as belonging to "lament," such songs were grouped by the *gala* priests with other *ershemma*s, an indigenous categorization that in fact could have important implications for classicists' understanding of the origin of tragedy. Because the overlapping of "lament" and songs for returning gods, which correspond in many ways to Greek kletic hymns or paeans, applies more broadly throughout the eastern Mediterranean, it should be considered to be an areal feature of the eastern Mediterranean, which in turn allows us to make a link between the *theoxenia* of Dionysus in the Athenian Dionysia and the lamentations that feature so prominently in the tragedies performed during his festival.[53]

The advent of the god anticipated with mingled fear and joy in the *ershemma* to Ishkur quoted above shares striking parallels to the epiphany of Dionysus in Euripides' *Bacchae* accompanied by a choral ode (519–603). The narration of the arrival of the Sumerian Storm God consumes the bulk of the hymn, as the advent of Dionysus does the tragic ode. Whereas in the *ershemma* Ishkur is sent forth by his father, in the ode performed before Dionysus's return the god is revealed by his father to Thebes (525–529). Just as Ishkur is sent to punish the rebellious and the hymn demands that his power and authority be recognized, so Dionysus punishes the house of Pentheus for its refusal to acknowledge his power. His minions fear injury at the hands of the Thebans, bemoan their rejection, and warn that he must be accepted, calling on him to appear (530–536, 545–548, 550–555). The earthquake that resounds at Ishkur's tread is paralleled by the earthquake unleashed at Dionysus's command, which overturns the palace (585–593), and the thunderbolt wielded by Ishkur is also made use of by Dionysus (594–595), whose byname is Bromios (thundering).[54]

The relationship between the neglect of the god within the frame of the story and the actual setting in which the story is told also shares similarities in the two hymns, although the situation presented in the *Bacchae* is somewhat more complex. In the *ershemma* the wish that the god may be acknowledged properly seems to be a formality as the song itself performs that function, while within the play the followers of Dionysus are being persecuted along with their god, and the demand that he be respected is quite serious. The members of the chorus do not fear the manifestation of their god's violent nature, confident that it will be loosed against their enemies, the unbelievers. Outside the frame of the action the spectators of course could take heart that the performance of the story assured Dionysus of their continuing devotion, even though they were aware of occasions when an improper welcome caused death and madness.[55]

A key difference between the *ershemma* for Ishkur and the ode in the *Bacchae* is the overtones of Dionysiac initiation in the latter. Although Seaford has been criticized for forcing every line and image in this play into the form of mystic initiation, in this case such an interpretation is persuasive.[56] Seaford compares the fear of the Bacchantes, who describe themselves as "possessing a lonely emptiness" without him (609), lest Dionysus "fall into the shadowy enclosure of Pentheus" (611), to the despair of the worshipper at the thought that his or her god has died, only to be replaced by rejoicing when he returns.[57] Seaford considers the use of the thunderbolt typical of mystic initiation and surmises that the thunder and shaking would have been simulated by beating drums and rattling bull roarers. The intent, to illustrate the destructive forces of nature, must have been very similar to that of the pounding of kettledrums during the *gala*'s performances as he bewailed the destructive powers of the gods.

The differences in the two hymns may be summed up as the difference between a religion that is practiced by initiates in order to ensure a happy afterlife and a religion whose primary function (as attested in the songs by and about the *gala*) is to serve the state. However, these are superficial differences produced by structural changes in society that should not be allowed to obscure important underlying archaic similarities. The later mystery religions that were the product of the first millennium were focused on the search for and retrieval of a dying or disappeared god, like the attested cults of the second millennium throughout the Near East, although now this mission was mapped onto the mission of finding personal salvation, a happy afterlife or rebirth for the worshipper.[58]

Neither the *ershemma* to Ishkur nor the Bacchantes' ode would be described as a lament according to the usual definition. They may be better defined as "complaint," a label that is useful insofar as it allows us to avoid some of the semantic baggage that has accrued to the English translation of "lament" for Greek terms such as *goos, thrênos,* or *klauô/klaiô.*[59] This use of a fearful, complaining tone by the ancients in odes to returning gods holds good for Anatolia, an area that was in direct contact with Greece at least since the second millennium, as classical scholars such as Latacz are beginning to acknowledge, and therefore must be considered a bridge between the Greek and Mesopotamian cultures, which were never in direct contact with each other.[60] The Hittite material from second-millennium Anatolia allows us in fact to postulate a connection between the two sets of data examined here that goes beyond a typological one.[61]

One Hattic-Hittite myth narrates the disappearance and return of the vegetation god Telipinu. The version of Telepinu ("Great Son" in Hattic) has been compared with the myth of Dionysus (son of Zeus) as a disappeared vegetation god who returns angry and must be propitiated.[62] A similar myth that tells of the disappearance and return of Hannahanna (Hittite "Granny") has already been compared with the story of Demeter and Persephone by Burkert, in an illuminating analysis of a complex set of Greek myths including that of Dionysus.[63] These myths narrating the disappearance of Telipinu and Hannahanna, themselves imbedded in invocation rituals meant to attract and soothe the god with pleasant smells and substances, are labeled *mugawar* or *mukessar.* The Proto-Indo-European root **mug^w* means "bellow," and this term is glossed in a lexical list as Akkadian *tazzimtu,* "lament, complaint," a noun formed from the verb *nazāmu,* "moan, complain."[64] Therefore, there is the same strong link here between an ostentatious vocal show of suffering and diverting the destructive fury of a god that we saw above in the *ershemmas.* However, the contents of the songs do not necessarily reveal a strong element of grief. Rather, *mukessars* contain elements that are found in a Greek kletic hymn and rely on analogic magic to soothe the angry god even as they draw him near:

Let evil, fury, anger, [sin] and rage go. But let it not go into
the ripe field, forest, (and) garden. Let it go along the path
of the Dark Earth. In the Dark Earth lie iron containers. Their
lids are of lead. What goes in does not come up again; it
perishes in this very place. And let Telipinu's evil fury, anger,
rage, sin, evil tongues, evil fetters go into this very place and
let it not come up again. Let it perish within.

Eat tasty things; drink tasty things. Look here! Let the path of
Telipinu be sprinkled with fine oil. Set out upon it. Your bed
is *sahis* and *happuriyasas* (boughs). Sleep on it. Just as fragrant
reed is fitting, so may you be fitting also with the king and queen
and to the land of Hatti.[65]

As one would expect of a text coming from an area in direct contact
with Greece, the Hittite story presents a much more familiar picture to the
classical scholar than the earlier Sumerian material, which, because it stems
from the heart of Mesopotamia, could not have been in direct contact with
Greek speakers but may have been known to the Anatolians directly to the
West across the Euphrates.[66] More likely, however, is the possibility that
we are getting a glimpse of an areal feature of the eastern Mediterranean,
that is, a cultural practice found throughout the eastern Mediterranean, whose
precise origin is unknown, although it is clearly connected to agriculture and
thus might have spread with Neolithic culture.

Interestingly, the bedding of boughs spread out invitingly for Telipinu
matches the *stibades* discussed by Sourvinou-Inwood in her analysis of the
theoxenia of Dionysus.[67] As in the *ershemma* to Ishkur, the worshipper
wishes his god to approach yet is deeply concerned that he could be angry
and destructive in his advent. He therefore attempts to propitiate the god
with a show of fearful respect in order to turn aside any negative feelings.
Not incidental to my comparison is the fact that when this type of invocation
is not directed to gods, it can be directed to the dead when they have been
called away from their loved ones or have died abroad, a situation parallel to
the one Electra imagines for Orestes in Sophocles' play.[68] Meanwhile,
modern Greek laments, which make parallel the distant traveler and the
dead, are considered to "call up" (*anakaleisthai*) the dead.[69] In one fragmentary text, recently discussed by Polvani, the Hattic goddess Kamrusepa,
who is frequently involved in the return of the disappeared god, is in fact
described as dying. Polvani links this text with *mukessar*s, noting that the
story differs in that the goddess is not just disappeared but dead. In another
fragment, probably part of the same tablet, we can pick out the words "[his
or her] tears" and "my tears." Thus, we can infer that Hattians also had a
myth with some similarities with the Mesopotamian myths we have been
discussing, involving the temporary death of a god and mourning.[70]

To sum up, we have broadened our understanding of the scope of the
genre of "lament/complaint" to include songs that, instead of mourning

the dead and disappeared, call back and propitiate the dead and disappeared. Whereas some songs in the genre contain only mourning, and some contain only invocation, in the Near Eastern material mourning and invocation are inextricably intertwined. The mode of delivery, passionate and wailing, delimited the genre and was considered to be effective for appealing to both dead humans and the gods. As one would expect from these findings concerning the genre of "lament/complaint," ritual wailing is closely connected with necromancy. Thus the Sumerian phrase "man of the *balag*" (*lú-balag-gá*), that is, the man who uses the characteristic instrument of the *gala* priest, is translated as "raiser of a ghost" (Akk. *mu-še-lu-ú* [*e-dim-me*]) in the matching Akkadian entry of a lexical list.[71] One thinks of the *goês* (necromancer, lit., "man of the wail"), whom Johnston has argued drew on Mesopotamian knowledge to ply his craft.[72]

Turning now to the peculiar effectiveness of feminine men, including *gala* priests, to activate, recall, and propitiate dying gods, we will first examine two etiologies for the *gala* priest and then turn briefly to their descendants, Cybele's *galloi*, again drawing on Hittite material to postulate a direct connection between the first-millennium worshippers of the Anatolian goddess and the Sumerian priests. Not surprisingly, one myth refers to propitiation; the other, to resurrection.

The first myth of origin appears in an Old Babylonian *balag* to Inanna that draws on lamentation themes already illustrated above:

Queen of Ibgal, what has your heart wrought! How heaven and
earth are troubled!
What has your raging heart wrought!
What has your flood-like raging heart wrought!
Enki heard these words, took counsel with himself in the *kigal*,[73]
He fashioned for her the *gala*, him of the heart-soothing laments . . . ,
He arranged his mournful laments of supplication . . . ,
He placed the *aḫulap*-uttering *ub* and *lilis* in his hand.[74]

Here the *gala* is shown to be particularly proficient at performing laments that soothe and propitiate the enraged and destructive goddess.

On the other hand, the Sumerian narrative "Inanna's Descent" connects the invention of the *gala-tura* (young/little *gala*) and the *kurgarrû* to the resurrection of the goddess.[75] Inanna has taken it into her head to rule over the Netherworld as well as the upper world. She descends into the realm of her sister Ereshkigal, where she is forced to strip naked and then is executed. Her grieving servant Ninshubur seeks aid from a series of gods to no avail, until Enki the Trickster God invents two mourners to propitiate Ereshkigal:

Father Enki answered Ninšubura: "What has my daughter done?
She has me worried.

What has Inana done? She has me worried. . . . " (217–219)

He removed some dirt from the tip of his fingernail and created the *kurĝara*. He removed some dirt from the tip of his other fingernail and created the *galatura*. To the *kurĝara* he gave the life-giving plant. To the *galatura* he gave the life-giving water. (222–225)

Then father Enki spoke out to the *galatura* and the *kurĝara*: "Go and direct your steps to the underworld. Flit past the door like flies. Slip through the door pivots like phantoms. The mother who gave birth, Ereškigala, on account of her children, is lying there. Her holy shoulders are not covered by a linen cloth. Her breasts are not full like a *šagan* vessel. Her nails are like a pickaxe (?) upon her. The hair on her head is bunched up as if it were leeks." (226–235)

"When she says: 'Oh my heart,' you are to say: 'You are troubled, our mistress, oh your heart.' When she says: 'Oh my liver,' you are to say: 'You are troubled, our mistress, oh your liver.' (*She will then ask:*) 'Who are you? Speaking to you from my heart to your heart, from my liver to your liver—if you are gods, let me talk with you; if you are mortals, may a destiny be decreed for you.' Make her swear this by heaven and earth." (*one line fragmentary*) (236–245)

"They will offer you a riverful of water—don't accept it. They will offer you a field with its grain—don't accept it. But say to her: 'Give us the corpse hanging on the hook.' (*She will answer:*) 'That is the corpse of your queen.' Say to her: 'Whether it is that of our king, whether it is that of our queen, give it to us.' She will give you the corpse hanging on the hook. One of you sprinkle on it the life-giving plant and the other the life-giving water. And so let Inana arise." (246–253)[76]

Note that here Ereshkigal exhibits the same ritualized behavior of the female mourner that caused her to release Inanna when it was enacted by Inanna or her mother in the "*Ershemma* of Ningirgilu." When the *gala-tura* and the *kurgarrú* imitate her behavior, showing sympathy for her, she is grateful enough to allow them to take back their queen.

Although the ruse is successful, the doorkeeper demands in addition a substitute for Inanna, and she treacherously orders that her consort, the shepherd Dumuzi, be captured and dragged down to the Netherworld. In turn, Dumuzi's sister Geshtinanna grieves so for her brother that Inanna decrees that each in turn will spend half of the year in the Netherworld. As with the Hittite myth of Hannahanna, the parallels with the story of Persephone's abduction as told in the *Hymn to Demeter* have been frequently noted.[77]

In the Akkadian version of this story, the consequences of Ishtar's disappearance are made clearer. Just as Demeter's grief and absence caused agricultural sterility, so does the absence of Ishtar:

Ishtar has gone down to the netherworld,
she has not come up.
As soon as Ishtar went down to the netherworld,
The bull will not mount the cow,
the ass will not impregnate the jenny,
The young man will not impregnate the girl
in the thoroughfare.[78]

The return of Dumuzi/Tammuz is also associated with the return of the
ordinary dead to enjoy the sacrifices provided by the mourning living, as
the close of the poem makes clear:

On the day Tammuz (says) "Hurrah!"
the lapis flute and carnelian ring (say) "Hurrah!"
With him (say) "Hurrah!" the wailing men and wailing women,
Let the dead come up and smell the incense.[79]

Just as the *gala-tura* and the *kurgarrú* transcend their male gender by
imitating the feminine mourning of the queen of the Underworld, Inanna
herself is able to transcend genders, an ability that should be associated
with her return from the Underworld, for two of the barriers that "cannot
be crossed" are that of biologically determined gender and that between
living and dead: "Inanna-Ishtar shatters the boundaries that differentiate
the species: between divine and human, divine and animal, human and
animal."[80] Other scholars have noted the connection between transgen-
dering and the ability to mediate between the mundane world and the
world of the divine or the dead with respect to Siberian shamans, to whom
kurgarrús and *assinnus* have been compared, and I contend that *galas*
should be included among the number of feminized men who can communicate with the dead and the divine.[81]

The connection between highly emotional, transgendered, transgressive behavior and communicating with dead, angry, or disappeared gods
that is made explicit in the Mesopotamian texts supports the theory that
cross-dressing and other behavior usually explained simply as carnivalesque
were also considered to make the Dionysia as a whole a more effective
invocation and propitiation of Dionysus. I turn briefly now to the Dionysiac
evidence for gender-bending and otherwise transgressive behavior, to well-
known material that we can now look at in a new light. Athenian men did
not impersonate women only on the tragic and comic stage. Male celebrants
also appeared on the street in drag even as they hoisted large *phalloi* or wore
phalloi during the City Dionysia, engaging in riotous behavior. Dionysus
himself dressed in an outfit that was considered feminine and sported the
long curly hair of women.[82] He is accused both of being effeminate and of
seducing women in Euripides' *Bacchae* (225, 455–459, 487), and he tricks
Pentheus into dressing like a woman, who is then dismembered by his
female family members. It is difficult to avoid comparison between the

violent and transgressive behavior alluded to in the *Bacchae* and engaged in
by Cybele's *galloi*, with a procession described in the Sumerian "Iddin-
Dagan A" hymn in which humans cross-dress and slash themselves in
honor of Inanna, the goddess in charge of transsexuality. Harris has indeed
compared the Dionysiac and Mesopotamian rites, focusing on the carnival-
esque function of the two cults.[83]

It has long since been acknowledged that the myth of Dumuzi/
Tammuz and its concomitant rituals were regional examples of a phenomenon spread widely throughout the eastern Mediterranean ranging from
the Greek cult of Adonis, the ill-fated consort of Aphrodite, to the myth of
"Phrygian" Cybele and Attis. There are obvious parallels between the
emotional rites of Cybele, performed by her effeminate, cross-dressing,
castrated *galloi*, who would wail and beat on drums, and the rites performed by the Sumerian *gala* priests, who were so closely connected with
Inanna/Ishtar.[84] Taylor has argued persuasively that Cybele's *galloi* and
the Sumerian priests were in fact related.[85] As he notes, there are striking
similarities between the famous depictions of the *galloi* confronting a lion
in Hellenistic epigrams and a Sumerian proverb that states, "A lamentation
priest ($= gala$), after he had met a lion in the desert, said, 'Let him come!
In the town . . . , at Inanna's gate, oh dog, chased away with potsherds,
what is your brother doing in the desert?' "[86] Taylor finds the missing link
between the Mesopotamian institution and the Phrygian cult in a Hittite
description of a Luwian festival for the cult of the pantheon of the city
Istanuwa, describing the men from the town of Lallupiya filling a cymbal
with a drink offering, as the *galloi* were known to do, and singing "like a
woman" (MUNUS-*nili*) in Luwian.[87] Taylor compares this to the high-
pitched singing of the first-millennium castrated *galloi*, but as Rutherford
shows in the following chapter, lament was a female-gendered activity in
the Hittite cult, assigned primarily to "Old Women" (^{MUNUS.MEŠ}ŠU.GI),
and therefore the reference is to a style of emotive singing expected of
women.[88] Taylor further compares the "songs of conciliation" and
"songs of thunder" performed in the cult of Istanuwa to the songs of
the *gala*, with their apotropaic lamentation meant to "soothe the liver" of
the gods.[89] The songs of thunder remind one of the advent of Dionysus as
described in the *Bacchae*. Here is yet another development in what seems to
have been a multifarious eastern Mediterranean tradition expressing a deep
structure of associations among sexuality, death, transgressing boundaries,
lamentation, and propitiation that organized how humans understood their
world, to which I argue Athenian tragedy must have been in part indebted
and which Attic tragedy joins as a fifth-century example.

When considering the reasons for the correspondences discussed in this
chapter, I agree to some degree with the "typological" approach used by
Casadio in order to explain parallels such as those between the dying gods
Dionysus and Attis.[90] Yet the correspondences among such gods, both
Greek and Near Eastern, are not simply the result of how humans think
but must be at least in part the result of contact across the Mediterranean.

Although I owe an obvious debt to the work of Burkert, Morris, and West, I hasten to note that I am not discussing here East-to-West influence in the Orientalizing period.[91] Rather, I am thinking of the eastern Mediterranean as a cultural area (a concept that has been applied to the modern Balkans and to South Asia) with overlapping "dialect areas," beginning at least in the third millennium B.C.E. and probably much earlier.[92] Furthermore, I hasten to make clear that the Hittite *mukessar*s that were brought into the discussion should not be interpreted as proof that Anatolia was the only link between East and West. Rather, the Anatolian material is one extant link we can trace among the many that must have existed.

The Anatolian sources are particularly valuable to those who wish to understand the prehistory of Greek tragedy and of other manifestations of Greek religion, first of all because of the types of texts found at the Hittite capital. Descriptions of festivals are particularly abundant, for example, providing comparanda that are otherwise lacking. Second, as befits its location midway between Greece and Mesopotamia, Anatolia, while sharing generally the characteristics of Near Eastern cultures, also shows extensive similarities with Greek culture, in part because of similarities in climate. Thus, both Greeks and Anatolians in the second and first millennium were heavily involved in viticulture, and the Anatolian god of the vine provides a key comparandum to Dionysus. Winiyanta, or "he of the vine," was one of the gods who were toasted in the cult of Istanuwa.[93] And we know from other sources, especially first-millennium Hieroglyphic Luwian monuments, that he was a particular manifestation of the Luwian Storm God, Tarhunza of the Vineyard, a deity sharing similarities with the Hattic vegetation god Telipinu. Eighth-century monuments from the southeastern Anatolian plateau depict him with bunches of grapes and stalks of barley and praise him for bringing agrarian fertility to those who worship him: "I set up this Tarhunzas of the Vineyard, (saying): 'We will set (him) up afterwards with an ox and nine monthling sheep.' *When* I presented him, he came with all his goodness, and the *corn-stem(s)* burgeoned forth at (his) foot and the vine was good here. And Tarhunza of the Vineyard gave [to] Wasusarmas, [. . . ki]ng, a mighty courage, and for him he put his *enemies* under his feet."[94] Finally the Hieroglyphic Luwian term for "vine" (*tuwar(i)sa-*) is obviously related to the Greek term *thursos*, "the staff of Dionysus." These correspondences make one suspect that the connection made by the Greeks between the Lydians and the youthful Dionysus was based on more than the perceived effeminateness of the luxury-loving Lydians.[95] Rather, the Greeks acknowledged some essential similarities between their worship of Dionysus and Anatolian worship of a god of wine, both of whom brought thunder and plant growth with their advent and could be persuaded by the right offerings to turn their powers of destruction on the enemy.

We can use the conclusions arrived at here to modify and unify several different theories about the origin of tragedy, beginning with the archaeology-based approach of Sourvinou-Inwood, who explains the origin of tragic drama as an expansion from the etiological myth of the advent of Dionysus and his subsequent punishment of Athenian men for their unfriendly reception of him by causing them sexual dysfunction.[96] This triggered the founding of a recurring compensatory festival for Dionysus, which morphed into "prototragedy." The new form of religious art then began to explore other myths with similar themes. While her analysis has the advantage of facing head-on a crucial problem facing scholars interested in the origins of tragedy—Why did so many tragedies have "nothing to do with Dionysus"? (Plut. *Symp.* I 1.5, 615a)—Sourvinou-Inwood does not take into consideration the question of how the lamentation onstage relates to the female folk genre of lamentation. She focuses on explaining tragedy as a "locus of religious exploration," an explanation that rings true to me.[97] Yet it seems to me that we must fit into our account of the origin of tragedy and provide a unified explanation for the peculiarly self-confident and powerful female characters in tragedy, which seem so unlike the socially accepted personae of contemporary women, as well as the cross-dressing that was characteristic of Dionysiac ritual and the performance by male actors of a female genre acknowledged to wield great power. Although it cannot explain all of these elements, the comparative material adduced here can link the gender-bending behavior and the performance of laments by men to the etiological myth of the angry divinity, which is the keystone of Sourvinou-Inwood's theory of the origin of tragedy. The sexual dysfunction attributed to Dionysus's anger may be connected to the sexual abnormalities attributed to Mesopotamian functionaries such as the *galas*.

Finally, the material used here can be applied to a second and complementary theory about the origin of tragedy, which sees the redirection of family funerary cult and hero cult praxis to benefit the state rather than a (fictional) kin group as an important factor in the development of tragedy. Hero cult, already in part a refocusing of private funeral lament and already involving male lamenters, was refocused away from the seasonal lamentation for and propitiation of one's own divine ancestors and toward the worship of state-sanctioned pseudo-ancestors and the performance of analogous lamentations in dramas within the Athenian celebration of the Dionysia.[98] The material discussed here shows that in the second millennium Mesopotamians already saw a connection between state-sponsored worship of disappeared gods and the dead and performances of lamentations by males, who took over the pleading and propitiatory role of women operating within their family unit in order to apply it to relations between the city and its gods. Moreover, the Near Eastern material indicates that recalling the dead and recalling a disappeared god could be considered simply two strains of the same ritual praxis. This allows us to postulate a link between hero-worship and Dionysiac worship.[99] Tragedy, by telling the stories of dead heroes in a festival honoring Dionysus, simply recombined the two distinct but ultimately linked rituals.

The gender-bending in Dionysiac ritual thus had multiple functions, just as tragedy itself and the festival in which it was imbedded served multiple purposes. It allowed men and women a socially sanctioned moment in which they could throw off the trammels of the good, sober, male citizen or female bearer of citizens. While relationships between men and women and the constraints and powers of male and female gender roles were explored when the dichotomy between male and female was momentarily transcended, it also allowed for a further bridging between the worlds of the living and the dead. Finally, men co-opted the powers of women to propitiate the gods and dead through lamentation, applying in a male public setting female powers that were used for the good of the family to the good of the state.

The comparative discussion here can only be preliminary. Yet I hope to have shown that material from the Near East can be used to provide context that supports and unifies some of the current theories concerning the origin of tragedy, by showing the connections between transgendered behavior and recalling the human dead and disappeared gods, and the use of lament/complaint in impelling and receiving the returning god. The Athenian state had a strong interest in harnessing female lament by using it in tragedy, not only because this provided a safe outlet for dangerous and divisive emotions but also because women could be a soothing and propitiating force in the relations between mortals and the divine, pleading the case of the injured and oppressed. The Mesopotamian texts can help us not only to recognize the references to hero-worship and the worship of dying gods in the themes of tragic odes that the original audience of tragedy would have noticed but also to understand that the conflation of paean and lament that was so disturbing to Plato and other ancient scholars of literature was an archaic feature imbedded in the cult practices from which tragedy developed.

ACKNOWLEDGMENTS

I would like to thank Hebrew Union Press for permission to use extracts from Mark E. Cohen's *Sumerian Hymnology* and Graham Cunningham, Eleanor Robson, and Gábor Zólyomi for permission to use an extract from *The Literature of Ancient Sumer*. I would also like to thank the editor of this volume for help in revising this chapter.

NOTES

1. For modern ethnographic studies, see especially Alexiou 2002; Holst-Warhaft 1992, 14–97.

2. The worship of Adonis is best represented in the record: Sappho 140a, 168 L-P, Ar. *Lys.* 387–398, Theocritus 15, Bion *Lament for Adonis*. Also see Alexiou 2002, 55–62, on laments for dying gods and heroes and their "Oriental" connections.

3. Henshaw 1994, 105–113.

4. Ibid., 91–93.

5. Ibid., 91.

6. Gelb 1976.

7. Ibid., 65. See Al-Rawi 1992; Henshaw 1994, 88–89. Cf. Frymer-Kensky's (1992, 32–44) discussion of the restriction of female roles, which she connects to

gala priests imitating women. Female mourners sponsored by the temple continued to ply their craft (Harris 2003, 100).

8. Henshaw 1994, 88.

9. I (1997) have used comparative data of the perceptions of literary dialects in ancient Greek and Old and Middle Indic. For other discussions of *emesal*, see Diakonoff 1976; Krecher 1966, 1967; Langenmayr 1993; Schretter 1990; and the brief review by Rubio (2001, 269–271, with further references). The other proposed translation of the term as "slender tongue" sees it as referring to a mode of performance that imitates the vocal register of women. This analysis ignores the fact that the dialect's idiosyncratic features include lexical items and morphemes.

10. Most interesting is the fact that the hymns of Enheduanna, Sargon the Great's daughter and the high priestess of Inanna, are not in *emesal*. (For a biography of Enheduanna, the first named poet in history, see Hallo and van Dijk 1968, 1–12; and, further, Westenholz 1989, with caveats of Bachvarova 1997, n. 10.) *Emesal* is used in the following documents outside of laments: a few so-called proverbs, short sayings that were used to train scribes in points of grammar; quotes from goddesses in narrative literature, especially in the "marriage songs" of Dumuzi and Inanna; two scurrilous dialogues between women that remain untranslated, as far as I know; and a "lullaby" (see Farber 1989 for the latter). Given the lack of context for these texts, the genre labels only reflect our own ideas of what these songs would be used for, rather than indigenous categories. The latter three all indicate a connection between a literary genre derived from a women's folk genre and the "women's language." A final very interesting example, a song commemorating the birth of a child to the Ur III king Shu-Sin, which has been assigned to a *lukur* priestess (Sefati 1998, 344–352), must remain undiscussed here. The *lukur* priestess was often a concubine of the king, and several erotic songs are attributed to her; see Leick 1994, 111–129.

11. Henshaw 1994, 89. The *assinnu* (Akkadian term) was a "man/dog-woman," Sumerian UR.SAL, a catamite, sometimes appearing to be impotent. He is thus reminiscent of the Indian *hijra*, on which see Nanda 1999 and Jaffrey 1999. The *kurgarrû* (Akkadian term) could carry female implements such as spindles, and they are described as slashing themselves with knives in a ritual procession (Inana and Iddin-Dagan = Iddin-Dagan A [translation by Black et al., http://etcsl.orinst.ox.ac.uk/cgi-bin/etcsl.cgi?text=t.2.5.3.1). See Henshaw 1994, 284–301, and Leick 1994, 157–169, for a discussion of the full range of "sexual deviants." On "free love," sacred prostitution, and priestesses who engaged in sexual activities with the king, see Leick 1994, 147–156. Also see the brief summary on sexuality and cult in Bottéro 2001, 122–124. Nissinen (1998, 28–36) provides an insightful discussion on the cult of Ishtar and what we know about such characters as the *gala* and the *assinnu*.

12. Cf. the Sumerian proverb: "The lamentation priest (= *gala*) wipes his bottom: 'One should not remove what belongs to my mistress Inana'" (2.100 [translation by Black et al., http//etcsl.orinst.ox.ac.uk/cgi-bin/etcsl.cgi?text =t.6.1.02). As Rubio (2001, 270) discusses, the Sumerian sign for *gala* is a combination of the signs for "penis" and "anus." See also Bottéro and Petschow 1975; Henshaw 1994, 88 n. 22.

13. See Groneberg 1986, 33–41, and 1997a, with earlier references; Henshaw 1994, 292–295; Roscoe 1996, 213–217. The character of Inanna is conveniently summarized in Leick 1991, 86–89, and Black and Green 1992, 108–109. Also see the insightful discussion by Harris (2003, 158–171), who compares her with Dionysus.

14. A summary of the information on the *gala* is provided by Henshaw (1994, 88–96). Also see Gelb (1976, 64–74), although some of his conclusions are outdated. See Cohen 1988, 13–14; Rubio 2001, 270–271.

15. Lee (2002, 47–73) discusses the use of the female voice ("Jerusalem's poet") in counterpoint to a male voice ("Jeremiah") in the biblical Book of Jeremiah and analyzes the Book of Lamentations as a similar dialogue between a male voice and a female voice (2002, 42).

16. Gwaltney (1983, 205–210) compares the formal and thematic features of the first-millennium Sumerian city laments and Lamentations, a comparison also made by Ferris (1992) and Dobbs-Allsop (1993). The history of the scholarly comparison between the city laments and Lamentations is briefly surveyed by Lee (2002, 37–40, with earlier references). Roberts ([1992] 2002) compares Jeremiah to the city laments. See Alexiou 2002, 83–101, on Greek city laments. Also see the general summarizing discussion by Hallo (1995).

17. These are all available online at *The Electronic Text Corpus of Sumerian Literature* (ETCSL; http://etcsl.orinst.ox.ac.uk [Black et al. 1998–2006]). The standard print editions with English translations are "The Nippur Lament" (Tinney 1996), "Lament over Sumer and Ur" (Michalowski 1989; also J. Klein, in Hallo and Younger 1997, 535–539), "The Eridu Lament" (Green 1978), and "The Uruk Lament" (Green 1984). "Lament over Ur" lacks a recent print edition but may be found in English translation in Jacobsen 1987, 447–477. See ETCSL for more details.

18. I leave aside the "Curse of Agade," also available at ETCSL and in a print edition by Cooper (1983), a standard Sumerian composition popular in the Old Babylonian scribal curriculum of Nippur, which seems to draw on both the lament tradition and royal inscriptions.

19. See Civil 1973; Krecher 1967; Michalowski 1992, 241–242.

20. Tinney 1996, 23–24, with earlier references.

21. There has been much debate over whether the *balag* is a drum or a harp. Black (1991, 28 n. 39) argues that the instrument is a drum, but Franklin (2005, 2006) has argued that the instrument must be a seven-stringed lyre. Livingstone (1986, 187–204) presents a text describing the re-covering of the bronze *lillissu* drum (kettledrum), another characteristic instrument of the *gala* priest.

22. Cohen 1981, 6.

23. On the repertoire of *gala* priests, see especially Black 1991. Specific types of laments are edited, translated, and discussed by Cohen (1981, 1988) and Maul (1982). There are eight Old Babylonian examples of a fourth type of hymn, the *shirnamshub*, "incantation song," some in *emesal* and some in the standard dialect of Sumerian. It has been posited that the *emesal* examples were used by *gala* priests. These again are part of apotropaic rituals, when, for example, a statue of a god is divested of its protective amulets and clothing to be washed or when the king sets out on a journey. They are praise hymns extolling the powers of a god. A final type of *emesal* lament, the *shuilla*, "hand lifting," is only attested in the first millennium. There are four extant examples.

24. Cohen 1981, 59.

25. Black 1991, 34.

26. Caraveli (1986; Caraveli-Chaves 1980) and Seremetakis (1991, 1993) provide the most important analyses of the use of lament in modern traditional Greece for social protest and fomenting revenge, whereas Holst-Warhaft (1992), Loraux (1998), McClure (1999), and Foley (2001) have applied their results, along with those of other scholars, to the study of tragedy. The updated bibliography in

Alexiou 2002 is a good source for primary materials and studies of lamentations, to which may be added Briggs 1992, which provides another good ethnographic parallel to the use of lament by women to manipulate responses to events.

See also Frymer-Kensky 1992, 38; Harris 2003, 98–99. See Wood 1999 for an illuminating example from the Gabra, a nomadic group based along the border between Kenya and Ethiopia, of men co-opting the mediating power of women.

27. In fact, this rhythm, frequently characterized by critics as indicative of great excitement, both good and bad (Dale 1968, 190, and 1969, 254–255), is only used for "good" excitement in such recognition scenes, in which a male—more often than not Orestes—previously mourned as dead is revealed to be alive to a female relation (Sophocles' *Electra*; Euripides' *Electra, Ion, Helen, Iphigeneia Among the Taurians*). The only recognition scene of this sort in which the dochmiac is not used is in Aeschylus's *Libation-Bearers*. Dochmiacs are the featured meter of Euripides' *Orestes*, perhaps somehow a parody of recognition scenes proper to Orestes. The possible connection between the arrival of the polluted Orestes and the annual return of the dead during the Anthesteria, which Hamilton (1992, esp. 118–119) has argued was an innovation of Euripides, lies beyond the scope of this chapter. On the formal features of the dochmiac, a lively and peculiar rhythm that may be found in modern Balkan folk music, see Dale 1968, 104–119, 207–208; West 1982, 108–115, and 1992, 142–147. West (1992, 387) suggests a possible non-Indo-European origin. The dochmiac first appears with Aeschylus and is nearly exclusive to drama (the only exception is the Hellenistic Grenfell fragment, *lyr. ad.* 1 [in Powell 1925, 177 ff.], a lament sung by a woman). Herington (1985, 114–115), noting that the dochmiac is original to tragedy, has suggested that it was a folk rhythm elevated to the tragic stage, whereas Else (1977, 79) has suggested that it was used in Attic folk laments. Other scholars attempt to derive the dochmiac from Indo-European verse forms: see Korzeniewski 1968, 170; Koster 1962, 279–282; White 1912, 295–297. Wright (1986, 52) claims that a feature of "full laments" (which number only eight in all of Greek tragedy according to her classification) is a division into two sections, the second of which contains iambo-dochmiac meter, but her analysis is based in part on a textually problematic section of the final lament in *Persians* (1073–1076), which in any case is not a mimesis of Greek lament.

28. Caraveli-Chaves (1980) notes the use of lament to help the dead cross over to the other side, but in this case the addressee is the dead woman herself, not God. Danforth (1982) also discusses how lament effects the transition between living and dead, and Stears (1998 [reprinted in this volume]) discusses the similarities among the three great rites of transition for women, birth, marriage, and death. I agree that women, because of the way they are involved in key transitions across boundaries such as childbirth and exogamous marriage, may be particularly efficacious in aiding the transition between life and death, but the point I make here is that their skills as intercessors between humans are also relevant.

29. The Moon God.

30. Heaven.

31. "Lord of the Steppe," god of Nippur.

32. Italics indicate that the translation is provisional.

33. *Ershemma* no. 79 (translated in Cohen 1981, 64–65).

34. On this role of women, especially older women, see Frymer-Kensky 1992, 38; Harris 2003, 98–99; and the discussion below.

35. Compare the similar function of Cornelia's lament in Keith's contribution to this volume.

36. For the different interpretations of this narrative, see Cohen 1981, 62–63 n. 205.

37. In Aeschylus's *Persians*, of course, the performance to raise Darius's ghost is successful. See Johnston 1999, 117–118; and Suter, this volume.

38. Dumuzi's mother, *Ershemma* no. 88 (translated in Cohen 1981, 85–87).

39. On the ritual gestures, see Frymer-Kensky 1992, 36–38; Kramer 1983.

40. See the Sumerian lament edited and translated by Black (2004) in which Dumuzi's two sisters mourn for him.

41. Death as exile is a topos of modern Greek laments, and the supposed return of Orestes as nothing but a heap of ashes in an urn, soon to be revealed as a ruse when he appears safe and sound, inverts the motifs of modern Greek secondary burial, in which the mourners act as if they truly will be united with the dead as their bones are exhumed, only to realize they are in fact truly gone forever and the few remnants of their mortal being must be interred in the crypt (Danforth 1982, 58–69). On laments for travelers abroad, see Alexiou 2002, 118–119.

42. Seaford 1994, 377–378.

43. See n. 27 on the dochmiac.

44. *Ershemma* no. 184 (translated in Cohen 1981, 59–60).

45. See McClure 1999, 52–54, on the female *ololygé* and the male paean.

46. Stehle 2004, 144–148.

47. The observation that it is appropriate for men to lament the destruction of their city is borne out by the chart of tragic laments provided by Suter (this volume), derived from Wright 1986. Males lament only in the following situations: destruction of their city, the death of persons on whom they are dependent, their own destruction (I consider *OT* 1307–1366 by Oedipus to be for himself, as he barely mentions Jocasta but, rather, dwells on his own crime and fate), or the death of their children and therefore their family line.

48. Also see Stehle 2005, 102–103.

49. Ibid., 101.

50. Ibid., 119–120.

51. See Rutherford 1993, 1995.

52. For an example of modern scholars, see most recently Stehle 2004, 2005. This is not the place to argue the issue fully, but I provide some discussion of the nonseparation of prayer and curse in Alcaeus 129 in Bachvarova 2007. The distinctions listed above were not important in the ancient Near East. Scullion (1994) discusses evidence that shows that the ways in which heavenly and chthonian divinities were worshipped in ancient Greece were not as consistently different as one might imagine, although his conclusions from the evidence are not the ones drawn here. Scullion describes the opposition as "not an absolute dualism but as a true polarity, with given gods and rituals located not only at the two poles but at various degrees between them" (2000, 163). Also see Ekroth 1998, 2000, and 2002 on the epigraphic and archaeological evidence. See n. 27 on the dochmiac rhythm, and see Rutherford 2001, 24–25, and West 1982, 54–55, 106–108, 145–146, and 1992, 140–142, 387, on the cretic-paeonic.

53. See Alexiou 2002, 55–62.

54. For more on the natural phenomena unleashed by the god, see Seaford 1997b.

55. Apollodorus 1.9.12, 2.2.2, 3.5.2; Aelian *VH* 3.42; Schol. Ar. *Ach.* 243a. This last is discussed below.

56. Seaford 1997a; see also Friedrich 2000.

57. Seaford 1997a, 195–197, 200.

58. Sourvinou-Inwood 2003a; see also Alexiou 2002, 62.

59. The Greek noun *goos* is built on a Proto-Indo-European root meaning "speak, cry out" (Julius Pokorny, *Indogermanisches etymologisches Wörterbuch*, 2 vols. [Bern, 1959–1969], 1.403), while *thrênos* has no secure etymology and could be onomatopoetic, and *klauô/klaiô* means "weep" (R. S. P. Beekes, "The Greek Etymological Dictionary"). Both works referred to here were accessed via the Internet at the Indo-European Etymological Dictionary Project (http://www.indo-european.nl/index2.html).

60. Bachvarova 2002; Latacz 2004.

61. On the terminology, borrowed from linguistics, see Watkins 2001.

62. Tassignon 2001. These myths are conveniently translated by Hoffner (1998, 14–29).

63. Burkert 1979, 123–142. Also see the review of connections by Suter (2002, 229–236). Besides the story of Demeter, the Telipinu narrative presents a precedent for Pandora's box (Fauth 1974, 120–121; Haas 1993, 78–83). Also see the discussion in Alexiou 2002, 55–82, on lamenting the departure and rejoicing for the return of harvest gods.

64. *Keilschrifturkunden aus Boghazköi* (1921–1990; henceforth KUB) 3.103 obv. 5. Discussions of this genre may be found in Bachvarova 2002, 151–165; de Roos 1995, esp. 2000–2001; and Lebrun 1980, 431–440. The term *mukessar* can be replaced by the Sumerogram SISKUR, "sacrifice." See the discussion and examples in *The Hittite Dictionary of the Oriental Institute of the University of Chicago* (Güterbock and Hoffner 1989–) and the *Hittite Etymological Dictionary* (Puhvel 1984). *The Hittite Dictionary* is puzzled by the Akkadian gloss discussed here.

65. KUB 33.8 iii 3–22, filled in with *Istanbul Arkeoloji Müzelerinde Bulunan Boghazköy Tableteri(nden Seçme Metlinler)* (IBoT) 3.141 iii 21–23. Also see the translation in Hoffner 1998, 19–20, and a discussion of the similarities between Greek and Anatolian invocations in Bachvarova forthcoming a.

66. On Mesopotamian influence on Anatolian literature, see most recently Richter (2002, with earlier references), who distinguishes between earlier unmediated influence and later influence mediated by the North Syrian Hurrians.

67. Sourvinou-Inwood 2003b, 79–88.

68. *Keilschrifttexte aus Boghazköi* (henceforth KBo) 14.70 i 15–16 (Laroche 1971, 154); KUB 30–27 obv. 7–9 (Otten 1958, 98).

69. Alexiou 2002, 59, 109–110.

70. KBo 43.4 ii? 5', 31.77 i 7', 12' (Polvani 2007). I thank Professor Polvani for sharing her article with me in advance of publication.

71. *Materials for the Sumerian Lexicon = Civil 1969* (MSL) 12.120 27' (see Henshaw 1994, 107).

72. Johnston 1999, 80–90.

73. Lit., "great place."

74. *Aḫulap* seems to be a mourning cry; *ub* and *lilis* are two kinds of drums. Translated in Kramer 1981, 5.17–23.

75. See the discussion in Alster 1982. On the *kurgarrû*, see n. 11.

76. Translated in Black et al. 2004, 72. Interestingly, in the Akkadian version of this story, Enki creates an *assinnu/kulu'um* instead of the *kurgarrû* and *gala* (Henshaw 1994, 288). Also see the discussion of this scene by Taylor (2003, 162–163).

77. Penglase 1994, 128–158, with earlier references.

78. "Descent of Ishtar to the Netherworld" (translated in Foster 2005, 502; Jacobsen 1987, 205).

79. Translated in Cohen 1993, 481; Foster 2005, 504–505; Henshaw 1994, 109. Also see the general discussion in Cohen 1993, 454–481.

80. Harris 2003, 166.

81. See Balzer 1996; Eliade 1972, 257–258, 351–354. See n. 11 for the comparison. See Burkert (1979, 183 n. 12), as well as Groneberg (1997b, 153–154, with earlier references), who connects *kurgarrûs*' and *assinnus*' sexual ambiguity with Ishtar's, which causes her to see Ishtar herself as a shaman.

82. See discussions by Csapo (1997), who elucidates some odd imagery involving *phalloi*, and Hoffmann (1989, 93–100), who focuses on the carnival-esque aspects of exaggerated sexuality and transvestism. Maurizio (2001) provides another interesting analysis of the practice of playing the Other. Henrichs notes the connection between "Dionysiac" ritual and transvestism, even while insisting, "In any case, ritual transvestitism was never prominent in Dionysiac cult" (1982, 158–159). Bremmer (1999) connects the youthful Dionysus's feminine appearance with rites of passage. Gherchanoc (2003) provides thorough coverage of the theme of feminized men in ancient Greece. In an iconographic study Caruso (1987) shows that maenads may appear with phallic costumes, just as men may be represented as dressed in *peploi*, and Miller reviews scholarly explanations for transvestite komasts and Greek transvestism in general, arguing that "emphatic crossing of the gender boundary. . . functioned as a strategy for coping with elite anxieties" (1999, 253).

83. Harris 2003, 167–171. See n. 11.

84. The tangled origins of the Anatolian goddess Cybele/Kubaba lie beyond the scope of this investigation. The reader is referred to the discussion in Roller 1999.

85. Taylor 2003, 150–181, pace Lane 1996.

86. Gow and Page 1965, 6.10, 32, 217–220; SP 2.1.01 (translated in Alster 1997, 65).

87. *Catalogue des textes hittites* (Laroche 1971, CTH) 771.1; KUB 25.37 i 46'–51', 35.131 i 6'–11' (Güterbock 1995, improving Starke 1985, 344); see discussion in Taylor 2003, 166, and Taylor 2007

88. Also note the "thin voice" (*leptaleei phonei*) in which the Linos lament is sung (*Il.* 18.571, schol. 18.580), discussed by McClure (1999, 42–44) and West (1992, 45–46).

89. "Songs of conciliation of the men of Istanuwa" are mentioned in a catalog (KUB 30.42 i 1) and were performed by the men of Lallupiya (KBo 20.56; KUB 32.13 [Starke 1985, 352–353, discussion at 299–300]). "Songs of thunder" (KBo 4.11 left edge) were performed during a series of animal sacrifices to the pantheon, beginning with a bull to the Storm God of Istanuwa (KBo 4.11 obv. 1 [Starke 1985, 339–342, discussion at 299–300]).

90. Casadio 2003.

91. See Burkert 1992, 2004; Morris 1992; West 1997.

92. See Watkins 2001 for an explanation of this approach.

93. KUB 55.65 iv 16 (Starke 1985, 313).

94. Sultanhan §2–9 (translated in Hawkins 2000, 465–466), dating to 740–730 B.C.E. See the discussion in Ivanov 2001, 144 nn. 87–89. For depictions of the Storm God of the Vine, see Ivriz 1, plates 292–295 (Hawkins 2000, descriptions at 516–517), 738–710 B.C.E.; Niğde 2, plate 301 (Hawkins 2000, description at 526–527), end of the eighth/beginning of the seventh century B.C.E.

95. On scholarly theories concerning the connection, see the critique in Miller 1999, 235–236.

96. Schol. Ar. *Ach.* 243a (see Sourvinou-Inwood 2003b, 104–105). Other analyses of tragedy are critiqued by Suter (this volume).

97. Sourvinou-Inwood 2003b, 5.

98. On this, see Alexiou 2002, 14–23; Foley 2001, 27; Seaford 1994, 106–143.

99. Not only were offerings for the ordinary dead linked to offerings for Dumuzi, but, as Cohen notes, "[t]he kings of Ur identified themselves with Dumuzi the shepherd....So too there was a strong bond between Ur and the traditions of Uruk, where Dumuzi in ancient times supposedly reigned as king. And this identification persisted after the ruler's death—the dead king was Dumuzi who had been carried away by demons.... It seemed natural that festivals for the deceased Dumuzi evolved into festivals for the deceased kings" (1993, 476–477).

BIBLIOGRAPHY

Alexiou, Margaret. 2002. *The Ritual Lament in Greek Tradition*. 2nd ed. Rev. Dimitrios Yatromanolakis and Panagiotis Roilos. Lanham, Md.

Al-Rawi, Farouk N. H. 1992. Two Old Akkadian Letters Concerning the Offices of *kala'um* and *nārum*. *Zeitschrift der Assyriologie und vorderasiatische Archäologie* 92: 180–185.

Alster, Bendt. 1982. The Mythology of Mourning. *Acta Sumerologica* 4: 1–16.

———. 1997. *Proverbs of Ancient Sumer: The World's Earliest Proverb Collections.* Bethesda, Md.

Bachvarova, Mary R. 1997. The Literary Use of Dialects: Ancient Greek, Indic and Sumerian. In *CLS 33: Papers from the Panels on Linguistic Ideologies in Contact, Universal Grammar, Parameters and Typology, the Perception of Speech and Other Acoustic Signals*, ed. Kora Singer, Randall Eggert, and Gregory D. S. Anderson, 7–22. Chicago.

———. 2002. From Hittite to Homer: The Role of Anatolians in the Transmission of Epic and Prayer Motifs from the Ancient Near East to the Ancient Greeks. Unpublished Ph.D. dissertation, University of Chicago.

———. 2007. Oath and Allusion in Alcaeus fr. 129. In *Horkos: Proceedings of the International Conference on the Oath*, ed. Alan H. Sommerstein and Judith Fletcher, 179–188. Woodbridge, Conn.

———. Forthcoming. Hittite and Greek Perspectives on Traveling Poets, Festivals and Texts. In *Poeti Vaganti*, ed. Richard Hunter and Ian Rutherford.

Balzer, Marjorie Mandelstam. 1996. Sacred Genders in Siberia: Shamans, Bear Festivals, and Androgyny. In *Gender Reversals and Gender Cultures: Anthropological and Historical Perspectives*, ed. Sabrina Petra Ramet, 164–182. London.

Black, Jeremy. 1991. *Eme-sal* Cult Songs and Prayers. In Velles Paraules*: Ancient Near Eastern Studies in Honor of Miguel Civil on the Occasion of His Sixty-fifth Birthday*, ed. Piotr Michalowski, Piotr Steinkeller, Elizabeth Caecilia Stowe, and Richard L. Zettler. 23–36. Aula Orientalis 9. Barcelona.

———. 2004. Dumuzid and His Sisters. *Orientalia* N.S. 73: 228–234.

Black, Jeremy, Graham Cunningham, Jarle Ebeling, Esther Flückiger-Hawker, Eleanor Robson, J. Taylor, and Gábor Zólyomi, eds. 1998–2006. *The Electronic Text Corpus of Sumerian Literature*. Oxford. (http://etcsl.orinst.ox.ac.uk/)

Black, Jeremy, Graham Cunningham, Eleanor Robson, and Gábor Zólyomi, eds. 2004. *The Literature of Ancient Sumer*. Oxford.

Black, Jeremy, and Anthony Green, eds. 1992. *Gods, Demons and Symbols of Ancient Mesopotamia: An Illustrated Dictionary.* Austin.

Bottéro, Jean. 2001. *Religion in Ancient Mesopotamia.* Trans. Teresa Lavender Fagan. Chicago.

Bottéro, Jean, and H. Petschow. 1975. Homosexualität. In *Reallexikon der Assyriologie und vorderasiatischen Archäologie 4,* ed. Dietz O. Edzard, 459–468. Berlin.

Bremmer, Jan N. 1999. Transvestite Dionysos. In *Rites of Passage in Ancient Greece: Literature, Religion, Society,* ed. Mark Padilla, 183–199. Lewisburg, Pa.

Briggs, Charles L. 1992. "Since I Am a Woman, I Will Chastise My Relatives": Gender, Reported Speech, and the (Re)Production of Social Relations in Warao Ritual Wailing. *American Ethnologist* 19: 337–361.

Burkert, Walter. 1979. *Structure and History in Greek Mythology and Ritual.* Sather Classical Lectures 47. Berkeley.

——. 1992. *The Orientalizing Revolution: Near Eastern Influence on Greek Culture in the Early Archaic Age.* Trans. Margaret E. Pinder and Walter Burkert. Cambridge.

——. 2004. *Babylon, Memphis, Persepolis: Eastern Contexts of Greek Culture.* Cambridge, Mass.

Caraveli, Anna. 1986. The Bitter Wounding: Lament as Social Protest. In *Rural Greece, Gender and Power in Rural Greece,* ed. Jill Dubisch, 169–194. Princeton.

Caraveli-Chaves, Anna. 1980. Bridge Between Worlds: The Greek Women's Lament as Communicative Event. *Journal of American Folklore* 93: 129–157.

Caruso, Christiane. 1987. Travestissements dionysiaques. In *Images et société en Grèce ancienne: Iconographie comme méthode d'analyse,* ed. Claude Bérard, Christiane Bron, and Alessandra Pomari, 103–110. Lausanne.

Casadio, Giovanni. 2003. The Failing Male God: Emasculation, Death and Other Accidents in the Ancient Mediterranean World. *Numen* 50: 232–268.

Civil, M. ed. 1969. *The Series lu = sa and Related Texts,* with the collaboration of R. D. Biggs, H. G. Guterbock, H. J. Nissen, E. Reiner. Rome.

Civil, Miguel. 1973. The Sumerian Writing System: Some Problems. *Orientalia* N.S. 42: 21–34.

Cohen, Mark E. 1981. *Sumerian Hymnology: The Eršemma.* Hebrew Union College Annual Supplements 2. Cincinnati.

——. 1988. *The Canonical Lamentations of Ancient Mesopotamia.* 2 vols. Potomac, Md.

——. 1993. *The Cultic Calendars of the Ancient Near East.* Bethesda, Md.

Cooper, Jerrold S. 1983. *The Curse of Agade.* Baltimore.

Csapo, Eric. 1997. Riding the Phallus for Dionysus: Iconology, Ritual, and Gender-Role De/Construction. *Phoenix* 51: 253–295.

Dale, Amy Marjorie. 1968. *The Lyric Metres of Greek Drama.* 2nd ed. Cambridge.

——. 1969. *Collected Papers.* Cambridge.

Danforth, Loring M. 1982. *The Death Rituals of Rural Greece.* Princeton.

de Roos, J. 1995. Hittite Prayers. In *Civilizations of the Ancient Near East,* ed. J. M. Sasson, 1997–2005. New York.

Diakonoff, I. M. 1976. Ancient Writing and Ancient Written Language: Pitfalls and Peculiarities in the Study of Sumerian. *Assyriological Studies* 20: 99–122.

Dobbs-Allsop, F. W. 1993. *Weep, O Daughter of Zion: A Study of the City-Lament Genre in the Hebrew Bible.* Rome.

Ekroth, Gunnel. 1998. Altars in Greek Hero-Cults: A Review of the Archaeological Evidence. In *Ancient Greek Cult Practice from the Archaeological Evidence,*

Proceedings of the Fourth International Seminar on Ancient Greek Cult, Orga-nized by the Swedish Institute at Athens, 22–24 October 1993, ed. Robin Hägg, 117–130. Skrifter Utgivna av Svenska Institutet i Athen 8° 15. Stockholm.

———. 2000. Offerings of Blood in Greek Hero-Cults. In *Héros et héroïnes dans les mythes et les cultes grecs: Actes du Colloque organisé à l'Université de Valladolid du 26 au 29 mai 1999,* ed. Vinciane Pirenne-Delforge and Emilio Suárez de la Torre, 263–281. Kernos supplément 10. Liège.

———. 2002. *The Sacrificial Rituals of Greek Hero-Cults in the Archaic to the Early Hellenistic Periods.* Liège.

Eliade, Mircea. 1972. *Shamanism: Archaic Techniques of Ecstasy.* Princeton.

Else, Gerald. 1977. Ritual and Drama in Aischyleian Tragedy. *Illinois Classical Studies* 2: 70–87.

Farber, Walter. 1989. *Schlaf, Kindschen, schlaf! Mesopotamische Baby-Beschwörun-gen und -Rituale.* Winona Lake, Ind.

Fauth, Wolfgang. 1974. Der Schlund des Orkus: Zu einer Eigentümkeit der römisch-etruskischen Unterweltsvorstellung. *Numen* 21: 105–127.

Ferris, Paul Wayne, Jr. 1992. *The Genre of Communal Lament in the Bible and the Ancient Near East.* Atlanta.

Foley, Helene P. 2001. *Female Acts in Greek Tragedy.* Princeton.

Foster, Benjamin R. 2005. *Before the Muses: An Anthology of Akkadian Literature.* 3rd ed. Bethesda, Md.

Franklin, John Curtis. 2005. Lyre Gods of the Bronze Age Musical *Koine. Journal of Ancient Near Eastern Religions* 6: 39–70.

———. 2006. The Wisdom of the Lyre: Soundings in Ancient Greece, Cyprus and the Near East. In *Musikarchäologie im Kontext: Archäologische Befunde, histor-ischer Zusammenhang, soziokulturelle Bezeihungen und andere Bindungen,* ed. E. Hickmann and R. Eichmann, 1–19. Studien zur Musikarchäologie 5. Berlin.

Friedrich, Rainer. 2000. Dionysus Among the Dons: The New Ritualism in Richard Seaford's Commentary on the *Bacchae. Arion Third Series* 7 (3): 115–152.

Frymer-Kensky, Tivka. 1992. *In the Wake of the Goddess: Women, Culture, and the Biblical Transformation of Pagan Myth.* New York.

Gelb, I. J. 1976. *Homo Ludens* in Early Mesopotamia. *Studia Orientalia* 46: 43–76.

Gherchanoc, Florence. 2003. Les atours féminins des hommes: Quelques repré-sentations du masculin-féminin dans le monde grec antique. Entre initiation, ruse, séduction et grotesque, surpuissance et déchéance. *Revue Historique* 35: 739–791.

Gow, A. S. F., and D. L. Page, eds. 1965. *The Greek Anthology: Hellenistic Epigrams, Vol. 2.* Cambridge.

Green, Margaret W. 1978. The Eridu Lament. *Journal of Cuneiform Studies* 30: 127–167.

———. 1984. The Uruk Lament. *Journal of the American Oriental Society* 104: 253–279.

Groneberg, Brigitte. 1986. Die sumerisch-akkadische Inanna/Ištar: Hermaphroditos? *Die Welt des Orients* 17: 25–46.

———. 1997a. Ein Ritual an Ištar. *Mari, Annales de Recherches Interdisciplinaires* 8: 291–303.

———. 1997b. *Lob der Ištar: Gebet und Ritual an die altbabylonische Venusgöttin.* Groningen.

Güterbock, Hans G. 1995. Reflections on the Musical Instruments *arkammi, galgalturi,* and *ḫuḫupal in Hittite.* In *Studia historiae Ardens: Ancient Near Eastern Studies Presented to H. J. Houwink ten Cate on the Occasion of His 65th Birthday,* ed. Theo P. J. Van den Hout and Jan de Roos, 57–72. Istanbul.

Güterbock, Hans G., and Harry A. Hoffner Jr., eds. 1989–. *The Hittite Dictionary of the Oriental Institute of the University of Chicago.* Chicago.

Gwaltney, W. C., Jr. 1983. The Biblical Book of Lamentations in the Context of Near Eastern Literature. In *Scripture in Context II: More Essays on the Comparative Method,* ed. William W. Hallo, James C. Moyer, and Leo G. Perdue, 191–211. Winona Lake, Ind.

Haas, Volkert. 1993. Ein hurritscher Blutritus und die Deponierung der Ritualrückstände nach hethitischen Quellen. In *Religionsgeschichtliche Beziehungen zwischen Kleinasien, Nordsyrien und dem Alten Testament. Internationales Symposium Hamburg 17.–21. März 1990,* ed. Berndt Janowski, Klaus Koch, and Gernot Wilhelm, 67–85. Göttingen.

Hallo, William W. 1995. Lamentations and Prayers in Sumer and Akkad. In *Civilizations of the Ancient Near East,* ed. J. M. Sasson, 1871–1881. New York.

Hallo, William W., and J. J. A. van Dijk, eds. 1968. *The Exaltation of Inanna.* Yale Near Eastern Researches 3. New Haven.

Hallo, William W., and K. Lawson Younger Jr., eds. 1997. *The Context of Scripture: Vol. 1: Canonical Compositions from the Biblical World.* Leiden.

Hamilton, Richard. 1992. *Choes and Anthesteria: Athenian Iconography and Ritual.* Ann Arbor.

Harris, Rivkah. 2003. *Gender and Aging in Mesopotamia: The Gilgamesh Epic and Other Ancient Literature.* Norman, Okla.

Hawkins, John David. 2000. *Corpus of Hieroglyphic Luwian Inscriptions, Vol. 1: Inscriptions of the Iron Age.* Untersuchungen zur indogermanischen Sprach- und Kulturwissenschaft 8. Berlin.

Henrichs, Albert. 1982. Changing Dionysiac Identities. In *Jewish and Christian Self-Definition, Vol. 3: Self-Definition in the Greco-Roman World,* ed. Ben F. Meyer and E. P. Sanders, 137–160. Philadelphia.

Henshaw, Richard A. 1994. *Female and Male: The Cultic Personnel: The Bible and the Rest of the Ancient Near East.* Allison Park, Pa.

Herington, John. 1985. *Poetry into Drama.* Sather Classical Lectures 49. Berkeley.

Hoffmann, R. J. 1989. Ritual License and the Cult of Dionysus. *Athenaeum* 77: 91–115.

Hoffner, Harry A., Jr. 1998. *Hittite Myths.* 2nd ed. Writings from the Ancient World 2. Atlanta.

Holst-Warhaft, Gail. 1992. *Dangerous Voices: Women's Laments and Greek Literature.* London.

Ivanov, Vjacheslav V. 2001. Southern Anatolian and Northern Anatolian: As Separate Indo-European Dialects and Anatolian as a Late Linguistic Zone. In *Greater Anatolia and the Indo-Hittite Language Family: Papers Presented at a Colloquium Hosted by the University of Richmond, March 18–19, 2000,* ed. Robert Drews, 131–183. Washington, D.C.

Jacobsen, Thorkild. 1987. *The Harps That Once . . . : Sumerian Poetry in Translation.* New Haven.

Jaffrey, Zia. 1999. *The Invisibles: A Tale of Eunuchs of India.* New York.

Johnston, Sarah Iles. 1999. *Restless Dead: Encounters between the Living and the Dead in Ancient Greece.* Berkeley.

Korzeniewski, D. 1968. *Griechische Metrik*. Darmstadt.

Koster, W. J. W. 1962. *Traité de métrique grecque suivi d' un précis de métrique latine*. 3rd ed. Leiden.

Kramer, Samuel Noah. 1981. BM 29616: The Fashioning of the *Gala*. *Acta Sumerologica* 3: 1–11.

———. 1983. The Weeping Goddess: Sumerian Prototypes of the *Mater Dolorosa*. *Biblical Archaeologist* 46: 69–80.

Krecher, J. 1966. *Sumerische Kultlyrik*. Wiesbaden.

———. 1967. Zum Emesal-Dialekt des Sumerischen. In *Adam Falkenstein zum 17. September 1966*, ed. Otto E. Dietz, 87–110. Heidelberger Studien zum alten Orient. Wiesbaden.

Lane, Eugene N. 1996. The Name of Cybele's Priests: The "Galloi." In *Cybele, Attis and Related Cults: Essays in Memory of M. J. Vermaseren*, ed. Eugene N. Lane, 117–133. Leiden.

Langenmayr, Arnold. 1993. Sprachpsychologische Untersuchung zur sumerischen Frauensprache (eme-sal). *Sprache und Kognition* 12: 2–17.

Laroche, Emmanuel. 1971. *Catalogue des textes hittites*. Paris.

Latacz, Joachim. 2004. *Troy and Homer: Towards a Solution of an Old Mystery*. Trans. K. Windle and Rosh Ireland. Oxford.

Lebrun, René. 1980. *Hymnes et prières hittites*. Homo Religiosus 4. Louvain-la-Neuve, Belgium.

Lee, Nancy C. 2002. *The Singers of Lamentations: Cities Under Siege, from Ur to Jerusalem to Sarajevo*. Leiden.

Leick, Gwendolyn. 1991. *A Dictionary of Ancient Near Eastern Myth*. London.

———. 1994. *Sex and Eroticism in Mesopotamian Literature*. London.

Livingstone, Alisdair. 1986. *Mystical and Mythological Explanatory Works of Assyrian and Babylonian Scholars*. Oxford.

Loraux, Nicole. 1986. *The Invention of Athens: The Funeral Oration in the Classical City*. Trans. Alan Sheridan. Cambridge, Mass.

———. 1998. *Mothers in Mourning: With the Essay of Amnesty and Its Opposite*. Trans. Corinne Pache. Ithaca, N.Y.

Maul, M. Stefan. 1982. *"Herzberuhigungsklagen": Die sumerisch-akkadischen Eršaḫunga-Gebete*. Wiesbaden.

Maurizio, Lisa. 2001. Performance, Hysteria and Democratic Identities in the Anthesteria. *Helios* 28: 29–41.

McClure, Laura K. 1999. *Spoken like a Woman: Speech and Gender in Athenian Drama*. Princeton.

Meier, Christian. 1993. *The Political Art of Greek Tragedy*. Trans. A. Webber. Baltimore, Md.

Michalowski, Piotr. 1989. *The Lamentation over the Destruction of Sumer and Ur*. Winona Lake, Ind.

———. 1992. Orality and Literacy and Early Mesopotamian Literature. In *Mesopotamian Epic Literature: Oral or Aural?* ed. Marianna E. Vogelzang and Herman L. J. Vanstiphout, 227–245. Lewiston, Pa.

Miller, Margaret C. 1999. Reexamining Transvestism in Archaic and Classical Athens: The Zewadski Stamnos. *American Journal of Archaeology* 103: 223–253.

Morris, Sarah P. 1992. *Daidalos and the Origins of Greek Art*. Princeton.

Nanda, Serena. 1999. *Neither Man nor Woman: The Hijras of India*. 2nd ed. Belmont, Calif.

Nissinen, Martti. 1998. *Homoeroticism in the Biblical World: A Historical Perspective*. Trans. Kirsi Stjerna. Minneapolis.

Otten, Heinrich. 1958. *Hethitische Totenrituale*. Deutsche Akademie der Wissenschaften zu Berlin, Institut für Orientforschung, Veröffentlichung 37. Berlin.

Penglase, Charles. 1994. *Greek Myths and Mesopotamia: Parallels and Influence in the Homeric Hymns and Hesiod*. London.

Polvani, Anna Maria. 2007. The "Death" of Kamrušepa. In *Tabularia Hethaeorum: Hethitologische Beiträge Silvin Košak zum 65en Geburtstag*, ed. Detlev Groddek and T. M. Zorman, 569–574. Wiesbaden.

Powell, I., ed. 1925. *Collectanea Alexandrina*. Oxford.

Puhvel, Jaan. 1984. *Hittite Etymological Dictionary.* Berlin.

Richter, Thomas. 2002. Zur Frage der Entlehnung syrisch-mesopotamischer Kulturelemente nach Anatolien in der vor- und frühen althethitischen Zeit (19.–16. Jahrhundert v. Chr.). In *Brückenland Anatolien: Ursachen, Extensität und Modi des Kulturaustasches zwischen Anatolien und sein Nachbarn*, ed. Hartmut Blum, Betina Faist, and Peter Pfälzner, 295–322. Tübingen.

Roberts, J. J. M. [1992] 2002. The Motif of the Weeping God in Jeremiah and Its Background in the Lament Tradition of the Ancient Near East. *Old Testament Essays* 5: 361–374. Reprint, in *The Bible and the Ancient Near East: Collected Essays*, ed. J. J. M. Roberts, 132–142. Winona Lake, Ind.

Roller, Lynn E. 1999. *In Search of God the Mother: The Cult of Anatolian Cybele*. Berkeley.

Roscoe, Will. 1996. Priests of the Goddess: Gender Transgression in Ancient Religion. *History of Religions* 35: 195–230.

Rubio, Gonzalo. 2001. Inanna and Dumuzi: A Sumerian Love Story. *Journal of the American Oriental Society* 121: 268–274.

Rutherford, Ian. 1993. Paeanic Ambiguity: A Study of the Representation of the παιάν in Greek Literature. *Quaderni Urbinati di Cultura Classica* N.S. 44: 77–92.

——. 1995. Apollo in Ivy: The Tragic Paean. *Arion Third Series* 3: 112–135.

——. 2001. *Pindar's Paeans: A Reading of the Fragments with a Survey of the Genre*. Oxford.

Schretter, Manfred K. 1990. *Emesal-Studien: Sprach- und Literaturgeschichtliche Untersuchungen zur sogenannten Frauensprache des Sumerischen*. Innsbrucker Beiträge zur Sprachwissenschaft 69. Innsbruck.

Scullion, Scott. 1994. Olympic and Chthonian Gods. *Classical Antiquity* 13: 75–119.

——. 2000. Heroic and Chthonian Sacrifice: New Evidence from Selinous. *Zeitschrift für Papyrologie und Epigraphik* 132: 163–171.

Seaford, Richard. 1994. *Reciprocity and Ritual: Homer and Tragedy in the Developing City-State*. Oxford.

——. 1997a. *Euripides' Bacchae with an Introduction, Translation and Commentary.* Warminster, U.K.

——. 1997b. Thunder, Lightning and Earthquake in the *Bacchae* and the Acts of the Apostles. In *What Is a God? Studies in the Nature of Greek Divinity*, ed. A. B. Lloyd, 139–152. London.

Sefati, Yitschak. 1998. *Love Songs in Sumerian Literature: Critical Edition of the Dumuzi-Inanna Songs*. Jerusalem.

Seremetakis, C. Nadia. 1991. *The Last Word: Women, Death, and Divination in Inner Mani*. Chicago.

Seremetakis, C. Nadia. 1993. Durations of Pain: The Antiphony of Death and Women's Power in Southern Greece. In *Ritual, Power and the Body: Historical Perspectives on the Representation of Greek Women*, ed. C. Nadia Seremitakis, 119–149. New York.

Sourvinou-Inwood, Christiane. 2003a. Festival and Mysteries: Aspects of the Eleusinian Cult. In *Greek Mysteries: The Archaeology and Ritual of Ancient Greek Secret Cults*, ed. Michael B. Cosmopoulos, 25–49. London.

———. 2003b. *Tragedy and Athenian Religion*. Lanham, Md.

Starke, Frank. 1985. *Die keilschrift-luwischen Texte in Umschrift*. Studien zu den Boğazköy-Texten 30. Wiesbaden.

Stears, Karen. 1998. Death Becomes Her: Gender and Athenian Death Ritual. In *The Sacred and the Feminine in Ancient Greece*, ed. Sue Blundell and Margaret Williamson, 113–127. London.

Stehle, Eva. 2004. Choral Prayer in Greek Tragedy: Euphemia or Aischrologia? In *Music and the Muses: The Culture of "Mousikê" in the Classical Athenian City*, ed. Penelope Murray and Peter Wilson, 121–156. Oxford.

———. 2005. Prayer and Curse in Aeschylus' *Seven Against Thebes*. *Classical Philology* 100: 101–122.

Suter, Ann. 2002. *The Narcissus and the Pomegranate: An Archaeology of the Homeric Hymn to Demeter*. Ann Arbor.

Tassignon, Isabelle. 2001. Les éléments anatoliens du mythe et de la personnalité de Dionysos. *Revue de l'histoire des religions* 218: 307–337.

Taylor, Patrick John. 2003. Studies in Ancient Anatolian Language and Culture. Unpublished Ph.D. dissertation, Harvard University.

———. 2007. The GALA and the *Gallos*. In *Anatolian Interfaces: Hittites, Greeks and Their Neighbors. Proceedings of an International Conference on Cross-Cultural Interaction, September 17–19, 2004, Emory University, Atlanta, Ga.*, ed. Billie Jean Collins, Mary R. Bachvarova, and Ian C. Rutherford. Woodbridge Conn.: 175–182.

Tinney, Steve. 1996. *The Nippur Lament: Royal Rhetoric and Divine Legitimation in the Reign of Išme-Dagan of Isin (1953–1935 B.C.)*. Occasional Publications of the Samuel Noah Kramer Fund 16. Philadelphia.

Watkins, Calvert. 2001. An Indo-European Linguistic Area and Its Characteristics: Ancient Anatolia. Areal Diffusion as a Challenge to the Comparative Method? In *Areal Diffusion and Genetic Inheritance: Problems in Comparative Linguistics*, ed. Alexandra Y. Aikhenvald and Richard M. W. Dixon, 44–63. Oxford.

West, Martin L. 1982. *Greek Metre*. Oxford.

———. 1992. *Ancient Greek Music*. Oxford.

———. 1997. *The East Face of Helicon*. Oxford.

Westenholz, Joan Goodnick. 1989. Enheduanna, En-Priestess, Hen of Nanna, Spouse of Nanna. In *DUMU-E$_2$-DUB-BA-A: Studies in Honor of Åke W. Sjöberg*, ed. Hermann Behrens, Darlene Loding, and Martha T. Roth, 539–256. Occasional Publications of the Samuel Noah Kramer Fund 11. Philadelphia.

White, J. W. 1912. *The Verse of Greek Comedy*. London.

Wood, John C. 1999. *When Men Are Women: Manhood Among Gabra Nomads of East Africa*. Madison, Wisc.

Wright, Elinor Scollay. 1986. The Form of Laments in Greek Tragedy. Unpublished Ph.D. dissertation, University of Pennsylvania.

3

"WHEN YOU GO TO THE MEADOW..."

The Lament of the *Taptara*-Women in the Hittite *Sallis Wastais* Ritual

IAN RUTHERFORD

The Hittite Kingdom that dominated central Anatolia for about four centuries during the middle of the second millennium B.C.E. is gradually revealing itself to modern scholars, thanks to the discovery and deciphering of extensive archives from its capital at Hattusa (modern Boghaz Köy) in the early decades of the twentieth century. Hittite religion and society are turning out to have been a complex, multilayered structure with Indo-European elements fused with a pre-Indo-European ("Hattic") substrate, heavily influenced by the civilization of North Syria. Most of what has been learned about it relates to the experiences and activities of the royal family, the festivals they took part in, their prayers, their intrigues, and their dreams; and for death too the treatment of royalty is much better documented than that of any one else in the society.[1]

Most of our information about the royal funerary ritual is textual; archaeology has made little contribution (a point of contrast with mortuary practice in the roughly contemporary Mycenaean civilization in Greece, for which the sources are almost exclusively archaeological).[2] The most important document for Hittite funerary ritual is the fourteen-day royal funerary ritual, known as the "*Sallis Wastais* Ritual" (henceforth SWR), named after the expression *sallis wastais* (great loss), which occurs in the opening lines:

> If a great loss occurs in Hattusa—either king or queen becomes
> a god—everyone, adult and young, takes away their reed
> *SULPATE*-objects and begins to wail.[3]

53

The death of the king or queen is described as "becoming a god," anticipating the ideology of Roman imperial funerals a millennium later. The idea that the king has to wait till death to become divine differentiated Hatti from contemporary Egypt, where the pharaohs were immanent deities on earth. Equally, the idea that a king or queen becomes a god at all is probably quite distinct from the much bleaker expectations of ordinary Hittite men and women about their own deaths.[4]

The end of the quotation above states that the inhabitants of Hattusa "begin to wail," the first of many references to wailing and lamentation in the SWR.[5] In this chapter, I will discuss the role of lamentation and lamenters in the ritual, an endeavor that will require a brief survey of the ritual itself, followed by an overview of episodes of lamentation within it, with special focus on the performances of one group, the so-called *taptara*-women. Finally, I will address the issue of why the most important performance by the *taptara*-women, the only utterance of theirs for which the words are actually supplied in the text, comes almost at the end of the SWR, during the night between Day 13 and Day 14, accompanying the symbolic burning of a cord.

THE SWR

The surviving copies of the texts of the SWR date mostly from the thirteenth century B.C.E., the final decades of the Hittite New Kingdom, but there is reason to believe that the texts themselves were many centuries older and had their origins in the earliest stages of Hittite civilization.[6] The texts are of several types: the primary text is a complete description of the festival, but there is also a summary outline tablet, a ration list, and a liturgy giving the words of individual participants. The primary text is written like a description, in third-person singular (like all Hittite ritual texts), but in fact the point of it must be to prescribe what has to be done. The first edition of the whole text was completed by Heinrich Otten; the most recent and most complete is by Kassian, Korolëv, and Sidel'tsev (henceforth KKS), which also includes an English translation.

The SWR mentions a whole cast of participants who might be thought of as ritual actors, for the whole action resembles in many respects a macabre drama. Some of these are familiar from other Hittite ritual and festival texts: the Cup Bearer (SAGI.A), the Comedian (ALAN.ZU$_9$), the Barbers ($^{LU.MES}$SU.I), and the Old Woman (SU.GI), one of the most common figures in Hittite rituals.[7] Besides these ritual actors, agency in the ritual is also frequently attributed to an unidentified "they." Some persons one might expect to be mentioned are not: the new king is not involved, as far as we can see; and there is little involvement of members of his family, although there is a role for "a relative of the deceased."[8]

One group of participants found only in the SWR are the *taptara*-women, specialized wailers who formed a kind of chorus; in fact, in Hittite the expression "*taptara*-women" is a collective noun (i.e., $^{MUNUS.MES}$*taptara* rather than ^{MUNUS.MES}*taptares*) and governs a singular verb.[9] *Taptara*-men are not attested (i.e., the word is always accompanied by the determinative for "woman/women" rather than the one for "man/men"), with the exception of one problematic text that uses the determinative for man: ^{LU}*taptara*.[10] This, then, would seem to be an instance of the common tendency (of which several instances are studied in this volume) for female performers to have a central role in funerary ritual.[11] Little is known of the *taptara*-women outside funerary ritual. One text refers to a "house of the *taptara*-women," which suggests a degree of institutional organization.[12] Is it possible that when they were not involved in the SWR they performed rituals in royal mausoleums?[13]

Most of the content of the ritual can be reconstructed, though there are a few gaps and many obscurities. During the first three days, the king or queen's body was cremated, and the bones were gathered together and housed in a mausoleum, the "stone house" (É.NA4), usually one located in the Hittite capital at Hattusa.[14] This part of the SWR has been thought in the past to bear some resemblance to Homer's account of the cremation of the Greek hero Patroclus.[15] After the cremation, an effigy of the deceased was placed on the pyre, which was decorated with fruit and other things.[16] Day 3 included the mysterious ritual of the balance (KKS 267–269):

> The Old Woman speaks opposite her colleague as follows, calls
> the deceased by name "(Someone) brings him, so-and-so. Who
> brings/leads him?" And her colleague says: "The men of Hatti, the
> *uruhha*-men bring him." And she says "Let them not bring him."
> And her colleague says "Take the silver and gold for yourself."
> And she says "I shall not take it for myself." She says likewise
> thrice. For the third time, however, she says once the following: "I
> shall take the clay mortar for myself." And she smashes the balance
> into smithereens, and holds it towards the Sungod. She laments.
> The *taptara*-women begin wailing.[17]

Days 4–6 are the least well preserved, but they seem to have included a ritual of conciliation (*lilawar*), which was performed alongside the main part of the ritual and apparently not always performed.[18]

Days 7–13 were occupied by a sequence of subrituals, performed in the presence of an effigy of the deceased (constructed soon after the cremation), which was each day placed in a chariot.[19] These subrituals were apparently designed to ensure the convenience of the king or queen in the afterlife; in each of them, some special item representing an aspect of the deceased's life in this world was destroyed, apparently so that its essence might be transported to the afterlife where the king or queen could make use of it. Thus, the purpose of this part of the SWR was to "secure for the deceased an afterlife modeled on his former existence."[20] So, for example, on Day 8, when a piece of turf, symbolizing a meadow, is dedicated to the deceased, the Old Woman says (KKS 385):

And this meadow, O Sungod, make rightful for him. May no
one take it away from him, nor sue him! May the oxen and sheep,
the horse and mules graze for him on this meadow.

The king, who becomes a god in the afterlife, takes on the role of a farmer
tending an otherworldly "meadow," like the paradisiacal fields of Yarru in
Egyptian mythology or the asphodel meadow in book 11 of Homer's
Odyssey.[21]

The same background is to be assumed for the ritual on Day 10, when
a plough was destroyed, presumably to provide the king (or queen) with
something to farm with. On Day 12, grapes were cut from a special
grapevine and destroyed, an action that may reflect a widespread symbolic
association between the grape and life.[22] Not all the rituals in this sequence
are equally pellucid: thus, no one has yet explained the significance of the
models of a special type of duck, the *lahhanza,* which were destroyed on
Day 13. (Could the association of birds with death, attested also in
Mycenaean iconography, be a factor here?[23]) Difficult too is the subritual
conducted on the night following Day 13, when a group of people prayed
to the statue of the king not to be angry and the *taptara*-women sang a
special song as a cord was burned (see below).

The SWR thus had various functions: it mourned the dead king (or
queen); it propitiated his spirit (at least in the optional *lilawar* section);
and it ritualized the transition between the king's life on earth and his
existence in the afterlife by providing things he would need there. These
functions may seem inconsistent: why mourn the king's death when
paradise awaits him? Should we think of two sequential stages of a process,
the royal soul going first to the underworld (which seems to have been the
destination for most peoples' souls in Hittite belief) and then to a better
place? In that case the SWR could be considered analogous to classic rites
of passage, effecting a transition between two social states through an
intermediate period of ritual inversion. More likely, as Theo Van den
Hout has argued, the two dimensions should be seen as corresponding
to the fates of two parts or aspects of the royal personage, the physical part
being destroyed and the institutional part, symbolized by the image (the
"body political"), achieving immortality.[24]

WAILING AND LAMENTATION IN THE SWR

The SWR contains many instances of ritual speech (*memian*), often delivered by the Old Woman and sometimes by an anonymous group. A whole
tablet is devoted to the words uttered at various points by the Old Woman
(KKS 641 ff.), mostly ritual dialogues and prayers. Utterances in Hittite
are also attributed in various points in the ritual to an indeterminate
"they," introduced by the two verbs that mean "they say" (*taranzi* and
memianzi).[25] It also included many musical performances by professional
singers or musicians ([LU.MES]NAR), including in one case the "singers of

the sun-goddess of heaven" (Day 8, KKS 379). As far as we can tell, these performances were instrumental without lyrics.[26]

In addition, the SWR mentions two types of performance that are specially connected with mourning:

1. Individual participants sometimes perform an action referred to by the verb *kalkalinai-* (third singular *kalgalinaizzi*), such as the "Cup Bearer" and the "Old Woman." This verb has generally been interpreted as "lament."[27]
2. Groups of people wail, the wailing being expressed by the verb *wiya-* (singular *wiyaskizzi*, plural *weskanzi*, periphrastic inchoative *weskiwan tianzi*).

Of these types of performance, "wailing" is the more widely attested. At the beginning of the ritual the whole community of the Hittites wails (Day 1, KKS 47, cited above). This is the only reference to communal "wailing" in the SWR, though there may be other communal activities, such as a communal covering of the head (Day 4, KKS 305). Elsewhere, the only people said to wail (*wiya-*) are the *taptara*-women. In a few cases, the verb *wiya-* occurs in the third-person plural without an explicit subject, and modern editors generally suppose that in such cases we should understand the *taptara*s as the subject.[28]

It will be helpful now to survey briefly the SWR for evidence of lamentation and wailing. We can distinguish three phases in the ritual.

Days 1–3

The SWR starts with communal wailing. At some point during Days 1–2 there is antiphonal wailing by the *taptara*-women (KKS 177): the Cup Bearer smashes the "cup of baked clay of his (the king's) soul" and laments (*kalkalinai-*); the *taptara*-women wail. Then they (unspecified) chase them (the *taptara*-women) out, and the Barbers sweep; and they give loaves of a certain sort to the *taptara*-women. The "chasing out" of the *taptara*s happens only here and on Day 13.[29] But the most interesting event is at the end of Day 2 (KKS 151): "They let them in for wailing. They begin wailing. The second day is finished." The place referred to seems to be the house where the body is laid before cremation. The wailers here are likely to be the *taptara*-women, and, as the text does not specify that the wailing stops (contrast Day 7, cited below), it is possible that it continues for a sustained period through the night, even up to the point of the cremation itself.

Days 7–13

During Days 7–13 the *taptara*-women accompany the statue of the deceased as it is moved around. On Day 7 (entitled in the outline tablet "Burning of Straw"), they accompany the bringing out of the statue from the house (KKS 323). A bonfire of straw is kindled at the gatehouse, and on it various items are burned, nine animals are sacrificed, and vessels of wine and beer are broken; and then the *taptara*-women "turn round" (whatever that may mean).[30] After this, a major sacrificial meal takes place in honor of the gods and the deceased, followed by some ritual performances; here the text includes an obscure passage that may mean either "they wail a little" or "they wail 'small place.' "[31] After further offerings, the day ends with the lines (KKS 335):

> It is finished. They sweep. After that, the *taptara*-women do not
> cry any more on that day. The seventh day is finished.

Wailing is mentioned only once in the account of Day 7 up to this point (KKS 329), which suggests that a certain amount of wailing by the *taptara*-women is presupposed in the background at all times.

On Day 8 ("Pig diverts the water; cutting off of the meadow"), a ritual drama takes place involving pigs and the symbolic presentation of a piece of turf to the deceased. The *taptara*-women are mentioned apropos of the sacrificial feast at the end, where they are given food (KKS 387); they wail when the Cup Bearer smashes an *isqaruh*-vessel (KKS 389); and they accompany the statue as it is taken from the tent (KKS 391). They were probably present also during the arrival of the statue of the deceased, which must have been described in the lost opening of the tablet.

On the first and better preserved part of Day 10 ("The plough, the threshing floor"), the arrival of the statue accompanied by the *taptara*-women is followed by the ritual destruction of a plough and oxen. To begin with, somebody drives the plough; an unidentified group says, "[M]ay the plough not drive it"; then someone else *kalkalinais*; the *taptara*-women wail (KKS 451); and then the plough is destroyed.

On Day 12 ("The cutting of the grapevine"), again, the statue is brought from tent to chariot while *taptara*-women walk behind and wail (KKS 477). A special grapevine is adorned with a belt, fruit, and wool, and the *taptara*-women bring it into the tent of the deceased (KKS 479). Further rituals follow, including some relating to an unidentified ritual object called a *tarse*.[32] Then, after the statue has been carried back to the tent, there is a sacrificial feast, and a relative of the deceased cuts clusters from the grapevine. That is followed by the Cup Bearer smashing an *isqaruh*-vessel and doing a *kalkalinai*-performance, whereupon the *taptara*-women wail as the statue is carried from the tent to the chariot (KKS 489).

On Day 13 (*lahhanza*-ducks), a ritual involving *lahhanza*-ducks and figurines of them takes place. The *taptara*-women are chased out of "the house," and it is swept; then they are fed (KKS 499). Later the *taptara*-women bring in two *allantaru*-trees and decorate them, tying ducks to them (KKS 499 = 589). Then further rituals take place, and three times they are interrupted by the formula "the *taptara*-women wail, then fall silent."

The Night of Day 13

On the night between Day 13 and Day 14, those staging the ritual spend the night awake (*ispandan luganuwanzi*, lit., "they light the night"). A loaf of bread is put on the statue's knees. A Cup Bearer smashes the cup of his soul and *kalkalinai*s, and the *taptara*-women wail. An object called a *summanza*, which is probably a cord, is smeared with oil and thrown on the hearth; then the *taptara*-women wail: "[W]hen you go to the meadow, do not pull the *summanza*-cord." The "meadow" here seems to be paradise, a standard trope in many mythographies and reminiscent of the ritual role of the "meadow" on Day 8. The account of the following Day 14 is poorly preserved, but we can make out reference to chasing out the *taptara*-women and Barbers sweeping and apparently to the tying of ducks to trees, as on Day 13 (KKS 603). This nocturnal performance by the *taptara*-women perhaps looks back to the performance at the end of Day 2 before the cremation.

THE ROLE OF THE *TAPTARA*-WOMEN

The role of the *taptara*-women in the ritual is not confined to wailing, and they sometimes perform ritual actions, as, for example, on Day 7 and Day 13. But wailing is the central activity. Several forms can be distinguished: Sometimes the wailing accompanies a ritual action, such as the transportation of the statue of the deceased, and in these cases the women may themselves be processing, as on Day 12 (KKS 477):

They bring the statue out of the house and set it up on the sitting chariot. *Taptara*-women walk behind and wail.

More commonly, the wailing is a response to a lament (*kalkalinai-*) by the Cup Bearer or the Old Woman, which itself responds to another ritual event, such as the smashing of a significant object, particularly a vessel.[33] Destruction of vessels is common in many funerary traditions and must itself have had ritual significance.[34] In these cases the *taptara*-women probably did not process; rather, they may have stood or perhaps circled.[35] We can call this second form "antiphonal." The one exception to this antiphony comes at the end of Day 2 (KKS 151). When the body is stored in "the house" before cremation, "they" let the *taptara*-women in to wail. This sounds like a more sustained performance, in which the *taptara*-women wail in the direct presence of the corpse. In fact, it is possible that wailing provided the background noise to the whole SWR. I observed earlier that the statement that the *taptara*-women "do not wail any more" on Day 7 (KKS 335/355) suggests that most wailing on that day is not mentioned explicitly in the text. Possibly, the same is true of the SWR as a whole.

The first two patterns could occur in close succession, as we find on Days 8–9 (KKS 389–391/427):

> The Cup Bearer smashes the *isqaruh*-vessel against the ground.
> Then he *kalkalinai*s. And the group of *taptara*-women begin
> wailing. They carry the statue out of the tent and set it up on the
> sitting chariot. The *taptara*-women walk behind. They drive it
> away and (the *taptara*-women) wail.[36]

Both forms of performance are well established in other ritual texts. In
one text, a group of girls (*zintuhis*) sings songs as they ascend a sacred
mountain; in another the girls of Tahurpa stand at the side of the road and
sing as salt is transported; in yet another the girls of Kasha sing as the god is
taken down to a river.[37] Antiphonal performance shows up in many ritual
texts from the Hattic sphere, for example, the "songs of the women of
Tissaruliya," for which a lengthy sequence of antiphonal performance can
be reconstructed. Notice, however, that the terminology for the solo
and communal performance is different: the soloist normally "calls out"
(*halzai*), whereas the chorus "sing in response" (*kattan ark-*).[38] Another
significant difference is that while true antiphonal performance requires a
succession of solos followed by choral responses, the sequence of solo
kalkalinai followed by communal *wiya-* is not explicitly stated to have
been repeated in our texts, though it may have been.[39] Despite these
differences, it seems that there are significant resemblances between the
taptara-women and groups of choral singers in other Hittite texts in
respect of performance or at least in the way in which performances are
described or prescribed.

   In fact the *taptara*-women function as a chorus throughout the SWR.
That sense is intensified by the fact that they are generally referred to by a
collective noun with a singular verb (see above) and also by the fact that
they are sometimes referred to as the *pankus*, which means "totality" or
"congregation," as on Days 8–9 (KKS 389):

> The Cup Bearer smashes the *isqaruh*-vessel against the ground.
> Then he *kalkalinai*s and the *pankus* begins to wail.[40]

In principle, the word *pankus* could refer to everyone present, the "congregation" (as in the second line of the SWR, cited above), but the former
interpretation is confirmed by the fact that we sometimes find the expression *pankui taptaras* in the sense of "to the group of *taptara*-women" in
the context of offerings of food, as in KKS 387.[41]

THE RITUAL OF THE *SUMMANZA*-CORD

Another principal difference between the account of the *taptara*-women
in the SWR and accounts of choral song in other Hittite ritual texts is that
we never learn the content of what the *taptara*-women sing or the content
of the laments that sometimes precede their wails. The fact that we do not
have texts for the *taptara*-women may indicate either that the content of

the laments or wails was inarticulate or that it was so formulaic that it did not need to be reproduced.

There are only two exceptions to this pattern.[42] One is a difficult passage from Day 7, where in the middle of a long series of drinking offerings in honor of various deities, there is an interlude describing some utterances and performances, beginning with the statement (KKS 329/351): *nu tepu pedan weskanzi*, which means, on the face of it, "and they wail small place." The subject will be the *taptara*-women, if the principle holds that the instances of the verb *wiye-* with unspecified subject refer to the *taptara*-women.[43] Some scholars think the words *tepu pedan* give the content of the wailing, and perhaps refer to the grave, contrasting with a cry of *halentuwa* (palace!) that follows below; others think the words mean "a little" and describe the degree of wailing.[44] In the end, there are too many uncertainties about this passage for us to make much of it.

The other case is from the night between Days 13 and 14. A special "soldier loaf" is placed on the legs of the statue, and an unidentified group says the following:

> Behold, we have put the soldier loaf on your legs, do not be
> angry henceforth! Be dear to your children! May your
> kingdom be eternal down all generations! Your own temple
> will be revered and the offering will be provided for you.

What follows concerns an object called in Hittite a *summanza*, which, having been smeared with oil, is burned on the hearth. The word *summanza* has generally been interpreted as "cord" or "rope," although it has also been suggested that the primary meaning might be "bulrush."[45] As the *summanza*-cord burns, the *taptara*-women wail the following words:

man-[wa]-kan welluwa paisi	[W]hen you go the meadow
nasta summanzan le huitiyasi.	do not pull the cord.
tuel-[wa]-za istanza kisari.	May your will be done.

The verb introducing the utterance here is *alalamniya-* in at least two of the three copies, though in one copy Kassian, Korolëv, and Sidel'tsev suggest that a form of *wiye-* could possibly be read.[46] The verb *alamniya-*, which only occurs in these texts, may be derived from the ritual cry "alala-" (comparable to Greek *alalazo* and *ololuzo*, meaning basically "shout *alalai*, shout *ololoi*"), which is combined with *lamniya-*, meaning "name."[47]

It is not clear whether the type of utterance referred to here is to be interpreted as singing or speaking. Singing might, perhaps, be thought more likely in view of the fact that there is an observable correlation between choral utterance and singing in Hittite ritual texts. On the other hand, the fact that the lines are in Hittite (slightly archaic Hittite, in fact) tells against that, because although choral singing was a staple of Hittite rituals, the language of the songs was usually anything other than

Hittite.[48] Hattic, the non-Indo-European language of the people who lived in the territory of Hatti before the "Hittites" arrived, is probably the best-attested language for choral performance, but we also find Luwian, a language related to Hittite and spoken in the west and south of Anatolia in this period. Songs in Hittite are almost unattested, although ritual speech could be in Hittite.[49]

The significance of pulling/not pulling the *summanza*-cord has been the subject of much speculation. Why should the king (or queen) not pull it, and what is the relationship between this request and the king's will? Because this is the end of the ritual, possibly the king is being instructed to sever links to the world of the living, in which case the cord could be one that symbolically connects him with this world. Or perhaps the cord is one that binds the king in his place, and pulling it loosens its effectiveness, like pulling on a knot.[50] In the latter case, the point of burning the cord would be to transfer it to the other world, where it would bind the king.[51] In the former case, the point of the burning might be partly to destroy the rope, severing the link between that world and this. The statement "May your will be done," if that is the correct interpretation, may be an attempt to mollify the king's soul by assuring him that, despite the cessation of direct contact between the two worlds, his wishes will continue to be respected.[52] As such, the *alalamniya*-performance perhaps complements the speech about not being angry mentioned earlier.

Thus, though our understanding of the end of the SWR is imperfect (not least because the account of Day 14, which would provide the greatest insight, is one of the sections least well preserved), it appears that the rituals on the night of Day 13 mark a fundamental shift. After the cremation and interment in the stone house, the main agenda has been ensuring the prosperity of the king or queen in the afterlife. But now comes a ritual of separation by which the conventional barrier between the world of the dead and this world, open during the main part of the ritual, is again closed. It may be significant that this is the one episode in the SWR that happens at night, with the exception of the cremation on the night of Day 2.[53]

CONCLUSION: THE SIGNIFICANCE OF THE *TAPTARAS*

Two things define the *taptara*s. The first is that they seem to have been a specialized troupe with no connection to the family of the deceased. I take them to have been a permanently constituted group of ritual specialists concerned with royal funerals and possibly a mortuary cult. Being a specialized group of mourners, they perhaps resembled the *praeficae* of ancient Rome; one might also think of the semi-professional Carian women who performed laments in ancient Greece.[54] Specialized wailers might have been used either because of their perceived expertise—in performing laments or in funerary ritual in general—or because performing ritual was perceived as dangerous or polluting, so that it was more expedient to delegate it to a group of surrogates who were more or less separate from the community as a whole. The latter explanation suits the "ritual of the *summanza*-cord," where, as I have suggested, any pollution or divine displeasure resulting from the *alalamniya*-performance would be deflected from the community and fall on the *taptara*-women alone.

The second thing that defines the *taptara*s is that, like many of the performers of lament studied in this volume, they were women. In fact, there is some reason to think that the association between death and women was well established in the Hittite mentality. It may be significant that a frequent Hittite euphemism for "the day of one's death" was "the day of one's mother," an expression that suggests that birth and death were regarded as analogous. One of the texts where that expression is attested is a much-cited ritual, one of whose participants is a *patili*-priest who stands on the roof of a house; it is significant that the usual sphere of the *patili*-priest was birth.[55]

The strong tendency for women to be the agents of lamentation is seen by the anthropologist Maurice Bloch as part of a more general association of women with death, an association with deep ideological roots in human culture. Early tribal societies tended to perceive the death of individual human beings as a threat to their long-term stability, and they developed strategies for dealing with the threat. For example, we find in them the idea that for important individuals at least, physical death is not the end of their existence but, rather, they survive within the framework the institutions and rituals. Or they may have used funerary ritual as an occasion to reaffirm and celebrate the structure of society and try to limit the contact that members of the society had with death and the decay of physical bodies. One way of achieving the last is to delegate the task of dealing with death to the women of the family or the community. A consequence of associating women with death is that death henceforth comes to be seen as analogous to birth, both fundamental biological processes over which women have control, an association we have just seen in the Hittite evidence.[56] Men, whose position in society is more public, are thus left comparatively free of death's pollution. In some societies, for example, that of Madagascar (the focus of Bloch's own anthropological research), funerary ritual has two stages: a primary burial carried out by women and accompanied by lamentation and a secondary burial (the *famadihana*) carried out by men some time later when the bones of the deceased are interred in a tomb. The second stage marks the point when the deceased is symbolically reintegrated into the community as an ancestor, and the mood is not one of mourning but of celebration.[57]

The Malagasy case studied by Bloch resembles the SWR in some respects and is in some ways a little different. As Van den Hout has demonstrated, the Hittite funerary ritual too draws a distinction between the disposal of the physical body of the deceased and his or her institutional afterlife. But whereas in the Malagasy case these two processes happen a long time apart, in the SWR they are combined within the frame of the same macroritual. As for a division of roles in the funerary ritual between the genders, if we think of the first three days of the SWR as concerned with the body and the remaining part as dealing with institutional afterlife, then no clear division of task between female and male performers emerges. Women are well represented, but men are involved as well, and usually the two genders seem to perform in cooperation. On the other hand, there is reason to think that the *taptara*-women had a critical role in dealing directly with the body and soul of the deceased, gathering the bones after the cremation and at the end of the ritual appealing directly to the king's soul and facilitating its separation from the world of the living. On the basis of this, one might speculate that the special concern of the *taptara*s was the body and soul of the king and that they were not so involved in the other concern of the ritual—preparing for the establishment of a royal cult that would symbolize the continuing presence of the dead king in this world. In this context, it is also worth reminding ourselves that although the relationship of the *taptara*s to the other performers within the ritual drama seems in general to have been one of cooperation, nevertheless on two occasions in the ritual they are "chased out" after their wailing. If the point of the SWR was simply to mourn the dead king, banishing the *taptara*s in this way would be difficult to explain, but it makes more sense if we remember that the SWR was not only the last stage of the existence of the dead person as a human but also the first stage of his existence as an institution. In this way, then, one might read the SWR as articulating in quasidramatic terms the conflicting claims of the two major concerns of a royal funerary ritual.

NOTES

1. On the subject of death in Hittite civilization, the best treatments in English are Haas 1995 and Van den Hout 1994. See also Haas 2000.

2. See Burke, this volume; Cavanagh and Mee 1998; Gallou 2005.

3. Kassian, Korolëv, and Sidel'tsev 2002 (henceforth KKS), 47. In translating the word *wastais* as "loss," I follow Van den Hout 1994, 56; Gurney (1974, 59) translates it as "calamity." It has more usually been translated as "sin." For the root and its Greek relatives, see Catsanicos 1991.

4. For the bleakness of Hittite attitudes to death, see Haas 1976.

5. The significance of "taking away the reeds" here is still not certain, but it most likely refers to drinking straws; see Van den Hout 1994.

6. See most conveniently KKS 12–13. Haas (1994, 219) seems to suggest Hurrian origin.

7. Capital letters indicate a Sumerian word; where these are used, the Hittite equivalent may not be known. See, e.g., Gurney 1974, 44–45; the Hittite word for the Old Woman may have been *hasawas*, which could mean "midwife," in which case it is worth bearing in mind that there are some signs that death was considered analogous to birth in the Hittite mentality.

8. See Van den Hout 1994, 42.

9. See KKS 336–337, which points out that when a verb immediately follows the noun it is singular, but if a second verb follows in a second clause, it is plural. For collectives in Hittite syntax, see Friedrich 1960–1970, 115–116.

10. *Keilschrifturkunden aus Boghazköi* (1921–1990; henceforth KUB) 57.120R.17': ^{LU}*taptaras* ^{URU}Z[i (see Tischler 1977–, 135–136).

11. See, in this volume, Burke on the Tanagra larnakes, Dutsch on the Roman *praeficae*, Stears on Classical Greece, Martin on the keening women of Ireland, and Bachvarova on the gender-transgressive mourners of the Near East.

12. KUB 16.34.

13. Notice that KUB 57.120R17' links the male *taptara* to the city of Zi[, which could be the site of a royal mausoleum.

14. It has been suggested that Chamber B in the rock sanctuary at Yazilikaya was a stone house, and there may have been another just south of the citadel of Hattusas but within the greater city wall at Nisantepe. On stone houses, see Hawkins 1998.

15. See Bittel 1994, 23 ff.; Christmann-Frank 1971; Haas 2000, 66–67; and Rutherford2007.

16. On the text, see Van den Hout 1994, 73. The use of fruit in this context recalls the common association in many cultures between death and regeneration; see Bloch and Parry 1982.

17. On the meaning of this, see Gurney 1974; Van den Hout 1995. Balances have been found in Mycenaean Greek tombs; see Cavanagh and Mee 1998, 53.

18. See KKS 21–22.

19. Van den Hout 1994, 73, and 1995.

20. See Van den Hout 1994, 60. On the ritual destruction, see Testart 2005.

21. Haas 1976, 103, 111; Puhvel [1969] 1981b.

22. Böcher 1970, 56; Haas 1994, 226.

23. See Gallou 2005, 39–40. Cf. Burke, this volume; notice in particular the bird models found in graves at Tanagra.

24. See Van den Hout 1994. For a different view, see Taracha 1998.

25. The indexes in KKS 844–845 are a useful guide here. Sometimes these indeterminate references might be to the principal actors in the ritual, e.g., the Old Woman and her colleague, as at KKS 643: "when the old woman pours . . . they speak as follows," and KKS 645: "They speak as follows, she calls the deceased by name." As for the *taptara*s, it is not an objection that the plural verb is used because it is used sometimes of the *taptara*-women (see above).

26. Whether the Hittite word *isamia*- (SIR 3 in Sumerian) always means "sing" or can also mean "play (musical instruments)" has been debated recently. See Kümmel 1973; Schuol 2004, 136–142.

27. Cf. KKS 528–529. Puhvel (1984–, 4.25) suggests the alternative interpretation "clang, clash," but, as Kassian, Korolëv, and Sidel'tsev observe, this does not fit all the attestations. See also Schuol 2004, 153.

28. In some cases two copies of the ritual differ insofar as one says "the *taptara*-women wail" and the other says "they wail," as at the end of Day 7 (KKS 335). The association is so constant that editors assume it even when it is not explicit, e.g., at the end of Day 2 (KKS 151, cited below).

29. The Barbers (^{LUMES}SU.I, here and elsewhere restored from KKS 88 and 130) sweep (KKS 177; cf. KKS 499/603 from Day 13). So at the end of Day 7, they (the Barbers?) sweep, and the *taptara*-women "do not wail any more" on that day (KKS 335/355). In other Hittite festival texts even ordinary musicians can exceptionally be "chased out" at the end of a performance, as in *Keilschrifttexte aus Boghazköi* 4.9iii 23–25 (Hinrichs 1916), from the *antahsum*-festival, cited in *The Hittite Dictionary of the Oriental Institute of the University of Chicago* (hereafter

CHD; Güterbock, Hoffner, and Van den Hout 1980–), P fasc2, 145; and Badalì 1991, 51–52. So too "silencing" musical instruments is common in festival texts; see Puhvel 1984–, 117, citing Badalì 1991, 8–9, 18, 163.

30. Kassian, Korolëv, and Sidel'tsev interpret this as "stir the crocks," though Haas (1995, 2025) thinks it means "circle around."

31. See below.

32. In Kassian, Korolëv, and Sidel'tsev's reconstruction, the *taptara*-women appear again when the vine is removed, but this is speculative (KKS 35, 481, 526): "[I]f it is winter, they take the *habustija*-beverage. If it is spring, the *taptara*-women keep wailing much. Their tears flow into the GAL GIR4-vessel. They give the vessel (with *habustiya*-beverage or tears) to the deceased."

33. A complete lists of contexts for *kalkalinai* + *wiye* is as follows: Day 1/2, KKS 177, the Cup Bearer smashes the cup of his soul; Day 3, KKS 269, the Old Woman smashes the balance; Day 8/9, KKS 389 = 427, the Cup Bearer smashes the *isqaruh*-vessel; Day 10, KKS 451 (fragmentary), a group says, "[M]ay the plough not drive," then someone laments, and the *taptara*-women wail; Day 12, KKS 489 (grapevine), the Cup Bearer smashes the *isqaruh*-vessel; Day 13 (night), KKS 579 = 519, the Cup Bearer smashes the cup of the king's soul and the *lelundali*-vessel; fr. 16, KKS 757, someone smashes the *zalhai*-vessel. The exception is the one on Day 10, because nothing is smashed then.

34. See Carsten 2001; Soles 1999. On modern Greece, see Alexiou 1974, 27, 45.

35. Compare two fragments: in one they stand and wail (KKS 701); and according to the liturgy at one point they "wail around" (KKS 643).

36. Day 1/2, KKS 177; Days 8–9, KKS 389, 401, 427; Days 12–14, KKS 489, 495 (damaged), 579.

37. On the ascent of Mt. Daha, see Popko 1994, 156–157. On the salt song, see KUB 11.73; KUB 58.4. On the *hazqara* women of Hanhana standing on the right side of the road and singing opposite the king as he passes, see Klinger 1997, 720; on the *zintuhis* of Kasha, see Haas and Jakob-Rost 1984.

38. On antiphonal performance, see Klinger 1997, 277; Melchert 1998; Schuol 2004, 149–152.

39. The nearest we get to a refrain is perhaps the passage on Day 13, where there are three antiphonal performances by the *taptara*-women in succession. After each they fall silent or "they" silence them (KKS 505–509).

40. Kassian, Korolëv, and Sidel'tsev restore *pankus* in several other cases as well.

41. On *panku* elsewhere, see Melchert 1998. The same problem arises in KUB 12.8, the ritual for the town of Tuhumiyara. In Luwian texts the group is sometimes described as the *panku*. *Panku* is also the term for the governing council in the Old Kingdom; see Bryce 2003.

42. I am assuming here that none of the statements of ritual speech with unspecified subject is to be attributed to the *taptara*-women.

43. But Haas (1995, 2025) does not follow this here.

44. For the interpretation as "wail a little," see KKS 329 with 338–339; for the interpretation as "small place," see Haas 1995, 2025; Van den Hout 1994, 57 n. 81.

45. See Burde 1974, 47; both senses are attested -for the Akkadian word *aslu*; see *The Assyrian Dictionary of the Oriental Institute of the University of Chicago* (1956–), *s.v. aslu* A and *aslu* B.

46. KKS 517, 542, citing *Hethitisches Wörterbuch* 1:55 (Friedrich and Kammenhuber 1952–1954) for the synonymous nature of these words.

47. Puhvel 1984–, *s.v.* LAMNIYA.

48. The form *welluwa* (meadow = Ú.SAL*wa*) is an example of the obsolete directive case. See KKS 544.

49. Possibly, cult songs by the "singer of Kanesh" would have been in Hittite, but the text of these does not survive. See Archi 2004.

50. Haas (1994) compares death rituals involving a cord from Ireland and Armenia, suggesting that this might be an Indo-European element.

51. Thus the song would in fact be a sort of "binding song," to apply the poetical expression used by the Furies in Aeschylus's *Oresteia*. "Binding spells" are, of course, a common category in Greco-Roman magic and religion; see Faraone 1991.

52. Haas does not agree. On the concept of "will" in Hittite culture, see Starke 1996.

53. On rituals at night, see CHD, *s.v. luganu-*.

54. On Carian mourners, see Plato, *Laws* 800e.

55. On the "day of one's mother," see Van den Hout 1994, 42, with references in n. 25. On the ritual of the *patili*-priest, see KUB 30.28, with Van den Hout 1994, 42 n. 25; CHD, *s.v.* (Vol. P, fasc. 3, 245–246). See also n. 7 above.

56. See Bloch 1982; Bloch and Parry 1982, 24–27, passim. Comparable in some respects is the prominent role of women in funerary rituals in modern Greece, memorably analyzed in Danforth 1982. On the matter of the pollution incurred in death rituals in ancient Greece, see Stears, this volume.

57. See Bloch 1982, 215–217, and the fuller treatment in Bloch 1971.

BIBLIOGRAPHY

Abeghian, M. 1899. *Der armenische Volksglaube*. Leipzig.

Alexiou, M. 1974. *The Ritual Lament in Greek Tradition*. Cambridge.

Archi, A. 2004. The Singer of Kanes and His Gods. In *Offizielle Religion, lokale Kulte und individuelle Religiosität*, ed. M. Hutter and S. Hutter-Brausar, 11–26. Münster.

The Assyrian Dictionary of the Oriental Institute of the University of Chicago. 1956–. Chicago.

Badalì, E. 1991. *Strumenti musicali, musici e musica nella celebrazione delle feste ittite*. Heidelberg.

Beckman, G. 1993. From Cradle to Grave: Women's Role in Hittite Medicine and Magic. *Journal of Ancient Civilizations* 8: 36–39.

Bittel, K. 1994. Hethitische Bestattungsbräuche. *Mitteilungen der Deutschen Orient-Gesellschaft* 78: 20–28.

Bloch, M. 1971. *Placing the Dead: Tombs, Ancestral Villages, and Kinship Organization in Madagascar*. London.

——. 1982. Death, Women, and Power. In *Death and the Regeneration of Life*, M. Bloch and J. Parry, 211–230. Cambridge.

——. 1989. *Ritual, History, and Power: Selected Papers in Anthropology*. London.

Bloch, M., and J. Parry. 1982. *Death and the Regeneration of Life*. Cambridge.

Böcher, O. 1970. *Dämonenfurcht und Dämonenabwehr; ein Beitrag zur Vorgeschichte der christlichen Taufe*. Beiträge zur Wissenschaft vom Alten und Neuen Testament, 90. Stuttgart.

Brentjes, B. 1999. Das Bestattungsritualder Hethiter—Ein Erbe aus den euraischen Steppen? *Altorientalische Forschungen* 26: 58–76.

Bryce, T. 2003. *Life and Society in the Hittite World*. Oxford.

Burde, C. 1974. *Hethitische medizinische Texte*. Wiesbaden.

Carsten, A. M. 2001. Drinking Vessels in Tombs—A Cultic Connection. In *Ceramics in Context*, ed. C. Scheffer, 89–102. Stockholm.

Catsanicos, Jean. 1991. *Recherches sur le vocabulaire de la faute, Hitt. "wastu"1 et Gr. "a(F)a-te."* Paris.

Cavanagh, W., and C. Mee, eds. 1998. *A Private Place. Death in Prehistoric Greece*. Jonsered Sweden.

Christmann-Frank, L. 1971. Le rituel des funérailles royales hittites. *Revue Hittite et Asiatique* 29: 61–111.

Danforth, L. 1982. *The Death Rituals of Rural Greece*. Princeton.

del Monte, G. 1987. Inferno e paradiso nel mondo hittita. In *Archeologia dell' Inferno. L' aldilà nel mondo vicino-orientale e classico*, ed. P. Xella, 95–115. Verona.

Faraone, C. 1991. Blinding and Burying the Forces of Evil: The Defensive Uses of "Voodoo Dolls" in Ancient Greece. *Classical Antiquity* 10: 165–220.

Friedrich, J. 1960–1970. *Hethitsiches Elementarbuch*. 2 vols. Heidelberg.

Friedrich, J., and A. Kammenhuber, eds. 1952–1954. *Hethitisches Wörterbuch*. 2nd ed. Heidelberg.

Gallou, C. 2005. *The Mycenaean Cult of the Dead*. BAR International S1372. Oxford.

Gurney, O. 1974. *Some Aspects of Hittite Religion*. Oxford.

Güterbock, H. G., H. A. Hoffner, and T. Van den Hout, eds. 1980–. *The Hittite Dictionary of the Oriental Institute of the University of Chicago*. Chicago.

Haas, V. 1976. Die Unterwelts- und Jenseitsvorstellungen im hethitischen Kleinasien. *Orientalia* N.S. 45: 197–212.

——. 1994. *Geschichte der hethitische Religion*. Leiden.

——. 1995. Death and the Afterlife in Hittite Thought. In *Civilisations of the Ancient Near East*, vol. 3, ed. J. Sasson, 2021–2030. New York.

——. 2000. Hethitische Bestattungsbrauche. *Altorientalische Forschungen* 27: 52–67.

Haas, V., and L. Jakob-Rost. 1984. Das Festritual des Gottes Telipinu in Hanhana und in Kasha. Ein Beitrag zum hethitischen Festkalendar. *Altorientalische Forschungen* 11: 10–91.

Hartmann, H. 1952. *Der Totenkult in Irland*. Heidelberg.

Hawkins, H. David. 1998. Hattusa: Home to the Thousand Gods of Hatti. In *Capital Cities. Urban Planning and Spiritual Dimensions*, ed. J. Goodnik Westenholz, 65–82. Jerusalem.

Hinrichs, J. C., ed. 1916. *Keilschrifttexte aus Boghazköi*. Vols. 1–6. Leipzig.

Kassian, A., A. Korolëv, and A. Sidel'tsev, eds. 2002. *Hittite Funerary Ritual: Sallis Wastais*. Münster.

Keilschrifturkunden aus Boghazköi. 1921–1990. Berlin.

Klinger, J. 1997. *Untersuchungen zur Rekonstruktion der hattischen Kultschicht*. Studien zu den Bogazköy Texten 37. Wiesbaden.

Kümmel, H. M. 1973. Gesang und Gesanglosigkeit in der hethitischen Kultmusik. In *Festschrift Heinrich Otten 27. Dez. 1973*, ed. E. Neu and C. Rüster, 169–178. Wiesbaden.

Melchert, H. C. 1991. Death and the Hittite King. In *Perspectives on Indo-European Language, Culture and Religion. Studies in Honour of Edgar C. Polome*, ed. P. Pearson, 182–188. McLean, Va.

——. 1998. Hittite *arku-* "Chant, Intone" vs. *arkuwa(i)* "Make a Plea." *Journal of Cuneiform Studies* 5: 45–51.

Mouton, A. Forthcoming. Entry *"taptara."* In *The Hittite Dictionary of the Oriental Institute of the University of Chicago*, ed. H. G. Güterbock, H. A. Hoffner, T. Van den Hout. Chicago.

Otten, H. 1958. *Hethitische Totenrituale*. Berlin.

Pecchioli-Daddi, F. 1982. *Mestieri, professioni e dignità nell'Anatolia ittita*. Rome.

Popko, M. 1994. *Zippalanda: Ein Kultzentrum im hethitischen Kleinasien*. Heidelberg.

——. 1995. *Religions of Asia Minor*. Warsaw.

Puhvel, J. [1969] 1981a. Hittite *annas siwaz. Zeitschrift für vergleichende Sprachforschung* 83: 59–63. Reprint, *Analecta Indoeuropaea*, 205–263, Innsbruck.

——. [1969] 1981b. Meadow of the Underworld in the Indo-European Tradition. *Kuhns Zeitschrift* 83: 64–69. Reprint, *Analecta Indoeuropaea*, 65–69, Innsbruck.

——. 1984–. *Hittite Etymological Dictionary*. Berlin.

——. 1992. Shaft-Shedding Artemis and Mind-Voiding Ate: Hittite Determinants of Greek Etyma. *Historische Sprachforschung* 105: 4–8.

Rutherford, I. 2007. Achilles and the *Sallis Wastais* Ritual. In *Performing Death. Social Analyses of Funerary Traditions in the Ancient Near East and Mediterranean*, ed. N. Laneri, 223–236. Chicago.

Schuol, M. 2004. *Hethitische Kultmusik*. Orient-Archäologie Band 14. Rahden/West.

Singer, I. 1981. Hittites and Hattians in Anatolia at the Beginning of the Second Millennium B.C. *Journal of Indo-European Studies* 9: 119–134.

Soles, J. 1999. The Ritual Killing of Pottery and the Discovery of a Mycenaean Telestas at Mochlos. In *Meletemata: Studies in Aegean Archaeology Presented to Malcolm Wiener as He Enters His 65th Year*, ed. P. P. Betancourt, V. Karageorghis, R. Laffineur, and E.-D. Niemeier, 787–792. *Aegaeum* 20 (3). Liège.

Soysal, O. 1987. KUB XXXI 4 + KBo III 41 und 40 (Die Puhanu-Chronik). Zum Thronstreit Hattusilis I. *Hethitica* 7: 173–253.

Starke, F. 1996. Zur "Regierung" des hethitischen Staates. *Zeitschrift für Altorientalische und Biblische Rechtsgeschichte* 2: 140–182.

Taracha, P. 1998. Funus in effigie: Bemerkungen zu den hethitischen Totenritualen. *Kwartalnik historii kultury materialnej* 1–2: 189–196.

Testart, A. 2005. Le texte Hittite des funérailles royaux au risque du comparatisme. *Ktema* 30: 29–36.

Tischler, J. 1977–. *Hethitisches etymologisches Glossar*. Innsbruck.

Van den Hout, T. P. J. 1994. Death as a Privilege. The Hittite Royal Funerary Ritual. In *Hidden Futures. Death and Immortality in Ancient Egypt, Anatolia, the Classical, Biblical and Arabic-Islamic World*, ed. J. M. Bremer, T. P. J. Van den Hout, and R. Peters, 37–76. Amsterdam.

——. 1995. An Image of the Dead? Some Remarks on the Second Day of the Hittite Royal Funerary Ritual. In *Atti del II Congresso Internazionale di Hittitologia. Pavia 28 giugno—2 Luglio 1993*, ed. Onofrio Carruba, Mauro Giorgieri, and Clelia Mora, 95–211. StudMed 9. Pavia.

4

MYCENAEAN MEMORY AND BRONZE AGE LAMENT

BRENDAN BURKE

R itual lament in the ancient Greek world, as it is primarily understood
through epic poetry and Athenian tragedy, was a controlled, performative act of memory and mourning. In contrast to the Hittite material
discussed by Rutherford (chapter 3), Greek prehistory, or the Aegean
Bronze Age, has not left us any literature from which we can reconstruct
belief systems about death and lament. We do, however, have a great deal
of archaeological evidence for how the Mycenaeans buried their dead,
beginning with the great Shaft Graves of Mycenae, dating to the early
Mycenaean period, and continuing into the postdestruction phase of the
Bronze Age, with the famous Warrior Vase from Mycenae. This chapter
relies heavily on funerary imagery and archaeology to understand lament
in Greek prehistory.

Many scholars of the late nineteenth and early twentieth centuries
looked back at the Aegean Bronze Age through a philological lens to re-
create funerary rites based on their understanding of later Greek practice.
Emily Vermeule's work, however, attempts to bridge the literary and
archaeological evidence, and she has succeeded remarkably well. She
states, "The unbroken continuity of funeral imagery and behavior between the Bronze Age and the classical world is very clear in the artistic
documents that survive from the earlier period."[1] Building on this approach I would like to examine the archaeological record of Mycenaean
funerary art on its own to see what the visual record for lament is, without
the inherent bias of later literary sources.

The evidence, and the subject of this chapter, centers on funerary iconography and burial customs and demonstrates that some types of lament of the late second millennium B.C.E. differed from what was to become the standard Archaic Greek image of women with upraised arms in gestures of mourning. Several well-known works of Aegean funerary art are examined: the Late Bronze Age larnakes, or burial chests, from Tanagra; clay figurines from Perati; the painted sarcophagus from Ayia Triada; and the Warrior Vase from Mycenae. These objects give a prominent role to women actors that has been the key feature cited for continuity with later Greek funeral rites.[2] One goal of this chapter is to highlight these participants but also to show that a variety of types of lamentation are visible in Bronze Age iconography, some of which are not present in later Greek art.

TANAGRA LARNAKES

Funerary iconography of the Late Bronze Age Aegean demonstrates a complex relationship between the mainland Mycenaeans and the Cretan Minoans, each borrowing from the other similar themes and motifs in their art. Painted larnakes excavated in two cemeteries, Dendron and Gephyra, in eastern Boeotia, near the modern village of Tanagra, illustrate lament and funerary ritual from the Mycenaean period and show connections to the funerary art of contemporary Crete.[3]

The painted panels are a bit of an enigma in Aegean prehistory. As early as 1946 there were rumors in Athens of painted slabs coming from tombs at Tanagra.[4] Most of the Tanagra larnakes were excavated in the late 1960s by T. Spyropoulos. As several scholars have commented, sometimes vociferously, this important material has not yet been thoroughly published as a whole, which is truly regrettable. Consequently, it is difficult to give an exact number of the painted chests or even the number of tombs excavated.[5] A recent catalog prepared by Cavanagh and Mee lists fifty painted panels, yet each decorated side of a chest is counted as a separate entry.[6] It should also be stressed that some of the chamber tombs produced more than one painted larnax, sometimes up to six in one tomb. At least sixteen are on display in Room D of the Thebes Museum.[7] Because of their stylistic parallels with figural pottery, the larnakes and the two cemeteries are thought to have been in use during the Late Helladic IIIA–B period, from circa 1350 to 1250 B.C.E.

Before the discovery of the Tanagra larnakes it was thought that the use of painted coffins was primarily a Minoan practice. The earliest terracotta larnakes on Crete date to the mid–third millennium, becoming common in the fourteenth century B.C.E., roughly contemporary with the Tanagra examples.[8] After they were discovered some scholars suggested that the Tanagra larnakes were Cretan imports (modern or ancient) or that ancient Tanagra was a Minoan colony. However, the clay and the decoration are clearly not Minoan but part of the local Mycenaean *koine*, and it is highly unlikely that such large, friable, decorated chests would have been shipped from Crete to the mainland. The forms of the Tanagra examples also differ remarkably from the Cretan versions. The mainland chests are open boxes of varying size, made up of four terra-cotta slabs fitted together. Only a few have lids, either a flat terra-cotta tile or, rarely, a gabled roof. Examples on Crete, in contrast, are generally either bath-tub shaped with no lid or boxlike with a gabled removable lid, and occasionally they will have attached handles.[9] The decorative themes and style of execution of the Tanagra larnakes link them to Mycenaean wall painting and pictorial vases much more strongly than to Minoan funerary art.

The Tanagra larnakes have raised many questions with respect to their style, artistic inspiration, and derivation. Although the corpus of tombs and their contents remains unpublished, several scholars have investigated the iconography for a link between Mycenaean funerary customs and early Greek rites.[10] Scenes of *prothesis*, laying out the dead, and a procession of mourning women with hands raised to their heads find parallels in later Geometric art found on funerary vases of the Kerameikos in Athens, for example.

The Tanagra larnakes give primacy to human actors involved in rituals associated with funerary rites. On at least two examples figures are shown carefully making a *prothesis*, depositing what look like dead children into burial containers similar to the actual chests on which the scenes are shown (figs. 4.1–4.2).[11] Several other female figures are shown with arms raised to their heads in what became the standard gesture of lament. The *protheses* here are touching scenes among the Tanagra panels and demonstrate that even though the style of painting is sometimes crude or sketchy, the artists of these funerary monuments had great sensitivity.[12]

On the long sides of the larnax from Tomb 22 there are additional scenes related to funerary ritual (figs. 4.3–4.4). The upper register of side A (fig. 4.3) shows a long procession of thirteen individuals in dark heavy garments with arms raised over their heads, indicating mourning. These figures wear long robes cinched at the waist and are most likely women. In the register below, horse-drawn chariots carry two or three individuals from the left and right and two thin, unclothed figures thought to be male face each other in some sort of contest in the middle.[13] Most likely this illustrates a funeral game in honor of the deceased, or it recalls a scene from the life shared between the participants and the deceased.[14]

The upper register of side B (fig. 4.4) shows eighteen horned animals and a male figure in the center holding a sword or leash to the neck of the largest animal. This panel depicts a scene of hunting, and its prominent placement on a burial chest also connects it with the deceased and funerary imagery. As Vermeule and Marinatos have noted, hunting imagery is an important aspect of funerary art in Egypt, Etruria, and prehistoric Greece.[15] It is particularly common on Late Bronze Age painted larnakes found on Crete, and it is not surprising to find a hunt scene at Tanagra. Themes of hunting and bull jumping, however, are not found in later Greek art of the Geometric period.

Figure 4.1 Tanagra larnax from Tomb 22. Short end, lower panel. Copyright B. Burke. Drawn by A. Richards 2007.

Figure 4.2 Tanagra larnax from Tomb 3. Side B. Copyright B. Burke. Drawn by A. Richards, 2007.

Figure 4.3 Tanagra larnax from Tomb 22. Side A. Copyright B. Burke. Drawn by A. Richards 2007.

Figure 4.4 Tanagra larnax from Tomb 22. Side B. Copyright B. Burke. Drawn by A. Richards 2007.

On the lower register of side B is a scene of three male bull leapers holding onto the horns of rushing bulls. This scene attempts to show man mastering the natural elements, perhaps as a way of indicating the struggle of life or as a way of representing a rite of passage for some young man. Again, the context of the scene—on a burial chest—suggests that bull jumping, hunting, and chariot battles are part of funerary art in the Mycenaean period. And although men in Bronze Age art are never shown in a pose of mourning with arms raised to their heads, they are active participants in othertypes of ritual behavior and lament.

The standard funerary scene of the Geometric period depicts women mourners with arms raised to their heads, but this is not commonly found in Mycenaean art. Other than the two chests from Tanagra described above, the other prominent example of mourners in this position comes from the Mycenaean cemetery at Perati in Attica. In 1953, S. Iakovidis found at Perati six interments in Chamber Tomb 5; the remains of two individuals, presumably older than the other occupants, were pushed aside to make room for the four complete skeletons. Among the grave goods was a red clay *lekane*, or basin, with two cups and four small triangular projections with small perforations attached to the rim. Nearby were found four female figurines with small attached breasts, in various degrees of preservation, approximately 10 cm. in height, painted with the similar red paint of the *lekane* (fig. 4.5). The figurines had broken off the *lekane* and have been reattached by conservators, showing that the original vessel had a circle of lamenters placed around the rim (fig. 4.6). The use of figurines in a pose of lament found in a burial context is remarkable and provides additional evidence that this gesture in Mycenaean art probably

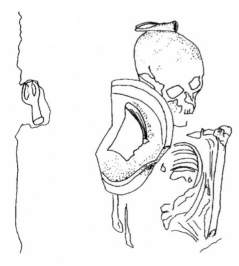

Figure 4.5 Perati tomb 111a, lekane and figurines as found. Drawn by B. Burke 2007 after Iakovidis *AJA* 1966 (70) fig. 5.

Figure 4.6   Perati lekane no. 65, from Tomb 5. National Museum in Athens.
(B. Burke)

replicates behaviors and postures of living funerary celebrants. This posture, which is common in the Geometric period, most likely has its origins
in the Mycenaean age. The Perati example is unique among Mycenaean
figurines; the majority typically have arms raised straight up, not touching
their heads, in a posture we might associate with prayer (the psi-type), or
they have no arms indicated at all (the tau- and phi-types).

THE PAINTED SARCOPHAGUS AT AYIA TRIADA

As we can see, the picture of Bronze Age lament is a composite, and there
is no single source that tells us exactly how the Mycenaeans buried and
lamented their dead. This situation is similar to the Athenian funeral of the
Archaic and Classical periods, as noted by K. Stears in chapter 7. Our most
reliable sources are archaeological remains and representational art from
funerary contexts.

The single most informative "text" from the Bronze Age Aegean is the Ayia Triada sarcophagus, dating to about 1370 B.C.E.[16] The tomb in which this painted chest was found differs significantly from earlier burial traditions on Crete. This type of tomb is new and is also found at Knossos. It contains weapons that are ascribed to a class of elite warriors who may have been related to newly arrived Mycenaeans on the island. The tomb construction and corpse deposition also differ significantly from older Minoan burials. This rather dramatic change in burial practice suggests new arrivals to the island and may mark the beginning of the Mycenaean occupation of Crete that culminated in an extensive economic network of centers, administered by the palace at Knossos.[17]

The historical context of the Ayia Triada sarcophagus, therefore, gives this work of art even greater significance, not only because it illustrates well a Late Bronze Age funerary rite contemporary with the transition from Minoan to Mycenaean culture on Crete but also because it is a materialization of Mycenaean ideology, as I have discussed elsewhere.[18] The sarcophagus was found in a small enclosure, Tomb 4, at Ayia Triada in south-central Crete by R. Paribeni on 23 June 1903. It is the only Aegean painted chest made of four limestone slabs, which are painted in fresco with scenes clearly illustrating a funerary rite celebrated by a roster of ritual actors. These figures are perhaps comparable to those described in the contemporary Hittite *Sallais Wastais* Ritual, the royal funerary ritual discussed by I. Rutherford in chapter 3. The specific aspect of Aegean Bronze Age death ritual reflected here is variously interpreted. Some scholars have reconstructed a cult for the dead, where the deceased was deified and subsequently worshipped.[19] Others read the painted panels as an illustration of ritual centered on a young vegetation god, where death and rebirth were the central aspects of the cult, comparable to the later Greek worship of Hyakinthos.[20] What is also interesting is that fragments of a nearly identical fresco were found associated with a large public building at Ayia Triada, Megaron ABCD; it also shows figures in procession accompanied by musicians.[21] The style and technique of these fragments are so similar to those of the sarcophagus panels that most scholars agree the same artist created them.

On the long side panels of the sarcophagus there are lyre players, men playing auloi, priestesses, vessel bearers, and what is thought to be an image of the deceased standing in front of the tomb (figs. 4.7–4.8). This is a cast of characters involved in the funerary rite, and we are again reminded of Hittite ceremonies. The figures on the sarcophagus, it should be noted, are not shown in the midst of vigorous emotional wailing or in positions of lament that became standard in later Greek art. In contrast, the controlled dignity of the funerary processions and the attendant musicians demonstrate that scenes of lament in the Bronze Age differ from those from later Greece, but this is lament nonetheless.

Side A (fig. 4.7) of the sarcophagus illustrates two ritual events associated with funerals: libation on the left and a presentation or offertory

Figure 4.7 Ayia Triada sarcophagus, side A, libation and presentation. Heakleion Archaeological Museum, CR 8. (Alison Frantz Photographic Collection, American School of Classical Studies at Athens)

Figure 4.8 Ayia Triada sarcophagus, side B, procession and sacrifice. Herakleion Archaeological Museum, CR 9. (Alison Frantz Photographic Collection, American School of Classical Studies at Athens)

scene on the right, presumably to the dead. The libation scene shows three figures in profile, two women and a male musician moving toward the left in procession toward two double axes on stepped stands with a bird atop each. At the far left, a woman pours some liquid into a blue cauldron positioned between the axes.[22] The red-skinned, male musician in a yellow robe follows behind the women in procession, playing a seven-stringed lyre, or *phorminx*, with duck-head finials.[23]

On the right of side A, three men with funerary offerings lead a procession. They are clad in white hide skirts similar to the one worn by the pouring woman of the libation scene. There is a change in the background color of these figures, perhaps indicating a later time of day for the ritual action. Yellow may represent early morning for the libation; white could stand for daylight; and the blue background could refer to night.[24] The figures carry two spotted animal figurines and a model boat.[25] The last figure on the right of the presentation scene is difficult to interpret. It is almost certainly some representation of the dead, and the red skin and short, curly, dark hair suggest that this is a male figure. He is smaller than any of the other individuals, and we cannot see his arms or feet.[26] A variety of suggestions have been made for his identity—that he is a deity, a mummy, or the spirit of the deceased.[27] The structure he stands before is interpreted as a tomb, possibly even Tomb 4 at Ayia Triada in which the sarcophagus was found.[28]

Side B illustrates a procession and the sacrifice of a bound bull on an altar with dripping blood collected in a rhyton stuck into the ground.[29] Another musician is found here, a double-aulos-playing man performing behind the bull, and two wide-eyed deer sit below the altar. The musician leads from the left a procession of five women toward the bound bull.[30] To the right another woman, wearing a white hide skirt decorated with a crocus-petal pattern, attends to a funerary sacrifice at a smaller altar.

Many scholars have noted the exceptional nature of the Ayia Triada sarcophagus, and some consider it the product of a Minoan craftsman working for a Mycenaean patron.[31] The heavy emphasis on musical performance and funerary procession suggests Bronze Age lamentations and rites of sacrifice, distinguishing the Ayia Triada sarcophagus from other examples of Minoan funerary art. As I have discussed elsewhere, the sarcophagus was contemporary with a major Mycenaean building program at Ayia Triada and was almost certainly made for a member of the Mycenaean elite.[32] The intentional fusion of mainland and Cretan elements makes the sarcophagus a remarkable work of Aegean art, documenting the Mycenaean presence on Crete, quoting the foreign while at the same time making it indigenous.[33] The elaborate decoration of the chest suggests high prestige for both the deceased and those attending to the funerary rites represented on the chest. Prominent displays of wealth and power in funerary art are typical of mainland elites beginning with the people of the Shaft Graves at Mycenae.[34]

The performative aspect of the sarcophagus—women performing lament, accompanied by male musicians, and elite figures brought in by chariots on the smaller side panels—along with the contemporary public architectural program at Ayia Triada, assists us in visualizing ritual events associated with Mycenaean funerals on Crete. The sarcophagus almost certainly was part of a ceremony for the dead that reaffirmed the elite group identity of the Mycenaeans in the Late Minoan IIIA2 period and visually transmitted symbols of power to a Cretan populace. By appropriating images from the Minoan past and combining them with contemporary Mycenaean elements, the creators of the sarcophagus produced a monument of memory that linked the Late Bronze Age present on Crete with a well-crafted view of the Middle Bronze Age past.

THE WARRIOR VASE AT MYCENAE

It is at the end of the Late Bronze Age that we might expect to find the strongest links to the succeeding Geometric style in Greek funerary art. The Warrior Vase from Mycenae is one example of Late Mycenaean pictorial vase painting that, after its discovery in the late nineteenth century, was thought to resemble art of the Geometric period so much so that scholars dated it to the seventh century B.C.E., citing similarities with vases from the Kerameikos in Athens.[35] However, by the mid–twentieth century, comparable Late Mycenaean vases also showing "warriors," with handles similar to the Mycenae example, were found on the Athenian acropolis and at Lefkandi in secure contexts, datable to the end of the Late Bronze Age, circa 1150 B.C.E.[36]

The Warrior Vase is one of the most well-known works of prehistoric Aegean art, but it is often cited as an illustration of the martial qualities of the Mycenaeans rather than as an example of Mycenaean funerary art (fig. 4.9).[37] Fragments of the pictorial krater were found by H. Schliemann in October 1876.[38] He reports that excavations were at a depth of 20 ft. below the surface in one of the chambers identified as the "Cyclopean house," which Schliemann thought belonged to the ruling family of Atreus.[39] This structure, within which the Warrior Vase was found, soon became known as the House of the Warrior Vase. The deposition of the krater in the house, however, is not certain because only basement rooms were preserved and the context of the vase was an eroded slump of fill from nearby.

According to Tsountas, under the House of the Warrior Vase there "were cuttings in the rock, perhaps graves."[40] Schliemann's Excavation Notebook (15 A) is helpful in understanding the original context of the Warrior Vase:

> p. 97, *Tuesday 3rd Octb*, I have dug and this chamber about 3 m deep and as there is neither a door nor a window either in this or in any other of house's chambers, I now believe that every one of the house's chambers served as a particular tomb. This seems also to be confirmed by the many bones found there.

Figure 4.9 Warrior Vase from Mycenae. National Museum in Athens. (B. Burke)

p. 98 *Wednesday 4th Octb:*....Among many other highly interesting potsherds were found there large fragments of vases with very primitive representations of warriors, some of whom have larg- a helmet in form of cap with thorns or [unreadable]. All of these have very long faces, very long noses, cuirasses, helmets with long [unreadable]; from the forepart of each helmet is protruding something in form of a horn; *Assyrian beards*, yellow shields; the objects on the lance [drawing of spear] may. All the features of the warriors are perfectly of the same cast.[41]

The archaeological context should not be overlooked and is of key importance for reading the image. The vessel was excavated at Mycenae in close proximity to Grave Circle A and near other burials of the Middle and Late Bronze Ages, suggesting that it may have functioned as a grave marker or was associated in some way with a burial. If there is a funerary context for the vase, it would suggest that the scenes painted on it are better viewed as a rite of lamentation rather than some vague reference to the supposed belligerent nature of the Mycenaeans.[42]

On side A, a partially preserved woman wearing a long robe raises an arm to her head (fig. 4.10). Her left half is obscured by the applied handle, which is poorly preserved. Her garment is a head-to-toe robe with a yellow panel in front, similar to those of the women lamenting on the Tanagra larnakes. She also seems to have a *polos*, or cap, on her head, a long nose

Figure 4.10   Detail Warrior Vase from Mycenae. National Museum in Athens. (B. Burke)

that overhangs pronounced lips, and a rather weak chin. The six bearded men marching away are dressed uniformly and wear white spotted, horned helmets with a plume at the back. They carry spears with an attached bag and wear greaves and short fringed skirts with spots and long-sleeved corselets. They carry circular, yellow shields.

On side B, five men in procession are dressed similarly to the six on side A, except they wear bristled helmets instead of horned ones, and they carry spears raised for throwing. The bristled helmets are the "hedgehog" type known in Mycenaean pictorial painting since the thirteenth century B.C.E., becoming common in the twelfth.[43] It has been suggested that this group of warriors is the same group as on side A but shown in a different phase of their action. If this is an illustration of funeral games or a hunt, the first group could be going off to start the proceedings and the second could be participating in spear-throwing events in honor of the dead.[44] This scene might in some ways be compared with the funeral games of Patroklos, as described by Homer, and illustrated by the early Athenian vase painter Sophilos on his famous dinos fragment.

The closest parallel to the Warrior Vase is the grave stele from Mycenae that was originally inscribed and then painted over in fresco, known as the reused Painted Grave Stele (fig. 4.11). By context and style, the stele is dated to the period contemporary with the Warrior Vase. The three registers of the painted stele show different themes: a fragmentary presentation scene

Figure 4.11   Photo of reconstructed Painted Grave stele from Mycenae. (B. Burke)

has a seated female figure receiving men in procession at the top; a row of armed figures march forward in the middle; and two horned and two unhorned deer plus a hedgehog are in a row along the bottom. The central panel shows armed soldiers in procession, which is strikingly similar to the Warrior Vase figures. The construction of the faces and the detail of the costumes suggest that both the stele and the Warrior Vase were made by the same artist, demonstrating that pictorial vase painters could work in color fresco. There is little dispute that the Painted Grave Stele is a work of funerary art, and its close similarity to the Warrior Vase further supports the identification of the vase from Mycenae also as a funerary monument. The themes of marching warriors or hunters in procession also should be taken as a reference to controlled ritual actions associated with burial.

In summary, what I wish to stress is not the historical context of the Warrior Vase but, rather, its depositional context. It was found in an area used as a cemetery of the Mycenaeans for centuries. It begins a tradition of large decorated ceramics used to mark burials. The themes on the krater should be read as funerary art, not an illustration of military prowess. The Warrior Vase may presage the later practice of using decorated ceramics with illustrations of lamentation and funerary rites to mark a grave.[45] If we consider the krater within its archaeological context—that it was found in the area of a Mycenaean cemetery and shows parallels with other examples of Mycenaean funerary art like the Painted Grave Stele—we can interpret the pose of the woman as a gesture of lamentation to the deceased whose grave was marked by the krater.[46] Most likely, if the illustration of the woman were complete, we would see that she has both her arms raised in what became the common position of lament. We should also view the male figures as engaged in a funeral procession or taking part in games associated with the funeral. They could also be going off to hunt, which would be appropriate for a funerary marker as well, as we have seen from the examples at Tanagra.

CONCLUSIONS

Our earliest representation of Bronze Age lament, it should be noted, comes from the mid–third millennium B.C.E., in the Cyclades. Sometimes marble figurines have painted details marked with red and blue pigment, possibly indicating blood from scratches or tears. The vertical painted striations such as those found on the head in the National Museum in Athens (inventory no. 3909; fig. 4.12) certainly look like streaks of tears, and if so, this would be the earliest Greek representation of mourning that we possess. The grinding tools and containers for such pigments have been found in Cycladic burials, and the color agents may have been used on the deceased's body or on those performing rites of lamentation. There is great consistency in terms of the style of carving and decoration of these figurines, suggesting a similar function. Because written sources from the Early Bronze Age are nonexistent and so few examples of figurines have secure archaeological provenance, our interpretations must be provisional. The tradition of representing tears or scratches to the face begins with these marble effigies of lamenters, which were placed in tombs. In the Late Bronze Age the tradition of placing figurines in tombs continued, as shown by those with upraised arms attached to the *lekane* from Perati (fig. 4.7). These demonstrate that the tradition of women mourners with their arms raised to their heads seems to have begun on the mainland in the Late Bronze Age and continued into the Geometric period.

The Tanagra larnakes (figs. 4.1–4.4) illustrate various funerary rites associated with a Mycenaean population in central Boeotia. Themes of hunting are also found on these clay chests and remind us that scenes not explicitly representing a burial rite may still refer to funerary rites. The

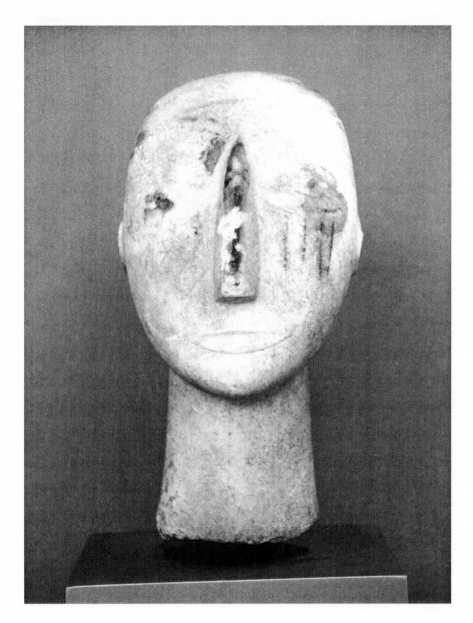

Figure 4.12 Cycladic head, mourning. National Museum in Athens. (B. Burke)

painted sarcophagus from Ayia Triada (figs. 4.8–4.9) illustrates funerary processions for newly arrived Mycenaeans on Crete and shows female participants in solemn acts of libation and musical procession. The Late Helladic IIIC Warrior Vase (figs. 4.10–4.11) from Mycenae shows both a lamenting woman and armed men in procession. The scenes of armed men on the vase and on the Painted Grave Stele from Mycenae more likely refer to funerary games than to military activities associated with the world of the living. The archaeological context of the vase suggests that this monument was intentionally created as funerary art. These examples, when examined with funerary lament in mind, allow us to reconstruct an image of Bronze Age burial rites that we would be otherwise unavailable to us if we relied solely on later literary testimonia.

ACKNOWLEDGMENT

I would like to thank Ashley Richards for her drawings of the Tanagra larnakes, figures 4.1–4.4.

NOTES

1. Vermeule 1979, 63.
2. Hoffman 2002, 525, 545.
3. Demakopoulou and Konsola 1981, 82.
4. Vermeule 1965, 124.
5. Multiple chests were found in the chamber tombs, and it is difficult to assess how many tombs have been excavated. The Mycenaean cemeteries are closer to the modern village called Tanagra, which is distinguished from the ancient city of this name, and the modern village of Grimadha surveyed by Roller (1987) and more recently by Bintliff et al. (2001).
6. Cavanagh and Mee 1995, 46, 60–61.
7. Demakopoulou and Konsola 1981, 82–87.
8. Vermeule 1965, 123. The Ayia Triada sarcophagus, discussed below, is not terra-cotta but is made of limestone slabs fitted together.
9. Marinatos 1997.
10. Cavanagh and Mee 1995; Immerwahr 1990, 154–158, and 1995; Marinatos 1997; Vermeule 1965, and 1979, 201–205.
11. Figure 4.1 is from Tomb 3, Thebes Museum catalog no. 4, and figures 4.2–4.4 are from Tomb 22, Thebes Museum catalog no. 1.
12. Cavanagh and Mee 1995, catalog no. 44; Spyropoulos 1970, plate 48a.
13. Benzi (1999) has recently suggested that they are boxing, which to my mind seems unlikely because they seem to be holding some kind of instrument, possibly swords. He also proposes that this larnax from Tomb 22 depicts rites of passage for a young male rather than an illustration of funerary rites. Thebes Museum catalog no. 1 notes: "The most important of the larnakes discovered so far in the course of the excavation. Length 0.73 m., width 0.31 m., height (including legs) 0.59 m." (Demakopoulou and Konsola 1981, 83).
14. This would parallel the practice in ritual lament of recalling a shared past with the deceased. See Perkell, this volume, on Homeric lament.
15. Marinatos 1997, 284–288; Vermeule 1979, 66–69.
16. Specifically, it dates to the early Late Minoan III A2 ceramic sequence. DiVita 2000, 480; La Rosa 1999, 2000a, and 2000b, 90.
17. Already in the Late Minoan II period at Knossos the Linear B texts from the Room of the Chariot Tablets attest to a prominent Mycenaean Greek presence,

perhaps even the establishment of religious activity focused on the mainland Bronze Age goddess Athena (*a-ta-na-po-ti-ni-ja*). Driessen 2000; Gulizio, Pluta, and Palaima 2001.

18. Burke 2005.

19. Cf. Rutherford, this volume, where one of the purposes of the funeral ritual was to deify the dead. Nilsson's (1950, 426–443) "heroization" of the dead man assumed that he was a Mycenaean overlord.

20. Nauert 1965. See also Pötscher 1997.

21. Fragments of a Procession Fresco at Hagia Triada illustrate musicians and deer, which originally decorated either the megaron or Stoa FG. See Immerwahr 1990, 102, catalog A.T. no. 3; Militello 1998, 154–155, and 1999, 345–352; Paribeni 1908, fig. 21; Rehak and Younger 2001, 447.

22. Long 1974, 36–37. For the libation scenes, see also Marinatos 1986, 25–27.

23. Carter has cataloged most examples of lyres and representations of lyres from the Bronze Age Aegean and notes that birds are summoned by musicians as "visualizations of a divine presence" (1995, 307). See also Immerwahr 1990, A.T. no. 3 and Py no. 14, plate xviii; Militello 1998; Younger 1998, 66–69, plates 10–12.

24. Pötscher 1990, 173–176, 1994, and 1997. However, Marinatos (1993) does not believe that this theory is supported by Aegean evidence.

25. For discussions of the boat, see Johnston 1985, 140, catalog representation no. 1; Wachsmann 1998, catalog 606. The boat is peculiar for Aegean funerary ritual, and Watrous (1991) sees parallels with Egyptian cult practices for the dead at Ayia Triada, comparing the presentation of a model boat and perhaps animal effigies to the dead to similar scenes found in tombs at Egyptian Thebes. See also Long 1974, 48–50, for further discussion of foreign influence on the Ayia Triada sarcophagus.

26. Rehak and Younger (2001, 448) compare this figure, presumed to be the deceased, to the fresco from Knossos named "La Parisienne" by Evans, in which a figure is also shown armless in profile, at a different scale from associated figures, and wearing an unusual garment.

27. Long 1974, 44–50.

28. La Rosa 1999, 186, fig. 9; Long 1974, 73.

29. Mantzourani (1995, 127) identifies this vessel as a two-handled vase and does not believe it is a rhyton stuck into the ground. I follow Long (1974, 36) and Immerwahr (1990, 101 n. 7) in identifying it as a rhyton.

30. One of the female figures is often reconstructed wearing an elaborate headdress, although there is no evidence for this.

31. Davis 1995, 14. N. Marinatos describes the sarcophagus as "one of the most valuable pictorial documentations of the Minoan cult of the dead that we possess" (1993, 31).

32. Burke 2005.

33. See Feldman 2002, 14–17, in reference to the exotic goods from Ugarit.

34. Dabney and Wright 1990, 50.

35. Dümmler 1888; Pottier 1896, and 1907, 248 n. 1. Pottier (1896, and 1907) suggests that it was painted by the seventh-century vase painter Aristonothos. Becatti (1965) discusses fully the aesthetic connection between Late Mycenaean painting and seventh-century art. D. Mackenzie (1906–1907) argues that the bull-head handles from the Warrior Vase show that the tradition had a much earlier history, originating in the Bronze Age. Even earlier examples are now known from the Mycenaean world. See Vermeule and Karageorghis 1982, 130.

36. Broneer 1939, 353–354; Popham and Sackett 1968, 20, figs. 38–39. The Warrior Vase from Mycenae dates to the mid–Late Helladic IIIC period, ca. 1150 B.C.E. See French 2002, 82; Immerwahr 1990, 150 n. 5. This date is based on comparisons with LH IIIC Close-style pottery from the mainland and from Cyprus.

37. Taylour (1983, 138) cites the Warrior Vase for its illustration of Mycenaean arms. Likewise Preziosi and Hitchcock describe it as a "virtual icon of Mycenaean militarism to modern archaeologists" (1999, 184–185).

38. National Museum Inventory no. 1426, from Mycenae. The krater was made on a potter's wheel, according to Schliemann, yet is "unusually bad and mixed with coarse sand; the fabric also is extremely rude; inside it is painted red" (1878, 137). For the date, see French 2002, 140.

39. Schliemann 1878, 131. This was thought to be the palace of the dynasts of Mycenae, appropriately located next to the so-called agora (Grave Circle A), based on a reading of Euripides' *Elektra* 170: "[T]he people of Mycenae are there called to the Agora to see the wonderful lamb with the golden fleece . . . (which) had been conveyed to the palace by Aerope, wife of Atreus."

40. In Wace 1964, 61.

41. The Gennadios Library of the American School of Classical Studies at Athens made Schliemann's notebooks available to me, and I would like to thank them. S. Kennel also was helpful in reading some of Schliemann's handwriting.

42. Drews (1993, 161–163) acknowledges that the vase dates to the period after the major destructions of the Late Bronze Age and that "the vase is probably funerary" (1993, 162), but he does not interpret the scene in terms of funerary iconography. Immerwahr (1990, 150–151) even suggests a connection with the Trojan War.

43. Vermeule and Karageorghis 1982, 122.

44. Ibid., 132.

45. French (2002, 82) also suggests that the Warrior Vase should be connected with a tomb.

46. Vermeule and Karageorghis 1982, 130, no. XI.42.

BIBLIOGRAPHY

Ahlberg, G. 1971. *Prothesis and Ekphora in Greek Geometric Art. SIMA* 32. Göteborg.

Alexiou, M. 2002. *The Ritual Lament in Greek Tradition.* 2nd ed. Rev. D. Yatromanolakis and P. Roilos. Lanham, Md.

Baxevani, K. 1995. A Minoan Larnax from Pigi Rethymnou with Religious and Funerary Iconography. In *Klados: Essays in Honour of J. N. Coldstream,* ed. C. Morris, 15–33. *BICS* Suppl. 63. London.

Becatti, G. 1965. *Interragativi sul vaso die Guerrieri di Micene.* Studi in Onore di Luisa Banti. Rome.

Benzi, M. 1999. Riti di passaggio sulla larnax dalla Tomba 22 di Tanagra? In *Epi Ponton Plazomenoi. Simposio Italiano de Studi Egei dedicato a Luigi Bernabò Brea e Giovanni Pugliese Carratelli,* ed. V. La Rosa, D. Palermo, and L. Vagnetti, 215–233. Rome.

Bintliff, J., N. Evelpidou, E. Farinetti, B. Music, I. Risnar, K. Sbonias, L. Sigalos, B. Slapsak, V. Stissi, and A. Vassilopoulos. 2001. The Leiden Ancient Cities of Boeotia Project: Preliminary Report on the 2001 Season. *Pharos* 9: 33–74.

Broneer, O. 1939. A Mycenaean Fountain on the Athenian Acropolis. *Hesperia* 8: 317–433.

Burke, B. 2005. Materialization of Mycenaean Ideology and the Ayia Triada
    Sarcophagus. *American Journal of Archaeology* 109: 403–422.
Carter, J. 1995. Ancestor Cult and the Occasion of Homeric Performance. In *The
    Ages of Homer: A Tribute to Emily Townsend Vermeule*, ed. J. Carter and
    S. Morris, 285–312. Austin.
Cavanagh, W., and C. Mee. 1995. Mourning Before and After the Dark Age. In
    Klados: Essays in Honour of J. N. Coldstream, ed. C. Morris, 45–61. BICS
    Suppl. 63. London.
———. 1998. *A Private Place: Death in Prehistoric Greece. SIMA* 125. Jonsered,
    Sweden.
Chippindale, C., and D. Gill. 1993. Material and Intellectual Consequences of
    Esteem for Cycladic Figures. *American Journal of Archaeology* 97: 601–660.
Cucuzza, N. 1997. The North Sector Buildings of Haghia Triada. In *La Crète
    Mycénienne: Actes de la table ronde internationale organisée par l'École fran-
    çaise d'Athènes*, ed. J. Driessen and A. Farnoux, 73–84. BCH Suppl. 30.
    Athens.
———. 2001. Religion and Architecture: Early LM IIIA2 Buildings in the Southern
    Area of Haghia Triada. In *POTNIA: Deities and Religion in the Aegean Bronze
    Age*, ed. R. Laffineur and R. Hägg, 169–174. *Aegaeum* 22. Liège.
———. 2003. Osservazioni sui costumi funerari dell'area di Festos ed Haghia Triada
    nel TM IIIA1–A2 iniziale. *Creta Antica* 3: 133–166.
———. 2004. Il volo del Grifo: Osservazioni sulla Haghia Triada "Micenea." *Creta
    Antica* 4: 199–272.
Dabney, M., and J. Wright. 1990. Mortuary Customs, Palatial Society and State
    Formation in the Aegean Area: A Comparative Study. In *Celebrations of Death
    and Divinity in the Bronze Age Argolid: Proceedings of the Sixth International
    Symposium at the Swedish Institute at Athens, 11–13 June 1988*, ed. R. Hägg
    and G. Nordquist, 45–52. Stockholm.
Davis, E. 1995. Art and Politics in the Aegean: The Missing Ruler. In *The Role of
    the Ruler in the Prehistoric Aegean*, ed. P. Rehak, 11–20. *Aegaeum* 11. Liège.
Demakopoulou, K., and D. Konsola. 1981. *Archaeological Museum of Thebes*. Athens.
DeMarrais, E., L. J. Castillo, and T. Earle. 1996. Ideology, Materialization, and
    Power Strategies. *Current Anthropology* 37: 15–47.
DiVita, A. 2000. Atti Della Scuola: 1996–1997. *Annuario della Scuola archeolo-
    gica di Atene e delle Missioni italiane in Oriente* 74–75: 467–586.
Drews, R. 1993. *The End of the Bronze Age: Changes in Warfare and the Catastro-
    phe ca. 1200 B.C.* Princeton.
Driessen, J. 2000. *The Scribes of the Room of the Chariot Tablets at Knossos:
    Interdisciplinary Approach to the Study of a Linear B Deposit. Minos* Suppl.
    15. Salamanca, Spain.
Dümmler, F. 1888. Bemerkungen zum ältesten Kunsthandelwerk auf griechischem
    Boden. *Mitteilungen des deutschen Archäologischen Instituts, Athenische
    Abteilung* 13: 288–291.
Feldman, M. 2002. Luxurious Forms: Redefining a Mediterranean "International
    Style," 1400–1200 B.C.E. *Art Bulletin* 84: 6–29.
French, E. 2002. *Mycenae: Agamemnon's Capital*. Charleston, S.C.
———, and A. Wace, eds. 1979. *Excavations at Mycenae 1939–1955*. BSA Suppl. 12.
    London.
Gates, C. 1985. Rethinking the Building History of Grave Circle A at Mycenae.
    American Journal of Archaeology 89: 263–274.

Getz-Preziosi, P. 1987. *Sculptors of the Cyclades: Individual and Tradition in the Third Millennium* B.C. Ann Arbor.

Gulizio, J., K. Pluta, and T. Palaima. 2001. Religion in the Room of the Chariot Tablets. In *POTNIA: Deities and Religion in the Aegean Bronze Age*, ed. R. Laffineur and R. Hägg, 453–461. *Aegaeum* 22. Liège.

Halbherr, F. 1903. Scoperti A.D. Haghia Triada presso Phaestos. *Monumenti antichi* 13: 6–74.

Halbherr, F., E. Stefani, and L. Banti. 1977. Haghia Triada nel periodo tardo-palaziale. *Annuario della Scuola archeologica di Atene e delle Missioni italiane in Oriente* 55, N. S. 39: 9–296.

Hamilakis, Y. 1998. Eating the Dead: Mortuary Feasting and the Politics of Mourning in the Aegean Bronze Age Societies. In *Cemeteries and Society in the Aegean Bronze Age*, ed. K. Branigan, 115–132. Sheffield Studies in Aegean Archaeology 1. Sheffield.

Hoffman, G. 2002. Early Cycladic II Mourning Figures. *American Journal of Archaeology* 106: 525–550.

Iakovidis, S. 1966. A Mycenaean Mourning Custom. *American Jouranal of Archaeology* 70: 43–50.

Immerwahr, S. 1990. *Aegean Painting in the Bronze Age*. University Park, Pa.

——. 1995. Death and the Tanagra Larnakes. In *The Ages of Homer: A Tribute to Emily Townsend Vermeule*, ed. J. Carter and S. Morris, 109–121. Austin.

Johnston, P. 1985. *Ship and Boat Models in Ancient Greece*. Annapolis, Md.

Kilian, K. 1988. The Emergence of Wanax Ideology in the Mycenaean Palaces. *Oxford Journal of Anthropology* 7(3): 291–302.

Knapp, A.B. 1996. Power and Ideology on Prehistoric Cyprus. In *Religion and Power in the Ancient Greek World: Proceedings of the Uppsala Symposium 1993*, ed. p. Hellström and B. Alroth, 9–27. Uppsala.

Kurtz, D. and J. Boardman. 1971. *Greek Burial Customs*. London.

Laffineur, R. 1991. À propos du sarcophage d'Aghia Triada: Un ritual de nécro-mancie à l'époque protohistorique? *Kernos* 4:277–285.

La Rosa, V. 1993. Haghia Triada in Eta Micenea. In *Mykenaïka: Actes du IXe colloque internationale sur les textes mycéniens st égéens organisé par le Centre de l' Antiquité Grecque et Romaine de la Foundation Hellénique des Recherches Scientifiques et l' École française d' Athènes*, ed. J.-P. Olivier, 617–620. BCH Suppl. 25, Athens.

——. 1997. Haghia Triada à l'époque mycénienne: L'utopie d'une ville capitale. In *La Crète Mycénienne: Actes de la table ronde internationale organisée par l'École française d'Athènes*, ed. J. Driessen and A. Farnoux, 249–266. BCH Suppl. 30. Athens.

——. 1999. Nuovi dati sulla tomba del sarcofago dipinto di H. Triada. In *Epi Ponton Plazomenoi. Simposio Italiano de Studi Egei dedicato a Luigi Bernabò Brea e Giovanni Pugliese Carratelli*, ed. V. La Rosa, D. Palermo, and L. Vagnetti, 177–188. Rome.

——. 2000a. The Painted Sarcophagus: Determining the Chronology. In *The Wall Painting of Thera: Proceedings of the First International Symposium*, vol. 2, ed. S. Sherratt, 996–997. Athens.

——. 2000b. To Whom Did the Queen Tiyi Scarab Found at Hagia Triada Belong? In Κρητη-Αιγυπτος Πολιτισμικοι δεσμοι τριων Χιλιετιων ed. A. Karetsou, 86–93. Athens.

Levi, D. 1956. The Sarcophagus of Haghia Triada Restored. *Archaeology* 9: 192–199.

Long, C. 1974. *The Ayia Triadha Sarcophagus: A Study of Late Minoan and Mycenaean Funerary Practices and Beliefs.* SIMA 41. Göteborg.

Mantzourani, E. 1995. Vases and Vessels in Aegean Wall-Painting. In *Klados: Essays in Honour of J. N. Coldstream,* ed. C. Morris, 123–141. BICS Suppl. 63. London.

Mackenzie, D. 1906–1907. Cretan Palaces and the Aegean Civilization III. *Annual of the British School at Athens* 13: 421–445.

Marinatos, N. 1986. *Minoan Sacrificial Ritual: Cult Practice and Symbolism.* Stockholm.

———. 1993. *Minoan Religion.* Columbia, S.C.

———. 1997. Minoan and Mycenaean Larnakes: A Comparison. In *La Crète Mycénienne: Actes de la table ronde internationale organisée par l'École française d'Athènes,* ed. J. Driessen and A. Farnoux, 283–292. BCH Suppl. 30. Athens.

Militello, P. 1998. *Haghia Triada I: Gli Affreschi minoici di Haghia Triada (Creta).* Monografie della Scuola Archeologica di Atene e Della Missioni Italiane in Oriente 9. Padua.

———. 1999. Oi mykenaikes ôopographies tes Ayias Triadas (The Mycenaean frescoes of Ayia Triada). In *Hperiphereia tou Mykenaikou kosmou* (The Periphery of the Mycenaan World), ed. N. Kyparisse-Apostolika and M. Papakonstantinou, 345–352. Lamia, Greece.

Nauert, J. P. 1965. The Hagia Triada Sarcophagus: An Iconographical Study. *Antike Kunst* 8: 91–98.

Niemeier, W.-D. 1982. Mycenaean Knossos and the Age of Linear B. *Studi Micenei ed Egeo-Anatolici* 23: 219–287.

———. 1983. The Character of the Knossian Palace Society in the Second Half of the Fifteenth Century B.C.: Mycenaean or Minoan? In *Minoan Society,* ed. O. Krzyszkowska and L. Nixon, 217–236. Bristol, U.K.

Nilsson, M. 1950. *Minoan–Mycenaean Religion and Its Survival in Greek Religion.* Lund.

Paribeni, R. 1908. Il sarcofago dipinto di Haghia Triada. *Monumenti antichi* 19: 5–87.

Popham, M., and L. Sackett. 1968. *Excavations at Lefkandi, Euboea 1964–66.* London.

Pötscher, W. 1990. *Aspekte und Probleme der minoischen Religion. Religionswissenschaftliche Texte und Studien,* Band 4. Hildesheim.

———. 1994. Der Termin des Festes auf dem Sarkophag von Hagia Triada. *Klio* 76: 67–77.

———.1996. Zum Sarkophag von Hagia Triada. *Atti e Memorie* 2: 857–859.

———. 1997. Tag und Nacht auf dem Sarkophag von Hagia Triada. *Klio* 79: 19–22.

Pottier, E. 1896. Observations sur la céramique mycénienne *Revue Archéologique* 28: 19–23.

———. 1907. Documents céramiques du Musée du Louvre. *BCH* 31: 115–138, 228–269.

Preston, L. 2004a. Contextualising the Larnax: Tradition, Innovation and Regionalism in Coffin Use on Late Minoan II–IIIB Crete. *Oxford Journal of Anthropology* 23 (2): 177–197.

———.2004b. A Mortuary Perspective on Political Changes in Late Minoan II–IIIB Crete. *American Journal of Archaeology* 108: 321–348.

Preziosi, D., and L. Hitchcock. 1999. *Aegean Art and Architecture.* Oxford.

Rehak, P., and J. Younger. 2001. Neopalatial, Final Palatial, and Postpalatial Crete. In *Aegean Prehistory: A Review*, ed. T. Cullen, 383–473. Boston.

Roller, D. 1987. Tanagra Survey Project 1985: The Site of Grimadha. *British School at Athens* 82: 213–232.

Rutkowski, B. 1968. The Origin of the Minoan Coffin. *Annual of the British School at Athens* 63: 219–228.

Schliemann, H. 1878. *Mycenae: A Narrative of Researches and Discoveries at Mycenae and Tiryns.* New York.

Spyropoulos, T. 1970. Excavation in the Mycenaean Cemetery at Tanagra. *Archaiologika Analekta ex Athenon* 3: 184–187.

Taylour, W. 1983. *The Mycenaeans.* London. (Originally published 1964)

Tsountas, C., and J. Manatt. 1897. *The Mycenaean Age: A Study of the Monuments and Culture of Pre-Homeric Greece.* Boston.

Vermeule, E. 1965. Painted Mycenaean Larnakes. *Journal of Hellenic Studies* 85: 123–148.

———. 1979. *Aspects of Death in Early Greek Art and Poetry.* Berkeley.

———.1991. Myth and Tradition from Mycenae to Homer. In *New Perspectives in Early Greek Art*, ed. D. Buitron-Oliver, 99–121. Studies in the History of Art 32. Washington, D.C.

Vermeule, E., and V. Karageorghis. 1982. *Mycenaean Pictorial Vase Painting.* Cambridge, Mass.

Wace, A. 1964. *Mycenae: An Archaeological History and Guide.* 2nd ed. London.

Wachsmann, S. 1998. Seagoing Ships and Seamanship in the Bronze Age Levant. College Station, Tex.

Watrous, L. V. 1984. Ayia Triada: A New Perspective on the Minoan Villa. *American Journal of Archaeology* 88: 123–134.

———. 1991. The Origin and Iconography of the Late Minoan Painted Larnax. *Hesperia* 60: 285–307.

Younger, J. 1998. *Music in the Aegean Bronze Age. SIMA* 144. Göteborg.

5

READING THE
LAMENTS OF *ILIAD* 24

Christine Perkell

RITUAL/POETICS/IDEOLOGY

Many recent studies of lament by classicists as well as by anthropologists have established that women's lament has the potential to be subversive of the dominant (male) value system, whether in Homeric epic or in funeral rituals as still practiced in remoter areas of contemporary Greece.[1] This observation has particular and provocative interest for readers of both Homeric and later heroic epic poetry, because women's laments mourn heroes' deaths instead of, in some sense, celebrating them. Therefore, laments in epic can seem to be inconsistent with or even subversive of the genre's defining purpose of memorializing heroic deeds. As Katharine Derderian has recently put it, in both "formulaic and thematic senses," lament functions as an "anti-epic within the epic poems."[2] Sheila Murnaghan's nuanced reading of laments in Homer develops the interpretation that laments are a constitutive element of epic, a crucial if prefatory element in the hero's glory. In this reading, the oppositional potential of lament is real but is subsumed by epic's larger ideological thrust, its "central claims."[3]

It is this latter reading of women's grief that Hektor assumes in his famous *homilia* with Andromache in *Iliad* 6:

> And some day seeing you shedding tears a man will say of you:
> This is the wife of Hektor, who was ever the bravest fighter
> Of the Trojans, breakers of horses, in the days when they fought about Ilion.
> So will one speak of you; and for you it will be yet a fresh grief,
> To be widowed of such a man who could fight off the day of your slavery.
> (6.459–463)[4]

In Hektor's reading, Andromache's enduring grief at his death in battle will be interpreted as a memorial to his own imperishable glory (*kleos aphthiton*). In so thinking Hektor exemplifies what I will term in this chapter the "heroic code," that "logical chain which links death, glory, art, and immortality. Death is inescapable . . . yet certain acts . . . can achieve the glory that outlives finite life, so long as they are perpetuated in art" (i.e., the tradition of heroic poetry).[5]

Yet as readers/audience of the *Iliad*, we may not all read Hektor's actions as he himself anticipates. Instead we may find that other perspectives on Hektor emerge through the laments of *Iliad* 24 that figure so significantly in the poem's closure. A remarkable feature of these laments, as Gail Holst-Warhaft observes, is that they do not praise Hektor's glory.[6] Other studies of these laments have noted the bitterness of Andromache in her explicit regret/ambivalence about Hektor's fatal pursuit of heroic glory.[7] In this chapter, I pursue these provocative observations about the *Iliad* 24 laments as they comment implicitly and explicitly on Hektor's pursuit of epic fame through glorious death. It is a feature of great texts that they challenge generic conventions in some degree. As Michael Silk argues, this is true of the *Iliad*: "The greatest literature is wont to subvert the dominant ideological categories that it purports to, and does indeed also, embody"; he adds that "thanks to Achilles, the *Iliad* surely does just this."[8] Although Silk does not include the laments in his discussion of the *Iliad*'s questioning of heroic ideology, I propose that the laments, too, function to put heroic ideology into question and thus participate in the pattern of genre subversion that Silk describes. Because the laments of *Iliad* 24 figure so importantly in the poem's closure, they have interpretive significance—greater than they would have elsewhere in the poem. Their presence in this emphatic position—a crucial fact of poetics—invites interpretation from the perspective of poetics and therefore should not be "underread."[9]

I would briefly distinguish between lament as a tool in the poet's armamentarium, as a poetic device, and lament as a cultural performance enacted by real women and susceptible to anthropologists' study and documentation. What we have learned about the continuity of the lament tradition in Greece and about the function of lament generally from comparative anthropology aids our attempts to appreciate the functions of laments in Homeric poetry. Additionally, as Murnaghan has so well observed, part of the fascination of lament for scholars is the possibility of accessing the authentic voices of women, laments being female-authored texts outside the mainstream of Western culture.[10] Derderian, among others, has isolated and cataloged various components and themes of laments as they appear in the Homeric poems in order to try to establish what may be considered traditional or conventional in lament. Christos Tsagalis, too, has described the typology of Homeric *gooi*—their formulas and motifs—also with a goal of discovering an ur-form of lament, to the degree that this can be inferred from the Homeric texts.[11] To the extent that the findings of these and other scholars correlate with later laments available to us, we may infer what constitutes tradition in the *Iliad*, as well as what might plausibly be seen to constitute *deviation* from tradition and thereby to function poetically to express individual characterizations of the poem's speakers. In this way anthropology, lament studies, and poetics all serve to enrich our interpretation of laments in the *Iliad*. When scholars such as Hélène Monsacré read the laments in the *Iliad*, they observe rightly that the women in the poem are represented as "infantilized," that their grief seems without power to affect action, unlike the grief of male characters that is actualized in vengeance on enemies.[12] For the male society represented in the poem, the *internal* audience, the laments, because they are spoken by women, are indeed powerless.[13] On the other hand, it is also the case that what is true for characters in the society represented in the poem is not necessarily true of the poet who composes a poem about that society. In seeking to appreciate meaning in the *Iliad* we do well to remember that meaning in a narrative comes from locating "a sensibility behind the narrative that accounts for how it is constructed."[14] Indeed, there is no principle of narratology more crucial than this for interpretation. Similarly, James Redfield has urged that "we abandon the point of view of the characters and take our stand with the poet" in order to appreciate the meaning of the *Iliad* as a poetic structure.[15] When we do this, we may become persuaded that the *poet* of the *Iliad*, from the perspective of his "more sublime thought-world," honors the women and their values more than the *characters* in the poem do.[16]

I propose, therefore, a reading of the laments of *Iliad* 24 primarily from the perspective of poetics. Without addressing the challenges of the "Homeric question," I assume that the *Iliad* is a purposeful artistic composition, structured throughout by a master poet in order to achieve a particular effect on the *external* audience/readers.[17] If, as Redfield proposes, we "take our stand with the poet" instead of with the characters, if we study the poem's strategies and structure from the poet's perspective, we aid ourselves in appreciating the *Iliad*'s meaning(s). In particular we must consider the character of the poem's closure—whether strong or weak, open or closed, resolved or unresolved—and the function of the laments, as significant elements within it, for creating and complicating closure.[18] To this end, even as we note that laments proliferate toward the end of the poem, we also note that the laments in book 24 are exceptional, for they are the only laments in the poem that may be termed *ritual* laments, that is, that participate in a shared public ceremony.[19] (In sequence and combined length, of course, they are exceptional as well.[20]) Through their laments for Hektor in the course of his funeral ceremony, Andromache, Hekabe, and Helen comment implicitly—in variously pertinent, tangential, and discontinuous ways—on Hektor's dedication to the pursuit of heroic glory.

This last issue, the "heroic code," and its importance in the *Iliad*, has been provocatively reconsidered in some recent scholarship. Several studies have, in fact, read the *Iliad* as a questioning of traditional heroic value (e.g., those by Silk, Lynn-George, Martin, Rose, Zanker).[21] The authors of these nontraditional readings locate their arguments primarily in Achilles' critical examination of and departures from the heroic code, ultimately in his pity for Priam that makes possible his return of Hektor's body for burial and emerges as the true heroic act and high moral value of the poem. Therefore the reading that the *Iliad* poet puts traditional epic values into question has support among contemporary Homeric scholars. On my reading, we can understand the laments of *Iliad* 24 as another one of the strategies by which the poet problematizes the traditional values of heroic epic. In their specificity these laments, especially when taken as a composition, go well beyond cataloged topoi of grief to respond to the life choices of Hektor in particular.[22] We will see how these laments at Hektor's funeral engage, variously and pointedly, the fundamental assumptions of heroic ideology as they are exemplified by Hektor and therefore to some extent more generally as well.

READING THE LAMENTS

There is no character in the poem more committed to pursuit of heroic glory than Hektor.[23] I cite here two passages that, in addition to the one cited above, express unambiguously Hektor's understanding of the dynamics of heroic memory. In *Iliad* 7.89–91 he announces to the assembled warriors that, if he kills Ajax in their duel, a future passerby will say:

> "This is the mound of a man who died long ago in battle,
> Who was one of the bravest, and glorious Hektor killed him."
> So he will speak some day, and my glory will not be forgotten.

In *Iliad* 22.305–308, facing Achilles at last, he says to himself:

> But now my death is upon me.
> Let me at least not die without a struggle, inglorious,
> But do some big thing first, that men to come may know of it.

Nevertheless, the three laments that close the poem—and thus constitute for *the external audience* the final memory of Hektor—ignore his overriding wish for *kleos*, in that they are silent about his glory.[24] In their silence (or even bitterness) about Hektor's glory, the women speak in ironic indifference to Hektor's own aspirations—the reading of his pursuit of glory that he himself proposes.

The laments at Hektor's funeral are the only laments in the poem that form part of a formal ceremony and therefore may be termed ritual laments. Thus they function to some degree differently from the informal, private expressions of grief that occur elsewhere.[25] The ritual aspect of these laments, as they are integrated into a formal ceremony and come at the poem's conclusion, renders them strongly closural. In narrative, as has been clarified in recent studies, the end is the significant moment, from which vantage point the narrative assumes structure and therefore meaning.[26] In the same way, by imposing structure—and therefore meaning—on life, ceremony gives coherence to the experience of individual lives. Deborah Roberts has shown how ceremony gives strong closure not only to individual lives through funeral rituals but to literary texts as well. Shared mourning, both in life and in literary texts, may be seen to give strong closure and to affirm the value of the individual as well as of the community in the face of death, which would seem otherwise to dissolve life and community.[27] This affirmative character of the *Iliad*'s closure, however, is complicated by attention to the specific content of the laments, to which I now turn.

ANDROMACHE

Andromache, as Hektor's wife, has the place of honor in the ceremony and therefore speaks the first, and by far the longest, lament of the three:

> Ἆνερ, ἀπ᾽ αἰῶνος νέος ὤλεο, κὰδ δέ με χήρην
> λείπεις ἐν μεγάροισι· πάις δ᾽ ἔτι νήπιος αὔτως,
> ὃν τέκομεν σύ τ᾽ ἐγώ τε δυσάμμοροι, οὐδέ μιν οἴω
> ἥβην ἵξεσθαι· πρὶν γὰρ πόλις ἥδε κατ᾽ ἄκρης
> πέρσεται· ἦ γὰρ ὄλωλας ἐπίσκοπος, ὅς τέ μιν αὐτὴν
> ῥύσκευ, ἔχες δ᾽ ἀλόχους κεδνὰς καὶ νήπια τέκνα,
> αἳ δή τοι τάχα νηυσὶν ὀχήσονται γλαφυρῇσι,
> καὶ μὲν ἐγὼ μετὰ τῇσι· σὺ δ᾽ αὖ, τέκος, ἢ ἐμοὶ αὐτῇ
> ἕψεαι, ἔνθα κεν ἔργα ἀεικέα ἐργάζοιο,
> ἀθλεύων πρὸ ἄνακτος ἀμειλίχου, ἤ τις Ἀχαιῶν
> ῥίψει χειρὸς ἑλὼν ἀπὸ πύργου, λυγρὸν ὄλεθρον,
> χωόμενος, ᾧ δή που ἀδελφεὸν ἔκτανεν Ἕκτωρ
> ἢ πατέρ᾽, ἠὲ καὶ υἱόν, ἐπεὶ μάλα πολλοὶ Ἀχαιῶν
> Ἕκτορος ἐν παλάμῃσιν ὀδὰξ ἕλον ἄσπετον οὖδας·
> οὐ γὰρ μείλιχος ἔσκε πατὴρ τεὸς ἐν δαῒ λυγρῇ.
> Τῶ καί μιν λαοὶ μὲν ὀδύρονται κατὰ ἄστυ,
> ἀρητὸν δὲ τοκεῦσι γόον καὶ πένθος ἔθηκας,
> Ἕκτορ· ἐμοὶ δὲ μάλιστα λελείψεται ἄλγεα λυγρά
> οὐ γάρ μοι θνήσκων λεχέων ἐκ χεῖρας ὄρεξας,
> οὐδέ τί μοι εἶπες πυκινὸν ἔπος, οὗ τέ κεν αἰεὶ
> μεμνήμην νύκτάς τε καὶ ἤματα δάκρυ χέουσα.

My husband, you were lost young from life, and have left me
a widow in your house, and the boy is only a baby
who was born to you and me, the unhappy. I think he will never
come of age, for before then head to heel this city
will be sacked, for you, its defender, are gone, you who guarded
the city, and the grave wives, and the innocent children,

wives who before long must go away in the hollow ships,
and among them I shall also go, and you, my child, follow
where I go, and there do much hard work that is unworthy
of you, drudgery for a hard master; or else some Achaian
will take you by hand and hurl you from the tower into horrible
death, in anger because Hektor once killed his brother,
or his father, or his son; there were so many Achaians
whose teeth bit the vast earth, beaten down by the hands of Hektor.
Your father was no merciful man in the horror of battle.
Therefore your people are grieving for you all through their city,
Hektor, and you left for your parents mourning and sorrow
beyond words, but for me passing all others is left the bitterness
and the pain, for you did not die in bed, and stretch your arms to me,
nor tell me some last intimate word that I could remember
always, all the nights and days of my weeping for you. (*Il.* 24.725–745)[28]

That Andromache expresses bitterness toward Hektor in this lament, although perhaps unexpected by most readers, is now not a new observation.[29] Andromache's passionate love for Hektor is established earlier in the
poem, thus intensifying for the reader her bitterness in this lament. She
makes three general plaints: because Hektor has died, she and their child
are unprotected from slavery or death; Hektor's ferocious fighting on the
battlefield will be avenged precisely by the murder of their own child; and,
finally, in dying Hektor spoke no final word to her for her to remember all the
days and nights of her weeping.

Andromache begins starkly, addressing Hektor simply as "husband."
This address stands in austere contrast to those in the poem's other laments,
which begin characteristically with what I call the "superlative expression of
affection." Thus Briseis begins her lament for Patroklos: "Patroklos, far
most pleasing to my heart in its sorrows" (19.287); in the two laments
following Andromache's, we find Hekabe saying, "Hektor, of all my sons
the dearest by far to my spirit" (24.748), and Helen says, "Hektor, of all my
lord's brothers dearest by far to my spirit" (24.762). Thus we may read
Andromache's opening "husband, you were lost young from life" as unelab-
orated, that is, as omitting an expected expression of affection. Instead,
Andromache moves immediately to the fearful consequences of Hektor's
death: destruction of the city, enslavement of the women and children, the
murder of their son. This last consequence she conceives as vengeance
for Hektor's ferocity in battle (735–739), which for her now has become
an outright "liability."[30] Her interpretation of the murder of Astyanax
as vengeance for Hektor's mode of battle rather than as, for example,
political calculation (which is another, perhaps more plausible, motivation
[as we find in Euripides' *Trojan Women* 723, 1160–1161]) is born of her
grief and sense of victimization. If Astyanax is killed for vengeance against
Hektor, then Hektor may be perceived, in this sense, as responsible for his
son's death.

The first part of Andromache's lament recalls for the reader or listener the famous *homilia* with Hektor in *Iliad* 6 (cited above), wherein she makes the point that Hektor's audacity in battle risks his life ("Dearest, your own great strength will be your death" [6.406–407]). Their exchange, one of the two most thematically crucial for interpretation of the poem as a whole, concerns precisely the ideology of the heroic code, which locates life's highest value in heroic achievement: specifically in achievement on the battlefield, to be memorialized (in Hektor's imagining) in the person of his grieving wife or in the tomb of his slain antagonist.[31] In *Iliad* 6 Andromache implicitly argues for an alternative ideology of life's purpose, one located in the value of life itself: she recalls to Hektor how she has lost everyone—mother, father, brothers (the males all killed by Achilles)—so that now Hektor embodies all life and connectedness and belonging for her. For this reason she urges that he not risk his life recklessly but, instead, guard a weak point in the wall, that is, fight defensively. The thematic importance of this proposal for the poem cannot be overestimated; for in urging a defensive strategy Andromache reveals that for her the purpose of the war is not glory but survival. In asking Hektor to fight for survival, to forgo personal honor in exchange for life (6.431–434), she makes the poem's strongest argument for the value of life itself, "unvalidated," over glory.[32] Therefore, in its way, Andromache's objection to the pursuit of heroic glory as an end in itself is as emphatic as Achilles' (*Iliad* 9.318–420, esp. 400–409):

> Please take pity upon me then, stay here on the rampart,
> That you may not leave your child an orphan, your wife a widow,
> But draw your people up by the fig tree, there where the city
> is openest to attack, and where the wall may be mounted. (6.431–434)

This is a request that Hektor's sense of shame does not allow him to grant:

> Then tall Hektor of the shining helm answered her: "All these
> Things are in my mind also, lady; yet I would feel deep shame
> Before the Trojans, and the Trojan women with the trailing garments,
> If like a coward I were to shrink aside from the fighting;
> And the spirit will not let me, since I have learned to be valiant
> And to fight always among the foremost ranks of the Trojans,
> Winning for my own self great glory and for my father.
> For I know this thing well in my heart, and my mind knows it;
> There will come a day when sacred Ilion shall perish,
> And Priam, and the people of Priam of the strong ash spear." (6.440–449)

The reader will note Hektor's recurrent themes: fear of shame and pursuit of heroic glory, both conjoined with a sure premonition of the futility of his heroism as far as his city and his family are concerned. Similarly, in *Iliad* 22 when Hektor faces Achilles alone outside the walls of Troy and reflects on his options in this dire strait, his need for honor continues to determine his actions. He concludes that it is better to risk death than to risk shame in the eyes of the Trojans, thereby confirming that, for Hektor, the purpose of the war above all has not been survival—either of himself or of the city—but personal glory. The poet movingly dramatizes this conflict of values between these two most sympathetic characters:

> Now since by my own recklessness I have ruined my people,
> I feel shame before the Trojans and the Trojan women with trailing
> robes, that someone who is less of a man than I will say of me:
> "Hektor believed in his own strength and ruined his people."
> Thus they will speak; and as for me, it would be much better
> At that time, to go against Achilleus, and slay him, and come back,
> Or else be killed by him in glory in front of the city. (22.104–110)

In *Iliad* 6.450–456 Hektor had accurately foreseen Andromache's future pain:

> But it is not so much the pain to come of the Trojans
> That troubles me, not even of Priam the king or Hekabe . . .
> As troubles me the thought of you, when some bronze-armored
> Achaian leads you off, taking away your day of liberty,
> In tears.

But, though troubled, he does not question his goals and strategy:

> But may I be dead and the piled earth hide me under before I
> Hear you crying and know by this that they drag you captive. (6.464–465)

Hektor is explicit about his motives for pursuing his fighting "in the foremost," although to some modern readers his dedication to personal glory verges on the irresponsible.[33] His wish that he might, by dying, avoid witnessing Andromache's enslavement is an implicit acknowledgment of the ethical weakness of his position.

Hektor's unquestioning commitment to the heroic code, as the poet represents it, is at one pole of a range of attitudes toward the pursuit of heroic glory in battle, from rejection to uncritical endorsement, that is expressed by the various speakers in the *Iliad*. Despite his physical fear of death (as expressed in 7.214–218 when he fears the duel with Ajax or at 22.136 when he runs from Achilles), Hektor has wholly internalized—or, as he says, "learned"—the values of the code, that is, to risk his life battling in the forefront in order to achieve lasting fame. As a consequence of this commitment, we see that even greater than his fear of death is his fear of shame, which determines his actions. The exchange between Hektor and Andromache allows the poet to put the heroic code vividly into question, as he illuminates sharply the competing goals of survival versus achievement that depends on risking life.[34] This thematically crucial conflict between Hektor and Andromache is left unresolved in *Iliad* 6, with neither speaker being endorsed by the poet. For a time Hektor and Andromache have shared goals, as Hektor's pursuit of glory coincides with the city's interest in survival. At the last, however, in *Iliad* 22, as Hektor stands alone outside the city walls, deaf to his parents' entreaties to withdraw to safety, the division between him, on the one hand, and the interests of Andromache, his parents, and the city, on the other, is unambiguous.

In the second half of her lament, Andromache expresses her "bitterness and pain" at Hektor's failure to say a last word to her, which she might remember "all the nights and days of [her] weeping" for him. Scholars have inferred that the term *pukinon epos* connotes urgency, importance, something that might change the outcome of events.[35] Yet it seems clear, in this context, that the final significant word that Andromache longs for is a word of love, as would be consistent with Hektor "reaching out his arms to" her to utter it. From Andromache's perspective, it would be a deeply painful irony to know that Hektor, in the last moments of his life, as the poet imagines them, gave no thought to her but only to his own shame.[36] Sadly, the relationship between these two most sympathetic characters is marked by haunting failure on both sides, as Andromache had consistently failed to understand Hektor's need for heroic validation, and he failed ultimately to protect her. In thus deftly sketching the moral and emotional disappointments of this thematically crucial relationship, the poet allows the contradictions of the heroic code to become painfully stark for the reader.

In summary, Andromache omits the conventional superlative expression of love for Hektor at the opening of her lament. In her grief, justifiably or not, she blames Hektor's particular mode of fighting for leaving her undefended, vulnerable to slavery or death. Thus she implies that Hektor was the virtual cause of his own death and that his ferocity in battle will bring on his own child's murder.[37] Her final reproach, that he left her no *pukinon epos*, speaks to her felt abandonment and to a perceived failure of love on Hektor's part. It is to be noted that Andromache is here portrayed not as hysterical (this is not tragic pathos) but, rather, as reflective. She expresses her pain with fluid eloquence and coherence.[38] Thus the poet allows Andromache, in her final speech in the poem, to speak with great dignity and moral authority.

HEKABE

Hekabe, Hektor's mother, speaks next:

Ἕκτορ, ἐμῷ θυμῷ πάντων πολὺ φίλτατε παίδων,
ἦ μέν μοι ζωός περ ἐὼν φίλος ἦσθα θεοῖσιν·
οἱ δ' ἄρα σεῦ κήδοντο καὶ ἐν θανάτοιό περ αἴσῃ·
Ἄλλους μὲν γὰρ παῖδας ἐμοὺς πόδας ὠκὺς Ἀχιλλεὺς
πέρνασχ', ὅν τιν' ἕλεσκε, πέρην ἁλὸς ἀτρυγέτοιο,

ἐς Σάμον ἔς τ᾽ Ἴμβρον καὶ Λῆμνον ἀμιχθαλόεσσαν·
σεῦ δ᾽ ἐπεὶ ἐξέλετο ψυχὴν ταναήκεϊ χαλκῷ,
πολλὰ ῥυστάζεσκεν ἑοῦ περὶ σῆμ᾽ ἑτάροιο,
Πατρόκλου, τὸν ἔπεφνες· ἀνέστησεν δέ μιν οὐδ᾽ ὧς.
Νῦν δέ μοι ἐρσήεις καὶ πρόσφατος ἐν μεγάροισι
κεῖσαι, τῷ ἴκελος ὅν τ᾽ ἀργυρότοξος Ἀπόλλων
οἷς ἀγανοῖσι βέλεσσιν ἐποιχόμενος κατέπεφνεν. (Il. 24.748–759)

Hektor, of all my sons the dearest by far to my spirit;
while you still lived for me you were dear to the gods, and even
in the stage of death they cared about you still. There were others
of my sons whom at times swift-footed Achilles captured,
and he would sell them as slaves far across the unresting salt water
into Samos, and Imbros, and Lemnos in the gloom of the mists. You,
when he had taken your life with the thin edge of the bronze sword,
he dragged again and again around his beloved companion's
tomb, Patroklos', whom you killed, but even so did not
bring him back to life. Now you lie in the palace, handsome
and fresh with dew, in the likeness of one whom he of the silver
bow, Apollo, has attacked and killed with his gentle arrows.

As Nicholas Richardson (ad 24.718–776)points out, the laments of
Hekabe and Helen resemble each other more than either resembles
Andromache's. Thus, both open with a superlative of affection; both set
off Hektor from others, either from the other sons or from the rest of the
family; both are unambiguously warm in their love of Hektor; and both
speak of the past, whereas Andromache's looks to the (dread) future.[39] We
observe again the thematic continuity of these laments with the earlier
speeches that the poet gives to these characters.[40] Thus, concern with
Hektor's physical well-being is a continuing motif in Hekabe's speeches
to and about Hektor. Her lament in *Iliad* 24 focuses on Hektor's divinely
restored physical perfection, as her first speech to him was concerned with
his physical exhaustion, for which she offered wine as remedy (6.253–
262). Her second speech to Hektor (22.79–89) implores him to retreat
within the city walls instead of facing Achilles alone. In her appeal she
pleads that he honor her bared breast, from which he nursed. Significantly,
in this fearful moment she, too, like Andromache, shows her greater care
for Hektor's very life than for his future glory.

Hekabe's lament, as noted above, begins with the familiar superlative
of affection, "most loved of my sons." This is not a mere topos, as Hekabe
continues to develop the motif of Hektor's singularity. Others of her sons,
she says, Achilles had been willing to ransom; Hektor he killed and
defiled—a bitter mark of singularity. Consistent with her earlier concern
for his physical well-being, she remarks on Hektor's perfect physical
beauty despite his defilement by Achilles and other Greeks (e.g., 22.371,
22.375, 24.12–18). She interprets Hektor's undefiled, perfect body as a

gift of the gods, a miracle. This interpretation is correct, as readers know that Aphrodite and Apollo had indeed intervened to preserve Hektor's body from Achilles' depredations and from decay (23.184–191). Zeus acceded willingly to this plan because of Hektor's sacrifices to him (24.66–69). Subsequently Apollo and Zeus intervene to bring about Hektor's burial because they remember his piety, to which multiple references are made (22.169–172, Zeus speaking; 24.33–38, Apollo). Hermes describes to Priam this miracle of the gods' care:

> You yourself can see when you go there
> How fresh with dew he lies, and the blood is all washed from him,
> Nor is there any corruption, and all the wounds have been closed up
> Where he was struck, since many drove the bronze into his body.
> So it is that the immortals care for your son, though
> He is nothing but a dead man; because in their hearts they loved him.
> (24.418–423)

As Hekabe divines, it is true even for the gods (as well as for herself and her co-lamenters) that glory is not the defining attribute of Hektor's life. Instead it is Hektor's piety that draws the miracle, that outlasts his death, protects his body from decay, and restores his physical beauty. In this sense, as the poet reveals to readers/audience, the gods have brought it about that Achilles' victory over Hektor is only limited and transient.

Piety is a high value in the poem and an element of Hektor's large humanity. It is not, however, the driving goal or transcendent value for Hektor. Thus, in terms of his own values, the perhaps undesirable result of this divine intervention is that Hektor looks as if he died a gentle, natural death.[41] In death Hektor does not look like a warrior. His restored perfection is a reflection of the gods' favor and therefore redounds unambiguously to his credit. Yet this manifestation of divine care has the curious effect of erasing all physical signs of the struggle for heroic glory that Hektor himself valued above his life. Thus, the burden of Hekabe's lament is to praise Hektor's piety, and the effect of the gods' intervention is to erase his heroic struggle. Hektor's miraculously restored physical beauty is an ironic honor much like the laments themselves—a gift of love, yet at odds with Hektor's own values.

It is pertinent to recall here that the heroic ideal of the "beautiful death" does not mean looking beautiful at death. An earlier speech by Priam illuminates this truth, as he explicates the difference between the aesthetics of dying young in battle and dying old:

> For a young man all is decorous
> When he is cut down in battle and torn with the sharp bronze,
> and lies there
> Dead, and though dead still all that shows about him is beautiful;
> But when an old man is dead and down, and the dogs mutilate

The grey head and the parts that are secret,
This, for all sad mortality, is the sight most pitiful. (22.71–76)

Jean-Pierre Vernant reiterates the same concept: "The blood, the wounds, and the grime on the corpse of a young hero recall his courage and enhance his beauty with masculine strength, but on an old man . . . their ugliness becomes almost obscene."[42] Hekabe's lament, as it memorializes Hektor's peaceful and perfect appearance in death, ignores this sort of reasoning.

In sum Hekabe's lament—like Andromache's, silent about heroic glory—focuses on the fact that Hektor's body bears no signs of heroic struggle, testament to his piety and to the gods' love. In collocation with the preceding lament by Andromache, Hekabe's lament contributes to a final memory of Hektor (for readers) that celebrates values tangential to those that he, in life, most esteemed.

HELEN

Last to speak is Helen, the "sister-in-law" (or stranger, depending on one's view of Helen's anomalous status in Troy):

Ἕκτορ, ἐμῷ θυμῷ δαέρων πολὺ φίλτατε πάντων,
ἦ μέν μοι πόσις ἐστὶν Ἀλέξανδρος θεοειδής,
ὅς μ' ἄγαγε Τροίηνδ'· ὡς πρὶν ὤφελλον ὀλέσθαι.
Ἤδη γὰρ νῦν μοι τόδ' ἐεικοστὸν ἔτος ἐστὶν
ἐξ οὗ κεῖθεν ἔβην καὶ ἐμῆς ἀπελήλυθα πάτρης·
ἀλλ' οὔ πω σεῦ ἄκουσα κακὸν ἔπος οὐδ' ἀσύφηλον·
ἀλλ' εἴ τίς με καὶ ἄλλος ἐνὶ μεγάροισιν ἐνίπτοι
δαέρων ἢ γαλόων ἢ εἰνατέρων εὐπέπλων,
ἢ ἑκυρή – ἑκυρὸς δὲ πατὴρ ὣς ἤπιος αἰεί –
ἀλλὰ σὺ τόν γ' ἐπέεσσι παραιφάμενος κατέρυκες,
σῇ τ' ἀγανοφροσύνῃ καὶ σοῖς ἀγανοῖς ἐπέεσσι.
Τῶ σέ θ' ἅμα κλαίω καὶ ἔμ' ἄμμορον ἀχνυμένη κῆρ
οὐ γάρ τίς μοι ἔτ' ἄλλος ἐνὶ Τροίῃ εὐρείῃ
ἤπιος οὐδὲ φίλος, πάντες δέ με πεφρίκασιν. (Il. 24.762–775)

Hektor, of all my lord's brothers dearest by far to my spirit:
My husband is Alexandros, like an immortal, who brought me
Here to Troy; and I should have died before I came with him;
And here now is the twentieth year upon me since I came
From the place where I was, forsaking the land of my fathers. In this time
I have never heard a harsh saying from you, nor an insult.
No, but when another, one of my lord's brothers or sisters, a fair-robed
Wife of some brother, would say a harsh word to me in the palace,
Or my lord's mother—but his father was gentle always, a father
Indeed—then you would speak and put them off and restrain them

By your own gentleness of heart and your gentle words. Therefore
I mourn for you in sorrow of heart and mourn myself also
And my ill luck. There was no other in all the wide Troad
Who was kind to me, and my friend; all others shrank when they saw me.

The thematic resonances of Helen's lament are multiple and have been much discussed in the critical literature.[43] As is the case with the previous two laments, Helen's lament takes up motifs that appear in her earlier speeches. We see how she characteristically attempts to bond (either through self-reproach/vulnerability or seductiveness) with a strong male, that is, Priam in 3.172 and Hektor in 6.349–358. Helen also addresses Hektor as *philtate* (762), "most loved" of her brothers-in-law, beginning her lament with the superlative of affection ("Hektor, of all my lord's brothers dearest by far to my spirit"), as appears conventional in *Iliad* laments. She praises Hektor's gentleness repeatedly (*aganophrosyne* [772], *aganois epeessi* [772], *epios* [775]). In conjunction with the lament of Briseis for Patroklos (19.287–300), we infer that gentleness in men is a quality valued by women in the *Iliad*. Note that in her exchange with Hektor in *Iliad* 6, Helen flatters not Hektor's gentleness but, instead, his exemplary manly honor and courage. By contrast, she scolds Paris for avoiding the fighting and acting shamefully. Therefore, as she implies, she would rather be the wife of Hektor than the wife of Paris (6.344–351). Hektor's rejection of Helen's invitation to sit by her ennobles him in the readers' eyes, for it confirms Hektor's dedication to his marriage with Andromache.

None of this, of course, finds a place in Helen's lament in *Iliad* 24. Her theme in praise of Hektor is that he protected her from his family's harsh words and from the perceived revulsion of all the Trojans generally. Now she must mourn for herself because she lacks a protector from such hurts. (Helen's self-absorption here perhaps gives insight into the self-indulgent passion with which she and Paris carelessly sparked the war to begin with.) Ironically, then, while Andromache feels herself to have been left defenseless by Hektor, Helen remembers and praises Hektor's defense of her.[44] For Helen, the protection in question is not, as with Andromache, a matter of life or freedom but only of social slights, so that, compared with the troubles of Andromache, those of Helen are inconsequential. Nevertheless, the opposition between the two is quite precise and painfully ironic: Helen remembers Hektor as her protector, while Andromache grieves that Hektor has failed to protect her. The opposition between Andromache and Helen is one index of the deep hostility between Helen, cause of the war, and the women in Hektor's family—not to mention the Trojans more generally. The possibility is raised by a comparison of the themes of these two laments that Hektor has in some sense ultimately protected the wrong woman.[45] Such tensions as these may be seen to contribute to the complexity of the *Iliad*'s closure.

Commentators note the anomalous inclusion of Helen as a lamenter at Hektor's funeral, for from one perspective she is not a member of

Hektor's family at all.[46] Indeed, her ambiguous kinship relation to Hektor is the very cause of the war and hence the fundamental subject of the poem. The several exact kinship terms that occur in Helen's lament bring this trouble explicitly to the fore. Thus she alludes with precise terminology to her husband's brothers, her husband's sisters, her husband's brothers' wives, her mother-in-law, and her father-in-law. In her lament for Hektor she refers to him as her brother-in-law, *daer*. However, in her first speech in the poem, to Priam in *Iliad* 3.180, it is Agamemnon whom she calls her brother-in-law, *daer*.[47] Whose sister-in-law, that is, whose wife, Helen is and will be is precisely the fatal question. As Helen says, *all* the Trojans, when they see her, shudder. *Pephrikasin* is the last word of her lament, in response to which the whole people, the poet says, join in (24.776). Richardson observes, in my view persuasively, that the ending of Helen's lament leaves a bitter taste, with its portrayal of her (tactless) self-pity and the Trojan people's implied fear or revulsion.

I have noted above the anomalous presence of Helen as a lamenter at Hektor's funeral. This anomaly is rendered more emphatic by Helen speaking in last position.[48] Although Andromache, as wife, speaks first and thus has the place of honor in the funeral ceremony (as we learn from the previously cited ethnographic studies of lament), it is Helen, speaking last, who has the emphatic place, the place of honor, *in the poem* (a fact of poetics). That the last place is the place of honor poetically speaking can be demonstrated by a comparison of the order of the laments with the order of Hektor's interviews with these same three women in *Iliad* 6. There the order is Hekabe, Helen, Andromache, where the poet builds up to Andromache, exploiting the folktale motif of the "ascending scale of affection."[49] When Hektor looks for Andromache at home, he does not find her and leaves again for the battlefield. Just as he is about to exit through the city gate, his passionate wife comes running to meet him. Thus, in the earlier passage, the poet delays even the last place entrance of Andromache in order to intensify the drama of her entrance into the poem. In book 24 this climactic place is Helen's. For the reader, this changed order brings about a formal closure, for Helen is both the first and the last female speaker in the poem. Emotionally, however, this order may feel off center to many readers, given that it does not conclude with the voice of the woman closest to Hektor and most sympathetic to the reader/audience. Thus the laments conclude with a tension between formal closure, on the one hand, and emotional (even, indeed, moral) disjunction, on the other.

LAMENTATION AND "MORAL MEANING" IN THE *ILIAD*

We are surely justified in supposing that the poet's choices in constructing closure reveal much about his thematic purposes. The laments of *Iliad* 24 achieve emphasis, thus moral authority, in the first instance and above all through their closural position. This placement is an unarguable fact of poetics. The authority of the laments is further confirmed by their ritual, public character as well as by the sheer number of verses that the poet gives to them. Additionally, all three lamenters are important characters in the poem in their own right, so that readers may follow in their laments a development of theme, characterization, and value. As we have seen, the three laments embody a range of perspectives on Hektor and how he lived his life. Thus, Hektor, who dies in pursuit of heroic glory ("Let me at least not die without a struggle, inglorious, / But do some big thing first, that men to come shall know of it" [22.304–305]), is memorialized in the *Iliad*'s final scene as pious by his mother, as gentle by his "sister-in-law," and with deep (or "faint" [see n. 7]) disappointment by his wife. Through silence or through explicit utterance, all have implications for Hektor's dedication to heroic glory. The contradiction between Hektor's aspirations, on the one hand, and the readers'/audience's final memory of him in the poem, on the other, invites interpretation. Through their concerns with love, piety, gentleness, and compassion the laments contribute importantly to the debate in the *Iliad* over what constitutes the high value of life—a debate that has pervaded the poem, from the *homilia* between Andromache and Hektor in book 6, to Achilles' rejection of the code of heroic glory in 9.400–409 ("not worth the value of my life"), to Hektor's decisive choice of hoped-for glory over dreaded shame in book 22. The laments thus express moral values that, like Achilles' pity for Priam, compete with heroic glory for the reader's allegiance. By allotting to the laments emphatic placement, sequence, length, and moral substance, the poet of the *Iliad* allows them to speak for values alternative to heroic glory and thereby to share emphatically in embodying the "moral meaning" of the *Iliad*.[50]

CONCLUSION: ON THE (DEBATED) FUNCTION OF LAMENT IN EPIC POETRY

The ritual character of the *Iliad*'s closure has led many critics to see affirmation in the close of the *Iliad*—an integration of desolating grief into communal reflections on the large conditions of human life. Therefore, to the degree that the laments are ritual, and to the degree that they adhere to forms traditional through centuries, they are experienced as affirmative by both internal and external audiences. On the other hand, to the degree that they are contrary to Hektor's imaginings and desires— to the degree that they give voice to values alternative to those of Hektor in particular and to those of most male characters in the poem generally— they are disruptive of closure and dramatically subversive of epic's "dominant ideology" or "central claims."[51] These tensions go far to explain the range of readings of this closure that one finds in the critical literature. I have argued that these particular laments in this particular closure serve, in an exceptional and authentic way, to endorse a range of moral values alternative to those embodied in the heroic code of glory and, thus, that they function in opposition to the poem's dominant ideology.

I have also tried to establish that readers ought not simply assume as a matter of course that laments in epic have uniform significance. For example, Alison Keith in this volume shows how laments in the *Bellum Ciuile*, both women's laments and men's funeral orations, serve the purpose, in conjunction with the poet's bias, of arousing opposition to Caesar. Here Cornelia's laments do not question or regret war (or the poem's ideological thrust) but, instead, encourage it. Analogously, in *Beowulf* the closing laments, spoken by men, explicitly and comprehensively affirm the values exemplified by Beowulf as man, warrior, and king. Beowulf is praised both as the "gentlest of men" and as the "keenest for fame."[52] In this closure, we find no haunting questions unresolved, no implied wishes of how it might have been otherwise. Instead we find congruence of all values held by poet, lamenters, and heroic deceased. We see, then, that laments carry the ideological weight that the *poet constructs* for them in the course of the text as a whole. Though it may perhaps be possible to generalize about the function of lamentation in the performance of actual funeral rituals, it is not possible to so generalize about the significance of lamentation in poetic texts.[53] In this latter case, meaning is a function of, for example, who laments, who is being lamented, the specific content of the lament, and where it occurs in the text. All these features of lament in a poem result from the poet's choices and operate in service of the poet's overall purposes in the text. Therefore, the meaning of lamentation in any given poetic text (as opposed to any actual ritual practice) must be seen to be a function of the poet's artistic or thematic choices.

ACKNOWLEDGMENTS

I would like to thank Peter Bing, Kevin Corrigan, Stephen Scully, Pura Nieto, and especially the editor of this volume, whose thoughtful, generous suggestions greatly improved this essay.

NOTES

1. The works of, e.g., Helene Foley (1993), Gail Holst-Warhaft (1992), and Nadia Seremetakis (1991) have observed the recurrent opposition between women's laments for the dead and the political or military ideology of the male/ruling class. Solon's legislation to restrict women's laments and death rituals (Plut. *S01*.21.5) confirms the perceived disruptive power of lament in antiquity. As Foley comments on lament in tragedy: "By concentrating on the negative effects that death and war itself have on survivors, lamentation can offer a muted reproach of the dead and of the ambitions of the dead for immortal fame celebrated in the funeral oration" (1991, 44). Seremetakis's study of lament in contemporary rural Greece traces the power of women's lament as a voice of resistance from antiquity to the present, suggesting that laments are "strategies of resistance that emerge and subsist on the margins" (1991, 1). It is to be noted as well, however, that lament may also function to reinforce male ideology, as in Inner Mani it is the prelude to murderous vengeance (Seremetakis 1991). Lament is not wholly uniform,

therefore, in its relationship to male authority. See Perkell 1997, 278–280, for a summary discussion of the oppositional potential of lament, with bibliography.

2. Derderian 2001, 10.

3. Murnaghan argues that lament is both necessary to epic, because it functions to promote praise of the deceased (e.g., 1999, 213), and subversive of epic's "central claims" (1999, 217). See Sultan 1991 for a comparable reading of more contemporary material: women's interests are opposed to male heroic action, and yet women's voices are essential to the process of making heroic glory immortal.

4. All translations are from Richmond Lattimore's The Iliad *of Homer* (1951).

5. Silk 1987, 70.

6. Holst-Warhaft (1992) anticipates my reading in two key respects. She notes that "[n]ot one of the women praises Hector as a hero in battle" (1992, 113). She notes also the heightened significance of the laments, given their placement at the end of the poem: "The position of the laments in the narrative suggests that they fulfil an artistic purpose of greater importance than the dramatic representation of female mourning. . . . [The women's] laments are a vehicle for summarizing the artistic and philosophical themes of the narrative" (1992, 110). My further contribution is to do a close reading of the three laments as a composition, maximally significant by virtue of their closural placement and their contents, specific to Hektor and, above all, in ironic contrast with his wishes for glory. In this way the laments comment implicitly and explicitly on Hektor's particular relationship to the heroic code and thus are subversive of closure as much as they are summarizing of themes.

7. Note the difference in degree in the readings of Alexiou and Holst-Warhaft. Alexiou writes: "Andromache opens and closes with a faint note of reproach" (2002, 183). Holst-Warhaft, more emphatically, says: "Andromache . . . is full of reproach and bitterness for the perilous situation in which he has left her and her son" (1992, 112). Foley observes the subversive quality of Andromache's lament but does not read it as problematizing the poem's overall meaning: "In the *Iliad* the themes expressed in lamentation also subtly counter the dominant ideology of the poem (see especially the lamentations of Andromache), which celebrates the immortal kleos acquired by the warrior in battle. But the poet does not problematize this tension in a comparable way [i.e., comparable to tragedy]" (1991, 44).

8. Silk's key formulation is as follows:

> The *Iliad* presents a coherent heroic ideology, which presupposes war. That ideology is celebrated and affirmed in the poem, in that it is what the heroes in general live by, and the poem unquestionably celebrates *them*. At the same time the supreme hero is Achilles, and it is clear that Achilles is an uncomfortable and even a destructive presence within the heroic world. . . . [T]he poem is so structured as to reveal the negative implications of heroic values *along with* their obvious splendour. . . . [T]he greatest literature is wont to subvert the dominant ideological categories that it purports to, and does indeed also, embody: and thanks to Achilles, the *Iliad* surely does just this. (1987, 96; emphasis in original)

9. Martin writes: "[B]eginnings and endings carry a significance far disproportionate to that of the midportion of any temporal artistic composition" (1989, 197). Famously, Kermode has written: "[W]e use fictions to enable the end to confer organization and form on the temporal structure" (1967, 45). See also Culler 1997, 83–94, on narrative. On "underreading"—the neglect of material signified within the text and thus the exclusion of possible meanings—see Abbott 2002, 79–82, 194.

10. Murnaghan 1999, 204.

11. The gestures of the lamenting women on the Bronze Age vases described by Brendan Burke (this volume) have no obvious analogue in the laments in *Iliad* 24. Burke, therefore, questions if the lament tradition is in fact as continuous as has been proposed.

12. Monsacré's study, which elaborates on the "radical impotence" (1984, 201) and private nature of women's laments (1984, 166) and the perceived difference between women's laments and men's (read as heroic grief, a display of force and vitality [1984, 201]), has significantly shaped more recent readings of lament.

13. Speakers in the *Iliad* vary in their evaluations of women. As Zanker (1994, 68) observes, "like a woman" expresses the honor-driven warrior's contempt for the affective appeal. MacCary's (1982, 99–108, 149–151, 152–162) psychological study discusses the anxieties underlying men's valuations of women. On the other hand, Achilles, who has no anxiety about his heroic status, compares himself to a woman twice in similes (*Il.* 9.323–327, 16.6–12).

14. Abbott 2002, 77.

15. Redfield writes:

> The characters in a poem are as the poet made them, and he made them as he would have them for the needs of his work. When we think of the poem as a made thing, a construct, we abandon the point of view of the characters and take our stand with the poet. We ask what sort of meaning the poet is conveying and how he seeks to convey it; we shall find this meaning conveyed, not in the represented experience of any single character, but in the poem as a whole. We thus shift our interest from character to plot, taking "plot" in a very broad sense as the implicit conceptual unity which has given the work its actual form. (1975, 23)

16. Zanker 1994, 45.

17. Alden writes: "The *Iliad* and the *Odyssey* are both highly integrated and carefully composed poems which can only be explained as the work of a brilliant and insightful poet carefully shaping and polishing his work over many years" (2000, 1–2). Similarly, see Latacz 2004. This view is not, of course, universally held among Homer scholars. Casey Dué (2002) exemplifies a different kind of reading of the Homeric texts. She rejects the concept of a master poet and reads seeming innovations as a means of adapting the tradition. Cf. Nagy 1979, 94–117, esp. 116–117, "Lamentation and the Hero."

18. See Roberts 1993 for a discussion of types or gradations of closure: closure may be read as strong or weak, as open or closed, as reductive or problematic, as resolving the conflicts of the text or extending them, or, by ignoring them, as perhaps implying their unresolvability. For another discussion, see Abbott 2002, 51–61.

What we might see as, in fact, even triple closure—of lamentation, funeral, and a shared meal—concludes the poem. The funeral ceremony of Hektor is described in detail, from the nine days of mourning in the palace and gathering wood to the burning of the body on the funeral pyre on the tenth; the extinguishing of the fire with wine poured over it on the eleventh; the gathering the bones into a golden casket, wrapped with soft (purple) robes; and the burying of the casket under piled-up stones and a grave mound, all concluded by the funeral feast (*Il.* 24.656–667, 719–722, 782–804).

19. See Tsagalis 2004, 112, tab. 2. Funeral ritual, with its shared formal mourning, brings consolation, as Roberts (1993) several times observes. She (1993, 586) notes further that ritual, even when marred, evokes order and regularity. Similarly Redfield writes: "In the funeral the community acts on its own behalf to reassert its own continuity in spite of the disorderly forces which assail it. By the funeral the community purifies itself [i.e., constructs meaning for itself through form]" (1975, 182). Again, Redfield notes: "By its treatment of the body the community enacts its determination that even qua organism a man belongs to the order of *culture* and not to the realm of *nature*" (1975, 185).

20. See Beck 2005, 247, 247 n. 30: "[T]hese laments are longer and more elaborate than the laments in other funerals described in the Homeric epics." For her discussion of the *Iliad* 24 laments and death of Hektor, see Beck 2005, 246–257.

21. See Lynn-George 1988; Martin 1989; Rose 1992; Silk 1987; Zanker 1994.

22. Derderian (2001) and Tsagalis (2004) both offer a discussion and cataloging of topics and forms of laments, establishing thereby a typology of lament, isolating what appear to be its conventional features. Tsagalis (2004, 27–52, 75–108) includes the following among topoi of lament: distance, separation, premature death, praise of deceased, comparison of deceased to others, common fate with deceased, death wish of lamenter, and contrast between past and present. The listing of topoi does not, of course, exhaust the possible meanings of laments, especially if they include highly specific, even idiosyncratic detail. See Tsagalis 2004, 38–39. For an earlier listing, see Alexiou 1974.

23. It is important to realize that several different attitudes toward the heroic code are represented in the *Iliad*. On the Greek side Diomedes is the exemplary warrior, consistently behaving in accordance with the code, as shown by Marilyn Arthur ([1981] 1992). Sarpedon's nuanced justification for the pursuit of heroic glory (*Il.* 12.310–328) is "in a way metaphysical," as Vernant (1991, 57) observes. Achilles, on the other hand, speaks the most pointed critique of the code:

> For not
> worth the value of my life are all the possessions they fable
> were won for Ilion, that strong-founded citadel, in the old days
> when there was peace. (*Il.* 9.400–403; see also *Il.* 9.307–420 throughout)

Cf. Silk 1987, 96; and n. 8 above.

24. See Silk 1987, 70.

25. The laments of *Iliad* 24 are the only ritual laments in the poem because of the public context and the presence of professionals. Richardson (1993, ad 720–722) notes that the terms *aoidos, threnos, threnein,* and *exarchos* occur only here in the poem and that *threnoi* do not occur in connection with Patroklos. *Iliad* 24.719–722 suggests the distinction between *threnoi* and *gooi,* the latter being the personal and less polished grieving of kinswomen. Tsagalis writes: "*Threnos* involves two groups of mourners, the professionals and kinswomen. The lament begins with a musical *threnos* sung by professionals and answered by the chorus' (of kinswomen) wailing, and is then continued by the next of kin, each uttering a *goos*-speech capped by a refrain of cries from the chorus" (2004, 3). Tsagalis offers further definitions: *exarchoi* are singers of the *threnos* who lead the lament; *aoide/aoidous* refers explicitly to the character of the *threnoi* and the professionals who utter them.

26. On the importance of closure in making meaning, see n. 9 above.

27. This power of shared mourning to affirm human value pervades the deeply felt readings of *Iliad* 24 by Charles Segal (1993, 64) and W. R. Johnson (1976, 121).

28. Alexiou (1974, 133) has established what scholars generally consider to be traditional in laments, namely, a tripartite structure, which she terms ABA: address to the dead, narrative section, return to direct address. The narrative section, as preserved in subsequent texts and summarized by Alexiou (1974, 177–178), has conventional, comprehensive themes, such as the speaker's memories of the past or images of the future, the desolation of those left behind, or a wish to have died *with* or instead of the dead one. (Also see n. 20 above.) For the antiphonal element in lament, which she also describes, see Alexiou 1974.

29. See n. 7 above.

30. See J. Foley 1991, 173, for "liability." For his treatment of the laments, see Foley 1991, 168–174.

31. The other thematically crucial exchange for interpretation, of course, is that between Achilles and Priam in *Iliad* 24 that establishes pity as the high value of the poem.

32. See Arthur [1981] 1992 for this crucial observation. These verses were athetized by Aristarchus on the grounds of being inappropriate content for a female speaker. (See Kirk 1990, ad 6.433–439, for a discussion.) However, the thrust of Andromache's position is manifest even without them. See Alden 2000, 311–318, app. E3 ("The Motivation Ascribed to Wives Entreating Husbands") n. 2, on Hektor's repeated rejections of others' entreaties interpreted as a moral failure. For her comprehensive discussion of Hektor, see Alden 2000, 262–290.

33. Contrast the wholly positive picture in, e.g., Andromache's speech about Hektor in Euripides' *Trojan Women* (742–744).

34. For Schadewaldt (1959), there is no such ambiguity as I propose. Hektor's needs for glory exemplify all admirable male strivings for achievement; Andromache is the hysterical, fearful wife, who fails to appreciate men's needs for greatness that transcend their love for family and render them immune to affective appeal. For another reading of this scene, along with a provocative and moving collocation of related texts, see Tatum 2003, esp. 96–115.

35. The phrase *pukinon epos*, translated here as "intimate word," occurs also at 7.375, 11.788, and 24.75. For Martin it "implies dense with meaning and filled with urgency" (1989, 35). For another discussion, see J. Foley 1991, 154–156, and Richardson 1993.

36. Hektor's parents urge him to withdraw into the city to save himself, which is thus the inverse of the Meleager paradigm, in which the true hero, the acknowledged greatest fighter, is urged by those close to him not to remain in the city but, on the contrary, to emerge from it in order to defend them against the enemy (*Il.* 9.573–596). This is not the only suggestion in the poem that Hektor is not the idealized heroic warrior that he wishes to be. See Alden 2000, 262–290.

37. It is a topos in later laments for the wife or mother to express a sense of abandonment or betrayal at the death of spouse or child, but in these cases the death is not attributed to the deceased's own agency. See Alexiou 2002, index, *s.v.* "Reproach of mourner to dead," and 106, for the following example:

Ammia, wise daughter, how is it you died so soon?
Why did you hasten to die, or which of the fates overtook you?
Before we decked you for the bridal garland in the marriage chamber
You left your home and grieving parents.
Your father and all the country and your mother lamented
Your most untimely and unwedded youth. (Kotiaion, fourth century C.E.)

38. Richardson's (1993) stylistic appreciation of Andromache's eloquence (fluidity, enjambment, *tricolon abundans*) establishes that she is not represented as hysterical.

39. Petersmann 1973, 12: Andromache refers to the future; the other two, to the past.

40. E.g., Murnaghan 1999, 209. My focus on poetics includes such considerations as who speaks the laments, where they occur in the poem, and if there is progression in the utterances of a particular speaker. Tsagalis (2004, 109–165) terms these relationships "intertextuality." Richardson, for example, calls Andromache's lament "a masterpiece of characterization" (1993, ad 762–775). Similarly, G. Petersmann suggests the poet was freely creative in composing the laments to express the individuality and humanity of the figures: "Der Dichter der Ilias hat neben dem Trauerritual, das noch immer machtvoll in der Dichtung aufscheint, jenen Raum geschaffen, den er brauchte, um Trauer und Leid seiner Gestalten in individuell verschiedener Weise zu gestalten" (1973, 13).

41. To die by the gentle arrows (*aganoisi belessin*) of Apollo or Artemis denotes a swift, easy death (e.g., Macleod 1982; Richardson 1993).

42. Vernant 1991, 64.

43. For other readings of Helen, see Martin, this volume; Ebbott 1999; Pantelia 2002; Suzuki 1989, esp. 54–56, on the *Iliad* 24 lament; Roisman 2006; Worman 2001.

44. See Zanker 1994, 40, on Hektor's motives for protecting Helen. In the first instance, he suggests the "noble treatment that the honor-constraint in the heroic code expected the warrior to extend to his dependents," adding that affection may also have played a part.

45. E.g., Zanker 1994, 42: "The heroic code has an internal ambiguity, when claims of honor override those of affection, justice, prudence, and appropriateness."

46. Alexiou (1974, 11–14) establishes that relatives or close friends are the conventional lamenters. There is scholarly discussion of Helen speaking in last place. See Monsacré 1984, 159: "On peut se demander pourquoi c'est Hélène, et non une soeur—Cassandre par exemple—, qui termine la lamentation des femmes autour d'Hector et fait gémir l'ensemble du people réuni." Monsacré (1984, 119) attributes Helen's presence as lamenter to her exceptional status as a woman in the poem, thus first and last to speak, and to affinity with the poet himself (e.g., she is weaving an account of the war). This is the reading of Pantelia (2002) as well. Martin (this volume) argues that through diction and rhetoric, even outside of formal lament, Helen is characterized in the *Iliad* as a "keening figure," i.e., identified with the lament genre generally. See also Martin, this volume, for the significance of the personal address to the dead.

47. Richardson (1993, ad 762–775) points to the kinship terms and the trouble signified by the use of *daer* for both Agamemnon at *Il.* 3.180 and Hektor at *Il.* 6.344, 355.

48. Others read this lament differently. (See n. 43 above.) For example, Holst-Warhaft suggests that it is because women's laments can encompass more than a single life, touching on mortal losses more generally, "that they occupy this position in the narrative, and that Helen, who has been the ostensible cause of all the suffering, should be the last to lament seems appropriate artistic license" (1992, 113). Pantelia (2002, 158–159) develops this universalizing reading of Helen's lament, followed also by Dué (2002, 81): Helen's lament turns the personal into the paradigmatic, as a necessary effect or function of lament.

Readers obviously have to come to their own understandings of the laments; for me, the thesis that there is something universalizing in Helen's lament, that she weeps for the human condition generally, is unsupported by the text and there-fore requires very special pleading. Richardson (1993) seems more on point in observing the pettiness and self-absorption of Helen's closing. Alexiou's 1974 chapter on historical laments for the fall of cities serves to bring to our attention the fact that public themes are not addressed in the *Iliad* 24 laments, although in fact a city is falling.

49. We see the same ascending scale of affection in the Meleager story. Meleager is supplicated first by the city elders and then by his father, his mother, his sisters, and his closest friends, all of whom he refuses in turn. He responds only, at last, to the appeal of his wife (*Il.* 9.573–596). See Kakridis 1949, 43–64, on Hektor, and 1949, 11–42, 127–148, on Meleager; see also Nagy 1979, 104–106.

50. Abbott 2002, 102: "To tell a story is to try to understand it." Cf. White 1987, 21: "The demand for closure in the historical story is a demand . . . for *moral meaning*, a demand that sequences of real events be assessed as to their significance as elements of a moral drama." On such questions, all readers do not read the same way. As Murnaghan (1999, 206–207) points out, different responses to hearing epic song are modeled by the poet in *Odyssey* 8, where, for example, Odysseus cries upon hearing Demodokos's song, whereas the Phaiakians take pleasure in it. Odysseus's own closeness to the song causes his grief. Personal context, therefore, is one variable in a listener's/reader's construction of a text.

51. See, for example, the editor's introductory question to Murnaghan: "Just How Subversive Can Lament Be in Epic?" (1999, 203). For the phrases "dominant ideology" and "central claims," see J. Foley 1991, 44; Murnaghan 1999, 217.

52. Richardson, citing the ending of *Beowulf*, comments: "So, too, *Beowulf* ends in mourning and praise for the hero" (1993, 350, ad 24.718–776). He cites the following from the end of the poem:

> Then the warriors rode around the barrow,
> twelve of them in all, athelings' sons.
> They recited a dirge to declare their grief,
> spoke of the man, mourned their king.
> They praised his manhood and the prowess of his hands,
> they raised his name; it is right a man
> should be lavish in honouring his lord and friend,
> should love him in his heart when the leading-forth
> from the house of flesh befalls him at last.
> This was the manner of the mourning of the men of the Geats,
> sharers in the feast, at the fall of their lord:
> they said that he was of all the world's kings
> the gentlest of men, and the most gracious,
> the kindest to his people, the keenest for fame. (*Beowulf* 3169–3182, trans.
> M. Alexander)

This lament is performed by men, not women. On female mourners in *Beowulf*, see Helen Bennett (1992) and Susan Signe Morrison (2000).

53. In fact, laments may not be uniform in ideological function even when performed as part of actual funeral ritual. Laments may subvert the dominant male ideology or reinforce it, as in Inner Mani, where lament is the catalyst and prelude to murderous vengeance (Seremetakis 1991).

BIBLIOGRAPHY

Abbott, H. Porter. 2002. *The Cambridge Introduction to Narrative*. Cambridge.

Alden, Maureen. 2000. *Homer Beside Himself: Para-Narratives in the* Iliad. Oxford.

Alexiou, Margaret. 1974. *The Ritual Lament in Greek Tradition*. Cambridge.

——. 2002. *The Ritual Lament in Greek Tradition*. 2nd ed. Rev. Dimitrios Yatromanolakis and Panagiotis Roilos. Lanham, Md.

Arthur, Marilyn. [1981] 1992. The Divided World of *Iliad* 6. In *Reflections of Women in Antiquity*, ed. Helene P. Foley, 19–44. Reprint, Philadelphia.

Barchiesi, Alessandro. 1978. Il lamento di Giuturna. *Materiali e discussioni per l'analisi dei testi classici* 1: 99–121.

Beck, Deborah. 2005. *Homeric Conversation*. Cambridge, Mass.

Bennett, Helen. 1992. The Female Mourner at Beowulf's Funeral: Filling in the Blanks/Hearing the Spaces. *Exemplaria* 4: 35–50.

Crotty, Kevin. 1994. *The Poetics of Supplication: Homer's* Iliad *and* Odyssey. Ithaca, N.Y.

Culler, Jonathan. 1997. *Literary Theory: A Very Short Introduction*. Oxford.

de Beauvoir, Simone. 1974. *The Second Sex*. Trans. H. M. Parshley. New York.

Derderian, Katharine. 2001. *Leaving Words to Remember: Greek Mourning and the Advent of Literacy*. Leiden.

Dué, Casey. 2002. *Homeric Variations on a Lament by Briseis*. Lanham, Md.

——. 2006. *The Captive Woman's Lament in Greek Tragedy*. Austin.

Easterling, P. E. 1991. Men's *Kléos* and Women's *Góos*: Female Voices in the *Iliad*. *Journal of Modern Greek Studies* 9: 145–151.

Ebbott, Mary. 1999. The Wrath of Helen: Self-Blame and Nemesis in the *Iliad*. In *Nine Essays on Homer*, ed. M. Carlisle and O. Levaniouk, 3–20. Lanham, Md.

Edwards, Mark. 1987. *Homer: Poet of the* Iliad. Baltimore.

Foley, Helene P. 1992. The Politics of Tragic Lamentation. In *Tragedy, Comedy, and the Polis*, ed. A. Sommerstein, S. Halliwell, J. Henderson, and B. Zimmerman., 101–143. Bari.

Foley, John Miles. 1991. *Immanent Art: From Structure to Meaning in Traditional Oral Epic*. Bloomington, Ind.

Griffin, Jasper. 1980. *Homer on Life and Death*. Oxford.

Holst-Warhaft, Gail. 1992. *Dangerous Voices: Women's Laments and Greek Literature*. London.

Johnson, W. R. 1976. *Darkness Visible: A Study of Vergil's* Aeneid. Berkeley.

Kakridis, Johannes Th. 1949. *Homeric Researches*. Lund.

Kermode, Frank. 1967. *The Sense of an Ending: Studies in the Theory of Fiction*. New York.

Kirk, G. S. 1990. The Iliad: *A Commentary. Vol. 2: Books 5–8*. Cambridge.

Latacz, Joachim. 2004. *Troy and Homer: Towards a Solution of an Old Mystery*. Trans. Kevin White and Rosh Ireland. Oxford.

Lattimore, Richmond. 1951. The Iliad *of Homer*. Chicago.

Lynn-George, Michael. 1988. *Epos: Word, Narrative, and the* Iliad. Houndmills, U.K.

MacCary, W. Thomas. 1982. *Childlike Achilles: Ontogeny and Phylogeny in the* Iliad. New York.

Macleod, C. W. 1982. *Homer:* Iliad, *Book XXIV*. Cambridge.

Martin, Richard P. 1989. *The Language of Heroes: Speech and Performance in the* Iliad. Ithaca, N.Y.

McClure, L. 1999. *Spoken Like a Woman: Speech and Gender in Athenian Drama.* Princeton.

Monsacré, Hélène. 1984. *Les larmes d'Achille: Le héros, la femme, et la souffrance dans la poésie d'Homère.* Paris.

Morrison, Susan Signe. 2000. Unnatural Authority: Translating Beyond the Heroic in *The Wife's Lament. Medievalia et Humanistica* N.S. 27: 19–31.

Murnaghan, Sheila. 1999. The Poetics of Loss in Greek Epic. In *Epic Traditions in the Contemporary World: The Poetics of Community,* ed. M. Beissinger, J. Tylus, and S. Wofford, 203–220. Berkeley.

Nagy, G. 1979. *The Best of the Achaeans: Concepts of the Hero in Archaic Greek Poetry.* Baltimore.

Pantelia, Maria C. 2002. Helen and the Last Song for Hector. *Transactions of the American Philological Association* 132: 21–27.

Perkell, Christine. 1997. The Lament of Juturna: Pathos and Interpretation in the *Aeneid. Transactions of the American Philological Association* 127: 257–286.

Petersmann, Gerhard. 1973. Die monologische Totenklage der *Ilias. Rheinisches Museum für Philologie* 116: 3–16.

Redfield, James M. 1975. *Nature and Culture in the* Iliad: *The Tragedy of Hektor.* Chicago.

Reiner, Eugen. 1938. *Die Rituelle Totenklage der Griechen.* Stuttgart.

Richardson, Nicholas. 1993. The Iliad: *A Commentary. Vol. 6: Books 21–24.* Oxford.

Roberts, D. H. 1993. The Frustrated Mourner: Strategies of Closure in Greek Tragedy. In *Nomodeiktes: Greek Studies in Honor of Martin Ostwald,* ed. R. Rosen and J. Farrell, 573–587. Ann Arbor.

Roisman, Hanna M. 2006. Helen in the *Iliad: Causa Belli* and Victim of War: From Silent Weaver to Public Speaker. *American Journal of Philology* 127: 1–36.

Rose, Peter W. 1992. *Sons of Gods, Children of Earth: Ideology and Literary Form in Ancient Greece.* Ithaca, N.Y.

Schadewaldt, W. 1959. *Von Homers Welt und Werk.* Stuttgart.

Schein, Seth L. 1984. *The Mortal Hero: An Introduction to Homer's* Iliad. Berkeley.

Segal, Charles P. 1993. The Female Voice and Its Contradictions from Homer to Tragedy. In *Religio Graeco-Romana: Festschrift für Walter Pötscher. Grazer Beiträge,* ed. J. Dalfen, Gerhard Petersmann, and Franz Ferdinand Schwarz., 57–75. Suppl. Band 5. Graz.

Seremetakis, C. Nadia. 1991. *The Last Word: Women, Death, and Divination in Inner Mani.* Chicago.

Silk, Michael. 1987. *Homer:* The Iliad. Cambridge.

Smith, Barbara Herrnstein. 1986. *Poetic Closure: A Study of How Poems End.* Chicago.

Spargo, R. Clifton. 2004. *The Ethics of Mourning: Grief and Responsibility in Elegiac Literature.* Baltimore.

Sultan, N. 1991. Women in "Akritic" Song: The Hero's "Other" Voice. *Journal of Modern Greek Studies* 9: 153–170.

——. 1993. Private Speech, Public Pain: The Power of Women's Laments in Ancient Greek Poetry and Tragedy. In *Rediscovering the Muses: Women's Musical Traditions,* ed. K. Marshall, 92–110. Boston.

——. 1999. *Exile and the Poetics of Loss in the Greek Tradition.* Lanham, Md.

Suzuki, M. 1989. *Metamorphoses of Helen: Authority, Difference, and the Epic.* Ithaca, N.Y.

Tatum, James. 2003. *The Mourner's Song: War and Remembrance from the* Iliad *to Viet Nam.* Chicago.

Tsagalis, Christos. 2004. *Epic Grief: Personal Laments in Homer's* Iliad. Berlin.

Van Wees, Hans. 1998. A Brief History of Tears: Gender Differentiation in Archaic Greece. In *When Men Were Men: Masculinity, Power, and Identity in Classical Antiquity*, ed. L. Foxhall and J. Salmon, 10–53. London.

Vernant, J.-P. 1991. A Beautiful Death and the Disfigured Corpse in Homeric Epic. In *Mortals and Immortals: Collected Essays*, ed. Froma I. Zeitlin, 50–74. Princeton.

White, Hayden. 1987. The Value of Narrativity in the Representation of Reality. In *The Content of the Form: Narrative Discourse and Historical Representation*, ed. Hayden White, 1–25. Baltimore.

Worman, Nancy. 2001. This Voice Which Is Not One: Helen's Verbal Guises in Homeric Epic. In *Making Silence Speak: Women's Voices in Greek Literature and Society*, ed. A. Lardinois and L. McClure, 19–37. Princeton.

Zanker, Graham. 1994. *The Heart of Achilles: Characterization and Personal Ethics in the* Iliad. Ann Arbor.

6

KEENS FROM THE ABSENT CHORUS

Troy to Ulster

RICHARD P. MARTIN

What experimentation is to science, comparison should be to philology—a way to test hypotheses and produce new ones that account for more of the data, more economically. What one chooses to compare, of course, will affect the results. On one end of the spectrum lies the tracing of curious resemblances among otherwise isolated words, motifs, or customs and the urge to weave around these an intriguing narrative, either of primitive origins, long-distance cultural contact, or deep genetic relationship.[1] The nineteenth century's fascination with atomistic and often obscure comparanda gave way in the twentieth century to a more dependable tendency to compare total structures, linguistics leading the way to the other end of the spectrum, with anthropology trailing some decades later.[2] Neither method was specifically designed for the study of verbal art, although Frazer's great work was prompted by a scene in Vergil's *Aeneid* and Lévi-Strauss's best-known article starts with the *Oedipus Rex* of Sophocles. Yet the philologist studying ancient or medieval texts has much to gain from a controlled use of ethnographic comparisons of both types—those based on telling Frazerian detail (now once again in fashion) as well as those concerned with global structures.[3] In fact, a twenty-first-century philology *without* strong affiliations to social anthropology, folkloristics, and performance study is increasingly untenable and in danger of exhausting itself on hermetic quests into the endlessly intertextual.[4]

An explication of two puzzling passages, one ancient Greek, the other medieval Irish, can illustrate the advantages of comparing old texts and modern cultures. My approach in this chapter will be quadrilateral: modern

Greek evidence illumines the Homeric *Iliad* and *Odyssey,* ancient Greek social practices can shed light on the medieval Irish *Scéla Muicce Meic Dathó,* and a famous modern Irish poem might be fruitfully reconsidered along the way. Underlying this approach is one key assumption: that typologically similar institutions often generate similar rhetoric and poetics.[5] That is to say, the details of the individual document or performance (the object of one sort of ethnography) can be brought into touch with larger structures (objects of a different sort of anthropology) so that we do not lose sight of either end of the data spectrum and we end up clarifying both in the process. Where our evidence from premodern periods is patchy and unsure, as is often the case with Greek and Irish materials, we can still look to mutually illuminating models for performances, ancient, medieval, and modern.[6] Such models do not "prove" anything about the texts in question but may provide better hypotheses—all that one can ask of most investigations.

First, the ancient Greek conundrum, a passage that was controversial already in the third century B.C.E.[7] In book 4 of the *Odyssey,* the hero Menelaus, now safely home from the Trojan War, reminisces, for the benefit of his young guest Telemachus, about the exploits of Odysseus in the final days of the siege. He recalls how his own wife, the exquisite Helen, nearly ruined Odysseus's plan of the Trojan Horse through a strange feat of ventriloquism—or so it seemed—enacted on the night that the Greek heroes lay hidden inside, waiting to make their sneak attack:

> Three times you walked around, handling the hollow ambush;
> You called by name the best of the Danaans,
> In voice resembling all the Argives' wives.[8]

Only the determination of Odysseus, claims his old friend, prevented the warriors with him inside the horse from crying out in response to Helen's near-fatal provocation. This extremely odd behavior by the Spartan queen has usually been connected with Helen's alleged resemblance to a sorceress, as scholars attempt to translate her adeptness at drug administration into something more sinister. Yet there is no other evidence to point the audience in that direction.[9] Then again, one can anachronistically psychologize Helen's character to ask why she nearly betrayed the Greeks (fear of her new Trojan relatives by marriage, the Stockholm syndrome, etc.).[10] But if we wish to base our explications on the immediate and more appropriate level of traditional conventions within Archaic Greek poetry, it is important to inquire first what other scenes this passage resembles in motif or diction. This is to ask, in another way: What might have resonated with a traditional Greek audience of oral-poetic craft, one aware of multiple performances that repeatedly featured the same characters, tales, and phrases? A close resemblance has sometimes been noted with the similar ventriloquist abilities of the maidens of Delos in the *Hymn to Apollo,* an anonymous composition in epic hexameter style, perhaps dating from the sixth century B.C.E. The marvel created by these young women is described as part of a longer passage celebrating the central festival of Apollo on his rocky sacred island, an event attended by travelers from all the Ionian city-states:

Calling to mind men of old and women
They sing a hymn and charm the tribes of mankind.
The voices and rhythm of all people they know to imitate;
Each might say that he himself was speaking:
that is how fine their song fits together.[11]

At the risk of explaining obscurum per obscurius, we can note that both performances, Helen's and the maidens', involve miming another's voice. But the lone figure of Helen is said in the *Odyssey* specifically to have imitated the voices of women, the wives of the Greek heroes inside the wooden horse. By contrast, the chorus of Delian women sings *about* a plurality, both men and women of an earlier age. Theirs is an epicizing act, overtly referring to distant heroic characters, yet their performance apparently represents the voices of all kinds of people actually present. The magic of the Delians' song lies in its ability to involve the audience so completely that each listener feels the closest affinity with the speaker—a beautiful image of the ultimate merging of singer and rapt audience.[12] That the stress falls on the *choral* nature of the maidens' performance can be deduced from the verb *sunareren*, "fits together," which denotes a joint production at the same time as it emblematizes, in context, the perfect "fit" between performers and listeners. In this highly charged scene, a distinctly Greek poetic ideology finds its summation: choral song has the power of modeling and enabling community cohesion.[13] This force of the preverb *sun*, "together," can be paralleled with reference to musical and vocal performance in a number of compound words, such as the verb *sumphônein*, which ultimately gives us "symphony."

The differences between these two vocal events strike one as much as the similarities: Helen's seems not to be a canonical performance but a spooky sort of improvisation. After all, the only "audience" is either the fearful concealed Greeks or Helen's latest husband, the Trojan Deiphobos, who accompanied her to see the horse. And where is the pleasure one expects, the regular concomitant of women's singing in Greek poetry? Furthermore, is it not perverse that one woman becomes a chorus? Then again, we might recall that Helen is herself a singular being, a divinity, outside epic, and a multiform of the Indo-European dawn goddess. Her abilities and practices have the right to be oddly different.[14]

The closest parallel for women's "choral" performance of this type within Homeric epic takes us to the end of the *Odyssey*. There it is not mortal women, however, but the Muses who once sang an antiphonal lament over the body of Achilles, toward the end of the war. As the shade of Agamemnon recounts the scene to Achilles, his companion now in Hades:

Around you stood the daughters of the Old Man of the Sea
Pitifully wailing, and clothed you in immortal clothes.

The Muses, all nine, with responsive lovely voice
Made the lament. Then you might have seen
No Argive tearless—in such a way did the clear-toned Muse arouse
them.[15]

Some critics have tried to explain the singular Muse of line 62 as a type of abstraction or even an (unparalleled) metonymy for "music," but the more functional explanation, through ethnopoetics, would interpret the scenario differently. One Muse leads the group and responds to them, as they respond to her and to one another, *ameibomenai opi kale*.[16] In this interpretation, the divine performance recounted in *Odyssey* 24 would match lament performance as attested in medieval and modern as well as other ancient texts.[17] It might show, in addition, a performance context (responsive song) whereby "one" and "many" are enabled to exchange roles, so that the boundaries of personality are blurred. But how can this lament at the death of Achilles help us to understand the original object of attention, Helen's weird imitative powers as she circles the Trojan Horse?

To take stock thus far, the Delian maidens present us with a chorus that can imitate the voices of others; so can Helen, but she is not a chorus. The Muses, on the other hand, operate in such a way that individual and choral voice naturally alternate; the vocal relation is symbiotic. If Helen is conceptualized as an *exarkhousa*—a chorus leader—we might be able to imagine that she crystallizes the power of choral song, within her own individual performance, in effect imitating call-and-response. But this suggestion seems to lead us into a further speculation, namely, that Helen is somehow connected with the performance, specifically, of lament, for that is the precise context—indeed, the only context—in which call-and-response is seen to function in Homeric descriptions of song. I suggest that, odd as it may seem at first sight, Helen, as we see her in Homeric verse, possesses a close affinity for lament. Furthermore, it can be demonstrated that the diction and rhetoric used by the Homeric poet to depict her in several key passages are permeated with markers of the lament genre. In addition, if we observe modern rural Greek practices of lament, as ethnographers have recorded them, a number of other puzzling features of Helen's character and story cohere in a new way. If Helen is thought of as an expert lamenter, a professional keener, her ambiguous status, mantic abilities, and ghostly double can start to make sense. Finally, we can begin to understand what she was doing that dark night outside the horse. Once we acknowledge the key role of choral poetry in the art of lament, we can understand the Irish material, even without reverting to reconstructions of Indo-European institutions, much as those have their attractions.

I

To establish Helen as keener, we need to work from both ends, drawing on traditional philological analysis of the ancient text (especially by comparing phraseology) but, equally, on contemporary examinations of a social-poetic genre, the *moiroloyia* (lit., "fate saying"), an enduring folk tradition on which there is now much careful ethnographic work. Scholarship of the past twenty-five years seeks to analyze Greek laments in terms of social categories and gender relationships; the role of performers in village life; and the attitudes toward kin, death, religion, and work that these songs embody. I rely in particular on the work of Nadia Seremetakis; among others studying lament and grief within Greek culture whose work has influenced me are Loring Danforth, Neni Panourgiá, Gail Holst-Warhaft, Margaret Alexiou, and Iannis Tsouderos.[18] For analysis of the ancient text, as will become clear, I rely on the fundamental insights of Milman Parry, Albert Lord, and the scholars who have followed in their tracks in treating Homeric epic as the product of an oral-traditional art.[19]

Helen makes one overt formal lament in the *Iliad*.[20] In a striking poetic moment, at the very end of the poem, the woman who caused the Trojan War weeps over the body of Hector, her brother-in-law (*Il.* 24.761–776):

> Helen, the third, began to lead their lamentation. "Hector,
> dearest to my heart of all my brothers-in-law...truly,
> Alexandros the godlike is my husband who led me to Troy
> I should have died before then! Already now this is the
> twentieth year for me since I came from there and left my
> native land; but never did I hear from you an ill, degrading
> word. Instead, if anyone else in the palace would curse me
> a sister-in-law, brother-in-law, or one's long-robed wife, or
> my mother-in-law (father-in-law was gentle as a father) it
> was you who restrained them with words you spoke aside,
> with your gentle-minded way and gentle words. So I weep
> for you and at the same time, myself—luckless one!—grieved
> at heart. For there is no one else for me, in broad Troy, mild
> or friendly: all are bristling in fear at me."

Helen has the right to lament publicly at this moment because she is kin by marriage to the murdered Hector. But by the time we see her in this official role of mourner at the end of the poem, Helen's language sounds familiar. The reason emerges when we go beyond an analysis restricted to speeches specifically designated as laments (*goos* or *threnos*) and look instead at the language of Helen elsewhere in the poem. Her other speeches, even though they are not called laments, more often than not contain the strategies and phrases of that genre. In other words, Helen in her appearances earlier in the *Iliad* would sound very much like a lamenting woman to the ears of a traditional audience aware of the deployment of speech motifs.[21] Primary evidence comes from book 3, when Helen first makes her entrance in the *Iliad*. At the moment she is called to come to the walls of Troy to see her present husband Paris battle her former husband Menelaus, Helen is weaving a story cloth depicting the sufferings that the warriors have already undergone for her sake (*Il.* 3.125–128). Thus, even before she utters a word, Helen is placed in the context of lamentation.[22] When she reaches the wall and begins to respond to Priam's questions about the Greek warriors whom they view on the plain below, the speech has an unmistakable tone that derives from lament phrasings found elsewhere in Homeric epic (*Il.* 3.171–180):

> Helen, glorious among women, answered him with strong words.
> "Dear father-in-law, you are revered and inspire awe.
> Evil death should have been my pleasure when I followed your son here,
> leaving marriage chamber, kin, dear daughter, my age-mates.
> But that was not to be. I melt with weeping for it.
> This, though, I'll tell you—which you ask and inquire:
> Over there is the wide-ruling son of Atreus, Agamemnon—
> Good king and strong fighter, both. And as well, to me,
> Shameful bitch, he was brother-in-law—if all that ever happened."

At 180, Helen refers to Agamemnon as one "who used to be" (with marked iterative-imperfect form *eske*) and adds "if he/it ever was"—a formulaic phrase regularly used of the absent or dead. Both recur in *Od.* 19.315 when Penelope recalls Odysseus, whom she thinks has perished: "The way Odysseus used to be among men, if ever he was."[23]

Although Agamemnon is very much alive and in view, Helen's diction treats her own past, and its figures, as the dead object. We can hear in this a brilliant poetic reworking of a traditional speech motif from another genre (lament), an innovatory enrichment pushing the poetic system to new expressiveness and characterizing Helen in the process.

At 172, Helen uses vocatives, *phile (*sw)ekure d(w)einos te*. The hexameter meter can only be scanned correctly here if we assume that the necessary long syllabic quantities were generated by the earlier presence of consonants that were lost in most dialects before the earliest possible fixation of any portion of the Homeric text (ca. 750 B.C.E.). In other words this double vocative, "dear father-in-law and held in awe," must have been already an old phrase in some ancient poetic tradition. What does this have to do with lament? Although it is certainly possible that such frozen archaic phrases were preserved in a number of contexts, one is struck by the predominant occurrence of designations of kin within the genre of lament as it is now practiced in Greece, especially among the women of Inner Mani. From fieldwork, Gareth Morgan and Nadia Seremetakis report that lament sessions regularly begin with highly conventionalized traditional greetings exchanged among kin, using kin titles—some of them not in common speech usage—rather than proper names. Thus *kafi' mou*—or *adhelfoúla mou*—can be used not just for blood sisters (the literal meaning in Modern Greek) but any female kin. Indeed, the lament performance arising in these modern occasions is a primary way of establishing and articulating the speaker's exact sentiment for degrees of kin affection, precisely through such designations. This is a striking case of social poetics in action.[24] In this regard, it is worth noting that Helen's single overt speech of lament (cited above) specifically singles out Priam as her "good" in-law: "father-in-law was gentle as a father" (*Il.* 24.770). The theme of Helen's relationship to Priam, which emerges fully in her lament for Hector at the poem's finale, revolves around the same phrase that we see in a highly traditional occurrence earlier in the poem. To put it pointedly, "dear father-in-law—*phile* (**sw)ekure*"—may well have arisen in a formal lament like the book 24 example and have been reused innovatively in the scene of Helen and Priam on the wall. Rather than continue the dense philological demonstration to show that Helen is always using lament language within the *Iliad*, and thus would sound like a constant and even professional mourner to an attuned audience, I turn now to three implications of the picture I have been drawing, of Helen as keening woman.[25]

1.

Helen's mantic abilities can be understood if we retroject to Archaic Greek times a belief found today concerning modern Greek lament experts. The modern Greek lore on lamenters makes them also consistently adept at interpreting signs that warn of imminent death. In the view of Seremetakis and others, they are the modern equivalent of diviners. Turning to *Od.* 15.173–178, let us imagine that an ancient lamenter might also have been credited with this capacity; Helen says:

> Listen—I will act as prophet (*manteusomai*), the way
> the gods put it in my spirit and I think it will turn out.

Odysseus will come home, she says, and punish the suitors just as an eagle has appeared and snatched a goose in the sight of all.

Helen's ability to foresee the future, and the persuasive ability she has at this, may well stem from her role as the paradigmatic lamenter for the heroic age. What I am suggesting can contribute to an economy of explanation. There is no need to resort to the rather ad hoc explanations that have depicted Helen as a witch. Knowing the poetics of a social institution, and retrojecting them, we can explain two aspects of Helen's characterization through one assumption.

2.

A second worrisome passage in the *Odyssey* can also be clarified in this way. The following lines have remained enigmatic, despite being a center of scholarly attention in recent years.[26] On her first entrance in the epic, Helen notices the newly arrived Telemachus with Nestor's son Peisistratos and says (*Od.* 4.138–140):

> Menelaus, god-nourished, do we know who these claim
> to be, among mortals, and who have reached our home?
> Shall I tell a lie, or speak the truth? My heart commands me.

As the lines that immediately follow these show, Helen has already divined, from his looks, that the guest is the son of her old acquaintance Odysseus. But what is the force of "Shall I tell a lie...?" The words have inevitably prompted comparison with those of other enigmatic females, in a passage that shares similar poetic diction: the Muses' own declaration to Hesiod in the beginning of the *Theogony* (27–28).[27] Here, the Muses, less tentatively, assert: "We know how to say many lies like true things, and when we want, we know how to sing truths." But do they tell the truth to Hesiod? And what does Helen's heart command her? Why is the disjunction of truth or fiction even made problematic in both passages?

It is in connecting these apparently isolated puzzles in Archaic Greek poetry that the value of a "performance model" attested from fieldwork in modern Greece can be shown. In a Maniot Greek lament recorded by Nadia Seremetakis in the mid-1980s we hear:

E, Aloghako, ela konda
na ze ta leou na t'aghrikas,
alithia leou ni psemata?

Alogako, come near,
so I can tell you, so you can hear:
am I speaking the truth or lies?[28]

What the modern ethnographer can make clear, however, is what we can never directly recover from the ancient text the context and force of this trope in actual performance. "Am I telling truth or lies," Seremetakis shows, is a rhetorical convention of the modern lament. It is a powerful, idiomatic expression that simply asserts the truth of what the speaker says: that is, the lamenter is *not* telling lies.

3.

But we should not characterize this as merely an assertion. To quote Seremetakis on the full force of the lament and its choral patterning: "The truth claims that arise from the ritual...depend on the emotional force of pain, and the *jural force of antiphonic confirmation*. By stating that they cannot properly sing laments without the help of others, Maniot women reveal that pain, in order to be rendered valid, has to be socially constructed in antiphonic relations. Antiphony is a jural and historicizing structure."[29] In other words, the assertion of truth is the prime marker for what the entire ritual undertakes to accomplish. Lament, in the words of the fieldworker, "has a built-in record keeping function." Once we realize, with the help of ethnography, that choral performance is not purely an aesthetic choice, but of the essence in lament, we can return to the passage with which we began: Helen "doing all the voices" as she circumambulates the Trojan Horse. It has not to my knowledge been noticed that the closest formulaic line to the description of Helen's action

(*Od.* 4.278: "You called by name the best of the Danaans") occurs in *Il.* 22.415, precisely when Priam laments Hector, "calling out each man by name." There, the "calling out" of individual names is a chilling part of the very public performance of Priam's grief by the old man himself. The comparative evidence of Maniot lament, meanwhile, shows that this calling out, either of living or dead, is an expected, conventional part of a lament performance.[30] What was Helen doing that dark night? Perhaps what she did was staged as a lament. This would fit the character that she had constructed already for her Trojan audience (recall her speech behavior in *Iliad* 3) and which she needed to maintain. At the same time, this would have been a frustrating and excruciating performance for another audience, the Achaean warriors hidden inside the horse. I suggest that in Helen's command performance, she becomes the keener *and* chorus, a lone choral leader calling out the dead. She provides the voices that would actually have lamented individual heroes had their wives been present (and were they already dead). But in this case the lament *for* the dead, like the call of the Sirens, is a summons *to* death unless one resists it.

To put it briefly, Helen is so closely associated with lament in Greek tradition that she becomes its metonym. I would submit that this phenomenon can be extended into a principle for traditional poetics as a whole: one character can embody a genre. It happens that lament, this antiphonal, foundational speech act, can be represented in Archaic Greece as the original authorizing act that lies behind *all* poetry of commemoration.[31] That may be why the Muses are women, for only women regularly take the professional role of praising and mourning the dead. It should not surprise us, then, that the Muses in Hesiod (*Theogony* 26), on the verge of declaring their powers, bandy about blame expressions, assaulting the shepherds as "mere bellies, wretched shames."[32] As we have seen, the rhetoric of ancient and modern lament resorts to exactly this, to spur the living to act or to express the survivor's aporia.

A final conclusion for Homeric poetics, emerging from this experiment in sociophilology, is that because Helen represents lament, which in turn can be taken as the source of a community's truth telling, its ranking of relations among dead and living, the place of Helen as the last person to utter a lament, at the very end of the *Iliad*, is entirely appropriate. She is the female Muse who counterbalances the Muse invoked at the poem's beginning. As another sort of goddess, she is the true inspiration for the Trojan War—and thus also for the stories told about it.

II

In most comparisons of Greek and Irish literature known to me, the transitional trope usually involves invoking a distant common source, a genetic relation based on shared Indo-European origins.[33] This is by no means to devalue such work, which stands as a monument to the finest controlled philological comparatism. Rather, my Helleno-Hibernian coda is an attempt to make connections at a broader typological level, without the precise matching of lexical items that is crucial to the Indo-Europeanist's demonstrations but with attention to cultural structures.[34] Two conclusions will flow from the comparison I propose: first, that ancient non-Homeric myths concerning the Greek Helen can be explicated by reference to Irish folklore on lamenters; and second, that the essential choral nature of lament in Greece can be used, by way of analogy, to clarify passages in medieval and modern Irish poetry.

The Greek myths have to do with Helen's infamous *eidolon* ("phantom" or "image"—the word gives us ultimately "idol"), which, according to a tradition attested in Stesichorus and Euripides was formed by the goddess Hera and sent to Troy as a substitute, while the real Helen innocently sat out the war in Egypt.[35] Whether or not Homer knew about this story and suppressed it is debatable. Yet the close connection between lament and Helen, which we can see in the Homeric representation of her, leads me to suggest the following, taking account of the sorts of lore that surround the social poetry of lamenting in modern Greece and (earlier) modern Ireland. In Inner Mani, it is thought that a vision of a dying person comes to his or her kin at the time of death, something like a ghost but more vital and convincing than such an apparition. Thus, expert lamenters—the *miroloyístres*—have been known to set out for the funeral rituals before they even get word, through normal channels, that someone has died. They simply realize, from their interpretation of signs, that someone has expired and they are needed as professional mourners. The presence of these elderly professional mourners on the roads is taken as a bad omen, and people try to avoid them.[36]

In modern Greek lore the lamenter herself, although she may be avoided and seen as a harbinger of death, is *not* seen in a vision. That is the communicative mode of the deceased. But in Irish tradition, as is well known, she is seen—or, perhaps more often, is heard, as an unseen presence. Both medieval and modern Irish keeners do unusual things, as Angela Partridge's analysis shows.[37] There are stories of the woman who hears about a death and then takes three leaps, upon which she arrives at the scene of the demise—not as good as bilocation but close. Even more relevant is the tradition of the *bean sídhe*, "woman of the otherworld people." Hearing or seeing her fearsome lamentation is thought to forebode death or disaster in a community.[38] If we assume that a traditional poetic role of Helen as a constant lamenter might have intersected with now lost Greek folk traditions that resembled the surviving Irish traditions, then the stories of her *eidolon* can be interpreted as emerging from a keener's banshee-like apparitions.[39]

Finally, the choral requirements of lament, which were used above to explicate odd moments in Helen's biography, can help us reconsider Irish women's performances in this genre. Although keening is a well-known and widely studied phenomenon in Irish culture and literature, it seems that its potential choral features have been neglected or misunderstood.[40] The quite literary focus on the "authorship" or ownership of lament encourages such readings. Thus, the most celebrated Irish lament, the *Caoineadh Airt Uí Laoghaire*, has to my knowledge always been taken as the solitary cry of a distraught wife, whose husband was shot dead by a sheriff's man in Macroom, Co. Cork, on 4 May 1773.[41] Attention should be drawn, however, to the odd "interruption" that occurs several times in the poem. The sister of Art breaks in, apparently scolding the wife, Eibhlín, while addressing the dead man:

Mo chara is mo stór tú!	My friend and my treasure!
Is mó bean chumtha chórach	Many fine-made women
ó Chorcaigh na seolta	From Cork of the sails
go Droichead na Tóime	To Droichead na Tóime
do tabharfadh macha mór bó dhuit	Would bring you great herds
agus dorn buí-óir duit,	And a yellow-gold handful,
na raghadh a chodladh 'na seomra	And not sleep in their room
oíche do thórraimh.	On the night of your wake.

To this the mourning wife reacts:

Mo chara is m'uan tú!	My friend and my lamb!
is ná creid sin uathu,	Don't you believe them
ná an cogar a fuarais,	Nor the scandal you heard
ná an scéal fir fuatha,	Nor the jealous man's gossip
gur a chodladh a chuas-sa.	That it's sleeping I went.

She goes on to explain that she had only left the room to settle the young children to sleep. The rhetorical dynamic can be compared with that in the modern Greek examples cited. Blame here elicits a confirmation that the closest kin is indeed doing what she must: the antiphonal mode works to stage and underline the assertion of proper ritual.

If we can see traces of a dramatized, interlocutory style in Irish lament in the eighteenth century, what of earlier periods? The songs that have made their way into our surviving manuscripts do not seem to offer help. I think especially of such poems as the lament of Créide for Dínertach.[42] A distinctive element, something we do not have, strictly speaking, in ancient Greek examples, emerges in such compositions: the lament is combined with expressions of passionate love. Créide's quatrains can be taken as either a love poem or a lament. The combination is beautifully shaped metaphorically so that the arrows that slew her beloved are transformed into thoughts that keep her awake:

It é saigte gona súain	Lamenting love are the arrows that kill sleep
cech thrátha i n-aidchi adúair	Each hour of the freezing night,
serccoí, lia gnása, íar ndé	From being with him, at end of day,
fir a tóeb thíre Roigne.	The man from beside Tír Roigne.

Just as Eibhlín Ó Laoghaire's lament is filled with terms of endearment, recollections of her husband's appearance, and their conversation, so Créide's words elide the realms of death and eros—a combination to which we shall return in a moment. For now, it is enough to note that such a focus on the loving association of the speaker with the object of her lament militates against the use of a choral voice, for how could many women, even in a stylized version, explicitly affirm this more intimate bond?

Yet there are situations in which this can be imagined. Créide's lament includes one quatrain (7) that seems to allude to choral praise—whether in lament or for the live hero is hard to tell: "In the land of glorious Aidne,... singing goes on (*canair*) about a glorious flame, from the south of Limerick of the graves, whose name is Dínertach." I note that, although Murphy translates the verb as "men sing," its impersonal-passive force leaves the gender of the subject unstated. I suggest that women might have been the singers, and if so we would have a parallel here for a strange passage from Irish saga.

Like the Greek, Irish tradition is immensely long and vigorous. Going back to the *Scéla Muicce Meic Dathó* (ca. 800 C.E.), we encounter a scene evocative of choral performances by women. The lines come at the end of the brawling story of the struggle between the men of Ulster and those of Connaught over the dog of Mac Dathó, which his owner has promised to both sides. In a shift ripe for structuralist myth analysis, the marvelous hound is temporarily trumped by a pig in a pot. The escalating contention for the Champion's Portion (*verbal, interior, spear fighting, Leinster centered, cooked*) breaks into a free-for-all chariot chase across Ireland (*physical, exterior, chariot-fighting, centrifugal, raw*).[43] The poor canine at the heart of the battle is carted around Ireland half-impaled on a war chariot until he gradually disintegrates, thus naming a number of topographical features—"Dog-head," "Dog-tail," and so forth. Women frame the tale. At the opening, we hear Mac Dathó in a dialogue with his wife, who urges him to adopt the plan of giving the hound to both parties. The tale ends with a mysterious passage concerning a group of women and a bit of cinematic plot business worthy of John Ford at his best. Ailill's Connaught charioteer, named Fer Loga, manages to leap onto the hurtling chariot of Conchobar, the Ulster king, taking him by surprise in a choke hold. Asked what he will take to spare the king's life, Fer Loga replies: "Nothing great: bring me with you to Emain Macha and let the single women of the Ulstermen (*mná óentama*) and their maiden daughters of an age to bear young (*a n-ingena macdacht*) perform a choral song (*do gabáil chepóce*) around me every hour saying 'Fer Loga is my darling' (*Fer Loga mo lennán-sa*)."[44] And so it happened, the tale concludes, "since they (the women) did not dare do otherwise." At the end of a year, Fer Loga was let go back west at Athlone, taking a pair of Conchobar's horses with him. The Rawlinson manuscript version (probably fifteenth century) adds a strange retraction at this point, after saying that Fer Loga's wish was granted: "and he did not get the choral songs though he got the horses" (*ní ruc na cepóca cé ruc na heocha*).[45] Both classicists and Celticists realize these days that such manuscript variants are usually loaded: no reading is without its politics. In this case, the stakes are quite clear. A version of the *Tale of Mac Dathó's Pig* asserting that the good women of Ulster spent a year in daily singing of a choral love song addressed to a Connaught hostage taker is unlikely to be generated by Ulster tale tellers. The counterassertion (he never got the songs) surely represents the remnant of an *Ulster* version struggling to defuse this insulting narrative.

But is there even more at stake? What harm after all is a onetime accession to the musical whim of a terroristic Connaught man, even an act so clearly charged with erotic overtones (which we might view as a verbal substitute for the conquest and rape of his enemies' women)? The mytho-historical threat, I submit, must lie in the assertion, through this minor saga detail, that Fer Loga thereby established in enemy territory a *continuing institution* to embarrass and taunt the Ulstermen, a recurrent song event that Ulster would rather deny. Furthermore, we should view that institution—even in a medieval, Christianized text—as alluding to something closely akin to ancient Greek hero cult.

To start at the lexical level, the uncommon word *cepóc* has been glossed as "panegyric sung in chorus ('possibly of an erotic character')."[46] But the lexicologists go on to note that the word is used frequently "of the eulogy of the dead." And as O'Curry's collection of material illustrates (although he does not make a point of this), the subjects of this choral performance are not just anyone.[47] A gloss on a fragment of an elegy for Colum Cille defines *cepóc* as a Scottish synonym for the Irish *aidbse*—the term used for the great choral song in the saint's honor, performed by the assembled poets of all Ireland in 590. In addition, the glossator cites a poetic tag showing that *cepóc* was used for praise of a king. Finally, the poem made on behalf of his peers by the chief poet Amergin on the death of his fellow poet and teacher Aithirne at the hands of the Ulstermen contains the quatrain:

> I will make a *cepóc* here
> And I will make his lamentation
> And here I will set up his tombstone
> And here I will make his graceful grave.[48]

While O'Curry sees the song for Fer Loga and for Colum Cille as expressions of joy, he acknowledges that the other two early attestations center on grief. Comparing the performance to the wide-ranging crooning called *cronán*, he speculates that "the Irish funeral cry, as it is called, of our times, is a remnant (though perhaps only a degenerate uncultivated remnant) of the ancient *Aidbsi* or *Cepóc* of the Gaedhil," and he ends with a personal note: in his own day, men and women sang choral laments at funerals in parts of the south of Ireland.[49]

The funeral context of *cepóc* might seem to be contradicted in some cases by the fact that the addressee is alive. Yet we need to allow for stylization. The poetic praise of Colum Cille in 590 may just as easily be a retrojection, a "live" version, of what we know became an elegiac post-mortem performance by 597, the *Amra Choluim Chille*. Similarly, I suggest, the song "Fer Loga is my darling" might be a stylized "live" version of what had become choral song in Ulster or elsewhere, a lament for a long-dead warrior whose story might gain annual, renewed relevance in the context of a (pagan or Christian) women's ritual. In effect Fer Loga lives again each time the performance is renewed. To represent the song as one dedicated to a notorious *living* man is to acknowledge this institu-tional continuity. As we have seen above, the erotic coloration is not foreign to lament (cf. the notion underlying *serc-coí*). The obvious Frazer-ian analogue would be to the cult of Adonis, which we know was repre-sented poetically by Sappho in the sixth century B.C.E. and was practiced in Athens through the fifth.[50] But an even closer comparandum brings us to notice the specific groups selected to sing the song: single (unmarried or widowed?) Ulster women and the (or their) maiden daughters of mar-riageable age. Compare the explanation for the women's rites for Hippo-lytos, which the radical antiquarian Euripides enshrines at the end of the tragedy named for this hero. Hippolytos, the object of his stepmother's love, spurns her, only to be falsely denounced as a seducer in her suicide note. Cursed by his father, he races away in a chariot that is then caused to crash. Artemis, *dea ex machina*, promises compensation for the hero's tragic death, as she addresses him in his last moments of life (1423–1430):

To you, long-suffering man, I shall give
In return for these evils the greatest honors in Troizen.
Girls, unyoked before their marriages, will cut
their hair for you, through long ages, as you harvest
from their tears the greatest griefs. On you forever
there will be the song-making thought of maidens,
and Phaidra's passion will not fall nameless and be hushed.[51]

Hippolytos will, in one sense, never die. His commemoration is, significantly, both erotic (it will concern Phaedra's love for him) and elegiac in tone. We might wonder whether the maidens reenact in some way their mythic counterpart, the woman who "died" for love, as they move (ritually) into the next world—that of their marriages.[52] Their choral song about love is civic and bears a social message: the necessity for passion, the requirement for women their age to enter the sphere of Aphrodite. That the Ulster women who are to hymn Fer Loga are specifi-cally "single" and ready for marriage appears to put their performance into the same initiatory category. This is not to say that some "archaic" ritual is just vaguely recalled, for certainly the scene in the *Scéla Muicce Meic Dathó* functions synchronically on its own as a fit ending to the tale. Yet in both— ritual origin and rhetorical stylization—at the same time as it revivifies memory, performance encodes power, whether that be the force of

Aphrodite, emblematized by her young victim, or the aggression of Connaught, planting its hero through maiden songs across the border.

AFTERWORD

Since the previous publication of this contribution, several relevant works have appeared or come to my notice. Fine, detailed readings of the laments of Helen and others are given in Tsagalis 2004. Pantelia (2002) offers a convincing explanation for the placement of Helen's lament for Hector. On Helen's self-blame, see Sultan 1999, 37–39 (also enlightening on the larger contexts of ancient and modern Greek lament); on how it colors her speeches in the *Iliad*, see Ebbott 1999. Dué (2002) provides a precise explication of Iliadic lament themes as focused through one character. Alexiou (2002a, 333–339) expands on several features of her classic 1974 study (now in revised edition, 2002b) dealing with the lament and ritual complex.

ACKNOWLEDGMENT

This chapter is reprinted from *Western Folklore* 62 (2003): 119–142. Copyright © 2004 Western States Folklore Society.

NOTES

1. Frazer is of course the major figure: "He could always find a minor superstition among frolicking harvesters or New Year celebrants to match any more grandiose theme. The switches of scale give us a sense of flippancy" (Douglas 1982, 284). Douglas's article offers a balanced assessment of Frazer's continuing importance (even after Wittgenstein's critique). Ackerman (1987) well analyzes the connection between the scholar's anthropology and his Classical philology. Hyman (1959) shows how Frazer's intellectual roots tangled with those of a number of other Victorian figures. On the aims and methods of Frazer's contemporaries, see Stocking 1987.

2. This is a well-known story, concisely told by Culler (1975, 3–54) and Donato (1972). Detienne (2001) traces the concomitant narrowing of the range of comparanda that this involved.

3. On the rediscovery of Frazer's rich (if not "thick") description, and resemblances to Geertzian practice, see Boon 1982.

4. For an incisive evaluation of intertextuality studies in Classics, see Edmunds 2001. Responses to the sterility of pure intertextuality, within my discipline, have gone in two directions: toward questioning the ways in which we construct any individual text (see Sharrock and Morales 2000) and toward broadening the text's boundaries by way of attention to social context whether through New Historicism or the slightly softer "cultural poetics," on which see Kurke and Dougherty 1993. On the modern relationship between anthropology and Classics, see Martin Forthcoming.

5. For an illustration of the principle in connection with a different pairing of Greek and Irish texts, see Martin 1984, with further bibliography on the approach. Masterly demonstrations of the method can be found in Benveniste [1969] 1973;

G. Nagy 1990b, 1999; and Watkins 1995. On finishing this article I came across McCone (1984, 27), whose formulation, applied to Greek and Irish as well, nicely fits the view expressed here.

6. I find an encouraging defense of my sort of intellectual poaching in Guneratne: "To be a successful fieldworker, one must be at least a little uninhibited about being conspicuous and unwittingly violating local norms, because the nature of field work makes this virtually inevitable" (1999, 4). She contrasts with this the diffidence felt accompanying her husband during fieldwork in Nepal. As a para-ethnographer and part-time Celticist, I was honored yet abashed to have been included in the University of California, Los Angeles, conference on performance models (February 2001) organized by Joseph Nagy. I wish to thank him for the kind invitation to that fascining event, at which my position was often more that of the anthropologist's spouse.

7. It appears that the Alexandrian critic Aristarchus questioned the authenticity of several lines in the passage, including the detail of Helen's mimetic behavior: see Heubeck et al. 1988, 211–212, where it is suggested that "there may be more to this curious detail than meets the eye."

8. *Od.* 4.277–279. Translations of all Greek and Irish passages in this chapter are my own unless otherwise noted.

9. Just before Menelaus tells his rather pointed story about her, Helen spikes the party's drinks with a powerful Egyptian painkiller (*Od.* 4.220–232). Austin (1994, 77–81) removes the first scene from the realm of sorcery but reads lines 277–279 as celebrating Helen for her "daimonic powers." See further Suzuki 1989, 66.

10. For bibliography and discussion, see Suzuki 1989, 69.

11. *Hymn to Apollo* 160–164. On the controversies surrounding this complex poem, which seems to offer a glimpse of epic song performed by female choruses, as well as a stylized reference to the (mythologized) Homeric poet himself, see Lonsdale 1995; Nagy 1995; and Martin 2000. For more on the vocal abilities of the Delian maidens, see Martin 2001, with further bibliography. For the translation "rhythm" of the Greek *krembaliastus* in line 163 (usually taken as "chattering" or "clacking") I am indebted to Anastasia-Erasmia Peponi, whose work concerning dance concepts in this passage is forthcoming.

12. Archaic Greek myth and poetics, from the stories of Orpheus to depictions of court bards in the *Odyssey,* fantasize in a number of ways about the power of song: good recent examinations of the topic are Segal 1994 and Aloni 1998.

13. On the concept, see Calame 2001, 207–263; Nagy 1995. The civic importance of choruses for an ancient city-state is repeatedly acknowledged by Plato in the *Laws* (e.g., 796b–c). On the institution in fifth-century Athens, see Wilson 2000.

14. On the ambiguous status of Helen, as mortal or goddess, see Clader 1976 and Austin 1994, 10–12.

15. *Od.* 24.58–62—another passage subjected to critical doubts since antiquity.

16. Russo et al. (1992, 366–367) trace the interpretive genealogy and propose tentatively that the singular Muse is an *exarkhousa* or chorus leader. Following them, I read *hupórore* as transitive but would submit that the understood object is *the lament of the other Muses*, as fellow chorus members (not the Greek heroes who observed this lament). Compare *Il.* 24.760 (of Hekabe's lament), "So she spoke, weeping, and raised incessant lamentation," where the same verb takes as explicit object the noun *goos* (a nonmusical, nonprofessional lament, as opposed to a

threnos, which the Muses performed over Achilles in *Od*. 24.61). The introduction to Hekabe's words significantly specifies that she is the *exarkhousa*, leader of the performance (*Il*. 24.747): "For them, Hekabe started out the pulsing lament." The proposal is in line with the dynamics within modern lament, as sketched further below.

17. Choral responsion to a single female leader is well documented: see Alexiou 1974.

18. I take this opportunity to thank the last four scholars named here for personal communications over the past few years on various aspects of Greek lament. Helpful also on the lament tradition are Caraveli-Chavez (1980), Kassis (1985), Morgan (1973), Motsios (1995), and Skopetea (1972).

19. The deeply traditional and precise nature of Homeric diction has been most fruitfully demonstrated by Gregory Nagy (see especially 1990a, 1990b, 1996, 1999) in a series of books and articles. See also Benveniste [1969] 1973 and, for a clear presentation of the theory underlying such analyses, the several works by Foley (1988, 1991, 1999).

20. For full analysis of the differences in Homeric rhetoric between formal and improvised laments, see Tsagalis 1998.

21. On the notions of speech motifs and speech genres as structuring devices within Homeric mimesis, see Martin 1989, 1997.

22. The word *aethlous*, "trials," not only is used to describe prize contests but is a formulaic complement for *algea* in the phrase *algea paskhein*, "to undergo griefs." On the polyvalence of the scene, see Austin 1994, 37–41, with further bibliography. He does not note lament associations, however.

23. See also Priam about the dead Hector, *Il*. 24.425–428. On the resonance of the phrase, see Kirk 1985, 290–291.

24. Morgan 1973; Seremetakis 1991, 86–92.

25. Cf. further *Il*. 6.343–358: Helen denigrates Paris in front of Hector in a speech filled with obvious mourning imagery applied to her own wished-for death. The blame elements in a "lament" speech are even clearer at *Il*. 3.426–438, when she hurls a *muthos* at Paris and wishes that he had died in his recent duel with Menelaus. A solution to the somewhat disturbing co-occurrence of blame and lament elements can flow from the evidence of modern Maniot laments, about which Holst-Warhaft (1992, 75–97) reports that movement between the themes of grief and revenge often occurs in the same song. See also Seremetakis 1991, 126–158, on violence as a topic in *moiroloyia*. Even in cases where death has been natural, the widow can blame the deceased for abandoning her to the cruelties of life without his protection. Death is figured as desertion. Cf. Caraveli-Chavez 1980, 137–138.

26. Heubeck et al. 1988, 203.

27. Ferrari 1988 is the most sensible view of the debate over the alleged deconstructive import of this couplet.

28. Seremetakis 1991, 103. Note that even surface lexical expressions (from *alethes* and *pseudos*) remain constant over 2,500 years of Greek performances.

29. Ibid., 120; emphasis added.

30. Caraveli-Chavez (1980) shows how call-outs structure lament. For other ways in which they can influence meaning in a lament, see Perkell, this volume.

31. On the varied mythic sources of song, see G. Nagy 1990a. For how another character may embody a genre, see Levaniouk, this volume.

32. For bibliography and a new solution to the meaning of the first phrase, see Katz and Volk 2000.

33. McCone (1984) offers a good critique of the sometimes less productive ways of constructing such origins in the case of Irish materials.

34. For this method, the work of J. Nagy (1990) on "talking heads" in Greek and Irish mythic traditions has been an inspiration.

35. Sources are analyzed in Gantz 1993; for further bibliography and discussions, see Suzuki 1989, 13–14.

36. Seremetakis 1991, 46–63.

37. Partridge 1980. An example occurs in the *Caoineadh Airt Uí Laoghaire* discussed below.

38. Lysaght 1986; ÓhÓgáin 1991, 45–46.

39. A glimmering of such a folk tradition can be seen in the episode at *Od.* 4.795–841 where an *eidolon* of the sister of Penelope comes to tell her to stop grieving, that her son is alive. Because the scene occurs in a section of the poem that has artful innovations in narrative, it may be that the tradition of a ghostly *eidolon* coming to tell of a death has here, too, been stylized and varied.

40. Ó Buachalla 1998, with analysis and recent bibliography.

41. Text and translation from Ó Tuama and Kinsella 1981, 200–219. I have also consulted the commentary in Ó Tuama 1961.

42. Murphy 1998, no. 36.

43. Recent treatments of the tale do not attempt such an overall reading, although McCone (1984) provides an interesting structural interpretation in terms of other hound and hero tales.

44. Text as in Thurneysen 1935, 19, ll. 9–13, from the Book of Leinster version (ca. 1160). The somewhat expanded version in Rawlinson B.512 omits the adjective *óentama* but adds a mark after the initial song verse to indicate "and so forth"—as if other verses had once been known to the scribe or his audience: see Meyer 1894, 56, 64.

45. Meyer 1894, 56.

46. Royal Irish Academy, *Dictionary of the Irish Language, s.v.*, citing *Scottish Gaelic Studies* 6.190. It is clear that the definition has been devised to fit our passage, the first cited after the lemma. The dictionary interestingly adds, from O'Mulconry's glossary, an etymology for *cepóc* (alleged to be "Greek," *graece*): *cae + bo*. "i. *laus*." Apparently the author of this gloss took *cepóc* as a compound of which the first element is *coí*, "lamenting" (cf. *serc-coí* in the lament of Créide, above).

47. O'Curry 1873, 371–374.

48. Ibid., 374, translating from the Book of Ballymote, f01.142a. Cf. Stokes (1903, 284–285), who translates the word in this passage as "death-chant," as he does earlier (1903, 282), when it is applied to lament over Luaine's death caused by Athirne's satire. It is worth noting that this tale features a male dialogic lament over the maiden Luaine, by Conchobar and Celtchair.

49. O'Curry 1873, 374.

50. Women lament the hero and grow fast-dying grasses as part of the ritual complex. See Detienne 1994.

51. This view of the Archaic Greek hero cult and its complex poetic stylizations is deeply indebted to Nagy 1999.

52. On the homology between women's marriage and death, see Rehm 1994. It is well known that change of status in initiation rite is stylized as a death: see Burkert 1985, 260–264.

BIBLIOGRAPHY

Ackerman, R. 1987. *J. G. Frazer: His Life and Work.* Cambridge.

Alexiou, Margaret. 1974. *The Ritual Lament in Greek Tradition.* Cambridge.

——. 2002a. *After Antiquity: Greek Language, Myth, and Metaphor.* Ithaca, N.Y.

——. 2002b. *The Ritual Lament in Greek Tradition.* 2nd ed. Rev. D. Yatroma-nolakis and P. Roilos. Lanham, Md.

Aloni, A. 1998. *Cantare glorie di eroi: Comunicazione e performance poetica nella Grecia arcaica.* Turin.

Austin, Norman. 1994. *Helen of Troy and Her Shameless Phantom.* Ithaca, N.Y.

Benveniste, Émil. [1969] 1973. *Indo-European Language and Society* (Originally *Le vocabulaire des institutions indo-européennes*). Trans. E. Palmer. Coral Gables, Fla.

Boon, J. 1982. *Other Tribes, Other Scribes: Symbolic Anthropology in the Compara-tive Study of Cultures, Histories, Religions, and Texts.* Cambridge.

Burkert, Walter. 1985. *Greek Religion: Archaic and Classical.* Trans. J. Raffan. Cambridge, Mass.

Buttimer, Cornelius. 1982. *Scéla Muicce Meic Dathó:* A Reappraisal. *Proceedings of the Harvard Celtic Colloquium* 2: 61–69.

Calame, Claude. 2001. *Choruses of Young Women in Ancient Greece: Their Mor-phology, Religious Role, and Social Function.* Rev. ed. Trans. D. Collins and J. Orion. Lanham, Md.

Caraveli-Chavez, A. 1980. Bridge between Worlds: The Greek Women's Lament as Communicative Event. *Journal of American Folklore* 93: 129–157.

Clader, Linda. 1976. *Helen: The Evolution from Divine to Heroic in Greek Epic Tradition.* Leiden.

Culler, Jonathan. 1975. *Structuralist Poetics.* Ithaca, N.Y.

Danforth, L. 1982. *The Death Rituals of Rural Greece.* Princeton.

Detienne, Marcel. 1994. *The Gardens of Adonis: Spices in Greek Mythology.* Trans. J. Lloyd. Princeton. (First published 1977.)

——. 2001. *Comparer l'incomparable.* Paris.

Donato, E. 1972. The Two Languages of Criticism. In *The Structuralist Controversy,* 89–97. Baltimore, Md.

Douglas, Mary. 1982. Judgments on James Frazer. In *In the Active Voice,* ed. Mary Douglas, 272–291. London.

Dué, C. 2002. *Homeric Variations on a Lament by Briseis.* Lanham, Md.

Ebbott, Mary. 1999. The Wrath of Helen: Self-Blame and Nemesis in the *Iliad.* In *Nine Essays on Homer,* ed. M. Carlisle and O. Levaniouk, 3–20. Lanham, Md.

Edmunds, Lowell. 2001. *Intertextuality and the Reading of Roman Poetry.* Baltimore.

Ferrari, G. 1988. Hesiod's Mimetic Muses and the Strategies of Deconstruction. In *Post-structuralist Classics,* ed. Andrew Benjamin, 45–78. London.

Foley, John M. 1988. *The Theory of Oral Composition: History and Methodology.* Bloomington, Ind.

——. 1991. *Immanent Art: From Structure to Meaning in Traditional Oral Epic.* Bloomington, Ind.

——. 1999. *Homer's Traditional Art.* University Park, Pa.

Gantz, Jeffrey, trans. 1981. *Early Irish Myths and Sagas.* Harmondsworth, U.K.

Gantz, Timothy. 1993. *Early Greek Myth: A Guide to Literary and Artistic Sources.* Baltimore.

Guneratne, K. 1999. *In the Circle of the Dance: Notes of an Outsider in Nepal.* Ithaca, N.Y.

Heubeck, A., Stephanie West, and J. B. Hainsworth, eds. 1988. *A Commentary on Homer's Odyssey.* Vol. 1. Oxford.

Holst-Warhaft, Gail. 1992. *Dangerous Voices: Women's Laments and Greek Literature.* London.

Hyman, Stanley Edgar. 1959. *The Tangled Bank: Darwin, Marx, Frazer and Freud as Imaginative Writers.* New York.

Kassis, Kyriakos D. 1985. *Tragoudhia notias Peloponnesou (Mani, Taygetos, Parnonas).* Athens.

Katz, J., and K. Volk. 2000. "Mere Bellies?": A New Look at *Theogony* 26–8. *Journal of Hellenic Studies* 120: 122–131.

Kirk, Geoffrey S. 1985. The Iliad, *a Commentary.* Cambridge.

Kurke, L., and C. Dougherty, eds. 1993. *Cultural Poetics of Archaic Greece.* Cambridge.

Lonsdale, S. 1995. *Homeric Hymn to Apollo:* Prototype and Paradigm of Choral Performance. *Arion* 3: 25–40.

Lysaght, Patricia. 1986. *The Banshee: The Irish Supernatural Death-Messenger.* Dublin.

Martin, B. K. 1992. The Medieval Irish Stories About Bricriu's Feast and Mac Dathó's Pig. *Parergon* 10: 171–193.

Martin, Richard P. 1984. Hesiod, Odysseus, and the Instruction of Princes. *Transactions of the American Philological Association* 114: 29–48.

——. 1989. *The Language of Heroes: Speech and Performance in the* Iliad. Ithaca, N.Y.

——. 1997. Formulas and Speeches. In *Le style formulaire de l'épopée homérique et la théorie de l'oralité poétique: Hommage àMilman Parry,* ed. Françoise Létoublon, 263–274. Amsterdam.

——. 2000. The *Homeric Hymn to Apollo* as Contest Piece. In *Una nueva visión de la cultura griega antigua hacia el fin del milenio,* ed. Ana González de Tobia, 403–432. La Plata.

——. 2001. Just Like a Woman. In *Making Silence Speak: Women's Voices in Greek Literature and Society,* ed. A. Lardinois and L. McClure, 55–74. Princeton.

——. Forthcoming. *Ethnographica Moralia: Experiments in Interpretive Anthropology.* ed. George Marcus and Neni Panourgiá. New York.

McCone, Kim. 1984. *Aided Cheltchair MaicUthechair:* Hounds, Heroes, and Hospitallers in Early Irish Myth and Story. *Ériu* 35: 1–30.

Meyer, Kuno, ed. 1894. *Hibernica Minora.* Anecdota Oxoniensia, Medieval and Modern Series Vol.3, pt. 8. Oxford.

Morgan, G. 1973. The Laments of Mani. *Folklore* 84: 265–298.

Motsios, I. 1995. *To Elliniko moirologi.* Athens.

Murphy, Gerald. 1990. *Greek Mythology and Poetics.* Ithaca, N.Y.

——.1995. Transformations of Choral Lyric Traditions in the Context of Athenian State Theater. *Arion* 3: 41–55.

——, ed. and trans. 1998. *Early Irish Lyrics: Eighth to Twelfth Century.* New foreword by Tomás Ó Cathasaigh. Dublin.

Nagy, Gregory. 1990a. *Greek Mythology and Poetics.* Ithaca N.Y.

——. 1990b. *Pindar's Homer: The Lyric Possession of an Epic Past.* Baltimore.

——. 1995. Transformations of Choral Lyric traditions in the Context of Athenian State Theater. *Arion* 3: 41–55.

Nagy, Gregory. 1996. *Poetry as Performance: Homer and Beyond.* Cambridge.

———. 1999. *The Best of the Achaeans: Concepts of the Hero in Archaic Greek Poetry.* Rev. ed. Baltimore.

Nagy, Joseph F. 1990. Hierarchy, Heroes, and Heads: Indo-European Structures in Greek Myth. In *Approaches to Greek Myth*, ed. Lowell Edmunds, 199–238. Baltimore.

Ó Buachalla, Breandán. 1998. *An Caoine agus an Chaointeoireacht.* Dublin.

O'Curry, Eugene. 1873. *On the Manners and Customs of the Ancient Irish.* Vol. 3. Ed. W. Sullivan. London.

ÓhÓgáin, Dáithí. 1991. *Myth, Legend and Romance: An Encyclopedia of the Irish Folk Tradition.* New York.

Ó Súilleabháin, Seán. 1967. *Irish Folk Custom and Belief.* Dublin.

Ó Tuama, Seán, ed. 1961. *Caoineadh Airt Uí Laoghaire.* Dublin.

Ó Tuama, Seán, and Thomas Kinsella, trans. 1981. *An Duanaire, 1600–1900: Poems of the Dispossessed.* Mountrath, Ireland.

Panourgiá, E. Neni K. 1995. *Fragments of Death, Fables of Identity: An Athenian Anthropography.* Madison, Wisc.

Pantelia, M. 2002. Helen and the Last Song for Hector. *Transactions of the American Philological Association* 132: 21–27.

Partridge, Angela. 1980. Wild Men and Wailing Women. *Éigse* 18: 25–37.

Rehm, R. 1994. *Marriage to Death: The Conflation of Wedding and Funeral Rituals in Greek Tragedy.* Princeton.

Russo, Joseph, M. Fernando-Galliano, and A. Heubeck, eds. 1992. A *Commentary on Homer's* Odyssey. Vol. 3, Books XVII–XXIV. Oxford.

Sayers, William. 1982. Conall's Welcome to Cét in the Old Irish *Scéla Muicce Meic Dathó. Florilegium* 4: 100–108.

———.1991. Serial Defamation in Two Medieval Tales. *Oral Tradition* 6: 35–57.

Segal, Charles. 1994. *Singers, Heroes, and Gods in the* Odyssey. Ithaca, N.Y.

Seremetakis, N. 1991. *The Last Word: Women, Death, and Divination in Inner Mani.* Chicago.

Sharrock, A., and H. Morales. 2000. *Intratextuality: Greek and Roman Textual Relations.* Oxford.

Skopetea, Sophia. 1972. *Ta maniatika moiroloyia.* Athens.

Stocking, G. 1987. *Victorian Anthropology.* New York.

Sultan, N. 1999. *Exile and the Poetics of Loss in Greek Tradition.* Lanham, Md.

Suzuki, M. 1989. *Metamorphoses of Helen: Authority, Difference, and the Epic.* Ithaca, N.Y.

Thurneysen, Rudolf, ed. 1935. *Scéla muicce Meic Da Thó.* Dublin.

Tsagalis, C. 1998. The Improvised Laments in the *Iliad.* Unpublished Ph.D. dissertation, Cornell University.

———. 2004. *Epic Grief: Personal Laments in Homer's* Iliad. Berlin.

Tsouderos, Ioannes. 1976. *Kretika moiroloyia.* Athens.

Watkins, Calvert. 1995. *How to Kill a Dragon: Aspects of Indo-European Poetics.* New York.

Wilson, P. 2000. *The Athenian Institution of the* Khoregia: *The Chorus, the City, and the Stage.* Cambridge.

7

DEATH BECOMES HER

Gender and Athenian Death Ritual

KAREN STEARS

A mourning woman is not simply a producer of pity, but dangerous.
—*Foley 1993, 143*

The lot of women in Archaic and Classical Athens has been characterized as an unhappy one. They were denied access to avenues of social, political, and economic power, their status has been identified as low, and their personal freedom of movement has been conceived of as being severely restricted. The funeral, so central to Athenian social and political life, has been singled out as a reification of the male and female power relationship, and the role of women within funerary practices has been adduced as evidence in the construction of this picture; the intensity of the display of their grief served as an outlet for their own repressed frustrations. Such analyses tend to focus on gender at the expense of other issues. It is doubtful whether gender functioned as the sole means of group identity in ancient Athens. In many circumstances other aspects of social identity and relationship may have been uppermost, most notably familial relationships. By using jointly the tools of gender and kin in assessing women's duties in funerary rituals, this chapter hopes to present an alternative, more sanguine view of female status and power.

There is no single account of a contemporary Athenian funeral in the Late Archaic or Classical periods. Instead, a composite picture has to be extrapolated from literary sources as disparate as the fifth-century tragedians, fourth-century orators, and Byzantine lexicographers, together with archaeological evidence from painted pottery and burials. Of all these sources, perhaps the pottery speaks most immediately, with its scenes depicting funerary ritual. Athenian potters chose in the main to portray three scenes, the *prothesis* (the laying out of the corpse), the *ekphora* (the procession to the

139

Figure 7.1   Attic black-figure pinax depicting, on the upper level, a prothesis, and on the lower level, chariots. (Ca. 510 B.C.E. Metropolitan Museum of Art, Rogers fund, 1954. 54.11.5)

grave), and the visit to the tomb. *Prothesis* and *ekphora* are attested in Geometric pottery of the eighth century B.C.E. as well as in later styles, with the *prothesis* being more common.[1] Scenes of funerary rituals are most common in the sixth century in the black-figure style (fig. 7.1) and are less well attested in the red-figure period, ending altogether at the close of the fifth century. *Prothesis* itself still existed, as is witnessed in the arguments among inheritors in the fourth-century law courts; perhaps it had lost something of its earlier significance.[2] However, in the fifth and fourth centuries it may well be that the tomb itself (a permanent arena for display as opposed to ephemeral funerary rituals) and expenditure on it became the center for familial display within the *polis;* this would account for its popularity in the iconography of white-ground *lekythoi* (oil jars specifically intended for the grave) and for it becoming the primary objective of funerary legislation.[3]

From what we know of the *prothesis* it seems to have been a standardized set of rites: regardless of its sex, the corpse appears to have been prepared for disposal in the same manner. Upon death the eyes and mouth of the corpse were closed.[4] The body was, whenever possible, returned to its *oikos* where it was further treated by the women of the household. It was washed and then wrapped in a number of layers of fabric, including a shroud and a top cover. On the bier it was laid out with the feet toward the door and a pillow under the head. It was then decked with herbs and sometimes with garlands and occasionally jewelry; an unmarried adolescent might be adorned as if for a wedding. A jar of oil was placed by the bier, and a pot of water was set by the street door of the house, measures effecting the containment and purification of ritual pollution (*miasma*).

Thus decorated, the body was ready to be visited. It is uncertain where in the house *prothesis* took place. Funerary legislation attributed to Solon restricted the *prothesis* to the interior of the house, but the iconographic evidence is inconclusive.[5] It may well be that the location depended on the size and form of the house, the weather, and the number of guests expected; the courtyard or the *andrôn* (the public room of the household reserved for men's dining) might have been particularly suitable given the semipublic nature of the proceedings.[6] What the legislation did prohibit was the conduct of the *prothesis* in an overtly public space outside the domestic sphere, as appears to have been the practice in the Geometric period.[7]

The *prothesis* lasted for one day, probably the day after death. Both men and women participated in mourning rituals, but the gestures of each sex are clearly differentiated in representations of *prothesis* scenes from the earliest examples onward. In Geometric iconography, women adopt a pose with both arms raised to the head.[8] Above the handles of some early pots, clay mourning women are attached, again with both arms lifted to the head but with the addition of dashes of brown paint on their white-slip cheeks to indicate laceration.

In black- and red-figure scenes there is a similar gender division of position and gesture. Typically, the men enter the scene in a procession from left to right, with their arms raised in salutation, palms facing outward, perhaps performing a prepared and orderly dirge.[9] They proceed no further than the feet of the corpse and are met by the male members of the household, who return their gesture. The women in the scene appear unresponsive to the procession but continue in their lamentation, standing closely around the corpse, which is their chief focus of interest. Children often appear near the corpse or under the bier. Occasionally, a male figure may stand nearby, and these individuals are often distinguished as old by their white beards and are perhaps to be recognized as fathers and grandfathers, their pose of lamentation marking them as distinct from the main body of male mourners.[10] Also in sharp contrast to the orderly procession of men, the women are depicted as being distraught. They tear at their hair as they sing their lament, moving around the bier as they grieve. The most important position in relation to the deceased appears to have been near the head, as this is where the chief female mourner (the mother?) stands, facing or behind the head, holding either it or the shoulders or sometimes plumping the supporting pillow. Occasionally this position is occupied by an older woman with short hair who might be identified as the old wet nurse of the deceased. Short hair, however, was a mark of grief as well as slavery and so may not be a simple indicator of servile status.

A black-figure plaque in the Louvre MNB 1905 attributed to the Sappho painter is of particular interest in helping to determine whether there were special places or roles for familial members at the *prothesis*, for identifying labels are placed next to some of the figures. An *adelphos* (brother) of the deceased is a member of the procession of men that is greeted by the *pater* (father). Around the head of the male corpse stand the grandmother (*thethe*) and three aunts, each marked as *thesis*, and one of these is further identified as being paternal (*prospatros*). The *meter* (mother) holds the head of her dead son, and next to her stands her daughter, his sister (*adelphe*). That the women are grieving is shown by the words *oimoi oimoi* placed next to the heads of the aunts.

On the third day after death, in the ceremony known as the *ekphora*, the corpse was taken out to the cemetery for burial. It was transported on either a bier or a cart in a procession that in vase paintings usually leads from left to right. Both men and women attended the *ekphora*, males usually leading the procession and the women following, lamenting openly. They may have been accompanied in their lamentations by musicians, for flautists also appear in depictions of the scene; perhaps this was meant to show that some of the women were hired professional mourners.

The burial or cremation of the corpse was presumably a male-led affair, for they would have had to manhandle the body, sacrifice animals, and perhaps dig or oversee the grave digging or tomb construction. At the end of the burial rites the mourners returned to the home of the deceased to partake in the *perideipnon*, the funeral meal, and bathe, purifying themselves from the ritual pollution to which they had been exposed. Further rituals were performed on behalf of the dead, the third- and ninth-day rites, *ta trita* and *ta enata*, in which food, libations, and other offerings were placed on the new tomb. Death was followed by a mourning period of thirty days, which was ritually closed by the performance of further rites on the thirtieth day (*triakostia*). At this point, the house of the deceased would be swept, and the sweepings, *kallysmata*, were probably placed on the tomb; the *oikos* and the wider kin groups were now free from the pollution of death.

It was these rites from *prothesis* to *triakostia* that were the kernel of Athenian funerary practice. Their correct performance might help to underpin a claim on the estate of the deceased by those who funded and dominated them. For this reason they could be rituals of great financial, legal, and even political importance and hence liable to be used as arenas for conspicuous consumption and associated rivalry, perhaps even revenge. Funerary laws attributed to Solon and, by Cicero, to a period some time after him are concerned with the size and extravagance of funerals. These laws, whatever their date, appear to be witness to the social and political tensions manifested at, and presumably by, funerals. These stresses on the system and the concomitant legislation have been associated with the rise of the Athenian *polis* and the changing relations between it and Athenian familial groupings, and with the growth of ideologies concerning political and legal equality—for instance, the establishment of the public burial of the war dead and the *epitaphios logos* (the annual state funeral speech)—as well as with the social control of women.[11]

The Solonian laws, while advocating a general diminution of funerary rites, such as forbidding the sacrifice of an ox at the graveside, specifically stipulate the expected roles and behavior of women mourners.[12] Only females within the kin group of the *anchisteia* (a bilateral kinship grouping centered on an *ego* and extending to the children of cousins) were allowed to attend either the *prothesis* or the *ekphora*; the latter had to take place before dawn, and in it the women walked separately from the men. The only exceptions to this general prohibition were women over the age of sixty years. Those participating were forbidden to lacerate their faces or sing set dirges (*threnoi pepoiêmenoi*). Enforcement of this legislation may not have been entirely successful as some time afterward a further law was enacted that attempted to limit large gatherings of men and women at funerals in order to control the amount of lamentation.[13]

This body of legislation should not be taken as being specifically aimed at women even though they were the central producers of noisy lamentation at the funerals.[14] The laws that prohibited the singing of *threnoi* and the laceration of the flesh, as well as the numbers of women, were probably aimed at curbing professional mourners as much as familial members; in which case, the legislation may have been specifically targeted against those families who were wealthy enough to indulge in such display. Thus the legislation was directed at excessively disruptive and even socially dangerous display by kin groups and not at women per se. The inference of these laws is that women mourned in a more extrovert fashion than did men.

From this brief outline of funerary practice it appears that the tasks and roles undertaken by participants were for the most part allotted along the lines of a sexual division. Women tended the corpse before and during *prothesis* and appear to have mourned in a more overt fashion than men, displaying greater levels of emotional grief. Furthermore, in general, men appear to have paid more attention to their guests than to the corpse at the *prothesis* but then seem to have taken charge of proceedings during the *ekphora*. Last, the Solonian funerary legislation restricted the number of women who could attend a private, and indeed public, funeral, but the attendance of men was unrestricted. We now need to ask why this division existed and what it signified.

During the period from death to *triakostia* and the final release of the soul from this world, those near the dead, both physically and by blood or marital ties, were thought to be ritually polluted.[15] This ritual pollution (*miasma*) has been considered a factor in accounting for the prominent role of women in death ritual.[16] Like death, birth was regarded as a source of *miasma*, and women, because of their childbearing capacity, were therefore seen as latently both polluted and polluting. For this reason, the argument goes, they were allotted the role of dealing with the pollution of death.

This argument requires closer examination. Here the parallel of child-birth is indeed instructive, though for reasons rather different from those outlined above. Like death, childbirth incurred a period of pollution for the household concerned and was followed by a series of purificatory rites of the fifth, tenth, and fortieth days. Anyone coming into contact with a woman who had just given birth was thought to be polluted for three days, and those who attended the birth were polluted until the fifth-day rites. The new mother was by this time no longer polluting, although she was apparently still regarded as polluted herself. It would seem then that it was the act of childbirth that was impure rather than the woman herself, although the *miasma* may have been centered on her.[17] One might maintain that "since women could not escape the pollution of giving birth, as men could, they were presumably better suited to deal with the pollution of death."[18] But there were other sources of pollution from which men could not escape, namely, the *miasma* surrounding sexual intercourse, which appears to have been centered on semen.[19] Thus the argument that the "natural" pollution of women made them particularly suitable as carers of the dead is inherently untenable. Indeed, women were not apparently considered to be any more affected than men by the pollution of death. Although measures were undertaken during *prothesis* to contain the *miasma* of the corpse, there is no evidence that it was considered less polluting at burial than at *prothesis*; thus, the men who carried the pall or buried the corpse were just as polluted as the women who prepared the body. Moreover, there is no evidence that women at Athens were obliged to undergo a longer period of mourning than were men. Rather, men and women associated with the household affected by death were considered equally ritually polluted until the *triakostia*. It was the degree of kin relationship to the deceased, rather than the sex of the mourner, that determined the level of *miasma* encountered and thus the level of correct ritual action necessary.

The ultimate implication of the line of argument linking women with the *miasma* of death is that men, as the power-holding section of society, would wherever possible have employed women to mediate pollution, which was seen as something to be feared and avoided. Females, in other words, were "given" death because they were of a lower social status and held less power than men.[20] This reasoning is based on a number of assumptions: that the mediation of pollution is indicative of lower social status and of marginality; and, even more importantly, that "power" is a unified concept. These are, I think, fundamental errors and ones that I shall attempt to rectify in the remainder of this chapter. Participation in funerals, it will be argued, served in fact as a means for the construction and display of women's power in both the domestic and the political arenas.

In seeking explanations for women's prominence in death ritual that go beyond that of inferior status, it is instructive to compare funerary practice with other rites of passage, such as those associated with marriage and, once again, childbirth. In these too, gender division was a significant feature.

Marriage, which like death was a crucial transitional stage for members of both sexes, was marked by elaborate rituals. Wedding scenes are common in Athenian vase painting, and, as with funerary scenes, the artists developed a limited repertoire concentrating on a small group of images, the most popular scenes being the adornment of the bride and the procession to the house of the groom.[21] These scenes betray a startling similarity to the funerary scenes. The bride is dressed within the interior of the *oikos*, surrounded by women. She is washed, anointed, bejeweled, and decked in fine clothes, a passive object just like the corpse. Then she makes the journey to her new home, often on a cart or chariot, accompanied by men and women and the sound of flutes. Whereas the funerary *ekphora* was restricted to the dark hours before daylight, the bridal journey seems to have taken place in the darkness of the evening; it was certainly lit by special torches held by the bride's mother. Females played a major part in these aspects of marriage ritual, although their presence was not required for the betrothal (*engye*) of the bride and groom. Indeed, the bride herself did not have to be at this ceremony, which took the form of a legally binding agreement between her present legal guardian, her father if alive, and her future husband, who would become her new legal guardian. This rite constituted a pledge that might be brought to public scrutiny if challenged or broken in any way. It was made between the head of an *oikos* and the potential head of another *oikos*; women did not need to be present, as this was essentially a public not a private concern. But the *gamos*, the marriage, was a different affair. The removal of a bride from her natal home and the consequent change in status from virgin (*parthenos*) to bride (*nymphe*), and ultimately through childbirth to that of woman (*gyne*), were personal rites that had to be undertaken carefully and properly in case of mistake. For, as with any rite of passage, the liminal state of those at its center was a potential cause for concern; the bride might be considered as an individual capable of pollution, as was the corpse.[22]

The rituals surrounding childbirth are less well documented than those at marriage and death. As death witnessed the loss of a member of a household, an event marked by rituals of separation between the deceased and the living and the incorporation of the former into the company of the dead, so birth was marked by rites incorporating a new member into the family. The new mother did not take a very active role in these rites, most notably because she was thought to be still polluted by the birth, perhaps until the cessation of postpartum bleeding (see above). But the baby would undergo a series of gradually more public appearances, overseen by his or her father. For it was the acceptance of legitimate paternity by the father that sanctioned full incorporation into both the *oikos* and the wider social, religious, and political body. The rituals concerning the mother, perhaps because of their private and therefore mainly female aspect, are largely unclear.[23]

In both wedding and birth ritual we find men taking the lead when the public domain impinged on the rite. But rites of passage affected not only the public but the private sphere, and here women as members and, indeed, the re-creators of the familial group were essential and sometimes dominant performers. Thus it may be useful when considering the different roles undertaken by the sexes at funerals to consider this public/ private dimension.

The *prothesis* was an event staged within the house. As an area devoted chiefly to private life, this may be thought to have been ideologically the space that was properly female; we might not be surprised to find women at the heart of this ritual.[24] A comparison with wedding ritual is particularly illuminating in addressing the argument that women prepared the corpse because of some link between themselves and pollution inherent in ideologies concerning their biology. Instead, let us view the *prothesis* as an adornment of the corpse, comparable to that of the bride. It was a time when females might employ their most expensive unguents, bring out their most finely woven and embroidered textiles, produce their specially bought pottery, and sing songs most expressive of their emotion, albeit sorrow rather than joy. Women were the center of the affair; it was their actions that held the attention of the pot painter and which were thought worthy of depiction. Their proper enactment of these rituals ensured not only the peaceful departure of the soul of the deceased to Hades but also the containment of the *miasma* of death and the ritual health of the household. It is easy for modern observers living in a society largely devoid of meaningful ritual to underplay the importance of correct praxis, but we should not underestimate the latent power that those in charge of ritual performance might wield. It may not have been the financial, legal, or political power that we ourselves value, but ritual knowledge was nevertheless a potent force. Hence, actions performed by women in the domestic domain may be thought of as enhancing their status rather than reinforcing their inferiority.

Men, usually associated with the "male" political world as opposed to the "female" domestic sphere (a distinction perhaps overemphasized in modern studies), also inhabited this domestic space. Therefore, we find them present at the *prothesis*, and sometimes, as close and in particular as elderly relatives of the deceased, they displayed their grief and mourned. But even within the house they were still linked to the public sphere; so it was they who greeted the visiting male mourners. At the *ekphora*, the funeral left the semipublic world of the *oikos* and entered fully the public world of the *polis*. Here the men, having played a secondary role at the *prothesis*, were required to take center stage, leading the procession and perhaps carrying the corpse. Women were still present, but in the Late Archaic and Classical city their attention-grabbing lamentations had been curtailed to some extent by legislation, and they were obliged to walk separately from the men behind the pall or cart. The sex-based divisions visible in Athenian funerary ritual may therefore be seen to be influenced by, as well as constructing, the concept of space as gendered. The distinction between private/female and public/male space should not be overstated, for males and females operated in both spheres; however, it is a useful tool in attempting to explain patterns of thought and associated behavior.

A distinction can also be discerned in the manner in which males and females expressed their grief. At the *prothesis* men are shown processing in orderly fashion, in contrast to the disheveled women who stand around the corpse. This restrained behavior may be as indicative of a form of social control as is the excessive emotionality of the women. Grief is a recognized psychological phenomenon comprising "a stereotyped set of psychological and physiological reactions of biological origin," whereas mourning consists of a set of conventional behavioral responses to death, both sanctioned and required by society.[25] As has long been noted, individuals who experience grief may be socially compelled either to restrict or to elaborate its display, and those who feel no emotion at all may be forced to undertake extreme forms of emotional behavior in mourning.[26] The contrast in male and female modes of mourning as portrayed in Athenian art may be witness to such strictures. The control of emotional display by Athenian men was a tenet central to the ideology of their gender construction and, moreover, their ethnic identity. Excessive emotionalism, of which mourning was a manifestation, was considered a typical female trait associated with lack of self-control. It was regarded not only as unmanly but also as un-Greek and something undertaken by those who were opposite to both constructs, namely, women and barbarians. Thus, the only male chorus that laments in Athenian tragedy is that of old men in *The Persians*.[27] That is not to maintain that men did not grieve or mourn; indeed, it was thought odd that Demosthenes did not mourn properly when his daughter died, even though he was attempting to make a political gesture.[28] The presence in the vase paintings of grieving older men who are distinct from the processing men who greet the corpse more calmly points to the conclusion that emotional distress may have been culturally permissible for aged fathers but not for younger men; this has implications for Athenian concepts of masculinity. It also suggests that the relationship between ceremonial display and gender construction may provide an additional explanation for the prominence of women in funerary rituals.

Just as men may have been obliged by social constraint to conceal emotion on occasions (whether consciously or subconsciously), so women may well have been encouraged to express a level of grief in lamentation that they themselves did not feel. The task of lamenting the dead noisily may not have come naturally to more distant members of the *anchisteia* who might not have been personally well acquainted with the deceased. However, such women may not have felt "compelled" to attend the funeral. On the contrary, they may have regarded attendance as a privilege. The fact that those who were allowed to attend were restricted by law may well have served to enhance their (self-perceived?) status, and this may have served as an encouragement to the level of emotion displayed, whether genuine grief or not. Moreover, the female members of a powerful kin group may well have realized that public recognition, by nonfamilial males attending the funeral, of both the extent and the care with which they carried out proper ritual, including lamentation, was a means of acquiring reputation and honor, *philotimia*, for the kin group as a whole. Modest and "correct" female behavior was after all a reflection of an ordered and properly run household. Such behavior may also have secured the rights of a woman's legal guardian (*kyrios*) to inherit; thus women may have been extremely willing to participate. We might remember that self-awareness of gender and the associated solidarity that it implies may often take second place to kin or other affiliations.

I am not suggesting that all the female members of the *anchisteia* would have participated in every burial. The variable structure of the *oikos* and *anchisteia* and the presumably varied reality of these terms for individuals in Athenian society imply that there was no single model for participation by relatives at an Athenian funeral. There is, however, an ideological and legal norm displayed within the forensic literature of the fourth century, which often draws on the Solonian legislation, with its references to the *anchisteia*. These speeches frequently imply that there was a direct correlation between, on the one hand, possession of a corpse (occasionally involving its theft) and being seen to bury it properly; and on the other hand, presenting a claim to an estate. And one aspect of a fitting burial was the requirement that the rites be overseen by the correct members of the deceased's household. Indeed at [Demosthenes] 43.63, the absence of the opponent's wife and mother at the *prothesis* and *ekphora* is used as ammunition by the plaintiff against the rival claim to the estate. In fact, the plaintiff very cleverly turns around the Solonian legislation that stipulates that women outside the *anchisteia* may not attend by arguing that the law actually obliges (*keleuei*) women within that kinship unit to participate in the rites. Might we not hypothesize that some women within kin groups may well have recognized and even exploited the centrality of their role in funerary ritual in legitimizing their *kyrios*'s claim to an estate? This may have especially been the case if the *kyrios*'s claim was dependent on a cognatic relationship, that is, a relationship through the female line.

As Van Gennep showed at the turn of the last century, death rituals are a means of "healing" a social group that has lost a member. That women were integral to the correct functioning of rites of passage, such as weddings, funerals, and birth rituals—and therefore responsible for the actual and ritual health of the *oikos* and, by wider association, the *polis*—has been underemphasized. It may well be further proof that women were not simply passively confined within the *oikos* but, rather, were its very lifeblood and that without them it could not exist properly, either physically, economically, or ritually. The establishment of an annual public funeral for the war dead may have directly impinged on women's ritual authority within the *oikos*. With no corpse to care for (the dead were cremated on the battlefield) and with their lamentations effectively suppressed by the institution in the early fifth century of a state funeral speech, the *epitaphios logos*, they were handicapped to the level of silence.[29] As with the funerary legislation enacted by Solon and others, when the *polis* wished to curtail the powers of kin groups in death ritual it struck out at its most vociferous members—its women.

Funerary legislation in particular shows that women's ritual activity within the *oikos* could be of significance for the *polis* as a whole. This link between private and public spheres is discernible in other aspects of women's involvement with rites of passage. These rites served to mark time within the history of a family, and it may be that as keepers of ritual knowledge, and as essential witnesses of past kin-based events, women could become powerful figures within the household and may have been the kernels of the *oikos*'s self-knowledge and memory. Athenian marriage patterns may have served to increase this likelihood. Middle-aged men tended to marry girls who had just passed menarche.[30] If a woman was lucky enough to survive childbirth and reach middle or even old age, she was also likely to have been widowed; thus she may have lived on to become the oldest member of a household. When old women were associated with the telling of old-fashioned traditions, might these not have included family histories? Plato writes of "the sort of things old women sing."[31] Might this not include old familial traditions and stories as well as myths in our sense of the word? These "songs" might have been sung to children to educate them about their ancestors, but it seems as likely that the "songs" were essentially laments.[32]

It is thus possible that female lamentations served as one of the media for the construction of a female and private history of the kin group. This memory may have told of the fate of individuals over generations, both men and women. Women's important role as overseers of familial rites of passage may have been integral in their ability to construct a history of the family. Indeed, women may be regarded in a sense as the guardians and perhaps inventors of aspects of familial tradition, a tradition that could well have been more detailed and personal than the familial record constructed by the archaeologically visible funerary inscriptions and tomb groupings.[33] Remembering the dead was of course only one aspect of lamentation; other elements might include the bewailing of one's loss and frustrations, expression of one's grief, and perhaps incitement to revenge.[34]

The funeral itself was not the only occasion at which laments might be sung: ethnographic comparisons suggest they may have been performed in nonfunerary contexts, such as when toiling in the fields or wool working.[35] But perhaps a more certain retelling of these familial histories within lamentation came at the monthly and annual visits to the tomb site. The tombs themselves may have served as mnemonic devices for the inspiration of lament singing, and groups of burials, *periboloi*, may well have occasioned extended singing of laments for a number of recent ancestors. Tombs were situated on roadsides and outside city gates and walls, both in cemeteries and on private land. Lament singing here would have been one of the means by which the familial group could construct and project a public face, to draw attention to and to elaborate on funerary monuments, which grew in size and expenditure through the fifth and fourth centuries.

The foregoing discussion suggests that women's lamentations may have fulfilled a number of social functions. By providing demonstrations of their observance of "correct" female behavior in relation to ritual, they enhanced both the women's status and that of their kin group. In addition, they may have helped to legitimate claims on an estate, have underpinned a family's ritual health, and have acted as a vehicle for the construction and promotion of family history. Functions such as these indicate that the impact of women's lamentations was by no means confined to the private sphere. In the course of funerary observances women were, moreover, able to cross the boundary between public and private in a more direct and physical way. It is something of a commonplace to write of women's confinement within the *oikos* in Archaic and Classical Athens, and while one would not wish to refute the ideology and ideal of the gendered division of Athenian space, it may be worth restating a point made by John Gould: "The world outside, the public world, is the world of men . . . with one striking exception. In the sacred and ritual activities of the community the active presence of women in the public world is not merely tolerated but required."[36]

Funerary ritual required not only that women should participate noisily at the *prothesis* and *ekphora* but also that they should continue to visit the tomb, certainly on the anniversaries of an individual's death and perhaps if they wished at other times. These visits, and the preparations for them, are a common motif on white-ground *lekythoi*.[37] We may need to reassess our picture of female usage of public space; it may be that women could use a visit to a tomb (and also a shrine or temple) to access the public world. A woman outside her house with no business to be so was an object of male concern, but a woman accompanied by other women, slaves, or otherwise and carrying objects for ritual use not only may have escaped censure but may have even earned praise. The singing of lament at grave-sides would have provided a meeting place for related women otherwise isolated in their respective *oikoi* and would have enabled them not only to become the focus of attention by lamenting but also to catch up on family news and to glean other information by observing comings and goings from the vantage point of the tomb, which was so helpfully placed in most conspicuous locations. We might characterize these actions as gossip and nosiness, but are they not also indirect ways of obtaining knowledge and hence a kind of power? Participation in birth and wedding rituals may have served much the same purpose. Clearly, the public/private distinction, though providing a useful basis for analysis, cannot be rigidly applied as an explanation for gender division in relation to funerary practices.

Death rituals are complex social and emotional phenomena, and my analysis touches on only some aspects. While arguing that women's partic-ipation in funerary rites needs to be reevaluated in a more positive light than has previously been the case, it must not be forgotten that at the center of women's lot in lamentation was a display of emotionality that both underpinned and reconstructed ideologies of the illogicality of a woman's nature and her essential lack of self-authority and control. For Aristotle, this was evidence enough that women needed to be controlled by men.[38] The display of emotion by women therefore confirmed and reinforced the belief that, if left uncontrolled, women would revert to a wild and untamed condition.[39] In this way women's behavior at funerals helped to strengthen the dominant ideology concerning female gender, and thus the construction of femininity was maintained. When women who did not conform to expected behavioral patterns (viz., adulteresses) were barred from participating in events, those who did take part may have valued their status of conformity all the more. This reinforced an imposed ideology that was already underpinning the women's behavior and treatment and indeed their very status and social value.[40] On this basis [Demosthenes] can claim that decent women would be outraged by the thought that Neaira, a former prostitute and of noncitizen status, participated in public ritual.[41]

It is always easy in this sort of study to overlook the fact that individuals in history did not merely function in terms of ideologies and structures but were sentient beings. Athenian men and women mourned because many of them felt acute grief and loss. But the fact remains that as a sex, women were also a medium through which a kin group was able to display "correct" grief and emotion, even if not actually felt, both for the kin group itself and for the social whole. This grief was "required" as one of the means by which the social crisis initiated by a death was resolved. As Rosenblatt, Walsh, and Jackson have shown, the fact that females cross-culturally display emotion more than males may be indicative of the cross-cultural subordination and socialization of women by men.[42] However, though as a gender group women might have had to conform to ideologically sanctioned norms of emotional behavior at funerals and were expected to handle the polluting corpse more than were men, this was nevertheless a situation that could be exploited by women. The overseeing and performance of rituals within the private domain, which often overlapped into the public, could serve to express and enhance the status of an individual or a group of women as powerful members of the *oikos* and indeed of their *oikos* within the *polis*. Women may be regarded as controllers of ritual pollution within society, as ritual timekeepers of the kin group, as guardians of familial traditions and histories, and as media for the display of kin group prestige. This is not to argue that females were empowered members of Athenian society, for in many important areas this was patently not the case. But these areas tend to be those most esteemed in our own societies: the economic, the legal, and the political spheres. In religion and ritual, arenas that our own societies value little or indeed may even denigrate, we may find an alternative picture.

Although the funeral may have been one of those arenas of ritual practice that served to construct dominant ideologies about female gender, and hence reinforce notions of the inferiority of women as a sex, in the actual performance of the rites, women may have been able to wield some power and attempt to assert and enhance their status as active individuals within the kin group. Ritual activity may also have functioned as an alternative access to other kinds of power, based on meetings with other women and on outings into the public world, a spatial domain that has for too long been viewed as simply male. Participation in funerary ritual would in this way have been one of the means of enhancing female status, rather than a way of emphasizing the social inferiority of women as a gender. Hence, ideologies dominant in social discourse may have been subverted in social action.

ACKNOWLEDGMENTS

This chapter is reprinted from *The Sacred and the Feminine in Ancient Greece*, edited by Sue Blundell and Margaret Williamson. Copyright © 1998 Routledge. Reproduced by permission of Taylor & Francis Books UK. I would like to express my thanks to Sue Blundell and Margaret William-son for their patience in extremis and to Sally Humphries, Lin Foxhall, and Mark Trewin for their comments on various versions of this chapter.

NOTES

1. Ahlberg 1971; Andronikos 1968; Boardman 1955; Kurtz 1984; Shapiro 1991; Zschietzschmann 1928. For other funerary scenes, see Kurtz and Boardman 1971, plates 36–37; Mommsen 1984.

2. There may have been a shift in artistic taste or fashion with regard to the extravagance of the practice, the scene itself, or the ritual pots it adorned. The popularity of sculpted funerary monuments from the end of the fifth century onward may also have been a contributing factor.

3. Shapiro 1991; Snodgrass 1980; Stears 1993.

4. But see Shapiro 1991 for gender differences in associated iconography.

5. Boardman 1955; Garland 1985, 1989.

6. Jameson 1990; Nevett 1995.

7. Ahlberg 1971.

8. Ibid.

9. Shapiro 1991.

10. Ibid.

11. Alexiou 1974; Foley 1993; Garland 1985; Holst-Warhaft 1992; Humphreys 1980; Loraux [1981] 1986; Seaford 1994.

12. [Dem.] 43.62; Plut. *Solon* 21; Cic. *de leg.* 2.64.

13. Cic. *de leg.* 2.65.

14. Plato *Laws* 800e; Hdt. 2.61.

15. Parker 1983.

16. Havelock 1982; Shapiro 1991.

17. Menstruation was not considered polluting (Parker 1983, 101–103). Contrast the lot of women as mourners among the Merina of Madagascar, where the pollution associated with menstruation is of relevance for their role in funerary ritual; Bloch 1971, 1982.

18. Shapiro 1991, 635.

19. Parker 1983.

20. On the danger of confusing gender roles with gender symbolism, see Dubisch 1986.

21. Oakley and Sinos 1993.
22. Van Gennep 1909.
23. Garland 1990; Parker 1983.
24. Gould 1980.
25. Averill 1968, 721; Bowlby 1961; Lindemann 1944.
26. Mauss 1921; Rosenblatt, Walsh, and Jackson 1971; Stears 1993.
27. Dover 1974; Fortenbaugh 1975; Hall 1989. (For another perspective on this point, see Suter, this volume.)
28. Plutarch *Demosthenes* 22.
29. Holst-Warhaft 1992; Loraux [1981] 1986. For a corrective to this statement, see Suter, this volume, esp. n. 24.
30. Garland 1990.
31. Plato *Lysis* 205b.
32. For examples of laments constructed around histories of past familial members, see Holst-Warhaft 1992.
33. Stears 1995.
34. Alexiou 1974; Foley 1993; Holst-Warhaft 1992.
35. Caraveli 1986.
36. Gould 1980, 50.
37. Shapiro 1991.
38. Dover 1974; Fortenbaugh 1975.
39. Gould 1980.
40. For a slur on virginity at Panathenaia, see Thuc. 6.56 ff.; [Arist.] *Ath. Pol.* 18. Cf. Ar. *Thesm.* 294; Isaeus 6.50; Luc. *Dial. Meretr.* 2.1.
41. [Dem.] 59.110 ff.
42. Rosenblatt, Walsh, and Jackson 1971.

BIBLIOGRAPHY

Ahlberg, G. 1971. Prothesis *and* Ekphora *in Greek Geometric Art. SIMA* 32. Göteborg.
Alexiou, Margaret. 1974. *The Ritual Lament in Greek Tradition.* Cambridge.
Andronikos, M. 1968. *Totenkult. Archaeologica Homerica* 3. Göttingen.
Averill, R. 1968. Grief: Its Nature and Significance. *Psychological Bulletin* 70: 721–748.
Bloch, M. 1971. *Placing the Dead: Tombs, Ancestral Villages, and Kinship Organisations in Madagascar.* London.
——. 1982. Death, Women and Power. In *Death and the Regeneration of Life,* M. Bloch and J. Parry, 211–230. Cambridge.
Boardman, John. 1955. Painted Funerary Plaques and Some Remarks on Prothesis. *Annual of the British School at Athens* 50: 51–56.
Bowlby, J. 1961. Processes of Mourning. *International Journal of Psychoanalysis* 42: 317–340.
Caraveli, Anna. 1981. Bridge Between Worlds: The Greek Women's Lament as Communicative Event. *Journal of American Folklore* 93: 129–157.
——. 1986. The Bitter Wounding: the Lament as Social Protest in Rural Greece. In *Gender and Power in Rural Greece,* ed. Jill Dubisch, 169–194. Princeton.
Dover, Kenneth J. 1974. *Greek Popular Morality in the Time of Plato and Aristotle.* Oxford.

Dubisch, Jill. 1986. Culture Enters through the Kitchen: Women, Food and Social Boundaries in Rural Greece. In *Gender and Power in Rural Greece*, ed. Jill Dubisch, 195–214. Princeton.

Foley, Helene P. 1993. The Politics of Lamentation. In *Tragedy, Comedy, and the Polis*, ed. A. H. Sommerstein, S. Halliwell, J. Henderson, and B. Zimmerman, 101–143. Bari.

Fortenbaugh, W. W. 1975. *Aristotle on Emotion*. London.

Garland, R. 1985. *The Greek Way of Death*. Ithaca, N.Y.

——. 1989. The Well-Ordered Corpse: An Investigation into the Motives behind Greek Funerary Legislation. *Bulletin of the Institute of Classical Studies* 36: 1–15.

——. 1990. *The Greek Way of Life from Conception to Old Age*. London.

Gould, John P. 1980. Law, Custom and Myth: Aspects of the Social Position of Women in Classical Athens. *Journal of Hellenic Studies* 100: 38–59.

Hall, Edith. 1989. *Inventing the Barbarian: Greek Self-Definition through Tragedy*. Oxford.

Havelock, C. M. 1982. Mourners on Greek Vases: Remarks on the Social History of Women. In *Feminism and Art History*, ed. Norma Broude and Mary DuBose Garrard, 45–61. New York.

Holst-Warhaft, Gail. 1992. *Dangerous Voices: Women's Laments and Greek Literature*. London.

Humphreys, Sarah C. 1980. Family Tombs and Tomb Cult in Ancient Athens—Tradition or Traditionalism? *Journal of Hellenic Studies* 100: 96–126.

Jameson, M. H. 1990. Domestic Space in the Greek City-State. In *Domestic Architecture and the Use of Space*, ed. S. Kent, 92–113. Cambridge.

Kurtz, D. C. 1984. Vases for the Dead, an Attic Selection. 750–400. In *Ancient Greek and Related Pottery Symposium 5*, ed. H. A. G. Brijder, 314–328. Allard Pierson Series. Amsterdam.

Kurtz, D. C., and J. Boardman. 1971. *Greek Burial Customs*. London.

Lindemann, E. 1944. The Symptomatology and Management of Acute Grief. *American Journal of Psychiatry* 101: 141–148.

Loraux, Nicole. [1981] 1986. *The Invention of Athens: The Funeral Oration in the Classical City*. Trans. A. Sheridan. London.

Mauss, M. 1921. L'Expression obligatoire des sentiments (rituels oraux funéraires australiens). *Journal de Psychologie* 18: 425 ff.

Mommsen, H. 1984. Der Grabpinax des Exekias mit den trauernden Frauen. In *Ancient Greek and Related Pottery Symposium 5*, ed. H. A. G. Brijder, 329–333. Allard Pierson Series. Amsterdam.

Nevett, L. 1995. The Organisation of Space in Classical and Hellenistic Houses. In *Time, Tradition and Society in Greek Archaeology*, ed. N. Spencer, 89–108. London.

Oakley, J., and R. Sinos. 1993. *The Wedding in Ancient Athens*. Madison, Wisc.

Parker, R. 1983. *Miasma: Pollution and Purification in Early Greek Religion*. Oxford.

Rosenblatt, P. C., R. Walsh, and A. Jackson, eds. 1971. *Grief and Mourning in Cross-Cultural Perspective*. New Haven.

Seaford, Richard. 1994. *Reciprocity and Ritual: Homer and Tragedy in the Developing City-State*. Oxford.

Shapiro, H. A. 1991. The Iconography of Mourning in Athenian Art. *American Journal of Archaeology* 95: 629–656.

Snodgrass, A. M. 1980. *Archaic Greece*. London.

Stears, Karen. 1993. Women and the Family in the Funerary Ritual and Art of Classical Athens. Unpublished Ph.D. dissertation, King's College, London.

———. 1995. Dead Women's Society: Constructing Female Gender in Classical Athenian Funerary Sculpture. In *Time, Tradition and Society in Greek Archaeology*, ed. N. Spencer, 109–131. London.

Van Gennep, A. 1909. *Les Rites de passage*. Paris.

Zschietzschmann, W. 1928. Die Darstellung der "prothesis" in der griechischen Kunst. *Mitteilungen des Deutschen Archäologischen Instituts (Athenische Abteilung)* 53: 17–47.

8

MALE LAMENT IN
GREEK TRAGEDY

Ann Suter

Much work has been done recently on the dramatic use of ritual lament in tragedy.[1] A pervasive assumption of this work is that, because ritual lament was a female responsibility in real life, it was a female activity in tragedy. McClure even calls it the "normative" speech genre for women in tragedy; it has come to be seen as the female genre par excellence both in real life and onstage.[2] In this essay I question that assumption and attempt to redress the imbalance in the focus of current scholarship by marshaling new material from tragedy. It will be seen that, if we had only the evidence of tragedy to inform us, we might not see lament as a particularly gendered genre. At the same time, it seems clear that ritual lament was a female activity in real life in fifth-century B.C.E. Athens, and it is argued that lamentation was perhaps discouraged, even scorned, in men in real life.[3] This essay, however, does not assume that lament *in tragedy* is a properly female activity. Rather, it undertakes to determine exactly how gender-related such activity in fact was *in tragedy* and then considers some possible patterns in male tragic lament and if attitudes toward males lamenting in tragedy were different from those determining what was expected of a man in everyday life. I will argue that the issue of the gendering of lament has not been posed precisely enough—everyone laments, both in tragedy and in real life. Rather, it is a question of the manner and gestures of male and female lamentation, which seem to have become more gendered over time, and perhaps also of the different dramatic functions performed by female and male lament in tragedy, each gendered in its own way.

I do *not* argue that ritual lament was not the most noticeable means of public expression permitted women in ancient Greece. It probably was—at least, the most noticeable to men. That is not the same thing as saying, however, that it was an exclusively or overwhelmingly female genre. It was not—at least in tragedy. What it was in real life is another question. The evidence of tragedy, however, has come to be used as evidence for real life, and it is important to assess that evidence correctly. It is argued that the treatment of lament in tragedy shows it to be a female genre and that males lamenting are in various ways criticized and stigmatized for doing so. At the same time, it is argued that the male in tragedy is taking over the female voice in lament. These arguments pose a logical problem: Does the lamenting male present an image of power, in that he is taking over the one means women had of speaking powerfully in public? Or is he an image of weakness, in that he is feminized? Finally, it is argued that efforts by males to control female lamentation in tragedy increased through the fifth century, reflecting both funeral legislation aimed at controlling it in real life and the introduction of the *epitaphios logos* as the preferred public way to commemorate the military dead in Athens.[4]

Rather than taking lament as properly a female activity and then saying that a lamenting male has "a compromised gender status," I will investigate just how gender related this activity is in tragedy.[5] Rather than seeing a reflection of real life in just a few passages of lamentation, I will investigate what a more comprehensive examination of the laments in their contexts in tragedy may show us.

I base my findings on a study by Elinor Wright, whose careful analysis of the meters and stylistic features of tragic lamentation permits the first comprehensive identification of represented lament for the human dead in tragedy by a set of objective criteria.[6] Beginning with passages where a ritual lament is surely being portrayed (*Pers.* 908–1077; *Seven* 961–1004), Wright isolates "essential recurring features" that "seem by their frequent appearance to represent laments for the audience."[7] She adds to standard guidelines for identifying lament (themes, metaphors, imagery; referred to as "topoi" by Wright and in this essay) certain stylistic features (anaphora, anadiplosis, polyptoton, cries, repetitions).[8] Then she identifies and analyzes the meters and metrical development characteristic of tragic lament.[9] The metrical signposts of tragic lament are antiphony and a bipartite progression in which the first part of the lament is in a lyric meter, usually anapests or iambs, and the second part, beginning always with a new strophe, is in iambo-dochmiacs and exhibits a heightening of emotion and a sudden increase in the speed of responsion.[10]

The essential factors that Wright isolates as diagnostic of lamentation in tragedy may or may not derive from actual ritual lament; it is not possible to know. Nevertheless, the persistent presence of certain features seems designed to trigger in the audience the emotional response that a lament would.[11] If all of these features are present, Wright terms the passage a "full" lament. Often, only some of the essentials appear together; these occasions she identifies as "reduced" laments. The missing elements are (always) a location at the end of the play (necessary for a full lament) and (usually) the complete and specific metrical progression outlined above. Dramatic context, subject matter, typical lament imagery and themes, and stylistic features indicate the presence of lament in these situations, as well as, sometimes, short runs of iambo-dochmiacs. The purpose of a reduced lament is similar in all its appearances: to integrate lamentation into an unclimactic moment of the play while permitting the action to progress.[12]

Wright identifies forty-two passages containing these lament elements. (See the appendix.[13]) In eighteen, a male laments; in twenty-six, a female does. These are usually solos. The respondent, usually the chorus, is male in fourteen and female in eleven. Five plays have only male lamentation; six have only female. These figures do not suggest an overwhelmingly female genre.[14]

First I will discuss several plays where males lament freely without provoking criticism, not old males, not barbarian males, not children males, but prime-of-life Greek males, the kind that current scholarship says should not. These passages qualify as lamentation by Wright's criteria but are seldom if ever discussed.

Teucer in the *Ajax* (992–1039) laments his brother.[15] This is a reduced lament because it is not at the end of the play and it is in iambic trimeter. It contains the requisite stylistic elements, however, and many of the standard topoi, and it takes place in the presence of the body. Wright describes it as a "eulogy": "[T]he effect of the non-lyric meter . . . is to make the lamenter seem brave and rational in grief." She compares Teucer's lament to Tecmessa's earlier one (866–973, also in iambs): "[T]he iambs are in character; like Tecmessa, [Teucer] is level-headed, ready to play the part of the orator to win Ajax a burial."[16] He laments freely, with no stigma attached. To be sure, the chorus (male) speaks at the end of his lament: "[C]ut short your speech." It might be easy to construe this as criticism, but see how they continue: "[Q]uickly consider/, How best to hide him in some sort of grave/and what you must say next" (1040–1042; trans. John Moore). They are not criticizing Teucer for lamenting; they see Menelaus coming, and quick action is necessary. In any case, they have just finished participating themselves in two laments earlier in the play (348–427 and 866–973), and surely they would not have let Teucer go on for forty lines already if they had wanted to express disapproval of his lamentation.

Ajax also, despite his apparent earlier disdain for emotional reactions to pain, for *gooi*, that Tecmessa tells us about (317–322), in a later, proleptic lament for himself, laments wholeheartedly and without criticism. The chorus begs him not "to say such things" when he asks for their help to die, but this is not criticism of his lamentation, in which they themselves join. It is sympathy and horror at his situation. He is discovering a new kind of pain, perhaps, not the battleground, physical kind he was so proud of scorning but a new kind, where lamentation is appropriate.

The laments of Creon in Sophocles' *Antigone* and Oedipus in his *Oedipus the King* may be discussed together because they have much in common. Both men have "lost family members, but are also facing their own misdeeds and stubbornness." Both lamenters "take the opportunity... to indulge in self lamentation."[17] The laments are both full laments; the antiphonal role of the chorus in each case is minimal. In each case, the chorus distances itself from the chief lamenter, showing its fear and dislike of the protagonist but not criticizing him.

Creon's is the only lament in the *Antigone*; Antigone's scene before she is taken to the cave to die is not a lament, although it is usually the only passage in the play discussed as such. She does lament—but offstage; it is reported by the guard (423). Even so, the play is accurately described as "a document of attitudes towards funerary activity" in contemporary Athens.[18] Exactly what evidence for contemporary attitudes does the play offer? Creon spends the whole play trying to control female "funerary activity," to the horror and concern of nearly everyone else. He is completely unsuccessful and, in the end, himself performs the only lament in the play. After a whole play of increasingly alienating himself from his family and fellow citizens because of these efforts, he finally imitates those, chiefly Antigone, whom he has been criticizing. It is unlikely that the contemporary audience was meant to carry away from this play a simple sense of the undesirability of lamentation, male or female. I do not think that the audience was meant to sympathize with Creon; they were probably meant to understand and think about the dilemma he is in but not sympathize with him personally, until, perhaps, the end when he does lament. Even then, the chorus does not give the audience much encouragement to sympathize.

Euripides' *Suppliants* has also been used as a template for fifth-century B.C.E. attitudes toward lament and its control in Athens. Several authors have used it in their search for information on the real-life situation and have commented on the feminization of Adrastus in his lament with the chorus. Nicole Loraux, in her inquiry into the origins and development of the *epitaphios logos*, finds the play to be a "dramatized reflection of the funeral oration"; she "examine[s]... the principal stages, from mourning to civic speech, enacted in this play."[19] These stages begin, she says, with Theseus's "intervention" (her word) in the lament by Adrastus and the chorus and end with Adrastus's speech in praise of the Argive heroes. The progression is clear: old-fashioned, unacceptably feminizing lamentation is "supplanted" by a civic, male *epitaphios logos*.[20]

Helene Foley also says that Theseus "intervenes to deprive them [the women and Adrastus] of the bodies and to suppress the extravagant lament that they had begun prior to his entrance."[21] She describes the content and possible effect of the women's lament on the younger generation of citizens, asserting that the dramatic situation argues that praise of the dead and the way they died (that is, an *epitaphios logos*–type speech) should be emphasized rather than the complaints and criticisms of the women.

Others agree with Loraux and Foley, saying that Theseus "intervenes" and that he "seems to be a mouthpiece for the establishment of wartime Athens in condemning such negative rhetoric. On the other hand, the play ends with the young men urging revenge and the women restraint."[22] The women's lament is "entirely suppressed in the course of the play," "document[ing] the subordination of women's ritual language to the city's collective eulogy."[23]

Several things should be noted in these interpretations: first, it might be more accurate to say that the mothers' lamenting is *followed* (rather than "supplanted") by a speech resembling in some ways an *epitaphios logos*. This is, in fact, the order scripted for the real-life funeral festivities for the war dead at that time in Athens.[24] Second, Theseus does not interrupt the lament. Wright's analysis shows that the lament's metrical structure is complete at 837. Theseus enters at 838, speaking to someone, variously identified (the text is problematic here): "During your long lament before the army/I would have asked you this, but I refrained/From speaking then, and now I let it pass."[25] Perhaps another male was lamenting, and Theseus did not interrupt him either. Then he turns to Adrastus and asks him to give a speech in praise of the dead. This speech turns out to be of debated similarity to an *epitaphios logos*, but it is nonetheless a speech, not a lament.[26] Third, there are two more laments in the play after this one, which are not considered in these discussions: Iphis's for his daughter Evadne and the full lament for the Argive dead by their mothers and sons at the end of the play. Theseus is not present at Iphis's lament; he stands to one side quietly as the mothers and sons bewail their dead. He may indeed be "echo[ing] mainstream Athenian ideology" at the time, but his behavior toward lamentation in the play is quite respectful.[27]

It is interesting to compare another detailed analysis of these scenes. Collard finds the "civic speech" and the laments (he considers them all) to be natural complements of one another and the speech itself to have a "close allusive association" with Adrastus's and the chorus's lament.[28] Indeed, why should we insist that they are hostile and contradictory rather than complementary?[29] Collard notes, "Praise of the dead was not exclusive to the public and epideictic epitaphios, but immemorial in everyday custom."[30] He goes further and argues that Adrastus's participation in the lament marks the end of the moral taint from his defeat at Thebes and the beginning of his refound "capacity as a feeling person together with his sense of kingly responsibility."[31] Collard was writing before gender concerns in the analysis of tragic lament became important, and there can be no doubt that his perspective has been enlarged and enriched by the addition of feminist sensibilities. I would like to propose here a perspective that includes both attitudes and admits the complexity of the issues in scenes of lamentation.

What Theseus *has* done is to refuse to permit the mothers to touch the bodies of their dead or, later, to receive their ashes. Their grandsons even refuse to let them touch the urns. This *is* a curtailment of the ordinary female role in burial rites and may reflect fifth-century efforts to restrict female funerary activity in the funerals of the war dead.[32] It is not a curtailment of lament, however. Further, if we use this play to assess the depiction of fifth-century Athenian attitudes toward lament, we should consider the whole play, not just the first half. An examination of all the laments reveals that Theseus does not suppress them in any way; rather, his silence while they take place suggests respect and patience.

Finally, what of the feminization of Adrastus in his earlier participation in the "feminine, private world" of lament?[33] He is not alone in participating in funeral ritual duties usually assigned to women. There is (if that textual reconstruction is correct) the unidentified male who lamented in front of the army (838), whom Theseus forbore to interrupt. And there is Theseus himself, who washed the bodies and spread the biers of the dead (766–777). Are they—even Theseus—being feminized here, as it is claimed Adrastus is? No one that I know of has ever said so, but it would seem to follow if the latter is argued.[34] I would suggest rather that none of them is being "compromised" by his actions.

The *Persians* of Aeschylus includes passages also often adduced to argue that lamenting males are presented as feminized by indulging in this "female" genre.[35] There are two laments in the *Persians.* The more well known is the full one at the end; it is the longest and most flamboyant of any lament in extant tragedy, male *or* female, Greek *or* barbarian, at least to judge from what the texts actually say. Holst-Warhaft calls this lament "the depiction of the Persians fulfilling what, to the Greeks of Aeschylus' period, was predominantly a female role. There will be no such extravagant display of male mourning in Greek tragedy."[36] We should remember, however, that we know very little about how any of tragedy's laments were staged. It may well have been, for example, that tragedy would make "no such extravagant display" of female mourning either; it does not seem as if it did, so far as we can tell from the texts. The remarkable extravagance in this lament perhaps has as much to do with the fact that Persians are the lamenters as the fact that they are men, as well as the specifics of how they lament.

This lament by Xerxes and the chorus (908–1077) has become the model for those arguing for the feminization of the male by lamentation; it forms an important part of Hall's arguments for the play's "serial images of Asia as Woman."[37] I do not disagree with Hall's general argument; in this lament, men perform what seem to have become actions of female lamentation. But once again, the full lament is not the only lament in the play, and an assessment of lament in the *Persians* should include all examples. The other is a reduced lament, given by the male chorus early in the play when they first hear the news of the Persian defeat (256–289). The messenger bringing the news alternates with the chorus's lyric lamentation; he maintains his iambic trimeter, even as he comes close to joining them in his last couplet (284–285). There is no indication here that the lament is excessive or undesirable. But the *messenger* is criticized, mildly, by the Queen; she asks him to control his grief and speak quietly (295).[38] He does and then reports more soberly the details of the disaster, listing those killed, describing the battle, praising the fallen.[39] Here we have, then, a female controlling justified male lamentation. What might that indicate about stereotyped gender roles in the play? Is the Queen acting the male, to the chorus's female? I have never seen it argued so, and I think rightly not. In fact, the scene follows the same pattern as the one in Euripides' *Suppliants* that we have just examined: first the lament and then the speech, a sequence that has been argued to be the suppression of female lamentation. In the *Persians* the sex/gender roles are changed: instead of the male Theseus, there is the female Queen, and instead of a female chorus, there is a male one; in only the Adrastus/messenger part is the biological sex the same. What does the scene from the *Persians* tell us about "mainstream Athenian ideology"? Is male lamentation being suppressed here? Should Theseus be seen as acting a female's role because his behavior resembles the Queen's? The female here does not collapse with emotion and need to be hushed when she hears the news; she and Theseus behave the same: she lets the chorus finish its lament and then asks for a reasoned speech. She is rational, in control, and saddened, as she has every reason to be; and she is Persian.[40] But it cannot be argued that her behavior is the result of reversed sex roles in Persia where the men are women and the women rule them: she is not portrayed as a masculinized monster, like Clytemnestra, whom I will discuss below.[41] It is perhaps only preconceptions of fixed gender roles in tragic lament, rather than anything intrinsic in the scene type, that, on the one hand, have led to the belief that the *Suppliants* scene is an example of the control of female lamentation by the male and the feminization of the male by lamentation and, on the other, have permitted scholars to ignore the scene in the *Persians*.

In a recent reading of the full lament performed by Xerxes and the chorus at the end of the play, Mark Griffith has suggested that the lament shows a progression from "abjectly answering the Elders' questions and complaints (918–1037), to a more assertive issuing of his own commands to them (1038 ff.)." The lament is an "operation of commiseration and reintegration . . . begin[ning] the process of restoring him to full authority."[42] This echoes in an interesting way the comment by Collard quoted earlier on the effect of Adrastus's lament in Euripides' *Suppliants*: that he begins to regain his kingly authority by his participation in the lament. Would it be too much to see a pattern here—the male lament as admission of and liberation from earlier mistakes and faults and the beginning of restoration of moral authority?

The lament of the messenger and chorus and that of Xerxes and chorus are the only two laments identified by Wright in the *Persians*, but another passage has been discussed as if it were: the scene where the chorus raises the ghost of Darius (532–680).[43] Indeed, this passage is three times called a *goos*, a lament (687, 697, 705), and is described as "having the shrieking, discordant tones . . . appropriate . . . [to] female *gooi*."[44] It does not fulfill Wright's criteria, however, and Sarah Iles Johnston's analysis of the scene suggests why. *Goeteia*, the summoning of dead spirits, appears to have been introduced into Greece in the Archaic age from the East, and at this period of history, it was a male activity. What "we witness [in this scene from the *Persians*] is the very *transformation* of female lament into male *goeteia*."[45] Rather than being feminized by performing female *gooi*, then, the chorus is here masculinizing a female activity: "[T]he professional craft of the male replaced female traditions."[46] Darius's response to the chorus is interesting. The Queen has not spoken a word since her speech (598–622) explaining her reasons for bringing libations and wishing to raise the ghost of her husband. The chorus alone in its *goeteia* has effected the raising of Darius; it then speaks with his ghost. Then, at 703, when the chorus is reluctant to tell him the bad news, he turns to the Queen and asks her to stop "these tears and laments" (κλαυμάτων λήξασα τώδε καὶ γόων) and "tell it me clearly" (σαφές τί μοι λέξον [705]). Is he asking *her* to stop lamenting?[47] What lament? Or is he asking her to quiet the chorus, as she has done earlier? In any case, he turns to *her* (a woman) to get a reasoned account, which she gives him in the following lines.

The message to be derived from the examples that the *Persians* offers of the gendering of lament is a mixed one. Certainly, the final lament with Xerxes and the chorus is a fantastic display of wild emotion, with men doing things onstage that Greek men in real life never or only rarely did at that time.[48] But Greek men do lament onstage, though not so wildly perhaps—again, we have only texts to guide us—but then, neither do women, Greek or foreign, appear to lament that wildly. In the other two passages we have examined, the gender roles clearly do not provide evidence for the standard argument. In one case, a woman urges a man to control his grief and give a reasoned account; in the other, a female real-life activity is being masculinized onstage.

There is another instance of a female controlling male lamentation, which might make an ideal example of the feminization of male lamenters: the final scene between Clytemnestra and the chorus of Argive elders in the *Agamemnon*.[49] She has just killed her husband and is glorying in the deed before the old men of the city, taunting them with her power over them. Clytaimestra's characterization as a male is well documented; she is monstrous, a freak of nature. We are meant to find her horrifying. The males who come in contact with her—Agamemnon, Aegisthus—seem correspondingly feminized. But I suggest that this is not true of the chorus of Argive elders in the final scene, when they begin to lament Agamemnon (φεῦ [1448]).[50] Clytaimestra, in anapests, repeatedly interrupts their efforts, refusing to join their iambo-dochmiacs; her refusal emphasizes her callousness as an unrepentant, boastful murderer.[51] Again (as with Creon in the *Antigone*), we are not meant to sympathize with her but, rather, with the chorus, who have every right to lament their dead king, whose body lies in front of them. Aeschylos's point here is not that the chorus is "feminized" by doing this "female" thing but that the masculinized Clytaimestra is outrageous in trying to silence them.

The laments just discussed provide an opportunity to examine the typical reactions of scholars when they cannot deny a man is lamenting but want to excuse it somehow as a special case of one sort or another. Some link lyrics to lamentation and point out that only Ajax and Theseus in Euripides' *Hippolytus* sing lyrics, which they feel feminizes them.[52] According to Wright's findings, however, a lyric meter is not necessary for a passage to count as a (reduced) lament, and nonlyric laments are performed by women as well as men (e.g., Tecmessa in the *Ajax*). Are they being "masculinized"? What of Orestes' lament with Elektra in Aeschylus's *Choephoroi*? We may excuse Orestes in this case, it is suggested, and hence maintain the position that tragic lamentation is a female genre, because "his youth may be critical."[53] Another excuse for Orestes' lament at Aeschylus *Choephoroi* 306–478 reads: "[A] man may—under circumstances of exceptional stress—have access to a language [lament] . . . normally restricted to women and/or foreigners."[54] Are not the circumstances of lament always "of exceptional stress," for women and foreigners too? What exactly do such circumstances excuse for a man that they do not for women and foreigners? An excuse for Teucer's lament in the *Ajax* was once suggested to me by a member of the audience when I gave a paper outlining the ideas of this essay: it was "all right" for Teucer to lament because he was a bastard. Another excuse sometimes offered for male lament is that it has "civic relevance," as in Peleus's lament for Neoptolemos.[55] Perhaps we can understand Xerxes' lament in this way, too, or Creon's.[56] So, if you are any foreign male or a Greek male who is old, young, a bastard, in great distress, or in a civic context, you may lament.[57] Is this not protesting too much? My point is that somehow we all work on the assumption, consciously or not, that lamentation is female in tragedy and so feel obliged to excuse males when we find they are lamenting unashamedly and uncriticized.

Let us take up again the pattern we noticed earlier in the *Suppliants* and the *Persians*, that of self-condemnation and a realization of failures in a lament leading to a moral restoration and reintegration of the lamenter into his proper place in society. This takes the form of a self-lament that may or may not be occasioned by an actual death; its function is similar to that of a confession.[58] Several other male laments follow this confessional pattern.[59] One could cite Creon in Sophocles' *Antigone*, or Oedipus in his *Oedipus the King*, or even Ajax in the *Ajax*. In each of these cases, the male has gone through a horrifying moral crisis and has admitted to it. He laments and condemns himself. Griffith comes close to saying as much of Creon, although his focus is elsewhere than on the function of male lamentation.[60] In his context, the pattern of the king's confession, repentance, and reemergence into a position of authority is seen as part of the restoration of order traditional at the end of tragic dramas. But for us this cannot be the whole story, for Adrastus's lament comes early in the play, as do several others.

Admetus, in the *Alcestis*, bewails not so much Alcestis's fate as his own, in a supremely self-centered lament (861–933). Immediately after the lament, however, he shows signs of remorse and self-criticism for what he has brought about (954–960). This follows the pattern of the lament/ *epitaphios logos* in the *Suppliants* and the *Persians*. After a response from the chorus, Herakles enters (1008), leading the veiled Alcestis, and persuades Admetos to accept her. The household is reestablished, and Admetus is once more the head of a flourishing *oikos*.[61]

Oedipus's lament (*Oedipus the King* 1307–1366) does not come quite at the end of the play either, although Wright counts it as a full lament on metrical grounds. There follows the scene of reconciliation between Oedipus and Creon and his reunion with his daughters in a reasoned speech in iambics. This serves as his reintegration because they will send to Apollo to find out if Oedipus may leave Thebes as he wishes.

Ajax's lament and suicide are also early in the play (348–427, 865). Once again, he follows his lament with a reasoned statement of his point of view in iambics. His situation is unique, in that he sees no possibility of reintegration into what he views as the corrupted society around him. Hence he finds in his suicide what is a reintegration into the heroic society he once belonged to.

In other plays, the pattern is simplified: Oedipus in the *Oedipus at Colonos* laments himself (1670–1750) and is then (we assume) transformed into the *daimon* of the grove. Peleus in the *Andromache* laments Neoptolemus (1173–1225), and immediately afterward, Thetis arrives to announce the survival of their line and her intention to deify him (1230–1272). I have not analyzed any of these passages in as much detail as they deserve, but there does seem to be a pattern: a lament, often accompanied by a restatement of the situation in a speech in iambics, followed by some kind of (re)integration into a desired and appropriate society.[62]

What does this fresh light on these difficult passages suggest? In a few cases, the laments identified by Wright's criteria corroborate the current *communis opinio* on gender roles in tragedy; in many other cases they provide counterexamples to those conventionally adduced. An example of the former would be the Phrygian slave—another Easterner, portrayed as feminized—in Euripides' *Orestes* (1381–1399); an example of the latter would be the male laments in the *Ajax*. It is noteworthy that in very few cases are male laments actually criticized in the texts as being feminizing, despite what Plato has been said to imply was the common feeling. Orestes' comments on the Phrygian slave in Euripides' *Orestes* are one instance.[63] The list of laments shows clearly one other fact: there is no difference between male and female laments in occasion, strophic structures, meters, topoi, or linguistic features. If lament were a female genre, one might expect to find variation by gender, in particular in the topoi and linguistic features, but one does not.[64] Nor does the presence or absence of the body correspond to the gender of the lamenter: both men and women lament in both the presence and the absence of a body.

Derderian finds that distinctions between "male and female forms of grief and lament" exist in the Homeric poems and that they persist into

Sophoclean tragedy (she does not examine Aeschylus or Euripides for evidence). Her textual examples are based on vocabulary that is used to describe lamentation (e.g., γόος, θρῆνος, κωκυτός, οἰμωγή, and their cognates), not on the characteristics of the laments themselves. This distinction she finds breaks down sometimes, however: οἰμωγή, for example, ordinarily a term for the male cry of grief, is extended to Tecmessa in the *Ajax*.[65] Nonetheless, her discussion shows clearly that, in Homer and in Sophocles, males lament in their own gender-specific way.

All the cases discussed above suggest that attitudes toward lament in plays with tragic lamentation are more complicated and diverse than is usually acknowledged. For example, the notion of "feminization" of Xerxes by lamentation in the final lament in the *Persians* works very well as part of Hall's argument for the general feminization of Asia in Greek texts. But the evidence for it is contradictory, and it works less well when you look at that one lament in the context of all the laments in the play. And there is a pattern of moral improvement and restoration for the male lamenter during and after his lament in at least half of those identified by Wright's criteria.[66] This does not suggest that lamentation is unacceptable for a male or dangerous for his masculinity.[67]

The material adduced here does not demonstrate, I think, that the female and male laments in tragedy are interchangeable. As indicated above, both female and male laments include the same metrics, topoi, and so on. Yet the function and result of each may differ.[68] Male lamentation often leads to the male's redemption and reintegration into his proper society, for example, whereas female lamentation does not. One difference that might be expected, however—that female lamentation provokes fear, whereas male lamentation does not—is not borne out in tragedy.[69] That is, the characters who are the internal audiences for lament (male or female) do not typically react with fear. I find only three laments that cause fear: Cassandra's in the chorus (*Ag.* 1072–1177), Elektra and Orestes' in the chorus (*Choeph.* 306–478), and Polymestor's in Agamemnon (*Hek.* 1108–1114)—a mixture of male and female lamenters as well as male and female fearful respondents.[70] A possible explanation for this might be found in the idea that tragedy has incorporated female lament into it and thereby "tamed" it.[71] If this is so, then the message of the internal audience to the external one is "Don't let laments upset you; they're under control." A nuanced examination of the dramatic functions of female and male laments in tragedy could perhaps produce a middle ground between the findings of this essay and previous work on tragic lament. It may be that the dramatic functions of laments are gendered, although the laments themselves are not.

These discussions suggest also how much we need accepted standards for identifying laments so that we can all talk about the same thing when we make claims for the evidence from tragedy. Wright's study is an excellent start toward this goal for laments for the human dead, offering much new material and specific text-based criteria for identifying that material. It does not support (at least as far as I have worked with it) the view that finds in tragedy the consistent denigration of male lamentation or the consistent condemnation of, or a developing effort to control, female lamentation.

Finally, what is it that legitimizes male lamentation in tragedy? Why was it acceptable for males to act "like women" in male roles? This is a specific question parallel to the larger issue of the convention of the theater where men took all roles, male and female, and most thinking on this topic has focused on the general issue. But there is a necessary distinction to be made between men taking women's roles, which are clearly "other" and clearly relinquished at the end of a performance, and men acting men's roles wherein the men behave in ways considered (at least in recent scholarship) the province of women in everyday life. This latter is the case when men lament in tragedy and is the situation described by Plato.[72] Thinking on the general issue offers useful insights, nonetheless, for the present concern, as some discussions hold good for both issues. Discussions fall into two general categories, psychological and religious.[73]

Zeitlin's view of the whole of tragedy as closely related to the Greek male idea of the feminine suggests that in tragedy the male can investigate that Other freely, indeed, that he has in part—consciously or unconsciously—created and developed tragedy for this purpose. She begins her analysis commenting on the convention of cross-dressing and the general inversion of gender roles in initiation rituals. Then she turns to "consider what . . . the actual experience [of cross-dressing in the theater] might imply for achieving male identity. . . other than [on the model of the initiation rites] to teach him the behaviors he must later scrupulously avoid."[74] She concludes that the opportunity to play the Other in tragedy offers men a "fuller model for the masculine self."[75] In other words, the male learns to be more fully male (or human, even) by experiencing the "often banned emotions of fear and pity." He does not, it would seem, learn to avoid this behavior, so much as to know it and make it his own through experience, so that he may have complete control over it. It is not clear, however, whether she is talking about the characters in the plays, or the actors playing the characters, or in some ways both. In my discussions above, I was talking about the characters only, but the border between the two (or between the characters and the audience) may be permeable.[76] This is of course what Plato feared, and it is important to keep the distinction in mind when comparing what men do onstage and what they do in real life.

"In the end," Zeitlin says, "tragedy arrives at closures that generally reassert male, often paternal (or civic), structures of authority, but before that the work of the drama is to open up the masculine view of the universe. It typically does so . . . through energizing the theatrical resources of the female and concomitantly enervating the male as the price of initiating actor and spectator into new and unsettling modes of feeling, seeing, and knowing."[77] This is very much like the pattern in male laments that was outlined above: the male, through his experience of lamentation, begins his reintegration into some desired and appropriate male structure. Once again it should be noted, however, that in the case of male laments, the "closure" can take place at any point in the play, not just at the end. The pattern in male laments, that is, is a function of lamentation itself, not of the structure of tragic drama.

Nicole Loraux agrees on many points with Zeitlin's analysis but approaches the matter from a different perspective. Whereas Zeitlin's organizing myth is taken from Euripides' *Bacchae*—Dionysus's persuasion of Pentheus to dress and behave like a woman—Loraux's is that of Zeus's incorporation of Metis into his body so that he may acquire her female powers.[78] Zeitlin's view of male/female depends on a judicious use of structuralism's paired opposites; Loraux's sees the male as seeking to encompass the Other. In her examination of this process in Greek myth, Loraux argues that "simple inversion" of the sexes (as when they cross-dress in certain ritual settings) is not sufficient to explain "the basic asymmetry that always redounds to men's benefit."[79] The male does not simply experience the feminine other; he integrates it into himself, thereby "gain[ing] in complexity" and "increas[ing his] . . . virility to its highest pitch."[80] This is getting closer to the situation of a man acting a male role that includes powerful "female" behavior in it.

Both Zeitlin and Loraux are careful in their discussions to warn against a simple inversion of gender roles—in dress, behavior, or speech. Zeitlin says it "runs the risk of assuming mutually inverted categories without looking to the internal dynamics of tragic conventions that shape and predict the conditions of this exchange."[81] Loraux puts it like this: "Greek formulations of the difference between the sexes must be approached via the notion of exchange: *all* exchanges between the sexes, and not only inversion . . . or even the exchange that operates by the mixing of opposites and the blurring of all boundaries."[82]

Simon Goldhill agrees. In his study of the relation between the pre-performance ceremonies at the Greater Dionysia and the tragic and comic performances, he finds the essence of Dionysos in the "interplay" between the "norm" of civic ideology, epitomized in the presentation of the sons of the war dead to the city and the "transgression" of the tragedies: "For tragedy. . . do[es] not simply reverse the norms of society, but inculcate[s] a questioning of the very basis of these norms, the key structures of opposition on which 'norm' and 'transgression' rest."[83] In the search for the roots of the propriety of male tragic lament, I would substitute *dissolution* for *transgression*. To my mind, Dionysos is more a dissolver of boundaries than a transgressor, although it may be transgressive to dissolve them. But in the present inquiry, the male/female opposition is dissolved in the male actor who plays a man lamenting; the male has absorbed the female into himself, as Loraux describes. Using Goldhill, then, perhaps we can connect Loraux's psychological phenomenon, of which the lamenting male is an example, to the nature of the god of tragedy and find a religious context that legitimizes the lamenting male. Some such context is necessary, for while the psychological approaches are well argued and believable as psychology, they do not suggest how male lamentation was regularized in tragic drama. What were the specific steps by which the possibility of this behavior came to be convention? How did the convention of acceptable male lamentation in tragedy develop?

Bassi acknowledges the importance of the Dionysiac too: "Dionysiac madness is homologous to theatre-like impersonations."[84] She contends that the theater is where an illusion of normative masculinity is produced for public view.[85] Like Zeitlin, she thinks that tragic drama was used, if not actually developed, in part as a way of (re-)creating a past ideal of masculinity. She calls it an exercise in nostalgia and focuses entirely on male actors acting female parts, never on male actors acting male parts that include "female" behavior, for example, lamentation. Bassi's theoretical framework of the theater as nostalgia for a past masculine ideal finds the earliest form of that ideal in the warrior of the *Iliad*: he is a male who is a doer of deeds and a speaker of words.[86] The premier example of this ideal for her is Achilles. And he, in Richard Martin's words, is "the one hero most practiced in the genre of lament, as we see in his speeches from Book 18 on," particularly 23.5–23.[87] It may be that Bassi's idea of tragedy as nostalgia for an idealized masculinity actually "testif[ies] to a desire to imitate what is no longer to be seen in the 'real life' of the city."[88] This idealized masculinity, then, must include males whose masculine identities are stable enough to permit them to lament without compromising their masculinity. By "males" I mean here at least the male characters of tragedy—and perhaps the actors too.

Richard Seaford's reconstruction of the ritual strands in the origin of tragedy is useful here.[89] He singles out several aspects of ritual to discuss in detail, among them the initiatory background of female Dionysiac *thiasoi*, the lamentation of Dionysus's death by maenads, and the lament of a hero in cult by those (men?) "of his circle."[90] He sees these ritual lamentations as parallel: in the one Dionysus is lamented by females; in the other, the hero, by males. When the female *thiasoi* that celebrated secret rites in honor of Dionysus became public, males took over celebration of the god, part of which was to lament his death.[91] In this way, according to Seaford's view of the origins and development of tragedy, male lamentation was intrinsic to drama from the very beginning.[92] He adduces an interesting vase painting of males lamenting before an image of Dionysus. (See fig. 8.1.) The vase dates to 500–490 B.C.E. and "shows men *lamenting* at a clothed pillar surmounted by a mask of Dionysus—just the kind of image associated in fifth-century Attic vase painting with the maenadic dismemberment of Dionysus."[93] The men raise their hands to their foreheads and appear to be beating their breasts. This reconstruction suggests an answer to the question posed above: the lamenting male is an image of power in tragedy, having arrogated to himself the power of female lament. If he is feminized at all, it is because he is an Easterner (e.g., Xerxes, the Phrygian slave), not because he is a man.

Iconographic evidence from the sixth and early fifth century B.C.E. supports the idea that men also lamented in funeral ritual. Stears discusses

Figure 8.1   Tragic chorus and cult statue of Dionysus. Frieze from a late black-figure lekythos. 500/490 B.C.E. (Munich Stattliche Antikensammlungen)

the male presence and role in lamenting the dead, referencing, among others, H. A. Shapiro's work.[94] Both cite black-figure vases showing male mourners, as well as later red-figure vases with the same male activities.[95] One black-figure phormiskos (not pictured) Shapiro describes thus: "A Doric column to the left of Myrrhine's bier marks the threshold of the house, approached by a group of six men led by her father. From his mouth spill the first words of his lament: *OIMOIO ΘΥΓΑ[THP]*."[96] In this scene, the behavior of the men differs from that of the women; they do not tear their hair or lacerate their faces. Rather, they make the raised-arm gesture of farewell as they sing their lament. They are nonetheless lamenting, in their own gender-specific manner.[97] There seem to have been, then, two kinds of behavior, male and female, which were regular and predictable. The behavior of each "consist[ed] of a set of conventional... responses to death, both sanctioned and required by society."[98]

It may be, then, that men lamented more than is usually claimed, in real life as well as in tragedy.[99] Our literary sources from Homer through the tragedians suggest that they did, and vase painting corroborates this.[100] Evidence such as Archilochus frg. 7 is not critical of lamenting males, despite arguments using it as such.[101] It is the "boys don't cry" attitude and has nothing to do with the religious demands for lamentation in funeral ritual. The manner of lamentation seems to have become increasingly gendered, with eventually only women tearing their hair, scratching their faces, and beating their breasts. It may even be that the scorn felt for lamenting males in real life began developing only in the fifth century and was not so great as is generally thought. Holst-Warhaft suggests that the introduction of the *epitaphios logos*—or rather the sentiments that lay behind its introduction—played a part in this development.[102] Even so, Plato seems to have been speaking only of the dangers of enjoying grief in poetry or drama, because that may lead to the "unmanliness" of expressing grief in real life. He does not seem to be talking at all about the ritually required expression of grief in lament. Bassi uses Plato's *Republic* as prime evidence when she argues that "the preservation of an idealized and normative masculinity is a motivating principle in ancient Greek analyses of dramatic production."[103] Clearly, tragic drama permitted men to lament.[104]

These suggestions deserve to be considered in greater detail, because it is clear from the comprehensive evidence adduced above from tragedy that the lamenting male (qua male) in tragedy was neither unusual nor criticized within the plays where he appeared. Such evidence from tragedy (if we think it is justified to use it) would suggest that neither was the lamenting male in real life.

APPENDIX

Male Lament in Greek Tragedy

Play and Lines	Lamenter	Respondent	Lament For
Aeschylus			
Persians 908–1077 (F)	Xerxes	male chorus	Persian dead
Seven 875–1004 (F)	Antigone/Ismene	female chorus	Polyneices/ Eteocles
Persians 256–289 (R)	———	male chorus	Persian dead
Agam. 1072–1177 (R)	Cassandra	male chorus	self
Agam. 1448–1576 (R)	———	male chorus	Agamemnon
Choephoroi 306–478 (R)	Elektra/Orestes	———	Agamemnon
Choephoroi 1007–1020 (R)	———	female chorus	Clytaimestra

(continued)

Male Lament in Greek Tragedy (continued)

Play and Lines	Lamenter	Respondent	Lament For
Sophocles			
Antigone 1261–1346 (F)	Creon	male chorus	Haimon
Oed. Tyr. 1307–1366 (F)	Oedipus	male chorus	Jocasta
Oed. Col. 1670–1750 (F)	Antigone/Ismene	male chorus	Oedipus
Ajax 348–427 (R)	Ajax	Tecmessa/ male chorus	animals/self
Ajax 866–973 (R)	Tecmessa	male chorus	Ajax
Ajax 992–1039 (R)	Teucer	———	Ajax
Elektra 86–120 (R)	Elektra	———	Agamemnon
Elektra 807–822 (R)	Elektra	———	Orestes
Elektra 1126–1170 (R)	Elektra	———	Orestes
Oed. Col. 510–548 (R)	Oedipus	male chorus	self
Euripides			
Suppliants 1114–1164 (F)	female chorus	male chorus	Argive dead
Andromache 1173–1225 (F)	Peleus	female chorus	Neoptolemos
Troiades 1287–1352 (F)	Hekabe	female chorus	Troy
Rhesus 895–914 (R)	Musa	male chorus	Rhesus
Alcestis 393–415 (R)	Admetus/son	———	Alcestis
Alcestis 741–746 (R)	———	male chorus	Alcestis
Alcestis 861–933 (R)	Admetus	male chorus	Alcestis/self
Medea 1021–1041 (R)	Medea	———	children
Hippolytus 811–885 (R)	Theseus	———	Phaedra/self
Hippolytus 1347–1388 (R)	Hippolytus	———	self
Hekabe 154–215 (R)	Hekabe	Polyxena	Polyxena
Hekabe 1056–1106 (R)	Polymestor	———	children
Suppliants 798–836 (R)	Adrastus	female chorus	Argive dead
Suppliants 1080–1113 (R)	Iphis	———	Evadne
Andromache 825–865 (R)	Hermione	Nurse	self
Troiades 577–607 (R)	Andromache /Hekabe Astyanax/Troy		female chorus
Troiades 740–763 (R)	Andromache	———	Astyanax
Troiades 790–798 (R)	Hekabe	———	Astyanax
Troiades 1167–1206 (R)	Hekabe	———	Astyanax
Troiades 1216–1237 (R)	Hekabe	female chorus	Astyanax
Elektra 1177–1232 (R)	Elektra/Orestes	female chorus	Clytaimestra/ Agamemnon/ selves
Helen 362–385 (R)	Helen	———	Greeks at Troy
Orestes 960–1012 (R)	Elektra	———	self/Orestes
Orestes 1381–1399 (R)	Phrygian slave	———	Troy
Iph. Aul. 1276–1335 (R)	Iphigeneia	———	self

Note: F = "full lament"; R = "reduced lament."

ACKNOWLEDGMENT

I thank Dorota Dutsch for her help on this essay. Edidit comiter illa editorem.

NOTES

1. See, especially, Derderian 2001; Foley 2001; Hall 1993, 1996; Holst-Warhaft 1992; Loraux [1981] 1986; McClure 1999. Alexiou 1974 is the seminal work.

2. McClure 1999, 93.

3. The *locus classicus* of this attitude for scholars is Plato's *Republic*: III.388a–e and X.604b–607a. I argue at the end of this essay against the propriety of using Plato to support this point of view. See also Bassi 1998, 18–23; Zeitlin 1996, 367–372.

4. This essay focuses mostly on the issue of lamenting males and their putative feminization and less on the male efforts to control female lamentation. For a discussion of that, and the difficulties with the argument that male efforts to control female lamentation in tragedy increased during the fifth century, see Suter 2003.

5. See McClure 1999, 148.

6. See Wright 1986. See also Suter 2003, which gives a fuller summary of Wright's study. Wright's work was undertaken as an objective analysis of metrical and textual data from within tragedy itself; she was not interested in issues of the gendering of lament and had no parti pris in this question. Hence her analysis is all the more valuable in the present investigation.

Note that her analysis does not include the two other lament categories that Alexiou (1974) outlines: those for the fall of cities and those for gods and heroes. These categories are present too in Attic tragedy; see Bachvarova, this volume, for a discussion.

7. Wright 1986, 3.

8. See Alexiou 1974.

9. Wright 1986, 52. Cf. the discussion of the meter of lament in lyric poetry in Levaniouk, this volume.

10. Wright 1986, 52. Compare the practice in modern Greece: "As the *korifea* [lamenter] passes into acoustic violence, the tempo of her song increases and her vocal tones move to higher pitches. The faster pace and the higher pitch increase emotional intensity for the singer and her chorus" (Seremetakis 1991, 119). See also Alexiou 1974, 41, where she links this increase to the traditional antiphonal form of lament.

11. Wright 1986, 3.

12. Ibid., 119, 123.

13. For the sake of clarity, I have collapsed three of Wright's categories: "reduced," "monodic," and "Euripidean innovations" are all designated "Reduced" in the appendix. It will come as a surprise perhaps that certain passages do not appear in this table whose treatment as laments has led to very interesting interpretations. I think in particular of Charles Segal's (1994) reading of the *Bacchae*, in which he analyzes Agave's speech over Pentheus's body ("Agave's formal lament over her son's body" [16]), or parts of Holst-Warhaft's (1992) reading of the *Oresteia*, where she uses both selected represented laments and descriptions of lamentation in her argument (see Suter, this volume, "Introduction," n. 1). Segal's comments on how ritual laments become fragmented in tragedy is very true; it does not follow, however, that every piece imitating a ritual lament should be counted as a represented lament (see n. 39 below, for example); these fragments are simply that,

included to give color to the scene. See also Bachvarova (this volume), whose Near Eastern comparanda indicate that Wright's criteria, developed exclusively from materials within the extant corpus of Greek tragedy, do not include some forms of lament, e.g., some city laments. See Suter 2003, however, for an extension of Wright's criteria to include most of the text of Euripides' *Trojan Women*.

14. Statistically speaking, these figures would probably be truly valid only if compared with the number of male and female characters in our corpus of tragic drama. The difficulties of determining how to count the characters has deterred me from attempting this: major characters only? How do you determine what "major" means? play by play? by author? in the whole corpus? including the fragments? Perhaps this problem can be solved by someone more gifted in statistics than I.

15. Wright 1986, 93–94.

16. Ibid., 93, 119. See also Ormand 1999, ch. 5, on Tecmessa's hardheaded rhetorical skills.

17. Wright 1986, 82–83.

18. Derderian 2001, 158.

19. Loraux [1981] 1986, 48.

20. McClure 1999, 46. See the discussion below.

21. Foley 2001, 39; see also Holst-Warhaft 1992, 167–168: "Theseus intervenes...," "One last intervention...."

22. Holst-Warhaft 1992, 168–169. Actually, the play ends with a lament for the dead by the mothers, Theseus's gift of the fathers' ashes to the sons, and an appearance by Athena ex machina.

23. McClure 1999, 46.

24. Thucydides, *A History of the Peloponnesian War* II.34. It is odd that so many who write on the subject of the curbing of female lamentation in this period seem to forget that women lamented for the war dead as part of the public ceremony commemorating them, as well as for all other deaths in private ceremonies. See, most recently, Goff 2004, 263; cf. Goff 2004, 33. Time, place, and numbers were restricted (several times, implying that the restrictions were not very successful; see also Alexiou 1974, 22), but not lamentation itself. Loraux ([1981] 1986, 48) does not make this mistake but does not consider the fact in the development of her argument on the *epitaphios logos*.

25. μέλλων σ᾽ ἐρατῶν, ἡνίκ᾽ ἐξήντλεις στρατῷ/γοούς, ἀφήσω (trans. Frank Jones). For another reading of the text here, see Collard 1975, 319: "Theseus, then, ... at first held back his request to Adrastus from a wish not to interrupt his lament for the dead: that is clear from the imperfect 'ἐξήντλεις.'"

26. For the full arguments, with references, see Collard 1972, 40; Zuntz 1963, 13–16.

27. Foley 2001, 44.

28. Collard 1972, 48.

29. Foley 2001, 44.

30. Collard 1972, 45. An early discussion of the development of panegyric and lament and their similarity to epic subject matter is in Bowra 1952, 8–23. See also Wright 1986, 11 and n. 26, citing Didymus: "[T]hrênos was a eulogy: ἔλεγος ὁ θρῆνος τὸ δι᾽ αὐτοῦ τοῦ θρήνου εὖ λέγειν τοὺς κατοιχομένους. ap Orion. 58.7, ed. M. Schmidt (Leipzig 1854): 387–388."

31. Collard 1972, 48.

32. Foley 2001, 40; Holst-Warhaft 1992, 168.

33. Holst-Warhaft 1992, 168.

34. See Rehm (2003, 94), who seems to share my feelings. See also Stears, this volume, for the sexual division of labor in Athenian funeral rituals.

35. E.g., Hall 1996, 13; Holst-Warhaft 1992, 130–133.

36. Holst-Warhaft 1992, 133. The statement as it is reads strangely. I assume she means "no such extravagant display of *Greek* male mourning."

37. Hall 1996, 13. See, e.g., Foley 2001, 29. See also Dué 2006, 77–78, 85, 88, where she argues how "[t]he laments of Aeschylus' *Persians* are infused with traditional themes of women's songmaking" (2006, 78) and that the "predominant song medium of the play is the Greek woman's lament" (2006, 88). Most of her examples of this come from parts of the *Persians* that are not laments, but that is not my point here. Her source for "traditional themes" is women's lamentation for the dead or likely to die in the *Iliad*, where the situation of war is similar to that in the *Persians*. But we should be careful not to assume that this feminizes the male chorus (Dué 2006, 89); the similarity of narrative context can account fully for the similarity of themes. Her assessment that "they are shown to be incredibly Greek, or perhaps simply all too human" (2006, 114) I think is more accurate.

38. πᾶν ἀναπτύξας πάθος/λέξον κατάστας, κεἰ στένεις κακοῖς ὅμως.

39. The Queen's response to the messenger has been called a lament (McClure 2006, 86–87), but I am doubtful that a simple "aiai" (331) constitutes lamentation and λιγεῖα κωκήματα (332) describes a lament; it does not reenact one (see Suter, this volume, "Introduction," n. 1).

40. Her political position as ruler in Xerxes' absence may influence her behavior also. I owe this observation to Dutsch. See also Keith, this volume, on the influence of social position on who laments in the Roman context.

41. Her characterization as an overprotective mother is better (Griffith 1998, 53–57), but in this scene her son is not present. See also McClure 2006.

42. Griffith 1998, 62–63. He calls it "an extended process of 'acceptance' by the representatives of his father's rule in the form of the lyric exchanges of lamentation and recrimination."

43. E.g., Hall 1993, 126; Holst-Warhaft 1992, 132.

44. Johnston 1999, 117.

45. Ibid., 116, 118; emphasis in original.

46. Ibid., 118. See also Griffith 1998, 57–58. Bachvarova (this volume) discusses Sumerian lament, in which the raising of the dead by *gala* priests was a frequent component. Aeschylus seems to have known his characters' customs!

47. See McClure 2006, 87. Perhaps she has been wailing inarticulately?

48. See the discussion below, of men on a vase painting from 500–490 B.C.E. Women did do these things, of course, tearing the hair and beating their breasts. Note that Achilles did also (*Il.* 18.22–27).

49. I have never found it discussed outside Wright 1986. I make a preemptive strike here.

50. Wright 1986, 70 n. 1.

51. Ibid., 70–71.

52. Foley 2001, 29 n. 30, citing Hall 1999, 112.

53. Ibid.

54. Griffith 2001, 121.

55. McClure 1999, 160–161. She includes "a *kommos* in which a father laments for his son" in the *Hippolytus* also in this excuse. I am uncertain as to what in the *Hippolytus* she is referring.

56. Perhaps we can see some female laments this way too: Ismene and Antigone's in the *Seven against Thebes*, Elektra's first two in Sophocles' *Elektra*, Iphigeneia in the *Iphigeneia at Aulis*, and so on. Civic relevance is not, it would appear, gender related when it comes to lament in tragedy.

57. Segal (1993, 64–67) also makes several of these excuses for men weeping. He does not distinguish between tears of grief and dramatic representations of ritual lament. Occasions of both are listed under "lament" in the index of his book.

58. For another possible function of the self-lament, see Levaniouk, this volume.

59. There are also obvious exceptions to this pattern: Iphis's lament in Euripides' *Suppliants*, Orestes' in Aeschylus's *Choephoroi*, and Teucer's in Sophocles' *Ajax* come quickly to mind. Neither would the laments of the choruses conform to the pattern.

60. Griffith 1998, 73–74.

61. Segal (1993) suggests that Admetus's series of reactions follows the clinically predictable stages of mourning. See esp. Segal 1993, 55–56.

62. An interesting modern comparandum may help to explain this lamentation. Seremetakis (1991, ch. 1) describes female ritual lament in Inner Mani as a location of female marginality to their communities. Through the "pain and confessional discourse" of the ritual lament, they "can vividly dramatize the dissonance between self and society" (Seremetakis 1991, 4–5). In their lamentation, they "generate entire categories of persons in conflict with the social structure" (Seremetakis 1991, 5). The men cited as examples from ancient tragedy are in just such a state of dissonance, though only temporarily to be sure; but the notion of lament as confessional pain from the margin can apply to them also. See also Karanika (this volume), who sees this confessional use of lament in Aristophanes' parodies of Euripidean lament.

63. Herakles' self-criticism when he is in pain from the poisoned robe at the end of the *Trachiniae* is sometimes analyzed this way, but this passage is not a lament. It is a criticism of his weakness; cf. Ajax's situation, discussed above.

64. See Wright 1986, 112, where she tabulates the criteria for the eight full laments and passim for the reduced laments.

65. Derderian 2001, 140. For further examples of where the distinction breaks down, and her suggested explanation for it, see Derderian 2001, 143–145, 158. In like manner, Loraux (1995, ch. 1) finds that there are gender-specific ways of describing pain, which overlap also sometimes.

66. Xerxes' experience follows this pattern. A brief survey does not suggest that the same pattern exists in female lamentation. This is perhaps an example of Loraux's "basic asymmetry that always redounds to men's benefit" in action (1995, 8). See the discussion below.

67. Again, see the discussion on Loraux 1995, below. A man is more of a man for his integration of the feminine within himself (Loraux 1995, 4).

68. I owe this insight to Dutsch's reading of this essay.

69. That female lamentation provoked fear is asserted with reason for ancient real-life ritual lament (Foley 1993, 2001; Holst-Warhaft 1992; Segal 1993). In evidence from modern Greek ethnography also this aspect of lament is quite clear (Danforth 1982; Seremetakis 1991).

70. Eteocles' reaction to the female chorus at the opening of Aeschylus's *Seven Against Thebes* is a candidate for this, certainly, but the chorus's song is, if a lament at all, a proleptic lament for the fall of a city, so I do not count it here. Though laments do not seem to alarm the plays' internal audiences, the playwright sometimes arranges matters so that they provoke fear in the external audience. See, e.g., my (2003) analysis of Hekabe's lament for Troy at the end of the *Trojan*

Women. For the necessity to make this distinction between internal and external audiences, see Perkell, this volume.

71. This is suggested, for instance,by Holst-Warhaft in Holst-Warhaft 1992, introduction and chapter 5.

72. Plato, *Republic* X.605.c–e. Bassi (1998, 16) feels that Plato's concerns are not about the actor. Indeed, he focuses his criticism on the audience, but I do not see how the actor could be exempt from the influences that he describes. In ch. 5 Bassi (1998) considers the actors too.

73. Zeitlin 1996 and Loraux 1995 are clear articulations of the psychological approach; Goldhill 1990, Bassi 1998, and Seaford 1994, of the religious. I apologize for oversimplifying their discussions; my focus is on the lamenting male, and theirs are not. I extract from them, I hope legitimately, what is useful for the present argument.

74. Zeitlin 1996, 345.

75. Ibid., 363.

76. See Calame 1999 for an intricate discussion of this phenomenon.

77. Zeitlin 1996, 364. I would urge caution, however, in claiming the "enervating" part.

78. Ibid., 343: "Through this scene we arrive at the dynamic basis of Greek drama, catching a momentary glimpse of the secrets of its ritual prehistory as it merges with and is imitated by the techniques of the theatre." Cf. the discussion of Seaford below. See also Loraux 1995, 12–13. This part of Loraux's collection ("Introduction: The Feminine Operator") was written originally in 1989 and translated into English in 1995. The overall model for the collection is that of Tiresias, who actually acquires a woman's body. For the purposes of this essay, the Zeus/Metis model is the better: the lamenting male actor/character retains his male body but acquires some womanly power by (supposedly) behaving like one in his lamentation.

79. Loraux 1995, 8.

80. Ibid., 14, 12. Loraux is referring here specifically to Herakles.

81. Zeitlin 1996, 345.

82. Loraux 1995, 7.

83. Goldhill 1990, 127.

84. Bassi 1998, 203.

85. Ibid., 41, quoting Butler 1990.

86. Ibid., ch. 5. Cf. Loraux 1995, 6, with bibliography, on Achilles.

87. Martin 1989, 86–87.

88. Bassi 1998, 220. She suggests this in relation to the pre-play ceremonies involving ephebes and the sons of citizens who died in battle, but it seems to me that the actors onstage too are seeking nostalgically to display that same ideal.

89. Seaford 1994.

90. Ibid., 142–143. Seaford's main focus, as everyone's, is on why and how men came to play all the parts in tragic drama. He comments that without the background of ritual transvestism, the transvestism of the Attic stage is "unthinkable" (1994, 272).

91. Ibid., 270–272.

92. Ibid., 323–327, summary on 385. See also Bachvarova (this volume), who adduces Near Eastern lament practices as influences in the development of Attic tragedy. She sees Dionysiac worship in the background too, but in a different way from this discussion. Her arguments are entirely compatible with these.

93. Seaford 1994, 323 and n. 182; emphasis in the original. See also several of the illustrations in Van Wees 1998, figs. 1.2, 4, 9, 18, 19, which show men lamenting on Geometric and Archaic pottery.

94. Stears, this volume; Shapiro 1991.

95. See Shapiro 1991, figs. 5–7, 11, 18 (discussed at 647).

96. Ibid., 638.

97. This tradition seems late, however. Achilles' behavior included "female" doings: he poured dust over his head and tore his hair when he learned of Patroklus's death (*Il.* 18.22–27); and cf. the Late Archaic vase with men mourning Dionysus in figure 8.1. Holst-Warhaft (1992, 2, 25, and ch. 4) sees this too.

98. Stears, this volume. See also Burke's Mycenaean iconographic evidence in this volume, which seems to corroborate this point of view.

99. It seems unlikely that men ever had a role in ritual lament comparable to women's, given the cross-cultural data that point to the primary role of women, but this is not the present argument. Alexiou (1974, 104–105, 108) traces the male *elegos* and the *epitaphios logos* to the Archaic *thrênos*, which included both lamentation and praise (cf. n. 30 above).

100. Tsagalis 2004 is a welcome piece of scholarship supporting this claim, although he comes close to rejecting his own evidence (2004, 68–70). See also Monsacré 1984.

101. See Campbell 1967, esp. 9–10: ἀλλὰ τάχιστα/τλῆτε γυναικεῖον πένθος ἀπωσάμενοι. It is worth reminding ourselves that such admonitions are not in any case confined to male discourse. See, for example, Dione to Aphrodite: τέτλαθι τέκνον ἐμόν, καὶ ἀνάσχεο κηδομένη περ (*Il.* 5.382); or Sappho 31.17: ἀλλὰ πὰν τόλματον. Cf. Van Wees 1998, 18 and n. 27.

102. Holst-Warhaft 1992, 121.

103. Bassi 1998, 12.

104. Cf. the participation of men in lamentation on occasion in parts of modern Greece (Caraveli 1986, 179–180). Seremetakis offers a possible comparandum for the early sharing of ritual lament by men and women: "In the past, we could identify two, distinct, male and female domains of social practice and cognition in Inner Maniat culture.... Although largely associated with the social practices of respective genders, individual members could cross back and forth between female and male domains. Women could kill and men could mourn" (1991, 222). She attributes the rigidification of gender polarities to "ideologies of modernization," where, with "the division of labor between genders and between city and country, and the magnification of the social distance between public and private spheres, male/female dichotomies have been essentialized" (1991, 222). One may compare the development of the *polis* in the sixth and fifth centuries B.C.E. and its attendant "modernization," which perhaps "essentialized" gender dichptomies. Cf. Pomeroy 1975, 71.

BIBLIOGRAPHY

Alexiou, Margaret. 1974. *The Ritual Lament in Greek Tradition*. Cambridge.

Bassi, Karen. 1998. *Acting like Men: Gender, Drama, and Nostalgia in Ancient Greece*. Ann Arbor.

Bowra, C. W. 1952. *Heroic Poetry*. London.

Butler, Judith. 1990. *Gender Trouble*. New York.

Calame, Claude. 1999. Performative Aspects of the Choral Voice in Greek Tragedy: Civic Identity in Performance. In *Performance Culture and Athenian Democracy*, ed. Simon Goldhill and Robin Osborne, 125–153. Cambridge.

Campbell, D. A., ed. 1967. *Greek Lyric Poetry: A Selection*. New York.

Caraveli, Anna. 1986. The Bitter Wounding: The Lament as Social Protest in Rural Greece. In *Gender and Power in Rural Greece*, ed. Jill Dubisch, 169–194. Princeton.

Collard, C. 1972. The Funeral Oration in Euripides' *Supplices. Bulletin of the Institute of Classical Studies* 19: 39–53.

———, ed. 1975. *Euripides'* "Supplices" *with Introduction and Commentary.* 2 vols. Groningen.

Connor, W. R. 1989. City Dionysia and Athenian Democracy. *Classica et Mediaevalia* 40: 7–32.

Danforth, Lorin. 1982. *The Death Rituals of Rural Greece.* Princeton.

Derderian, Katharine. 2001. *Leaving Words to Remember: Greek Mourning and the Advent of Literacy.* Leiden.

Dué, Casey. 2006. *The Captive Woman's Lament in Greek Tragedy.* Austin.

Foley, Helene P. 1993. The Politics of Lamentation. In *Tragedy, Comedy, and the Polis*, ed. A. Sommerstein, S. Halliwell, J. Henderson, and B. Zimmerman, 101–143. Bari.

———. 2001. *Female Acts in Greek Tragedy.* Princeton.

Garvie, A. F. 1986. *Aeschylus* "Choephoroi" *with Introduction and Commentary.* Oxford.

Goff, Barbara. 2004. *Citizen Bacchae: Women's Ritual Practice in Ancient Greece.* Berkeley.

Goldhill, Simon. 1988. Battle Narrative and Politics in Aeschylos' *Persae. Journal of Hellenic Studies* 108: 189–193.

———. 1990. The Great Dionysia and Civic Ideology. In *Nothing to Do with Dionysos?* ed. John J. Winkler and Froma I. Zeitlin, 97–129. Princeton.

Griffin, Jasper. 1998. The Social Function of Attic Tragedy. *Classical Quarterly* 48: 39–61.

Griffith, Mark. 1998. The King and the Eye: The Rule of the Father in Greek Tragedy. *Proceedings of the Cambridge Philological Society* 44: 20–84.

———. 2001. Antigone and Her Sister(s). In *Making Silence Speak: Women's Voices in Greek Literature and Society*, ed. André Lardinois and Laura McClure, 117–136. Princeton.

Hall, Edith. 1989. *Inventing the Barbarian: Greek Self-Definition Through Tragedy.* Oxford.

———. 1993. Asia Unmanned. In *War and Society in the Greek World*, ed. John Rich and Graham Shipley, 108–133. London.

———. 1996. *Aeschylos'* "Persians," *with Introduction, Translation and Commentary.* Warminster, U.K.

———. 1999. Actor's Song in Tragedy. In *Performance Culture and Athenian Democracy*, ed. Simon Goldhill and Robin Osborne, 96–122. Cambridge.

Holst-Warhaft, Gail. 1992. *Dangerous Voices: Women's Laments and Greek Literature.* London.

Johnston, Sarah Iles. 1999. *Restless Dead.* Berkeley.

Loraux, Nicole. [1981] 1986. *The Invention of Athens: The Funeral Oration in the Classical City.* Trans. A. Sheridan. London.

———. 1995. *The Experience of Tiresias: The Feminine and the Greek Man.* Princeton.

Martin, Richard P. 1989. *The Language of Heroes: Speech and Performance in the Iliad.* Ithaca, N.Y.

McClure, Laura. 1999. *Spoken like a Women: Speech and Gender in Athenian Drama.* Princeton.

McClure, Laura. 2006. Maternal Authority and Heroic Disgrace in Aeschylus's *Persae*. *Transactions of the American Philological Association* 136 (1): 71–97.

Monsacré, Hélène. 1984. *Les larmes d'Achille: Le héros, la femme et la souffrance dans la poésie d'Homère*. Paris.

Ormand, Kirk. 1999. Exchange and the Maiden: Marriage in Sophoclean Tragedy. Austin Tex.

Pomeroy, Sarah B. 1975. *Goddesses, Whores, Wives, and Slaves: Women in Classical Antiquity*. New York.

Pucci, Pietro. 1993. Antiphonal Lament Between Achilles and Briseis. *Colby Quarterly* 29 (3): 258–272.

Rehm, Rush. 2003. *Radical Theatre: Greek Tragedy and the Modern World*. London.

Scott, William C. 1984. *Musical Design in Aeschylean Theater*. Hanover N.H.

Seaford, Richard. 1994. *Reciprocity and Ritual: Homer and Tragedy in the Developing City-State*. Oxford.

———. 1998. In the Mirror of Dionysos. In *The Sacred and the Feminine in Ancient Greece*, ed. Sue Blundell and Margaret Williamson, 128–146. London.

Segal, Charles. 1993. Female Death and Male Tears. In *Euripides and the Poetics of Sorrow: Art, Gender, and Commemoration in* "Alcestis," "Hippolytus," *and* "Hecuba," 51–72. Durham, N.C.

———. 1994. Female Mourning and Dionysiac Lament in Euripides' *Bacchae*. In *Orchestra: Drama Muthos Bühne*, ed. Anton Bierl and Peter von Möllendorff, 12–18. Stuttgart.

Seremetakis, C. Nadia. 1991. *The Last Word: Women, Death, and Divination in Inner Mani*. Chicago.

Shapiro, H. A. 1991. The Iconography of Mourning in Athenian Art. *American Journal of Archaeology* 95: 629–656.

Simon, Erika. 1969. *Die Götter der Griechen*. Munich.

Sourvinou-Inwood, Christiane. 2003. *Tragedy and Athenian Religion*. Lanham, Md.

Stears, Karen. 1998. Death Becomes Her: Gender and Athenian Death Ritual. In *The Sacred and the Feminine in Ancient Greece*, ed. Sue Blundell and Margaret Williamson, 113–127. London.

Suter, Ann. 2003. Lament in Euripides' *Trojan Women*. *Mnemosyne* Series 4, 56 (1): 1–28.

Tsagalis, Christos. 2004. *Epic Grief: Personal Laments in Homer's* "Iliad." Berlin.

Van Wees, Hans. 1998. A Brief History of Tears. In *When Men Were Men: Masculinity, Power, and Identity in Classical Antiquity*, ed. Lin Foxhall and John Salmon, 10–53. London.

Vidal-Naquet, Pierre. 1981. *Le chasseur noir*. Paris.

Winkler, John J. 1990. The Ephebe's Song: *Tragôidia* and *Polis*. In *Nothing to Do with Dionysos?* ed. John J. Winkler and Froma I. Zeitlin, 20–62. Princeton.

Wright, Elinor. 1986. The Forms of Lament in Greek Tragedy. Unpublished Ph.D. dissertation, University of Pennsylvania.

Zeitlin, Froma I. 1996. *Playing the Other: Gender and Society in Classical Greek Literature*. Chicago.

Zuntz, Gunther. 1963. *Political Plays of Euripides*. Manchester.

9

GREEK COMEDY'S PARODY OF LAMENT

ANDROMACHE KARANIKA

This essay analyzes the parody of lament in Aristophanes' *Thesmophor-iazusae,* and discusses how lament is represented in a comic context and what this tells us about the lament genre. Much of current scholarship on lament focuses on reconstructing ritual lamentation based on evidence from early Greek epic poetry and Classical tragedy. As it has been argued, lament in epic poetry fulfils an important position of complement to heroic activity and "becomes the linguistic and generic inverse of heroic kleos."[1] Likewise, in elegy and tragedy it forms an integral part of the protagonists' situation. Tragedians go beyond that and use lament as women used it in real life, namely, to utter a voice on public matters.[2] Lamentation, however, is also present in the context of comedy and satirical texts that constitute witnesses about the genre that are worthy of more attention. As I argue in this chapter, the parody of lament in comedy plays a distinctive role, comparable to the role it plays in tragedy. Lament in the *Thesmophoriazusae* is used to make allusions to tragedy and, more than that, to create powerful political references to the politics of 411 B.C.E., the time of its performance.

Performances of ritual lamentation in real life traditionally involve an antiphonal dialogue between a central figure and a chorus of women.[3] The single lamenting voice stirs up the emotion among the chorus of other women. In this context, lamentation acquires sociopolitical force, becomes provocative, and challenges male-dominated societies. Recent research on lamentation has promoted an anthropological perspective on the represen-tation of laments in ancient literature. Vestiges of ancient lamentation are

181

preserved for us through ancient texts. Tragedy presents a crystallized tradition, behind which one can find rich cultural practices. As Foley remarks: "It is difficult to make sense of these aspects of Greek tragedy without assuming that the original audience brought to the plays not only contemporary experience of lamentation and death ritual but a cultural memory (one that Athenians themselves clearly believed to be genuine) of those aspects of the tradition that had been curtailed by law."[4]

Women are brought together in lamentation, and their voices are forceful. It is in this direction that the anthropological perspective has been most fruitful, helping us to understand more fully that lamentation may come from the periphery of the *polis* but nonetheless articulates and manipulates its audience in a complex manner on political and social matters.[5] Women's active role in handling the reputation of the deceased through ritual lamentation enables them to create social memory and channel public opinion and action.[6] Recent studies shed more light on the ethics and use of lamentation in tragedy and relate them to actual historical events. For instance, Suter relates the Euripidean representation of lament with the Sicilian expedition, an event that was crucial in the Peloponnesian War.[7] Likewise, Foley places her reading of the laments in the Sophoclean *Electra* in the context of the oligarchic revolution of 411 B.C.E.[8]

A perspective from comedy and the parody of lament can illuminate further the social function of lament, as well as the implicit references in comic texts. Aristophanic scholarship has been divided by the radical question of the presence or absence of politics in comedy.[9] Aristophanes' *Thesmophoriazusae* is thought by many to be the least politically engaged of all extant comedies. Indeed, at first reading, Aristophanes is simply invading and satirizing female ritual.[10] Euripides sends his Kinsman to the Thesmophoria on his behalf, dressed as a woman; the participants of the ritual find out his true sex and take him captive. The play stages four attempts to rescue the Kinsman from his captivity, all of which are carefully crafted parodies of plays by Euripides. Without undermining the importance of ritual, Aristophanes sets himself in an agonistic position vis-à-vis tragedy and Euripidean drama in particular. Recent studies have regarded the *Thesmophoriazusae* as a play that encapsulates the competition not only between Euripides and Aristophanes but ultimately between tragedy and comedy.[11] A comedy overtly inspired by tragedy, it testifies to the importance of theater in the spectators' lives.[12]

The Kinsman first attempts to escape by acting out a scene from Euripides' lost *Telephus* after seizing Mica's baby and running to the altar. This is when "para-tragedy" begins, namely, the parody of tragic scenes from Euripides. In the original *Telephus*, the hero, the Greek king of Mysia, disguised as a beggar, enters Agamemnon's palace, seizes Agamemnon's son, little Orestes, and threatens him with death.[13] He then takes refuge at an altar. In the parody of *Thesmophoriazusae*, the Kinsman seizes Mica's little girl, which, in a burlesque, is proven to be a wineskin. As the Kinsman runs to the altar in the orchestra with the "baby," Mica starts screaming. At that moment she first cries out and repeats the words:

Τάλαιν' ἐγώ, τάλαινα   (690)

Me, the wretched one.

This expression is typically used in lamentation scenes in tragedy.[14] As in real lamentation scenes, such cries are used to stir up emotion and bring the group of women together. At the beginning of the para-tragedy part of the *Thesmophoriazusae*, lamenting features are presented in parody and set the tone for what will follow. In tragic manner, Mica continues the poetics of self-pity in reproaching the other women:

ΓΥ. A' ὦ τάλαιν' ἐγώ.
Γυναῖκες, οὐκ ἀρήξετ'; Οὐ πολλὴν βοὴν
στήσεσθε καὶ τροπαῖον, ἀλλὰ τοῦ μόνου
τέκνου με περιόψεσθ' ἀποστερουμένην; (695–698)

Me the wretched one, women, won't you help me?
Won't you raise a loud war cry and a victory trophy, or
you will look at me as I become bereft of my only child.

The references to war cries and victory trophies make her cries even more intense. The commentators remark that this "zeugma" of war cry and victory trophy is "doubtless intended to be amusing."[15] Although this is certainly the case, at the same time this expression is part of several well-chosen political references to war and failure, as will be argued later on. In this light, the first parody lament carefully presents a woman in panic who yet manages to bring her fellow women together.

The chorus responds with cries:

ΧΟ. Ἔα ἔα.
ὦ πότνιαι Μοῖραι, τί τόδε δέρκομαι
νεοχμὸν αὖ τέρας; (699–701)

Ah, Ah, oh revered Fates, what new horror is the one that
I hold my eyes on?

The chorus's response and the reference to Fates are not accidental. It is yet another reference to tragedy.[16] The Fates are not simply a generalized notion of Destiny. As Fraenkel remarks, they are "the particular fate which causes the appropriate penalty to follow inevitably upon every sin" and who bring forth the connections between cause and effect, guilt and atonement.[17] The response by the chorus leader brings forth the notion of "shame":

'ως ἅπαντ' ἄρ' ἐστὶ τόλμης ἔργα κἀναισχυντίας   (702)

How everything is full of boldness and shamelessness.

This phrase acquires a different perspective when seen in the light of the political meaning in these parodies. Shame and shamelessness are powerful emotions that are encountered in epic lamentation. Helen's self-reproach in the *Iliad* demarcates the intensity as well as the manipulation of such emotions.[18] Lament becomes the vehicle of a primordial passing of judgment on what is right and what is wrong, what is acceptable and what is not, and, in its turn, defines shame and shamelessness. The leader's response in the parody scene is expressed in general terms, and despite the comic context, it becomes a commentary on contemporary politics around the Sicilian expedition. The theme of impudence is constantly reiterated in the words of the women (708, 720, 743).

The *Telephus* is aptly used in parody by Aristophanes in his *Acharnians*, performed at the Lenaea of 425 B.C.E. In that play, Aristophanes takes a serious political stance to promote peace while also establishing for the first time a relation with tragic poetry. It is mostly tragic speeches and in particular speeches of self-defense that are parodied.[19] In the *Acharnians*, the poet comes close to the parodied Telephus, as both had suffered slander. Just as Telephus, the king of Mysia, a Greek descendant of Herakles, was wounded by another Greek, Achilles, Aristophanes was at the time facing trouble from his indictment by Cleon.[20] At the same time, when the disguised beggar defends his countrymen, the Mysians, by saying that the Achaeans themselves would have reacted to a sudden, unprovoked attack on their country, in his use of the myth, he gives a Trojan perspective. The same happens in the *Thesmophoriazusae*, as Aristophanes brings to stage, through the parody of Telephus, the perspective from those in a faraway land.[21]

The final outcome in the *Thesmophoriazusae*, when Mica's baby is proven to be a wineskin, forms another link with the end of the *Acharnians*, where the associations among peace, wine, and comedy are overt.[22] For a man like Dikaiopolis, peace is translated into wine, and wine recalls the festivals in honor of the god of wine, Dionysus.[23] In the *Thesmophoriazusae*, however, peace is not a reality. Wine and drinking, references to peace in the *Acharnians*, are criticized by the Kinsman in the *Thesmophoriazusae*, when he realizes there is no baby but a wineskin:

> ὦ θερμόταται γυναῖκες, ὦ ποτίσταται
> κἀκ παντὸς ὑμεῖς μηχανώμεναι πιεῖν,
> ὦ μέγα καπήλοις ἀγαθόν, ἡμῖν δ᾽ αὖ κακόν,
> κακὸν δὲ καὶ τοῖς σκευαρίοις καὶ τῇ κρόκῃ.   (735–738)

O overheated women, o you most prone to drinking, constantly devising how to drink, a very good thing to bartenders but bad for us, our crockery, and our weaving.

The Kinsman's second attempt to escape involves a scene from another lost play by Euripides: *Palamedes*. The *Palamedes* was produced in

415 B.C.E., at the height of the Peloponnesian War, right before the Sicilian expedition. The Achaean hero is executed, while his brother sends a message to their father, writing it on oar blades. Aristophanes is making fun of the scene, as the Kinsman proposes as his safety plan to write a message on oar blades. Both *Telephus* and *Palamedes* present heroes related to the Trojan War who were trapped by Achaean mistakes: the land of Telephus was attacked by mistake on the way to Troy before the Trojan expedition, whereas Palamedes, after the Trojan War, was falsely charged with treason and then died. The first two parodies bring forth moments of tragedy at the beginning and end of the Trojan War, respectively, which evoke memories of political errors and treason. As Vickers argues, this could be a subtle reference to Alcibiades, who was in contact with the Persians around the time of production of the *Thesmophoriazusae*. The reference to oars and the use of the mythic material presented in a recent tragedy make an interesting choice for a parody in Aristophanes, as it could be used to refer to actual historical events in summer 411, when Andocides supplied oar spars to the Athenians at Samos but was later imprisoned by the oligarchs. Alcibiades' visit to Tissaphernes in 411 might also be hinted at.[24]

In the *parabasis*, the chorus seizes the opportunity and conveys its political messages. This is the point when the *Thesmophoriazusae* reaches the peak of its political commentary, in its direct references to politicians such as Hyperbolus and Lamachus (840–841). The leader of the chorus is trying to make an argument for women's superiority to men and pairs names of men and women. She mentions Charminus, the Athenian naval commander who was defeated in winter 412/411 at Syme, and finds him worse than a certain Nausimache, a female name that means "victory at sea."[25] She proceeds to compare Cleophon, another popular politician, to a certain Salabaccho, a courtesan also referred to in Aristophanes' *Knights* (765). She then produces two more female names: Aristomache, a name that means "excellent in battle" and possibly evokes a glorious Athenian past, and Stratonice, a name that means "army victory."

In his attempt to escape the women's captivity, the Kinsman parodies passages from Euripides' *Helen* at 850–928 and his lost *Andromeda*. Both these plays were produced in 412 B.C.E., about a year before the *Thesmophoriazusae*.[26] Both parodies focus on female heroines in danger in foreign lands: Andromeda and Helen. The parody of Euripides' *Helen* in the *Thesmophoriazusae* not only constitutes a comic version of the recently staged tragedy but comes right after explicit references to Lamachus, the Athenian commander who died in the Sicilian expedition (*Thesmo.* 841), also parodied in other comedies by Aristophanes.[27] Euripides' *Helen* presents a story in which the heroine at Troy turns out to have been a mere phantom, while the real Helen was in Egypt at the palace of Proteus. Menelaus finds out the truth about his wife, finds her in Egypt, and escapes with her. The parody draws mainly on Helen's prologue, Menelaus's confrontation with King Theoclymenus's doorkeeper, an old woman, and the recognition scene between husband and wife.

In the first, Helen's part in the prologue of Euripides' *Helen* has adapted the form of lament for its exposition. The disguised Kinsman plays the role of Helen, proclaims his identity as Helen, and plays with some typical lament features—reproach and refusal to live:

KH. Κἀγὼ μὲν ἐνθάδ᾽ εἰμ᾽· ὁ δ᾽ ἄθλιος πόσις
οὑμὸς Μενέλεως οὐδέπω προσέρχεται.
Τί οὖν ἔτι ζῶ;   (866–868)

And I am right here, whereas my wretched husband,
my Menelaus, is no longer coming. Therefore, why am I still alive?

At the same time the epithet for Menelaus, ἄθλιος, chosen to be echoed in comedy, shows how external lament features are manipulated to turn responsibility toward another character, while it also implicitly presents Menelaus as the one accountable for Helen's position. The word ἄθλιος is twice used in Euripides' *Helen* (49, 958), the first time by Helen, making the accusation toward her husband, and the second by Menelaus, responding to it. Real lamentation practices are evoked here. "Naming" and "calling out" are used often in ritual lament.

A closer look at *Thesmophoriazusae* 1008–1060 shows further how lament scenes are important in Aristophanes' parody. Ancient scholiasts noted long ago that in these lines Euripides' laments from the lost *Andromeda* are parodied.[28] In particular, the scene where Andromeda speaks lamenting her fate, addressing a chorus of young women, is the target of parody.[29] In this passage, Andromeda has been chained on a rock by her father, Cepheus, the king of Ethiopia, to be devoured by a sea monster, in an effort to appease the god of the sea, Poseidon. In the *Thesmophoriazusae* lament, the lines emphasize the external features of lamentation, namely, the antiphonic choral structure. The actor playing Andromeda carefully alludes to female lamentation scenes with the linguistic references to *goos* (1036), as well as the use of self-pity (1038, 1042) and blame. The voice of the leader of the chorus, Andromeda, seeks union with the voices of the other women:

Γαμηλίῳ μὲν οὐ ξὺν
παιῶνι, δεσμίῳ δὲ
γοᾶσθέ μ᾽, ὦ γυναῖκες, ὡς
μέλεα μὲν πέπονθα μέλεος,
– ὦ τάλας ἐγώ, τάλας, –
ἀπὸ δὲ συγγόνων ἄλλ᾽ ἄνομα
πάθεα, φῶτα λιτομένα,
πολυδάκρυτον Ἀίδα γόον φλέγουσα,
– αἰαῖ αἰαῖ, –   (1034–1042)

Lament me, women,
Not with a wedding hymn but a hymn

Of bond, for wretched do I suffer wretchedly
Alas, alas, woe—
And from lawless sufferings of my kinsmen,
I implored the man, igniting the tearful groans of Hades,
oh, oh.

In the beginning of the play, Andromeda speaks with the echo of her own voice, whereas later she is joined by a chorus of young girls, which is clearly a situation of ritual lamentation. She laments her own fate and invites the other girls to join her. As is befitting with lamentations for young women, a contrast is made between wedding songs and *gooi* (1034–1035).[30] The parody probably has musical elements, and Aristophanes imitates the words sung by Andromeda in the Euripides play.[31]

The references to chains in the text are extensive: on one hand, the bonds of Andromeda in the parody and, on the other, the bonds in which the Kinsman is held after his arrest (930–931, 940, 943, 1013, 1022, 1032, 1035, 1108, 1125). This particular emphasis could have its counterpart in contemporary political reality. As Austin and Olson remark, one of the things we know about the Athenian Thesmophoria is that prisoners in the city were released from their chains for the duration of the festival.[32]

In this particular case, though, the *goos* refers to the imminent death and the prisoner's bonds. Andromeda is chained on the rock, waiting to be eaten by a monster of the sea. I propose that the *Thesmophoriazusae*, far from being one of Aristophanes' least political plays, creates with its parody of lament and the allusion to prisoner's bonds as part of the parody the same effect as tragedy: it becomes a powerful commentary on the contemporary political situation and the outcome of the Sicilian expedition, as experienced in 411 B.C.E., the time of its first production. In that perspective, the reference in Andromeda's lament blaming her father for her "lawless sufferings" (1039) can be read as a comment on politics.[33]

Euripides' references to Helen and Andromeda were aptly presented a year earlier than the *Thesmophoriazusae*, in 412 B.C.E., evoking faraway places. Both plays involve a happy end and return of the hero, unlike the actual events in Sicily. The idea of a faraway land was appealing to the people of Athens. As Bury and Meiggs note: "The people, elated by their recent triumph over Melos, were fascinated by the idea of making new conquests in a distant, unfamiliar world; the ordinary Athenian had very vague ideas of what Sicily meant; and, carried away by dreams of a western empire, he paid no more attention to the discreet counsels of Nicias than to vote a 100 triremes instead of the 60 which were originally asked for."[34]

Parody in Aristophanes is more intricately woven, as the two plays with a happy outcome are unsuccessful when seen from the perspective of the Kinsman's attempt to rescue himself. Whereas both Helen and Andromeda are rescued, the comic burlesque fails, something that underlines further the point that Aristophanes is trying to make. Tragedy fails, as the Kinsman in his "tragic acts" is not able to escape until later. Tragedy

fails to convey the message of the danger in faraway lands. The parody of
tragic lamentation stirs through laughter the image of the impossible.
When Andromeda asks for help, she calls the chorus of maids. Instead, in
Aristophanes' version, the scene is parodied by having Echo as the respondent to the single lamenter. The scene with Echo focuses on the
centrality of the protagonist, who can hear only herself, the voice
in the desert sea that is able to reproduce itself alone. Taafe has analyzed
the shaving and cross-dressing of the Kinsman as a move that extends itself
beyond the move from male to female, to the transition from spectator to
actor.[35] The moment when he looks at the mirror marks the union
between spectatorship and acting. In like terms, the Kinsman as "Andromeda" mirrors his voice through the presence of Echo and does more than
just cause laughter. The dialogue with Echo consists of one of the funniest
moments of this play, while it underlines Andromeda's solitude and need
for rescue. She is the lamenter and recipient of her lament, unable to reach
her chorus, both agent and sole spectator of her crying and wailing that
she cannot fulfill (1064–1065).

Both the *Andromeda* and the *Helen* soften the friction between tragedy and comedy and stretch the boundaries of tragedies. Bowie suggests
that the *Thesmophoriazusae* forms an answer on behalf of Aristophanes to
the new boundaries that tragedy was developing.[36] In his view, comedy is
the winner by revealing more flexibility and potential. The use of Andromeda's lament in particular shows how comedy's boundaries are extended
to incorporate the quintessence of tragedy, lamentation. Aristophanes
reads and deploys lamentation that is usually present only in tragedy.
Lament in comedy is used as a means to underline its function in
tragedy: bring the community together and make a mark on shared
cultural memory. Andromeda's lament is parodied in all possible ways.
Her words in Aristophanes are welcomed only by Echo.

Inscriptional evidence on laws and regulations for funerary practices
emphasizes the link between women's lament and its effect on political life.
The state intervened to regulate lamentation. Special reference is made to
the clothes both men and women ought to wear at a funeral and purification rites, as well as to the duration of the lamenting period. An inscription
from Gambreion (ca. third century B.C.E.), situated eight miles away from
Pergamon in Asia Minor, is typical of such regulations in the Greek world.
This particular inscription makes specific reference to the Thesmophoria
and to the physical temple outside which a column inscribed with the law
would be erected. Let us investigate this law to see what it may tell us
about the *Thesmophoriazusae*:

Νόμον εἶναι Γαμβρειώταις τὰς πενθούσας φαιὰν ἐσθῆτα
μὴ κατερρυπωμένην· χρῆσθαι δὲ καὶ τοὺς ἄνδρας καὶ τοὺς
παῖδας τοὺς πενθοῦντας ἐσθῆτι φαιᾷ ἐὰμ μὴ βούλωνται
λευκῇ. Ἐπιτελεῖν τὰ νόμιμα τοῖς ἀποιχομένοις ἔσχατον
ἐν τρισὶ μησὶν, τῷ δὲ

τετάρτῳ λύειν τὰ πένθη τοὺς ἄνδρας, τὰς δὲ γυναῖκας
τῷ πέμπτωι καὶ ἐξανίστασθαι ἐκ τῆς κηδείας καὶ
ἐμπορεύεσθαι τὰς γυναῖκας ἤδη τὰς ἐξόδους
τὰς ἐν τῷ νόμῳ γεγραμμένας ἐπάναγκον.
Τὸν δὲ γυναικονόμον τὸν ὑπὸ τοῦ δήμου αἱρούμενον
τοῖς ἁγισμοῖς τοῖς πρὸ τῶν Θεσμοφορίων. ἐπεύχεσθαι
τοῖς ἐμμένουσιν. καὶ ταῖς πειθομέναις τῷ δὲ νόμῳ εὖ εἶναι
καὶ τῶν ὑπαρχόντων ὄνησιν, τοῖς δὲ μὴ πειθομένοις μηδὲ ταῖς
ἐμμενούσαις τἀναντία· καὶ μὴ ὅσιον αὐταῖς εἶναι, ὡς ἀσεβούσαις,
θύειν μηδενὶ θεῶν ἐπὶ δέκα ἔτη. Τὸν μετὰ Δημήτριον
στεφανηφόρον ταμίαν αἱρεθέντα ἀναγράψαι τόνδε τὸν νόμον
εἰς δύο στήλας καὶ ἀναθεῖναι, τὴν μὲν μίαν πρὸ τῶν θυρῶν τοῦ
Θεσμοφορίου, τὴν δὲ πρὸ τοῦ νεὼ τῆς Ἀρτέμιδος τῆς Λοχίας (4–33)[37]

There is a law among the citizens of Gambreion, that the women
who lament
wear dark clothes, not dirty ones; the men and children who lament should
also wear dark clothes, if they do not wish so, they can wear white. They
should conduct the necessary rites in three months the latest, and the men
should stop in the fourth month, whereas the women in the fifth. And
that the
women should be released from their funeral duties and return back
to public
life according to the law. The *gynaikonomos* who has been chosen by the
people in the purification rites preceding the Thesmophoria should pray
for those who abide by the law to be well and to have prosperity, whereas
for those who do not obey the law, the opposite. And it should not be
fitting for them, as they do not revere the sacred things, to sacrifice to any
of the gods for ten years. The one who was elected treasurer, in the year
after that of the*stephanephoros* Demetrios, should write up this law in two
columns and erect the one in front of the doors of the Thesmophorion,
and the other in front of the temple of Artemis Lochia.

This text reveals funerary practices and the need for regulations,
especially concerning women. The ordinance imposed law and order
while also linking the punishment with public rites. The first part
of the regulations concerns the physical appearance of both men
and women. Women were supposed to wear dark brown or dark
gray clothes as an external marker of their official lamenting status. It is
particularly noteworthy that the punishment for women who did
not abide by the regulations regarding their lamentation practices was
to be barred from sacrifices to the gods. The spatial references are
illuminating. Women's return to public life is referred to as an "exit"
(ἐξόδους [16]).

Bearing this inscription in mind, we may call Aristophanes' choice to
create parody with emphasis on the lamentation scene quite understandable.

As David Konstan argues, Aristophanic utopian worlds are not arbitrary fantasies but images of customary, though complicated, order. They are complex representations of Athens's contradictions and communal structures.[38] The *Thesmophoriazusae* presents the world of comic lament organized in the same way as the real one.

Women's lamentation is seen as a target for punishment if it remains outside of civic control. In this respect, just as a female congregation poses danger for Euripides in the *Thesmophoriazusae*, excessive lamentation poses danger for civic unity in the eyes of the lawmakers of Gambreion. Thus, it becomes imperative to impose laws and make them visible outside the places of female congregation. The very name of the festival, Thesmophoria, is thought to derive from Demeter Thesmophoros because she placed the laws and rites according to which people must work and earn their food:

Θεσμοφορία δὲ καλεῖται, καθότι θεσμοφόρος ἡ Δημήτηρ
κατονομάζεται τιθεῖσα νόμους ἤτοι θεσμούς, καθ' οὓς τὴν
τροφὴν πορίζεσθαί τε καὶ κατεργάζεσθαι ἀνθρώπους δέον.[39]

It is called Thesmophoria, because Demeter is called *thesmophoros*, as she placed the rites according to which people must find their food and work.

Bobrick emphasizes that these parodies reverse the women's relationship to their sacred space.[40] In ritual, women are the agents. In Aristophanes' parodies in the *Thesmophoriazusae*, they become spectators and interact with characters from tragedy. Unlike in the festival of the Thesmophoria, in Aristophanes' play, there is no longer the female rescue of the female that involves a mother and a daughter but, rather, the male rescue of the female, as with Menelaus and Helen, Perseus and Andromeda. In Aristophanes, women are depicted acting in cult contexts, several times: in the *Ecclesiazusae* the festival of Skira gives an opportunity, and in *Lysistrata* the female chorus's meeting coincides with the Boiotian festival for Hekate (700).[41] Ritual defines and marks the *Thesmophoriazusae* also, and it is now time to turn to that.

Lamentation in the *Thesmophoriazusae* is present in more ways than just the narrative of parodies. The Thesmophoria, a ritual dedicated to the rescue of Persephone by her mother, involved some type of presentation of the myth, but we do not know in any detail how it was reenacted. Although there is disagreement as to the exact activities about the Thesmophoria and their relation to the story in the *Hymn*, still there are striking similarities that cannot be disregarded. There is a correspondence between the festival calendar and the myth. The festival calendar started with the *Anodos* (Ascent) that signified Demeter's withdrawal. *Nesteia* (fasting) followed to mark Demeter's period of mourning and lamentation.[42] It is believed that the *aischrologia* (ritual obscenity) marked the transition between the second phase of the ritual to the third, that of celebration and sacrifice for the *Kalligeneia* (birth of fair offspring). The end of the festival involved activities that sought to ensure fertility.[43] Though there is no conclusive evidence about the relationship of the reunion theme in the *Hymn*, the theme is not incongruent with rites for the return of fertility that are believed to have taken place during the festival of the Thesmophoria.[44] It is noteworthy that the parodies of Euripides' tragedies are placed during *Nesteia*, the fasting period. In this respect, the theme of the Kinsman's captivity reflects the captivity of Persephone. Tzanetou, investigating the parallels among the myth, the events of the festival, and the complex dramatic structure of the play, remarks acutely that "the comic performance, which results in the Kinsman's liberation, suggests the transition to the third and final day (*Kalligeneia*), the return of Persephone. The end of mourning is signalled by the increasing comic obscenity in the parody of *Andromeda*, which marks the shift from tragedy to comedy as well as the transition from *Nesteia* to *Kalligeneia*."[45] Another similarity is when the Kinsman, a captive in the narrative of the *Thesmophoriazusae*, draws attention with his acting to another captive, namely, Andromeda. Andromeda's lyric monody can be read as an allusion to the story of Persephone, a girl who was also a captive. This is the crescendo of the play where ritual and dramatic and metatheatrical references all come to one, all become encapsulated in the theme of the captive maiden lamenting.

Malcolm Heath explores pervasive parallels between comedy and later political oratory and suggests the influence on Aristophanes of the contemporary practices of political rhetoric.[46] There are echoes of political discourse and cultural practices in Aristophanes. The problem is how one demarcates the line between the represented comic world and the real one. What kind of context can we give to the comic text when cultural practices such as lamentation are both the basis and the generator of the comic effect? The last question that needs to be answered, then, is how the use of lament can trigger the comic effect as well as sharpen the allusions to contemporary political realities.

Ritual lamentation is not incongruent with laughter, in either a mythical or a ritual and social context. Already in the *Homeric Hymn to Demeter* (199–204) Iambe eases the heart of grieving Demeter with her jokes. The words for joking and mocking suggest insult directed at someone.[47] Insult causes laughter that makes the goddess both abandon her sorrow and recapture her femininity. More important, Demeter's laughter at Iambe's performance places the divinity in the human social sphere.[48] The mythographer Apollodorus (1.5.1) assumes Iambe's jesting as a possible explanation for the ritual obscenity at the festival of Thesmophoria. Many scholars find a distinctive female voice in *aischrologia*, and indeed, it has a specific context and function in the narrative of the *Hymn*.[49] Obscenity is expected in comedy and used in many ways. Comic poets were allowed to go beyond the social norms.[50] But what is the parody of lament really doing?

Halliwell, in an influential article on Greek laughter, suggests that "at a deeper level, the licence allowed to Old Comedy may always have been precarious, for it presupposed in the city as a whole a climate which could accept the mockery of almost everything which the city itself took seriously."[51] Laughter in comedy plays with subjects "on which life outside the festival depended."[52] Lament, used throughout tragedy, is only scarcely touched on in comedy. Aristophanes inserts a parody of lament to test the genre's limits. He carefully constructs a parody of a captive heroine in faraway lands and carefully uses self-blame, a feature distinctive in real lamentation practices:

Εἴθε με πυρφόρος αἰθέρος ἀστὴρ
τὸν δύσμορον ἐξολέσειεν. (1050–1051)

May a fiery bolt from the skies
Obliterate the wretched one.

Presenting a parody of lament, with Echo's the only response, the lamentation is rendered weak, deprived of its empowering elements. One woman cannot lament. One voice cannot be heard only by its echo. Aristophanes is typically closing the *Thesmophoriazusae* with a message for unity and peace. His last parody of the lament emphasizes how his political message fails if followed by an echo of its own voice. Therefore the role of audience is critical. The metatheatrical element that the *Thesmophoriazusae* presents in abundance is emphasized through the character of Echo. The audience is necessary and constantly "negotiates" and "renegotiates" license and laughter.[53] Laughter is a potent medium in which contests can find a context and can be publicly declared. Yet the persistent Greek view was that laughter can also pose dangers to the social fabric of the *polis*.[54] And such laughing about a lament can be doubly dangerous, as it involves the worst fear of all, mockery after one's death.[55] Such references to cultural practices like lamentation present the opportunity to the poet to energize a tradition from which comedy constantly draws material while at the same time renegotiating that tradition's role. The poet does not simply play with established cultural practices. He "renegotiates" their function and defines new limits for both laughter and lamentation, bringing the two extremes together.

From an anthropological point of view, mockery and sarcasm constitute important means available for use by the lamenters. One of the most influential studies of contemporary lament practices is that by Seremetakis, who studied lamentation in the area of Inner Mani in the southern Peloponnese in Greece.[56] In this society, men practiced revenge, the "vendetta," killing the killer of one's kinsmen to avenge the death of their own kinsmen, and have traditionally managed violence through physical assault and retaliation of murder. Women, while often seen as agents in such retaliation practices, have another means of action, that of lamentation. As Seremetakis argues: "[W]omen, in contrast, manage violence with language and sound. Men do display violence linguistically, but their verbal power is dependent on the capacity to perform physical violence. Women's acoustic-linguistic violence has no external authorizing referent, unless one wants to consider the presence of the corpse in the *klama* as the authorizing agency."[57] This acoustic-linguistic violence, intertwined with the memorializing power of speech, as practiced by women, could be directed against the dead as well as toward the living, often exceeding the personal control of the singer. Seremetakis gives an important testimony from one of her informants: "Here, you see when one was killed, women could use in the lament all kinds of obscenities, too. In the laments, they could kill a person with language (*loyia*)."[58] This offers anthropological comparanda for the female authority in commemoration of the dead as well as direct invective against those responsible for a death of a kinsman, a *vendetta* in the female way.[59] At the same time, through this prism, we are urged to reconsider the sharpness that lament inherently exhibits.

There is one final question for which we must leave the sphere of comedy. How does the presence of parodied lament help us understand better the act of lamentation itself? Aristophanes, through the parody of Euripidean lament, adds another dimension to our understanding of the role of lamentation in real life. In both Euripides and Aristophanes, we see a clear emphasis on the relation that is established between the marginalized group and society through the use of confessional discourse. An anthropological comparison is illuminating here; as Seremetakis remarks in her study of lament in Inner Mani, pain is used by the lamenters to challenge and manipulate dominant ideologies.[60] The same pattern is also seen in Euripides in the presentation of lament by old men, where pain and its expression in confessional discourse dramatize the dissonance between margins and center in a society, marking further the state of dissonance.[61] Through lament and remembrance of the dead, the lamenter brings destruction to the absolute center of public attention. Restoration can only come after destruction; lamentation does exactly that, and it challenges the city. Aristophanes is a *didaskalos* seeking both to restore and to heal a city full of problems.[62] Restoration shines when it comes after destruction. The performance of comedies has a constructive and restorative role.[63] Aristophanic heroes are radical minds that often bring restoration through the destruction of current orders. Comedy criticizes and proposes different tracks of action.[64] Lysistrata is a destroyer of armies who proposes radical solutions that will bring peace. Strepsiades, in the *Clouds*, destroys the Socratic *phrontisterion*.[65] The pattern of restoration that follows destruction has its mythic—as well as tragic—counterpart in the worship of Dionysus, the god of theater, in Euripides' *Bacchae*, which presents the same themes of cross-dressing, theatrical illusion, and its rupture.[66] The *Thesmophoriazusae* is a unique comedy, as it presents the theme of restoration through multiple venues: lamentation, women's ritual, and ultimately theater itself. All the parodies of Euripidean drama present the theme of restoration. Ritual is thus reintegrated through lamentation into comedy and leads to restoration, as it does in tragedy.

Satire, sexuality, and lament are themes consciously used in this comedy. By parodying tragedy and creating his own adaptation of the female rescue pattern, Aristophanes situates himself in the contest between tragedy and comedy and also affirms the importance of women by presenting them in their ritual space. By bringing together his own versions of *Helen* and *Andromeda* in the *Thesmophoriazusae*, he alludes to the power of female lament and its role in tragedy—and uses it himself in his comedy. Lament is here defined and explicated by its parody.

ACKNOWLEDGMENT

I wish to thank the editor of this volume, Prof. Ann Suter, for all the time and effort she has put in reading and commenting on multiple drafts of this chapter and for her constant encouragement.

NOTES

1. Derderian 2001, 32.

2. Foley 2001; Suter 2003.

3. For a discussion on literary representations of the performance of lament in early Greek poetry in a choral or solo setting with comparative evidence from other cultures, see Martin, this volume.

4. Foley 2001, 153.

5. For an anthropological perspective on lament, see Caraveli 1981, 1986; Danforth 1982; Holst-Warhaft 1992, 2000; Morgan 1973; Seremetakis 1991, 1993.

6. See Stears, this volume.

7. Suter 2003, with references to earlier scholarship making the same connection.

8. Foley 2001, 170.

9. Some who favor the position that Aristophanes has political tendencies are de Ste. Croix 1972, 355–356; Henderson 1990. Against that position are Goldhill 1991, 167–222; Gomme 1938; Heath 1987.

10. For ritual in the *Thesmophoriazusae*, see Tzanetou 2002; Zeitlin 1996.

11. Gibert 1999–2000; Henderson 1990;Hubbard 1991; Stehle 2002; Zeitlin 1996.

12. For more on this, see Bobrick 1997, 191.

13. It is noteworthy that this scene had been parodied earlier in Aristophanes' *Acharnians* (325–351). For a study on the parody of Euripides' *Telephus*, see also Foley 1988.

14. For example, A. *Ch.* 743; S. *Ai.* 341, *El.* 807; E. *Med.* 511, *Hipp.* 300, *Hec.* 233, *IT* 549.

15. See Austin and Olson 2004, 245.

16. See A. *Ag.* 1535–1536.

17. See Austin and Olson 2004, 245, quoting Fraenkel on A. *Ag.* 1535–1536.

18. See Martin, this volume.

19. Foley 1988, esp. 33–36; Harriott 1962.

20. See the scholia to the *Acharnians* 378.

21. See also Miller 1948 for the view of Telephus as a dramatic prototype for Aristophanes' characters in both the *Acharnians* and the *Thesmophoriazusae*.

22. See in particular *Acharnians* 1225–1235, where the wineskin features prominently as a motif highlighting notions of victory and peace.

23. See Edmunds1980, 6.

24. See Vickers 1989, 47–48.

25. Sommerstein 1977, 116.

26. Sommerstein 1977; Vickers 1989, 42–43. The scholia to *Thesmophoriazusae* 1060 provide the information that the *Andromeda* was produced the previous year.

27. Lamachus is present in the *Acharnians*, where he is linked with Telephus. See Foley 1988, 39.

28. See Tzanetou, who remarks that "Andromeda's lyric monody and her lyric exchange with the chorus form part of the parody, when the Kinsman as Andromeda performs a lament that emphasizes 'her' captivity and exclusion from the ritual choruses of her co-evals and from wedding celebrations" (2002, 349).

29. As Petersen remarks on the fragments of *Andromeda*, Andromeda's "heart-breaking lament" ridiculed by Aristophanes with the device of making Echo repeat the last word of the lament "not only is a startling stage effect, but in an admirable way brings home to the spectator the absolute loneliness of the victim abandoned to a cruel death (fr. 114–116 Nauck). Then when the Chorus of Andromeda's companions arrives on the scene, Echo obeys the maiden's behest and is silent. This is far from unnatural, for the character of the lament alters, and instead of resounding in deserted space it is addressed to friends who are standing close by (fr. 117–122)" (1904, 100).

30. These lines evoke the girl's tragedy, namely, the pattern of a girl's violent death before her marriage. See Burkert 1979; Tzanetou 2002, 349; Levaniouk, this volume.

31. See MacDowell 1995, 269.

32. Austin and Olson 2004, li.

33. For a reading of the *Thesmophoriazusae* in its political context, see also Slater, who remarks that "the crisis of 411 casts its shadow over the *Thesmophoria-zusae*. Beneath the jokes about Agathon and Euripides lies a very real concern about the freedom of democracy to hear all advice and all information necessary to make its decision, a freedom threatened by the mutual hostility of the factions" (2002, 180).

34. Bury and Meiggs 1983, 294.

35. Taafe 1993, 84–87.

36. Bowie 1993, 219–220.

37. From Frisone 2000, 139–140.

38. Konstan 1997, 16–17.

39. *Scholia in Lucianum* 80.1.

40. Bobrick 1997, 184.

41. See Foley 1982, 12. For a further discussion on the presence of ritual in Aristophanes' *Lysistrata* and the representation of the female chorus as *hydrophoroi*, women who act according to mythic patterns familiar to them, see Faraone 1997.

42. See Suter 2002, 214–226. As Suter (2002, 216) writes, none of the Thesmophoria's activities requires the abduction and reunion part of the story in the *Hymn*.

43. For a detailed account of ritual in the *Thesmophoriazusae*, see Tzanetou 2002.

44. Even though the theme of abduction does not appear to be necessary in the Thesmophoria (for details, see Suter 2002, 215–219), the myth as presented in the *Hymn to Demeter* had an influence on the way it was perceived by the general Classical audience. After all, the male audience had no idea of what actually went on during the Thesmophoria. It is possible, then, that the version of the myth as presented in the *Hymn* was applied to the Thesmophoria, as they were celebrated in Aristophanes' times.

45. Tzanetou 2002, 339.

46. Heath 1997.

47. Foley 1994, 45, 126.

48. O'Higgins 2003, ch. 2.

49. See Brumfield 1996; Winkler 1990.

50. See Halliwell 1991, 295.

51. Ibid., 296.

52. Ibid.

53. Goldhill (1991, 188) examines the role of the audience and the concept of "negotiation" and constant "renegotiation" of license.

54. Halliwell 1991, 287.

55. Ibid., 286.

56. Seremetakis 1991.

57. Ibid., 118.

58. Ibid.

59. For a discussion on the ideology of heroic death and the role of women in memorialization in the *Iliad*, see Perkell, this volume.

60. Seremetakis 1991, 3–5.

61. See Suter, this volume, in particular her analysis on Adrastus in the *Suppliants* and Xerxes in the *Persians*.

62. Reckford 1987.

63. Ibid.

64. See Ober 2005, 122.

65. For further analysis of this thought, see Bobrick 1997, 192–193.

66. On the relation of the two, see also Bobrick 1997, 193; Foley 1980. One should note here that Aristophanes' *Thesmophoriazusae* precedes Euripides' *Bacchae*. Yet the two plays have a lot in common.

BIBLIOGRAPHY

Alexiou, M. *The Ritual Lament in Greek Tradition*. Cambridge.Austin, C. and S. D. Olson, eds. 2004. *Aristophanes:* Thesmophoriazousae, *with Introduction and Commentary*. Oxford.

Bassi, K. 1989. The Actor as Actress in Euripides' *Alcestis*. In *Themes in Drama 11: Women in Theatre*, ed. J. Redmond, 19–30. Cambridge.

Bobrick, E. 1997. The Tyranny of Roles: Playacting and Privilege in Aristophanes' *Thesmophoriazousae*. In *City as Comedy: Society and Representation in Athenian Drama*, ed. G. Dobrov, 177–197. Chapel Hill.

Bowie, A. M. 1993. *Aristophanes: Myth, Ritual and Comedy*. Cambridge.

Brumfield, A. C. 1981. *The Attic Festivals of Demeter and Their Relation to the Agricultural Year*. Monographs in Classical Studies. Salem, N.H.

————. 1996. *Aporreta*: Verbal and Ritual Obscenity in the Cults of Ancient Women. In *Role of Religion in the Early Greek Polis: Proceedings of the Third International Seminar on Ancient Greek Cult, Organized by the Swedish Institute of Athens, 16–18 October 1992*, ed. Robin Hägg, 67–73. Acta Instituti Atheniensis Regnae Suediae, 80 (24). Stockholm.

Burkert, W. 1979. *Structure and History in Greek Mythology and Ritual.* Sather Classical Lectures 47. Berkeley.

Bury, J. B., and R. Meiggs. 1983. *A History of Greece to the Death of Alexander the Great.* 4th ed. New York.

Caraveli, A. 1981. Bridge Between Worlds: The Greek Women's Lament as Communicative Event. *Journal of American Folklore* 93: 129–157.

————. 1982. The Song Beyond the Song: Aesthetics and Social Interaction in Greek Folk Song. *Journal of American Folklore* 95: 129–156.

————. 1986. The Bitter Wounding: The Lament as Social Protest in Rural Greece. In *Gender and Power in Rural Greece*, ed. J. Dubisch, 169–194. Princeton.

Clinton, K. 1992. *Myth and Cult: The Iconography of the Eleusinian Mysteries.* Stockholm.

Danforth, L. 1982. *The Death Rituals of Rural Greece.* Princeton.

de Ste. Croix, G. E. M. 1972. *The Origins of the Peloponnesian War.* Ithaca, N.Y.

Derderian K. 2001. *Leaving Words to Remember: Greek Mourning and the Advent of Literacy.* Leiden.

Dué, C. 2002. *Homeric Variations on a Lament by Briseis.* Lanham, Md.

Ebbott, M. 1999. The Wrath of Helen: Self-Blame and Nemesis in the *Iliad.* In *Nine Essays on Homer*, ed. M. Carlisle and O. Levaniouk, 3–20. Lanham, Md.

Edmunds, L. 1980. Aristophanes' *Acharnians. Yale Classical Studies* 26: 1–41.

Faraone, C. A. 1997. Salvation and Female Heroics in the Parodos of Aristophanes' *Lysistrata. Journal of Hellenic Studies* 117: 38–59.

Fine, J. V. A. 1983. *The Ancient Greeks: A Critical History.* Cambridge, Mass.

Foley, H. 1980. The Masque of Dionysus. *Transactions of the American Philological Association* 110: 107–133.

————. 1982. "The Female Intruder" Reconsidered: Women in Aristophanes' *Lysistrata* and *Ecclesiazusae. Classical Philology* 77 (1): 1–21.

————. 1988. Tragedy and Politics in Aristophanes' *Acharnians. Journal of Hellenic Studies* 108: 33–47.

————. 1994. The Homeric Hymn to Demeter: *Translation, Commentary and Interpretive Essays.* Princeton.

————. 2001. *Female Acts in Greek Tragedy.* Princeton.

Frisone, F. 2000. *Legge e Regolamenti Funerari nel Mondo Greco. I. Le Fonti Epigraphiche.* Lecce.

Garland, R. 1985. *The Greek Way of Death.* Ithaca, N.Y.

Gibert, J. 1999–2000. Fall in Love with Euripides (Andromeda). In *Euripides and Tragic Theater in the Late Fifth Century*, ed. Martin J. Cropp, K. H. Lee, and D. Sansone, 75–91. *Illinois Classical Studies* 24–25 (spec. issue).

Goldhill, S. 1991. *The Poet's Voice. Essays on Poetics and Greek Literature.* Cambridge.

Gomme, A. W. 1938. Aristophanes and Politics. *Classical Review* 52 (3): 97–109.

Hall, E. 1989. The Archer Scene in Aristophanes' *Thesmophoriazusae. Philologus* 133: 38–54.

Halliwell, S. 1991. The Uses of Greek Laughter. *Classical Quarterly* 41 (2): 279–296.

Hansen, H. 1976. Aristophanes' *Thesmophoriazusae*: Theme, Structure, Production. *Philologus* 120: 165–185.

Harriott, R. M. 1962. Aristophanes' Audience and the Plays of Euripides. *Bulletin of the Institute of Classical Studies* 9: 1–8.

Heath, M. 1987. *Political Comedy in Aristophanes*. Göttingen.

——. 1997. Aristophanes and the Discourse of Politics. In *City as Comedy: Society and Representation in Athenian Drama*, ed. G. Dobrov, 230–249. Chapel Hill.

Henderson, J. 1990. The Demos and the Comic Competition. In *Nothing to Do with Dionysos? Athenian Drama in Its Social Context*, ed. J. J. Winkler and Froma Zeitlin, 271–313. Princeton.

——. 1975. *The Maculate Muse. Obscene Language in Attic Comedy*. New Haven, Conn.

Holst-Warhaft, G. 1992. *Dangerous Voices: Women's Laments and Greek Literature*. London.

——. 2000. *Cue for the Passion: Grief and Its Political Uses*. Cambridge, Mass.

Hornblower, S. 1992. The Religious Dimension to the Peloponnesian War, or What Thucydides Does Not Tell Us. *Harvard Studies in Classical Philology* 94: 169–197.

Hubbard, T. K. 1991. *The Mask of Comedy: Aristophanes and the Intertextual Parabasis*. Ithaca, N.Y.

——. 1997. Utopianism and the Sophistic City in Aristophanes. In *City as Comedy: Society and Representation in Athenian Drama*, ed. G. Dobrov, 23–50. Chapel Hill.

Konstan, D. 1995. *Greek Comedy and Ideology*. Oxford.

——. 1997. The Greek Polis and Its Negations: Versions of Utopia in Aristophanes' *Birds*. In *City as Comedy: Society and Representation in Athenian Drama*, ed. G. Dobrov, 3–22. Chapel Hill.

Lateiner, D. 2001. Humiliation and Immobility in Apuleius' *Metamorphoses*. *Transactions of the American Philological Association* 131: 217–255.

Livingstone, R. 1960. *Thucydides, The History of the Peloponnesian War*. New York.

Loraux, N. 1998. *Mothers in Mourning*. Trans. by C. Pache. Ithaca, N.Y.

MacDowell, D. M. 1995. *Aristophanes and Athens. An Introduction to the Plays*. Oxford.

Martin, R. P. 1989. *Language of Heroes: Speech and Performance in the* Iliad. Ithaca, N.Y.

McClure, L. 1999. *Spoken like a Woman: Speech and Gender in Athenian Drama*. Princeton.

Miller, H. W. 1948. Euripides' *Telephus* and the *Thesmophoriazusae* of Aristophanes. *Classical Philology* 43 (3): 174–183.

Morgan, G. 1973. The Laments of Mani. *Folklore* 84: 265–298.

Morris, I. 1992. *Death-Ritual and Social Structure in Classical Antiquity*. Cambridge.

Muecke, F. 1977. Playing with the Play: Theatrical Self-Consciousness in Aristophanes. *Antichton* 11: 52–67.

Nesselrath, H. G. 1993. Parody and Later Greek Comedy. *Harvard Studies in Classical Philology* 95: 181–195.

Ober, J. 1989. *Mass and Elite in Democratic Athens: Rhetoric, Ideology, and the Power of the People*. Princeton.

——. 2005. *Athenian Legacies: Essays on the Politics of Going on Together*. Princeton.

O'Higgins, L. 2003. *Women and Humor in Classical Greece*. Cambridge.

Parke, H. W. 1977. *Festivals of the Athenians*. Ithaca, N.Y.

Petersen, E. 1904. Andromeda. *Journal of Hellenic Studies* 24: 99–112.

Pucci, P. 1993. Antiphonal Lament Between Achilles and Briseis. *Colby Quarterly* 29: 258–272.

Rau, P. 1967. *Paratragodia: Untersuchung einer komischen Form des Aristophanes.* Zetemata 45. Munich.

Reckford, K. 1987. *Aristophanes' Old-and-New Comedy.* Vol. 1. Chapel Hill.

Rehm, R. 1994. *Marriage to Death: The Conflation of Wedding and Funeral Ritual in Greek Tragedy.* Princeton.

Roilos, P., and D. Yatromanolakis. 2003. *Ritual Poetics in Greek Culture.* Cambridge, Mass.

Schlesinger, A. C. 1937. Identification of Parodies in Aristophanes. *American Journal of Philology* 58 (3): 294–305.

Seaford, R. 1994. *Reciprocity and Ritual: Homer and Tragedy in the Developing City-State.* Oxford.

Segal, C. 1993. *Euripides and the Poetics of Sorrow.* Durham, N.C.

Seremetakis, C. N. 1991. *The Last Word: Women, Death, and Divination in Inner Mani.* Chicago.

——, ed. 1993. *Ritual, Power, and the Body: Historical Perspectives on the Representation of Greek Women.* New York.

Simon, E. 1983. *Festivals of Attica: An Archaeological Commentary.* Madison, Wisc.

Slater, N. W. 2002. *Spectator Politics: Metatheatre and Performance in Aristophanes.* Philadelphia.

Sommerstein, A H. 1977. Aristophanes and the Events of 411. *Journal of Hellenic Studies* 97: 112–126.

——. 1994. Thesmophoriazusae. *The Comedies of Aristophanes,* vol. 8. Warminster, U.K.

Stehle, E. 2002. The Body and Its Representations in Aristophanes' *Thesmophoriazousai*: Where Does the Costume End? *American Journal of Philology* 123 (3): 369–406.

Suter, A. 2002. *The Narcissus and the Pomegranate: An Archaeology of the* Homeric Hymn to Demeter. Ann Arbor.

——. 2003. Lament in Euripides' *Trojan Women. Mnemosyne* 56 (1): 1–27.

Taafe, Lauren. 1993. Aristophanes and Women. London.

Tzanetou, A. 2002. Something to Do with Demeter: Ritual and Performance in Aristophanes' *Women at the Thesmophoria. American Journal of Philology* 123: 329–367.

Vickers, M. 1989. Alcibiades on Stage: *Thesmophoriazusae* and *Helen. Historia* 36: 41–65.

——. 1997. *Pericles on Stage: Political Comedy in Aristophanes' Early Plays.* Austin.

Winkler, J. J. 1985. *Auctor and Actor: A Narratological Reading of Apuleius'* Golden Ass. Berkeley.

——. 1990. Listening to the Laughter of the Oppressed: Demeter and the Garden of Adonis. In *The Constraints of Desire: The Anthropology of Sex and Gender in Ancient Greece,* ed. J. J. Winkler, 188–209. New York.

Worman, N. 2001. This Voice Which Is Not One: Helen's Verbal Guises in Homeric Epic. In *Making Silence Speak: Women's Voices in Greek Literature and Society,* ed. A. Lardinois and L. McClure, 19–37. Princeton.

Zeitlin, F. I. 1996. *Playing the Other. Gender and Society in Classical Greek Literature.* Chicago.

10

LAMENT AND HYMENAIOS IN ERINNA'S *DISTAFF*

OLGA LEVANIOUK

The *Distaff* of Erinna is a hexameter poem composed around the middle of the fourth century B.C.E. and so admired by its ancient audiences that it was compared to the poetry of Homer and Sappho.[1] Out of its original three hundred lines only some fifty survive on a badly preserved papyrus and in short quotations, and this incompleteness renders any study of the *Distaff* highly speculative.[2] If the poem is nevertheless not a complete enigma, this is in part because surprisingly much in its diction can be paralleled elsewhere. In what follows I view the genre of the *Distaff* through the prism of such parallels, some of them much discussed, others attracting little attention, and many with implications that remain to be fully appreciated.

At first glance the genre of the *Distaff* seems unproblematic: almost since its discovery the poem has been recognized as a lament.[3] "Erinna," named in the poem, laments the death of her companion Baukis, addressing and reproaching the deceased and recollecting past happiness.[4] These recollections seem to coalesce into a quintessentially feminine poem. As Arthur has observed, the *Distaff* contains "almost every known theme and motif having to do with the life of girls and women."[5] The question how these themes and motifs fit within a lament is usually left open, the presumption being that the death of Baukis simply provides Erinna with a chance to contemplate a young woman's life. As an alternative, I suggest that Erinna's recollections should be viewed in the light of the poem's genre, and I attempt to show that the *Distaff* is not just a lament but a lament that is so distinctly full of wedding diction as to constitute a wedding song for the dead Baukis. The wedding is the center of gravity for all the feminine themes of the *Distaff*: Baukis dies on the day of her wedding, while Erinna is waiting and preparing for her own. The importance of the theme is marked clearly by the double invocation of Hymenaios in lines 51 and 53.[6] The wedding song for Baukis, however, is transformed into a lament by its occasion, in this case an occasion created internally within the poem itself: the death of the bride. The genre of the *Distaff* is defined by the coincidence of the two events, wedding and death, and consequently by the coincidence of the two types of song, wedding song and lament. Further, I suggest that Erinna's Baukis (and to some extent even Erinna herself) is in fact an embodiment both of this genre and of its prototypical occasion, death at the moment of marriage.[7]

The background for the transformation of wedding song into lament is the well-known similarity between laments and certain love and wedding songs, abundantly documented in Modern Greek and certainly present in Ancient Greek.[8] This general similarity, however, allows for different degrees of likeness and contrast depending on the occasion. For example, Danforth observes that in the modern Greek village of Potamia in Thessaly certain songs are sung sometimes as laments and sometimes as wedding songs. Ordinarily, they are performed in different ways depending on the occasion: more somberly at funerals, more joyfully and ornately at weddings. However, for a person who has died before marriage, "they may even be sung in the musical style characteristic of wedding songs."[9] When death usurps the place of a wedding, musical style responds to the occasion not by means of conformity but by means of a contrast: a wedding song at a funeral brings to mind the happy occasion that ought to have taken place and thus underscores the "unfairness" of the occasion that is taking place instead. Erinna's poem, I suggest, belongs to this category of song, and this special effect is achieved in the *Distaff* primarily by the preponderance of wedding-related diction and also by formal features such as antiphony, anaphora, and even the dialect, which, I will argue, is also connected to genre. The diction, poetic features, and the dialect combine to substitute, in a sense, for the missing musical style.

I begin by citing in full a papyrus fragment that preserves part of Erinna's poem. For the moment I leave aside other lines from the poem that survive in quotations by later authors:

Col. I

[   ].ν[
[   ]εοίσ[α]ς
[   ]ε κώρας
[   ]ι νύμφαι
[   ]χελύνναν   (5)
[σ]ελάννα
[χε]λύννα

[   ]τελῆσ[
[   ]θμει
[   ]θα φυλλοις[(10)
[   ]αλάσσει·[
                                     ].ανναν[
                                     ]νίδα πέξα[ι
                                     [ἐς βαθ]ὺ κυμα[

Col. II

[λε]υκᾶν μαινομέν[οισιν ἐσάλαο π]οσσὶν ἀφ' ἴ[π]πω[ν]   (15)
αἰ]αῖ ἐγώ, μέγ' ἄυα· φ[ανεῖσα δὲ δηῦτε] χελύννα
]ομένα μεγάλας[   ] χορτίον αὐλᾶς
τα]ῦτά τύ, Βαῦκι τάλαι[να βαρὺ στονά]χεισα γόημ[ι]
τα]ῦτά μοι ἐν κρα[δίαι   ]παίχνια κεῖται
θέρμ' ἔτι·τῆν[α δ' ἃ πρίν ἀ]θύρομες ἄνθρακες ἤδη   (20)
δαγύ[δ]ων τε χ[οροὶ καὶ ἐταρ]ίδες ἐν θαλάμοισι
νύμ[φ]αι ν[   ]έες ἅ τε ποτ' ὄρθρον
μάτηρ αε[   ]οισιν ἐρείθοις
τήνας ηλθ[   ]να ἀμφ' ἁλίπαστον
..μικραις [   ]ν φόβον ἄγαγε Μορ[μ]ώ   (25)
τᾶς] ἐν μὲν κο[ρυφαῖ μεγάλ' ὤ]ατα ποσσὶ δὲ φοιτῆι.
τέτρα]σιν· ἐκ δ'[ἑτέραν ἑτέρας] μετεβάλλετ' ὀπωπάν
ἀνίκα δ' ἐς [λ]έχος [ἀνδρὸς ἔβας τ]όκα πάντ' ἐλέλασο
ἄσσ' ἔ[τι]..νηπία σι.τε[   ] μάτρὸς ἄκουσας,
Βαῦκι φίλα· λάθας [   ] ετ[   ] Ἀφροδίτα   (30)
τῶ τυ κατακλα[ί]οισα τὰ [μέν   ] ἄ[λ]λα δὲ λείπω
οὐ [γ]άρ μοι πόδες [ ] φ[υγῆν] ἀπὸ δῶμα βέβαλοι
οὐδέ σ' ἰδῆν φαέε[σσιν ἔχω νέ]κυν οὐδὲ γοάσαι
γυμναῖσιν χαίταισιν [φ]οινίκεος αἰδώς

Col. III

δρύπτε[ι] μ' ἀμφὶ πα[ρήιδας   (35)
αἰε[ὶ] δὲ π[ρ]οπάροιθ[εν
ἐννεα[και]δέκατος τ[
Ἤριννα[ ] ε[ ]ε φίλαι πα[ρὰ
ἀλακάταν ἐσόρει[σα
γνῶθ' ὅτι τοι κ[(40)
ἀμφέλικες γελ[
ταῦτ' αἰδώς μ' α[
παρθε[ν]ίοις· ἀ [
δερκομένα δ' ἐκ[
καὶ χαίτα μετ[(45)
πραϋλόγοι πο[λιαί, ταὶ γήραος ἄνθεα θνατοῖς
τῶ τυ φίλα φο[
Βαῦκι κατακλα[ίοισα

ἂν φλόγα μιν π[
ὠρυγᾶς ἀΐοισα ὁ[(50)
ὦ πολλὰν ὑμέν[αιε
π]ολλὰ δ' ἐπιψαύ[ην
π]άνθ' ἑνός· ὦ ὑμ[έναιε
αἰαῖ Βαῦκι τάλαιν[α

Col. I

                              of a girl
                              maidens
                              tortoise   (5)
                              moon
                              tortoise
                              with leaves   (10)
                              . . . . . .

                              . . . . . .
                              to card
                              deep wave

Col. II

from white horses (you jumped?) with maddened feet   (15)
"Aiai" I shouted loudly (and having become?) tortoise
leaping (?)   the yard of a great court
that's why, poor Baukis, I cry for you, deeply groaning
these   (games?) lie in my heart
still warm. But those (which we played before?) are already ashes, (20)
(dances?) of dolls . . .   . . . in the bed-chambers
maidens . . .   . . . at dawn
mother . . .   . . . to the wool-workers
those . . .   . . . sprinkled with salt
little . . .   . . . Mormo brought fear   (25)
on her head (were) big ears, and she roamed
on four feet and changed her appearance (from one form to another?)
but (when you went) into (a man's) bed, your forgot everything
which still innocent . . .   . . . you heard from (your? my?) mother,
dear Baukis . . .   . . . forgetfulness . . .   . . . Aphrodite   (30)
that's why, weeping . . .   . . . but I leave other things
for my feet are not permitted . . .   . . . from the house
nor (can I) look upon you, dead, nor lament
with uncovered hair . . .   . . . dark-red shame

Col. III

tears my cheek(s) on each side   (35)
always before

nineteenth
Erinna . . by the dear (mother?)
looking at the distaff
know that   (40)
twined (?)
therefore shame
maidenly. . .
looking
and hair   (45)
soft-speaking grey (strands of hair) which are for mortals the
    flowers of old age
that's why, you, dear
Baukis, lamenting
by (throughout?) the fire
hearing cries   (50)
o Hymenaios
to touch much
all for one, o Hymenaios
aiai wretched Baukis[10]

THE OCCASION

My starting point in analyzing the genre of the *Distaff* is the poem's internal occasion. According to the definition of Todorov as emended by Nagy, genre can be understood as "principles of dynamic re-production of discourse in society."[11] Nagy explains the implication of this formulation as follows: "The genre, the set of rules that generate a given speech act, can equate itself with the occasion, the context of this speech act. To this extent, occasion is genre. For example, a song of lament can equate itself with the process of grieving for the dead. Moreover, if the occasion is destabilized or lost, the genre can compensate for it, even re-create it."[12] It follows that without the occasion the meaning of the song can never be fully grasped; the meaning of the same words may be quite different, even opposite, depending on the occasion. Although Erinna's poem is not a song sensu stricto, it is a representation of one, and the impact of the poem depends critically on the interaction between its diction and formal features and the internally re-created occasion that frames it.

The extent to which this occasion defines the *Distaff* can be surmised from several epigrams, some (supposedly) by Erinna and others about her. The evidence of the epigrams is important because they all, together with the biographical tradition about Erinna, almost certainly derive from no other source than the *Distaff* itself and are based, of course, on the full text of the poem.[13]

Two of the epigrams ascribed to Erinna are in the form of grave inscriptions for Baukis, and the cornerstone of both is the fact that Baukis's death *coincided* with her wedding. In both epigrams Baukis is called νύμφη (here clearly "bride" as opposed to "young woman"), and Hymenaios is mentioned twice in *AP* 7.712:[14]

ὡς τὰν παῖδ᾽,᾽ ὑμέναιος ἐφ᾽ αἷς ἀείδετο πεύκαις,
ταῖσδ᾽ ἐπὶ καδεστὰς ἔφλεγε πυρκαϊᾷ·
καὶ σὺ μέν, ὦ Ὑμέναιε, γάμων μολπαῖον ἀοιδὰν
ἐς θρήνων γοερὸν φθέγμα μεθαρμόσαο.

[Say] that her father-in-law burned the body of the girl
on the pyre lit by the very torches that shone when her
wedding song (*hymenaios*) was sung, and you, o Hymenaios,
changed the tuneful song of wedding into the mournful
sound of lamentation.

The epigrams do not focus on the "personal" and "realistic" details of the *Distaff* that have attracted modern scholarly attention: Erinna's childhood together with Baukis, Erinna's attitude to marriage, the complexities of the relationship between the two women. Instead, they revisit the occasion of the poem, the transformation of a wedding into a funeral. Such an occasion is both highly symbolic and highly conventional: "marriage to death," death substituting for marriage, is one of the most traditional and enduring themes of Greek myth and poetry, embodied by a whole series of male and female figures such as Antigone, Iphigeneia, and Hippolytos, among others.[15]

There are dangers inherent in any transition and especially in such a decisive transition as marriage. In wedding songs, the girl before marriage is like a sheltered animal or plant, protected from the winds and rain, free of cares and nurtured by her parents.[16] Marriage at once exposes her to grown-up cares and the potentially lethal trials of childbirth. The happiest possible transition still entails danger because it may attract the jealousy of the gods, precisely because it may be so perfect. This seems to be exactly what happens to Baukis, for Hades is accused of jealousy in one of Erinna's epigrams: Βάσκανός ἐσσ᾽, Ἀΐδα, "You are jealous, Hades" (*AP* 7.12.3). The negative potentialities of the transition to married life, which are graphically expressed in myth, are meant to be overcome in ritual and, ideally, in life. Baukis, however, is on the side of myth: she is herself a paradigmatic expression of a life cut short.

Erinna's own literary fate is bound up with the occasion (and genre) of her poem. The epigrams and the ancient biographical tradition make Erinna virtually a double of Baukis. Like her friend, she dies a *parthenos*, and the Βάσκανός ἐσσ᾽,᾽ Ἀΐδα, uttered by "Erinna" about Baukis, is repeated in *AP* 7.13 about Erinna herself. Although the epigrams are concerned mostly with Erinna's success as a poet, the language in which they speak of her early death is shot through with thoughts of youth and intimations of marriage. For example, in *AP* 7.11 the smallness of her poem is associated with her young age:

ὁ γλυκὺς Ἠρίννης οὗτος πόνος, οὐχὶ πολὺς μέν,
ὡς ἂν παρθενικᾶς ἐννεακαιδεκέτευς. (1–2)

This is the sweet work of Erinna, not large in size—
as you would expect from a girl of nineteen.

In *AP* 7.13 Erinna is again called παρθενικά and carried off for a wedding
by Hades:

παρθενικὰν νεαοιδὸν ἐν ὑμνοπόλοισι μέλισσαν
Ἤρινναν Μουσῶν ἄνθεα δρεπτομέναν
Ἅδας εἰς ὑμέναιον ἀνάρπασεν. (1–3)

Erinna, the maiden honeybee, a new singer among the poets,
was plucking the flowers of the Muses when Hades snatched
her away to be his bride.

Similarly, Meleager in his *Stephanos* makes Erinna's poem a crocus of
"maidenly color" (παρθενόχρωτα κρόκον [*AP* 4.1.12]). The saffron color
of crocus features in rites of transition to adulthood for girls and gives its
name to the typical dress worn by the "bears" during their ritual services at
Brauron, the *krôkotos*.[17]

Erinna's age, nineteen (mentioned in the *Distaff* 37 and in *AP*
7.11.2), may mark her as a woman at a perfect point in her life to be
married, even if in practice women sometimes married at a younger age.[18]
In an ideal picture painted by Hesiod, a girl should be married five years
after reaching ἥβη, "puberty," which would normally mean at seventeen
or eighteen.[19] Plato in the *Republic* chooses twenty as an ideal age, while
Aristotle gives eighteen.[20]

Erinna, then, is a figure like Baukis, and this Erinna is certainly a
product of the poem, a personification of her poetry.[21] Externally, from
the point of view of the epigrams and the biographical tradition, both
Baukis and Erinna are defined by a death as symbolically untimely as can
be: a death that takes the place of marriage. As it responds to the occasion,
Erinna's lament, even those parts of it that look like recollections of
"everyday life," is marked by the themes and diction of wedding songs.

THE DICTION OF THE WEDDING

The first case in point is the very beginning of the *Distaff*, where, as Bowra
recognized, separate words must refer to a game known as *khelikhelônê*,
"torty-tortoise."[22] Pollux describes it as a game of tag: one girl would sit
in the middle and was called "the tortoise," while all the others ran in a
circle exchanging the following words with her:

χελιχελώνη, τί ποιεῖς ἐν τῷ μέσῳ;
ἔρια μαρύομαι καὶ κρόκην Μιλησίαν.
ὁ δ' ἔκγονος σου τί ποιῶν ἀπώλετο;
λευκᾶν ἀφ' ἵππων εἰς θάλασσαν ἅλατο. (Pollux 9.125)

> Torty-tortoise, what are you doing in the middle?
> I am carding wool and Milesian thread.
> And your child, how did he die?
> Off white horses he jumped into the sea.

Saying these words, the tortoise herself, presumably, would leap out of the middle and try to catch one of the other girls, who would then become a tortoise in her turn.

The tortoise game is thematically significant in the *Distaff*, as has been shown, but more can be said about the specifics of this significance.[23] The tortoise itself is associated with the goddess of love, Aphrodite, and specifically with Aphrodite as a patron of marriage. Plutarch, for example, comments on the chryselephantine statue of Aphrodite in Elis, where the goddess was represented with her foot on a tortoise. The tortoise symbolized the domestic qualities of a wife—staying at home and keeping quiet.[24] Elsewhere, Plutarch associates the tortoise specifically with married women.[25] This is also the role that *khelikhelônê* plays in the game: a mother, sitting at home and carding wool, an emblem of womanhood and domesticity.

Jumping off white horses and into the sea, on the other hand, is the opposite of domesticity. The leap of the child into the sea is paralleled in a tale about the tortoise preserved by Servius (in *Aeneid* 1.505): Khelone is a young woman who rejects marriage and refuses to attend Zeus's wedding feast. She prefers to stay at home. As a punishment, Hermes casts her house off a cliff into the sea. There, Khelone is transformed into a sea turtle, doomed to carry her house on her back forever. As in the game, Khelone's domesticity is opposed to a fall into the sea, and here it is also opposed to marriage. A wedding entails a departure from the mother's house and a journey to another one. Rejecting this departure, on the other hand, results for Khelone in a departure that is much more drastic and final: a fall into the sea.

Some of the same elements are present in Aesop 108, where the tortoise again refuses to attend Zeus's wedding feast, saying οἶκος φίλος, οἶκος ἄριστος, "home is dear, home is best" (108.4). In Aesop, as in Servius, the tortoise's attachment to the house is judged to be excessive, and Zeus punishes her by making her carry the house on her back. There is no leap into the sea, but here again the tortoise is associated with the opposition between leaving and not leaving the house specifically in the context of a wedding. The fact that both versions of the tortoise's story have a direct connection with a wedding suggests that this is also the subtext of the *khelikhelônê* game.

Further, the leap into the sea in the game is reminiscent of the mythological and poetic theme discussed in detail by Gregory Nagy, namely, the white rock of Leukas.[26] The theme is reflected for example in Anacreon *PMG* 376:

ἀρθεὶς δηὖτ' ἀπὸ Λευκάδος
πέτρης ἐς πολιὸν κῦμα κολυμβῶ μεθύων ἔρωτι.

Once again taking off from the rock of Leukas I dive
into the grey wave, intoxicated with love.

Nagy shows that falling off the white rock is parallel to losing consciousness through intoxication or love. A leap off the rock of Leukas was
believed to cure love—if it did not kill the sufferer. According to Menander, the first to jump off the rock was none other than Sappho, goaded by
desire (οἰστρῶντι πόθῳ) for Phaon.²⁷ The association of the leap with
madness and intoxication is present in Erinna's poem, where the adjective
μαινόμενος is used in the description of the game (λευκᾶν μαινομένοισιν
ἐσάλαο ποσσὶν ἀφ' ἵππων, "with maddened feet you jumped off white
horses" [line 15, as restored by Bowra]).²⁸ The concentric composition
of Erinna's verse emphasizes the central and irreversible act of leaping into
the sea: the expressions λευκᾶν ἀφ' ἵππων and μαινομέμοισι ποσσίν are
distracted, split in half by the verb, while the verb occupies the central
place between the caesura in the third foot and the bucolic diaeresis.

Moreover, the white rock has its own set of associations with horses. In
Alkman's *Partheneion*, Hagesikhora stands out among her peers like a
prizewinning horse "from dreams beneath the rock," τῶν ὑποπετρίδων
ὀνείρων (*PMG* 1.49). As Nagy has shown, the scholia of the Louvre papyrus
have good reasons to identify the rock in question with none other than the
White Rock, Λευκάδα πέτρην, in *Odyssey* 24.11.²⁹ The concept of sexual
release associated with the rock is also associated with horses. According to
the scholia on Pindar's *Pythian* 4.246, Poseidon Petraios falls asleep on a
rock and produces an emission of semen from which the first horse springs.³⁰

Horses, and especially white horses, are also one of the images most
strongly associated with both weddings and the pre-wedding activities of
young women. The *Partheneion* contains an elaborate set of comparisons
between young women and horses, and the same metaphor is developed in
Anacreon's comparison of a girl to a frolicking Thracian filly (πῶλε Θρηικίη
[*PMG* 417.1]). As Calame has argued, the *Partheneion* was probably
performed in a ritual setting associated with the girls' transition from
adolescence to adulthood, and Anacreon's "filly" seems to be at a similar
stage in her life: just about to know a rider for the first time.³¹ Horses in
general, not just white ones, appear in such contexts, and yet the particular
association of white horses with the transition to marriage is clearly indicated by the names of the Leukippoi and Leukippides, male and female
heroes who presided over this transition in Sparta.³² Regarding the Leukippides in particular, Calame concludes that the myth of their abduction
by the Tyndaridai (themselves associated with white stallions) "oscillates
between the domain of adolescence and the semantic values of the adult
world."³³ The abduction of the Leukippides leads to marriage (ταύτας
ἁρπάσαντες ἔγημαν Διόσκουροι [Apollodorus 3.118.1]) and constitutes an
entrance into the realm of Aphrodite, in whose honor young women,
presumably the Leukippides themselves, perform a dance in a lyric fragment ascribed to Bakkhylides.³⁴

Furthermore, themes reminiscent of the *khelikhelônê* surface in myths of transition to adulthood, for example, in that of Hippolytos. Like Khelone, Hippolytos refuses to give the realm of Aphrodite its due and has to face in their untamed form the very forces he rejects. The particular shape of his punishment is, of course, to be killed on the seashore by horses gone wild, spooked by a monster that appears out of a huge wave. The joint appearance of horses, sea, and death is reminiscent of the *khelikhelônê* game. Moreover, the fate of Hippolytos is specifically associated with preparations for marriage in Euripides' play (1424–1429), for Hippolytos is promised worship by unmarried maidens (κόραι ἄζυγες [1425]) prior to their marriage (γάμων πάρος [1425]). Hippolytos is at the stage of life when he is expected to become, in the social sense, a fully grown man, and that entails, among other things, coming in contact with Aphrodite. For reasons too complex to address here, Hippolytos fails or, rather, refuses to make this transition. Yet he is not permitted to remain, like a child, ignorant of the goddess, and the result is his untimely death. By the same token, Khelone is asked to come out and encounter Aphrodite's sphere of life by attending a wedding, but she wants to remain forever in her house and, like a little girl, be untouched by marriage. Because she refuses to make this transition willingly, she is forced out of her seclusion violently, with tragic consequences. Like the myth of Hippolytos, the game of *khelikhelônê* dramatizes a failed transition to the marital stage of life and the dangerous powers that come into play once it is time for the young to leave their homes.

Such an interpretation of the game is consistent with Pollux's statement that this game belongs to *parthenoi*—not little girls, as is often assumed, but marriageable maidens.[35] The age of the participants may help to explain why the moon is mentioned twice in the same lines as *khelikhelônê* (6, 12), something that has puzzled commentators because it seems strange for little girls to play in the dark. Two different ways to solve the problem have been proposed: to reject the game or to reject the moon. Magrini has suggested that the moonlit event in the *Distaff* is in fact Baukis's wedding and denies the whole notion of the game, translating χελύννα as "lyre" instead of "tortoise."[36] It seems to me that Baukis's wedding or the events leading up to it may indeed be the occasion in question, but, as West points out, the conjunction of carding wool, sea, white horses, and χελύννα is simply too peculiar not to refer to the game, especially in the light of παίχνια in 19. West's own solution to the problem, however, is to eliminate the moon. Instead of the simple reconstruction σελάννα, he suggests that]εαννα in 6 and].ανναν [in 12 may be part of a girl's name, Γέλαννα, an Aeolic form for Γαλήνη.[37] This seems somewhat unlikely because the name Γέλαννα is not actually attested (it is postulated on the basis of the supposedly Aeolic form γελήνη).

Although the moon may not suit the games of little girls, it does indeed suit the games of *parthenoi* on the occasion of marriage. Both the moon and games occur repeatedly in wedding contexts, as, for example, in Theokritos 18, where Helen's age-mates speak of "playing" all night long (παίσδειν ἐς βαθὺν ὄρθρον [14]). Moreover, as Bremer has argued, the full moon was seen as auspicious for weddings.[38] For example, Agamemnon's wish to give Iphigeneia away in marriage when there is a full moon (ὅταν σελήνης εὐτυχὴς ἔλθῃ κύκλος [717]) passes without further comment in Euripides' *Iphigenia in Aulis*. In Pindar's *Isthmian* 8.716–717, Thetis also wishes to marry Peleus under a full moon, and here, moreover, the theme of horses also makes an appearance (χαλινὸν...παρθενίας [717]).[39] The moon and horses are present again in Euadne's recollection of her wedding in Euripides' *Suppliants*, where the moon is said to ride as in a chariot (ἐδίφρευε [991]) and where there is an emphasis on speed (θοαῖσι [993], δρομάς [1000]). The text is corrupt, but it is clear that the mention of the wedding moon here coexists precisely with the equine themes associated with young girls (running, speed, leaping). Far from being inappropriate in the *Distaff*, the moon perfectly complements and frames the *khelikhe-lónê* game, once you realize that the girls playing are not children.

Moreover, the comparison between this game and Euadne's scene in the *Suppliants* can be extended. Euadne recollects her wedding as she looks on the dead body of her young husband, Kapaneus, whom she is determined to follow in death. She then casts her suicide as a wedding, wears wedding finery instead of mourning clothes (1054–1056), and, strikingly, utters her last words perched, like a bird, on a high cliff from which she then jumps onto Kapaneus's burning pyre, watched by her helpless father (1045–1047). Here again the rock and the jump occur in connection with a wedding, and Euadne's jump is in fact represented as a turning point in her deadly reenactment of her marriage to Kapaneus, the actual rejoining of the "newlyweds."[40]

It appears, then, that the traditional nexus of white rock, horses, moon, and leap into the sea is connected with the period leading up to the wedding and with the wedding itself. The elements of the *khelikhelónê* game, together with its setting in the *Distaff*, are part of the discourse of wedding and probably featured in wedding and pre-wedding songs. Just as Hippolytos's failure to make peace with Aphrodite became the subject of a pre-wedding song for the girls of Troizen, so Khelone's attachment to her house, contrasted with either her own or her son's fall into the sea, became a pre-wedding song and game. Every young woman coming in contact with sexuality has to leave her mother's protection and come into contact with the sea. It is hoped that she will travel safely into marriage, but the danger is always there that she will not.[41]

The game of *khelikhelónê* is followed in the *Distaff* by the mention of other games that seem to be set further back in a girl's life.[42] Erinna speaks of bridal chambers (θαλάμοισι [21]) and "figurines" (δαγύδων [21]), which are often taken to refer to dolls, as are the two mentions of νύμφαι at 5 and 22.[43] In the surviving sources, however, the word δαγύς never refers to the kind of dolls with which little girls play but only to depictions of young women. The word is applied to wax figurines used in love magic and also to figurative elements of female dress. For example, the scholia to Theokritos define δαγύς as κοροκόσμιόν τι, ᾧ αἱ παρθένοι κοσμοῦνται, "some ornament with which maidens decorate themselves," and as Ἀφροδίτης ἀπεικονίσματα, "representations of Aphrodite."[44]

Next comes the mention of someone's mother (23, whether Baukis's or Erinna's is not clear), hired workers (ἐρίθοις [23]), some food (ἀλιπάστον [24], cooked and salted meat, apparently), and then fear of Mormo. From *AP* 9.190 it is clear that in the *Distaff* Erinna is forced by her mother to engage in wool working, and it seems likely that the mother herself does the same.[45] From these household details Erinna moves on to Aphrodite and Baukis's forgetfulness. How these elements fitted together is impossible to tell, and the reconstruction of the text must remain uncertain. The range of possibilities, however, may be clarified by a comparison with what is certainly a pre-wedding scene in the *Odyssey*: the Nausikaa episode.[46]

The action of book 6 of the *Odyssey* is set in motion by Athena, who appears to Nausikaa in a dream in the guise of one of her friends and tells her that marriage is at hand: σοὶ δὲ γάμος σχεδόν ἐστιν (6.27). In the morning (αὐτίκα δ' Ἡώς ἦλθεν [48]), Nausikaa approaches her father and requests permission to go to the river and wash clothes, something her father rightly takes to indicate that marriage is on his daughter's mind. She also comes to her mother, who is weaving (ἠλάκατα στρωφῶσ' ἀλιπόρφυρα [53]) and receives food and wine (75–76). In the *Distaff* too, there is morning (ποτ' ὄρθρον [22]), mother (μάτηρ [23]), weaving, and a mention of food (ἀλιπάστον [24]). The word ἐρίθοις in 123 of the *Distaff* is usually taken to refer to the hired helpers that work along with the mother, and indeed Arete in the *Odyssey* is also surrounded by her servants (6.52).[47] There is, however, another possibility. Whereas Arete's servants are called ἀμφίπολοι, the word ἔριθος actually occurs in the *Odyssey* in the prefixed form, συνέριθος, and it refers to the girl in Nausikaa's dream who is coming out to wash clothes and play together with her (6.32).

This is not to say that a scene parallel to the Nausikaa episode should be reconstructed in the *Distaff*. The essential point is rather that in the *Odyssey* the household work is performed by girls in a markedly pre-wedding setting, just as their games are. The connection is signaled by Nausikaa's *sunerithos* herself:

καί τοι ἐγὼ συνέριθος ἅμ' ἕψομαι, ὄφρα τάχιστα
ἐντύνεαι, ἐπεὶ οὔ τοι ἔτι δὴν παρθένος ἔσσεαι.   (6.32–33)

And I will follow you as a companion in work, so that
you may complete your task as soon as possible, since
now you will not remain a maiden long.

It is therefore possible that references to household activities in the *Distaff* are in fact not simply recollections of the past but part of the discourse of wedding.

In the *Odyssey*, there is an emphatic contrast between the house-bound mother, Arete, who sits by the hearth and works the wool (just as mother tortoise in the *khelikhelônê* game), and Nausikaa, who is venturing off to play with her age-mates away from her house, by the river and the sea, places where encounters happen, depths open, and children are sometimes conceived. And, of course, Nausikaa does indeed have a potentially dangerous encounter with a male, an encounter seen as a possible match by all concerned.

When Nausikaa and her friends play on the shore, the prenuptial character of their games is made plain: in a telling gesture the girls cast aside their veils (ἀπὸ κρήδεμνα βαλοῦσαι [100]) and then play with a ball, which might itself have erotic connotations.[48] Most importantly, Nausikaa is compared to Artemis playing among the nymphs (6.101–109), a comparison that indicates both that a girl may be "abducted" from this dancing circle to enter adulthood and that Nausikaa is the one among them who is ready to make this transition. At the end of the dance description, Nausikaa's readiness for an able "rider" is summed up in the expression παρθένος ἀδμής, "untamed maiden" (109).

Odysseus, meanwhile, is asleep. The manner of his awakening, contrived by Athena, is both symbolic of Nausikaa's readiness and reminiscent of the prenuptial sea theme discussed above:

σφαῖραν ἔπειτ' ἔρριψε μετ' ἀμφίπολον βασίλεια
ἀμφίπολον μὲν ἅμαρτε, βαθείῃ δ' ἔμβαλε δίνῃ,
αἱ δ' ἐπὶ μακρὸν ἄυσαν. ὁ δ' ἔγρετο δῖος Ὀδυσσεύς. (6.115–117)

And then the princess threw the ball at one of her companions,
and missed the girl, but cast it into a deep eddy. And they shouted
loudly, and the godlike Odysseus woke up.

In this case, it is not Nausikaa herself who jumps into the sea but, rather, only the ball that falls in. Still, the ball's fall into the water, the emphasis on its depth and turbulence, and the reaction of the other girls are all reminiscent of the *khelikhelônê* game as it is described in Erinna. In the *Distaff*, too, Baukis's symbolic jump off the white horses is met with Erinna's shout (αἰ]αῖ ἐγὼ μέγ' ἄσα [16]). Baukis jumps into the wave (κῦμα), and if the reading βαθὺ κῦμα were correct, it would parallel very closely the Homeric βαθείῃ ... δίνῃ (6.116). West, however, observes that the traces are inconsistent with this reading and suggests τύ instead.[49] The reading κῦμα, at any rate, is certain.

To sum up, both in the *Distaff* and in the Nausikaa episode, a *parthenos* is playing among her age-mates, and the game is symbolic of imminent encounter with adulthood and sexuality. The potentialities of this transition are associated with the sea and expressed metaphorically as a leap or fall into the waves; the metaphor of an "untamed horse" typical of such transitions is present, as is the figure of the mother, associated with wool working and the house, a setting opposed to the one where the *parthenoi* are at play (could the word φύλλοις at *Distaff* 10 point to a natural setting?). In both cases, there is also a mention of morning/dawn, food, and attendants.

Nausikaa returns to her father's palace safely, having only toyed with the depths. Baukis does not return but, in fact, sets off on a journey over the sea, and the sea in the *khelikhelônê* game is only part of the nautical theme developed in the *Distaff*. Other instances include an excerpt from the *Distaff* quoted by Stobaios (see below) and two lines about a fish called *pompilos* quoted by Athenaios:

πομπίλε, ναύτῃσιν πέμπων πλόον εὔπλοον, ἰχθύ,
πομπεύσαις πρύμναθεν ἐμὰν ἀδεῖαν ἑταίραν. (Athenaios 7.283D)

Pompilos, the fish that sends sailors a fair voyage, escort my sweet companion [by granting a fair wind] from the stern.

The authenticity of these lines has been questioned because the alliteration is harsh and unlike the other parts of the *Distaff*, but these grounds seem insufficient given the fact that there probably was no other poem by Erinna. Thematically, the lines would fit very well, as has been demonstrated by Rauk.[50]

The fish addressed here is connected both with the sea and with Aphrodite: the *pompilos* is said to have been born together with the goddess from the blood of Ouranos, and Athenaios describes it as ζῷον ἐρωτικόν (7.282). This fish, it seems, has a habit of escorting boats and was believed to protect all seafarers, especially those who are in love.[51] Moreover, a story told by Apollonios of Rhodes links the *pompilos* precisely with the point of transition to sexuality in a young woman's life, the point marked by a festival of Artemis. According to Apollonios, Pompilos is a fisherman who is turned into a fish by Apollo after frustrating the god's amorous intentions. Apollo is after a nymph from Samos called Okyrhoe and plans to seize her while she is in Miletos celebrating a festival of Artemis. To escape the imminent rape, Okyrhoe begs Pompilos to rescue her, and he takes her back home in his boat.[52]

As Rauk suggests, the context for Erinna's invocation of the *pompilos* is surely Baukis's departure in marriage, and in this context the invocation joins other marriage-related elements of the poem.[53] In fact, both the address to the *pompilos* and the theme of the leap into the sea, discussed above, are parts of a developed system of sea-related concepts attested in connection with marriage, and this system is structured according to an internal logic. In contrast to lovers who dive into the sea, Okyrhoe remains untainted, conducted safely over the waves. In the same way, a bride is ideally conducted to the harbor of marriage, escaping the deep waves of the sea and completing the dangerous period of transition. To be sure, she comes in contact with the sea, but she emerges from it again safely.

Seaford suggests that the procession that conducts the bride to her new house at the end of the wedding is associated with nautical imagery.[54] For example, in Euripides' *Iphigeneia in Aulis*, Iphigeneia arrives as if for a marriage with Achilles, with her mother as νυμφαγωγός (610), and descends from the chariot to enter Agamemnon's tent. At this point, Agamemnon speaks of a voyage (πλοῦς [667]) that she is to undertake alone (669), and the reference has double meaning: for Iphigeneia, it refers to her departure to another household in marriage (οὔ πού μ' ἐς ἄλλα δώματ' οἰκίζεις, πάτερ, "Are you not settling me in another house, father?" [670]); for Agamemnon and the audience, Iphigeneia's sailing also refers to her imminent death, but the double meaning and Iphigeneia's reaction are only possible if a reference to sailing was customary in marital contexts.

Other examples abound. For instance, in Sophocles' *Oedipus Tyrannus*, Teiresias's dire predictions about Oedipus's marriage to Iocasta are couched in nautical imagery, with marriage pictured as a harbor (420–423), into which Oedipus sails with a fair wind (εὐπλοίας τυχών [423]). The word εὐπλοία occurs also in Aeschylus's *Suppliants* (1045), again in the context of marriage.

In the *Distaff*, it is precisely for an εὔπλοος sailing for Baukis that Erinna asks the *pompilos*. As Seaford observes, the double occurrence of εὐπλοία in connection with a wedding suggests that it has special meaning in this context.[55] If so, Erinna's εὔπλοος may also have been recognizable as part of the *Distaff*'s wedding-related diction.

In spite of Erinna's prayer, Baukis does not travel safely into marriage: instead, like the tortoise's child in the *khelikhelônê* game, she jumps or falls into deep waves. And just as Iphigeneia's πλοῦς comes to signify her death instead of marriage, so in a *Distaff* fragment preserved by Stobaios it seems that Baukis's death is described, like her wedding, in nautical terms:

τουτόθεν εἰς Ἀΐδαν κενεὰ διανήχεται ἀχώ.
σίγα δ' ἐν νεκύεσσι, τὸ δὲ σκότος ὄσσε κατέρρει. (Stobaios 4.51.4)

An empty echo sails across from here to Hades.
There is silence among the dead, and darkness comes over the eyes.

Beyond the theme of the sea, there are other elements of the *Distaff* that are also consistent with its overall orientation toward the theme of marriage. The mention of Mormo, for example, can be compared with Callimachus's use of μορμύσσεται to describe the fear instilled in girls by the *hymenaios*:

ἦ τοι Δηλιάδες μέν, ὅτ' εὐήχης ὑμέναιος
ἤθεα κουράων μορμύσσεται. (*Hymn* 4.296–297)

Indeed the girls of Delos, when the sweet-sounding *hymenaios*
spreads fear in their maiden haunts.

Even if the immediate role of Mormo in the *Distaff* is, as often, to bolster parental authority, the fear she instills belongs equally to the pre-wedding period in a girl's life.[56] Moreover, juxtaposition with Aphrodite (mentioned at *Distaff* 30) pulls the monster into the wedding discourse. As Stehle points out, "Aphrodite's effect is the opposite of Mormo's: rather than frightening her victims into immobility, she lures them into motion."[57]

Just as the theme of fear belongs to the wedding, so does the theme of shame, or modesty (*aidôs*), which is not only present but strikingly developed in the *Distaff*. Unmarried girls in general may be prone to maidenly shame, but there seems to be a specialized way of talking about *aidôs* in the context of the wedding. In Erinna, it is mentioned in the context of Baukis's funeral, but there are indications that it is very much of a wedding kind. First of all, Erinna's *aidôs* is called φοινίκιος, "red" or "crimson" (34), and the same lexical combination also occurs in Euripides' *Phoenissae* in association with a wedding. Here, Antigone bares her hair and casts off her headdress in the abandonment of grief over the death of her brothers and mother. She contrasts this behavior with how she would have acted at her wedding, as a modest bride, her blushing cheeks a sign of *aidôs*:

οὐ προκαλυπτομένα βοτρυχώδεος ἁβρὰ παρῆιδος
οὐδ' ὑπὸ παρθενίας τὸν ὑπὸ βλεφά-
ροις φοίνικ,' ἐρύθημα προσώπου. (1485–1487)

Not veiling the tender skin of my curl-shaded cheek[58] nor concealing
in maidenly shame the red below my eyes, my face's blush.

The image of blushing, of white turning to red, is also the basis for the striking effect of the scene in Sophocles' *Antigone* where the heroine's burial alive usurps the place of her marriage and is represented as a perverted wedding. Antigone's white skin is reddened here not by the blush of the bride but by the blood of her dying bridegroom, yet the adjective used is still φοίνιος, related to φοινίκεος, and it is precisely Antigone's cheek that is stained:

ὀξεῖαν ἐκβάλλει ῥοὴν
λευκῇ παρειᾷ φοινίου σταλάγματος. (1237–1241)

He ... spurts out a sharp stream of red blood onto her white cheek.

In the *Distaff*, too, *aidôs* reddens Erinna's cheeks, but here Baukis's death turns the red of her maidenly blush into the red of cheeks lacerated in grief, as wedding diction is combined with lament:

ἀτὰρ φ]οινίκιος αἰδώς
δρύπτε[ι] μ' ἀμφὶ πα[ρῆιδας. (29–30)

([B]ut) red shame tears my cheek(s) on each side.

The associations of Erinna's φοινίκιος αἰδώς specifically with marriage are confirmed by the fact that the second mention of αἰδώς (42) directly precedes an occurrence of the adjective παρθένιος (43). The noun this adjective actually modifies is lost, but the appearance of the adjective suggests that Erinna is thinking of her maidenhood.

By the same token, her unusual way of describing uncovered hair as naked (γυμναῖσιν χαίταισιν [34]) may be an example of wedding imagery acquiring a different meaning in the context of lament. The eroticism of the images of blushing cheeks and bared hair quite possibly reflects the eroticism of the actual wedding songs that accompany the sexual initiation of the young woman. In some sense the loss of virginity begins already with the removal of the veil, which is a moment of possibly even greater importance. It is precisely this moment of blushing cheeks that is evoked by Antigone in the *Phoenissae* (1485–1491).[59]

Another moment in the wedding distinctly recognizable as a sexual initiation is, I submit, the first touch, and this moment too is echoed in the *Distaff*. The exact referent of this symbol is hard to establish: it probably refers to the first night but could also point to the bridegroom's act of taking his bride by the hand in a traditional gesture of accepting and leading her away.[60] Erinna mentions touch in the *Distaff* (π]ολλὰ δ' ἐπιψαύ[ην [52]) precisely in her invocations of Hymenaios (51, 53). The notion of first skin contact crops up repeatedly in the ancient poetry in reference to the wedding. For example, in a Pindaric *thrênos*, Hymenaios, the wedding hymn personified, dies on his wedding night, just "touched" by marriage (ἐν γάμοισι χροϊζόμενον [fr. 128c7–8 Snell-Maehler]).

The same association is present in Euripides' *Suppliants*, where Euadne describes rejoining her husband in the underworld as placing skin next to skin (1021–1022), and in Theokritos 2.140 Simaitha recollects her first intimate contact with Delphis in similar terms.[61] Just like χρώς and its derivatives, the forms of the verb ψαύω (cf. ἐπιψαύ[ην [*Distaff* 52]) occur in such contexts. This marks, for example, the first sexual encounter of Euadne and Apollo in Pindar's *Olympian* 6.35:

ἔνθα τραφεῖσ' ὑπ' Ἀπόλλωνι γλυκείας πρῶτον ἔψαυσ' Ἀφροδίτας.

There, brought up by Apollo, she first touched [= came in contact with] sweet Aphrodite.

Given the occurrence of the same theme in Pindar, Euripides, and Theokritos, it is likely that the mention of touch in connection with Hymenaios would be easily recognizable as a wedding theme to the ancient audiences of the *Distaff*.

ERINNA AND BAUKIS

I further suggest that the overall narrative frame of the poem, Erinna's depiction of herself as she laments for Baukis, is suitable for a wedding song. The epigrams and the papyrus fragment paint a picture of Erinna engaged in wool working under her mother's supervision. Weaving was a normal activity for unmarried girls, but why is the whole poem entitled the *Distaff*?[62] One suggestion is that the title draws a parallel between Erinna and Moira (or the Moirai), who also spins and who is said to cut short Erinna's life in *AP* 7.12.4.[63] What this parallel does not explain, however, is the role of Erinna's mother, and the omission is significant: the Moirai do not appear in the surviving part of the papyrus, but the mother does, and in the epigram that is the most informative about the content of the *Distaff* it is her mother who compels Erinna to weave:

ἦ καὶ ἐπ᾽ ἠλακάτῃ μητρὸς φόβῳ, ἦ καὶ ἐφ᾽ ἱστῷ
ἑστήκει Μουσέων λάτρις ἐφαπτομένη. (*AP* 9.190.5–6)

Even occupied with her spindle in fear of her mother,
even at the loom she stood as a faithful servant of the Muses.

In view of this, I think there is another way of explaining the poem's title. The central theme of weaving, or rather, of not wanting to weave, is attested in the context of maidenhood, maternal compulsion, and love in Sappho 102 Voigt:

Γλύκηα μᾶτερ, οὔ τοι δύναμαι κρέκην τὸν ἴστον
πόθωι δάμεισα παῖδος βραδίναν δι᾽ Ἀφροδίταν.

Sweet mother, I no longer can ply the loom,
Subdued by desire for a boy at the hands of slender Aphrodite.

Here, the girl's weaving, supervised by her mother, is surely part of the preparation of her dowry, brought to an end at last, the girl hopes, by the power of Aphrodite. The weaving/wedding opposition is clearly expressed in *AP* 9.96, where a father instructs his daughter:

Παρθένε καλλιπάρῃε, κόρη δ᾽ ἐμή, ἴσχε συνεργὸν
ἠλακάτην, ἀρκεῦν κτῆμα πένητι βίῳ·
ἢν δ᾽ ἴκῃ εἰς ὑμέναιον, Ἀχαιΐδος ἤθεα μητρὸς
χρηστὰ φύλασσε πόσει προῖκα βεβαιοτάτην.

Pretty-cheeked maiden, my daughter, have as your work companion
your spindle, a sufficient property for a laborer's life.
But if you get married, keep to the honest habits of your Achaean mother—
this is the most secure dowry for your husband.

The idea that the girl's good character (rather than the products of her distaff) should be her dowry is surely based on the presumption of the opposite, namely, that normally the dowry would include the fabrics and clothes she produces.[64] It seems likely, therefore, that the distaff that gives its name to Erinna's poem is just such a maidenly distaff, the girl's cow-orker as she prepares for marriage. The mention of the distaff (ἀλακάταν [39]) occurs in the immediate proximity of *hymenaios*, maidenly shame, red cheeks, and other elements that belong to the discourse of the wedding. This distaff is not simply a typical feminine tool, but rather points specifically to Erinna's own preparation for marriage.

In the *Distaff*, then, we are dealing with a lament that is sung by a girl waiting and preparing for her own marriage over someone who tragically failed to accomplish this very transition, and this lament bears all the markings of a wedding song. In a sense, Erinna does the same thing as the girls of Troizen who perform laments for Hippolytos before their weddings, only her lament is not for a figure of myth but for her own συνεταιρίς Baukis. However, Baukis may herself be an archetypal figure.[65] She has a *nom parlant*, and both her name and her untimely death mark her as comparable to several mythological figures, especially to Adonis.

Aphrodite's young consort Adonis is associated both with sexuality and with premature death.[66] In Sappho, he is marked by a luxuriousness and sensuality captured by the term *habros*:

κατθνα<ί>σκει, Κυθέρη', ἄβρος Ἄδωνις·τί κε θεῖμεν;
καττύπτεσθε, κόραι, καὶ κατερείκεσθε κίθωνας. (140a Voigt)

Delicate Adonis is dying, Kythereia. What are we to do?
Beat your breasts, girls, and tear your robes.

As Nagy demonstrates, eroticism is inherent in the epithet *habros*, which also connotes luxury, wealth, and excess. The term is used about seductive youths, such as Pindar's Iamos (*Olympian* 6.55) and Hippolyta (*Nemean* 5.26) and is also associated with the figure of Lydian Croesus. Called Λυδὲ ποδαβρέ, "tender-footed Lydian," by the Pythia in Herodotos (1.55.7), Croesus epitomizes the Lydian reputation for wealth, luxuriance, and softness. The "Lydian" qualities of luxury, magnificence, and softness continue to be associated with Adonis from Sappho to Theokritos to Bion, who goes out of his way to describe the overflowing sensuality of Adonis both in love and in death (*Epitaphion Adonidos* 70–81).

Erinna's Baukis has a certain affinity with Adonis, signaled by her rare name, derived from the adjective βαυκός, which means "delicate, luxurious" and is regularly glossed as τρυφερός, "dainty, voluptuous," in lexica (e.g., Hesykhios and Photios, *s.v.* βαυκός).[67] Words with the same root include βαυκίδες, a type of shoe worn by Ionian women and described in various lexica as soft and luxurious and also as saffron colored, πολυτελὲς δ' ἦν ὑπόδημα κροκοειδές (*Onomasticon* 7.94.5).[68] The color of saffron in combination with luxuriousness brings to mind Antigone's "wedding" dress in the *Phoenissae* (στολίδος κροκόεσσαν ἀνεῖσα τρυφάν [1491]) and Iphigeneia's shedding of a saffron garment, probably her bridal veil, in the *Agamemnon*: κρόκου βάφας δ' ἐς πέδον χέουσα (239). Meleager selects the maiden-colored crocus to symbolize Erinna's poetry (*AP* 4.1.12). Moreover, elaborate footwear is a distinctive feature of a girl, already sexually attractive but still at play, in Anacreon (νήνι ποικιλοσαμβάλωι [*PMG* 358.3]).[69]

Elaborate footwear would shine most in movement, and the root of βαυκός in fact gives its name to a dance, βαυκισμός. This dance, said to be Ionian, is described by Pollux as an ornate, sensual, and whirling dance (ἁβρά τις ὄρχησις καὶ τὸ σῶμα ἐξυγραίνουσα καὶ στρόβιλος [4.100.7]). The same dance is called "tender" (ἀπαλή) by the Homeric scholia (*Iliad* 22.391b) and even "a type of vulgar dance" (εἶδος ὀρχήσεως φορτικῆς) by the scholia to Aristophanes (*Equites* 20a1). Such, then, are the associations likely to be evoked by the name Baukis: softness, luxury, youth, dancing, sensuality and sexuality, and, potentially, excess thereof. In all of these features the semantic field of the name is very close to that of the epithet ἁβρός, applied to Adonis.

As Nagy has shown, *habrosunê* has a negative side: built into it is the danger of excess, *hubris*, leading to destruction.[70] Neither Adonis nor Baukis is accused of *hubris*, but there is the sense, present both in the *Distaff* and in poetic references to Adonis, that the very magnificence of their blossoming invites its own demise. In Bion, for example, Adonis is a hunter, and the masculine trials of the hunt complement his sensual beauty, only adding to the desirability of the youth.[71] But the same occupation also gets him killed by a boar, and Aphrodite in Bion's lament reproaches Adonis for his "madness" in confronting the beasts (ἐμήναο θηρὶ παλαίειν [61]).

In a similar way, Erinna reproaches Baukis both for "madness" (μαινομέν[οισιν...]ποσσίν [15]) and for being forgetful (ἐλέλασο [28], λάθας [30]) and, presumably, not cautious enough. Erinna mentions Aphrodite, the marital bed (λέχος), and Baukis's forgetfulness in one breath. All of this suggests that Baukis entered the realm of Aphrodite either too early or too impetuously, and this aligns her with Adonis and his precocious growth and premature death, symbolized by the so-called gardens of Adonis, tender young shoots planted in shallow potsherds at the height of the summer, which grow quickly and vigorously but then equally quickly die.[72]

SONG AND THE DIALECT OF THE *DISTAFF*

Erinna's poem is full of recollections of daily life, but these recollections reflect traditional themes, and the occasion re-created in the *Distaff*, while presented as intensely personal, is transcendent and can stand for all similar occasions. In the way it creates its occasion internally the *Distaff* is like later Hellenistic poetry, in particular that of Theokritos's and of Callimachus's hymns. In keeping with its occasion, the poem emerges as a stylized representation of a wedding song for the untimely dead. In representing song through the medium of hexameter, Erinna is certainly not innovating. Homeric epic is known to incorporate and represent in a stylized form a wide array of genres, lament among them, and the hexameter can occasionally reflect not only the diction of such songs but also such stylistic features as antiphony, alternating question and answer, and various forms of repetition.[73] The same can be said about Erinna's poem, which is marked by the use of anaphora, reminiscent of popular song, for example:

τα]ῦτά τυ, Βαῦκι τάλαι[να βαρὺ στονά]χεισα γόημ[ι],
τα]ῦτά μοι ἐν κρα[δίαι   ] παίχνια κεῖται. (18–19)

That is why, poor Baukis, I cry for you deeply groaning,
these games lie in my heart.

Even within the small portion of the poem that survives, this device is used more than once: a little later in the poem, 32 and 33 begin with οὐ[γ]άρ and οὐδέ. A more complex example is the reversed echo between 30–31 and 47–48. Βαῦκι φίλα in 30 is followed by τῶ τυ κατακλαίοισα in 31, while τῶ τυ φίλα in 47 is followed by Βαῦκι κατακλα[ίοισα in 48. The repeated use of ὑμέναιε in 51 and 53 is reminiscent of the same invocation in wedding songs, which seems to have always been repeated. In this case, the effect is augmented by anaphora (ὦ πολλάν in 51, π]ολλά in 52) and the exclamation αἰαῖ in 53, which at once transforms the wedding shouts into lamentation and echoes Erinna's earlier cry αἰ]αῖ ἐγώ (16) in the khelikhelônê game.

Another distinctive feature of Erinna's poem is its dialect, which has attracted attention since antiquity.[74] An investigation of Erinna's dialect suggests that it is not a device for indicating her (imagined) place of origin or social status but, instead, a feature that correlates with the genre of Erinna's poem, that is, a wedding song performed as a lament.

The dialect of this poem is a mixture: a variety of Doric is combined with some Aeolic forms (see the appendix). Most of the Doric forms are of wide distribution, with the two exceptions (compensatory lengthening after the loss of digamma and the use of τῆνος as opposed to ἐκεῖνος, κῆνος) being characteristic of a narrower range of dialects.[75] The Aeolic element is specifically Lesbian, and although Lesbian features are few, they are highly typical and noticeable, such as feminine participles in -οισα and -εισα, geminate -νν from -σν (as in σελάννα, χελύννα), and athematic conjugation of contract verbs (γόημι). There are also some Ionic forms in Erinna, but they are characteristic of epic rather than any Ionic vernacular.[76]

It is hard to believe that such a dialect combination could reflect a particular place of origin, and the situation is not helped by the ancient biographical tradition, which provides too many conflicting views on where Erinna was from. The Suda (2.587) alone lists four possibilities: Teos, Telos, Rhodes, and Lesbos. Another Byzantine source, Stephanos of Byzantium, adds Tenos (*Ethnica*, epitome 622.4). The only epigram to mention Baukis's origins, *AP* 7.710, describes her as a native of Telos, and Telos is also a clear favorite in modern scholarship.[77] It is a small island off Knidos, in the south-east corner of the Aegean, and a Doric-speaking area, which invites the assumption that Erinna's dialect is an early example of dialectal experimentation, characteristic of the Hellenistic age. She took an old form, hexameter poetry, and used it for novel purposes: to compose a poem in a dialect that includes some elements of her Doric vernacular while also signaling her main literary antecedent, Sappho. This line of thinking is expressed by West: "The Doric element is meant to convey that she is an ordinary person, a homely little Telian maid.... The Aeolic element is meant to echo Sappho and so emphasize the female sex of the writer. Both elements are intended to define the poetic persona more piquantly, and the aim is certainly achieved."[78]

The question is, however, whether Erinna's audience would indeed assume that Doric dialect indicates a simple person, especially a Doric mixed with Aeolic. And although Erinna's poem certainly echoes Sappho, the effect is achieved as much by her sex and by her subject as by the Lesbian forms. After all, Pindar also composed in a variety of Doric with some Aeolicisms. As an alternative explanation, I suggest that Erinna's dialect correlates first and foremost not with the poet's place of origin, sex, or social status but with the genre of the *Distaff*.[79]

There are, broadly speaking, two kinds of antecedents to Erinna's dialect. One is choral lyric composed in a mixed Doric-Aeolic dialect. Like those of choral lyric (Alkman and Pindar), the Aeolicisms of Erinna are gratuitous from a metrical point of view. That is, they are metrically the same as corresponding Doric or Ionic forms, and accordingly their use does not entail any metrical advantages for the poets: a Doric or Ionic form could have been used instead without altering the meter. This distinguishes the Aeolicisms of choral lyric, and Erinna, from the Homeric ones, which are for the most part metrically distinct from the corresponding Ionic forms.

The ambit of choral lyric of course included both the genre of the *hymenaion* and the genre of lament, and by employing a stylized dialect reminiscent of such compositions, Erinna perhaps indicates that although her poem is in hexameters, it is not an epic/heroic narrative but, rather, represents a song such as those of Alkman. In this sense, Erinna could be seen as a forerunner of Theokritos: she imitates a song while "hexametriz-ing" it. The non-Ionic dialect remains as a sign of the poem's lyric rather than epic qualities.

The second type of antecedent for Erinna is poorly attested but important nonetheless: earlier hexameter poetry that is composed in a mixed dialect resembling hers. Very little of such poetry survives, yet even the scattered bits that do suggest that "hexametrizing" such as Erinna's may itself be a phenomenon much older than the Hellenistic age. In the remaining part of this chapter I present some evidence for the existence of a hexameter poetry that was distinguished by its use of Doric-Aeolic dialectal mixture and which included genres other than epic.

To start with well-known poetry, there are Sapphic hexameters in a toned-down Lesbian dialect, and the interesting thing is that these hexameters come mostly from wedding songs, such as, for example, Sappho 105 Voigt:

οἶον τὸ γλυκύμαλον ἐρεύθεται ἄκρῳ ἐπ᾽ ὔσδωι,
ἄκρον ἐπ᾽ ἀκροτάτωι, λελάθοντο δὲ μαλοδρόπηες
οὐ μὰν ἐκλελάθοντ᾽, ἀλλ᾽ οὐκ ἐδύναντ᾽ ἐπίκεσθαι.

Like a sweet apple glows red on the top branch,
top on the topmost branch, and the pickers forgot it.
No, they did not forget it, they could not reach it.[80]

In fragment 117B what seems to be a refrain consists of two dactyls: ἔσπερ᾽ ὑμήναον. This fragment is cited as an illustration of a particular meter, *hymenaicum*, and another illustration of the same meter looks like a refrain from a lament, a dactylic variation on the Adonian closure: ὢ τὸν Ἀδώνιον (cf. ὢ τὸν Ἀδώνιν, the Adonian closure).[81] These two snippets of Sappho provide an indication of a formal similarity between the *hymenaion* and a lament for Adonis. Moreover, the *adônion* is described by Hesykhios as a marching song and connected both with Aeolic Lesbos and with Doric Sparta: ἀδώνιον·τὸ παρὰ τοῖς Λάκωσιν αὐληθὲν ἐμβατήριον, ὅπερ ὕστερον παρὰ Λεσβίοις ὠνομάσθη (A 1228). It is noteworthy that Hesykhios mentions Sparta and Lesbos as the provenance of the *adonion*, a provenance that may reflect the dialect and the musical style of the song.[82]

A different kind of evidence for Doric and Aeolic hexameters is provided by the scant epigraphical poetry in varieties of Doric and West Greek, which also has some conspicuously Lesbian features. For example, there is a very badly preserved inscription from Boiotia (*CEG* 114, ca. 479 B.C.E.):

μ᾽ ἔθ]ραφσεν, ἐπ᾽ Ἀσοποῖ δὲ δαμασθὲς
θ]ρενον ἔθεκα,
ἑ τόδ᾽ ἐπέστ[ασε
]οισα τὸν ἡυιὸν Καφι[

[B]rought me up, but subdued on the banks of Asopos
I made a dirge
she set up this
. . . ing (her) son Kaphı . . .

This is a tombstone for someone who died in battle by the river Asopos. The end of the first line is easily paralleled in Homer:

Πάτροκλος δὲ θεοῦ πληγῇ καὶ δουρὶ δαμασθείς. (*Iliad* 16.816)

Patroklos, subdued by the blow of the god and by the spear.

The last line contains a form of participle that is neither Homeric nor Boiotian but Lesbian, a participle in -οισα. There is also a fragment of an inscription from Perakhora, which seems to be on a base for a dedication and which might form the beginning of a hexameter line containing an Aeolic participle: ε]υμενέοισα ηυπόδ[εξαι, "be favorable and receive" (*CEG* 352, ca. 650 B.C.E.).

Some equally fragmentary hints come from vases. There is a strange and famous "patchwork" hexameter line on a writing tablet in an early fifth-century school scene by the Attic vase painter Douris (*ARV* 431.48), which reads as follows:

Μοῖσά μοι/ἀ(μ)φὶ Σκάμανδρον/εὔρρων ἄρχομαι ἀείδεν.

Muse for me about the fair-flowing Skamandros I begin to sing.

Obviously this is a nonsensical verse or, rather, three chunks of it. But the form of the word *Muse* used here is not the Homeric and Ionic Μοῦσα but, rather, the Lesbian Μοῖσα. It is presumably from poetic sources, whether hexameter or not, that forms like this penetrate into inscriptions on the Corinthian vases, which bear such inscriptions as Μοῖσαι [Ἀπέλλ]ον (*COR* 36 Wachter, fragment of a Corinthian skyphos from Ithaka, 600–575 B.C.E.) and [Καλ(λ)?]ιάνερα Πνοτομέδοισα (*COR* 96 Wachter, fragment of a Corinthian krater of unknown provenance, possibly Gela, 570–550 B.C.E.).

A separate question is a strange imperative form, δίδοι, which appears both in Pindar and in inscriptions. Perhaps the most famous instance is *CEG* 326, circa 700–675 B.C.E.:

Μάντικλός μ' ἀνέθεκε Ϝεκαβόλοι ἀργυροτόξοι
τᾶς δδεκάτας· τὺ δε, Φοῖβε, δίδοι χαρίϜετταν ἀμοιβ[άν].

Mantiklos dedicated me to the far-shooter of the silver bow
from the tithe. But you, Phoibos, give a graceful recompense.

With this one can compare another inscription, also Boiotian, *CEG* 334 (550–525 B.C.E.):

καλϜὸν ἄγαλμα Ϝάνακτι Ϝ[εκαβόλοι Ἀπόλονι]
]ορίδας ποίϜεσέ μ' Ἐχέστροτος· αὐτὰρ ἔπεμφσαν
]ον ΠτοιεϜι
τὸς τύ, Ϝάναχς, φεφύλαχσο, δίδοι δ' ἀρ<ε>τάν [τε καὶ ὄλβον].

A beautiful statue for the lord, Apollo the far-shooter
Ekhestrotos son of...—or made me. But they sent
...to the Ptoian
Preserve them, o lord, and give them success and prosperity.

Both inscriptions are in hexameter. The end of the hexameter line in the Mantiklos dedication is a formula that also occurs in the *Odyssey*, where Athena, disguised as Mentor, prays to Poseidon (δίδου χαρίεσσαν ἀμοιβήν [3.58]).

It is an open question where these δίδοι forms come from. Strunk has explained them as secondary Lesbian formations, but there is not enough evidence to show that these forms were indeed used on Lesbos.[83] Rather than reflecting a spoken dialect, they may be poetic formations created by analogy with other forms where Ionic ου correlates to Aeolic οι, for example, μοῦσα/μοῖσα = δίδου/X. The origin of the forms, in any case, is not essential for my argument. What is essential is that they *look* like a Lesbian feature, and they occur in inscriptions where Homer would have had δίδου. In other words, the metrically gratuitous Lesbian forms of the type that is associated with choral poetry are also present in humble epigraphic hexameters in West Greek dialects.

Another hexameter fragment with similar characteristics is the *prosodion* of Eumelos (of uncertain date). Two lines are quoted by Pausanias, and he says that they are from a processional hymn:

τῶι γὰρ ᾿Ιθωμάται καταθύμιος ἔπλετο Μοῖσα
ἁ καθαρά [ ] καὶ ἐλεύθερα σάμβαλ᾿ ἔχουσα. (*PMG* 696)[84]

For he of Ithome had in his thoughts the Muse who is pure and
wears the sandals of freedom.

It is hexameter poetry that is essentially Doric, characterized, for example, by retention of the inherited long α and also by some "free" Aeolicisms: certainly Μοῖσα and possibly σάμβαλα.

Discussing the inscriptions on vases in connection with these lines by Eumelos, Wachter envisages a "dactylic-hexametrical tradition of prayer, possibly combined with hymns."[85] Two inscriptions with imperative δίδοι are prayers addressed to Apollo, but it is likely that the tradition was broader. One of the inscriptions just cited, *CEG* 114, mentions a lament; the vase with the inscription Μοῖσαι [᾿Απέλλ]ον (*COR* 36 Wachter) depicts Apollo and the Muses as part of a wedding scene, according to Wachter's analysis; and Eumelos's verse supposedly comes from a processional song, a *prosodion*.[86]

What seems to be behind these fragments is hexameter poetry, distinguished by its use of Doric/West Greek dialect with metrically free Aeolicisms and which is neither narrative nor heroic. This is the hexameter of small occasional genres, especially prayers, processional songs, *hymenaia*, and *thrênoi*. The occasionality of this poetry may in fact be the reason why so little of it survives. But even so, Doric-Aeolic hexameters crop up in Boiotia and the Peloponnese, and it may be that this tradition experienced a revival in the fourth century.

It is possible that in the *Distaff* Erinna imitates this preexisting kind of hexameter poetry. As with this poetry, the *Distaff* is strongly tied to its occasion and composed in a Doric dialect with metrically free Aeolicisms. Moreover, like some of the fragments considered above, the *Distaff* represents a song in spite of being hexametrical. Such hexametrizing of song combined with the use of Doric-Aeolic dialect seems to go back all the way to the Archaic period, and by employing these poetic devices Erinna responds to a particular tradition of occasional poetry. Further, by her use of dialect, repetitions, antiphonal structures, and marked diction, she reproduces the effect of a particular genre of song: a lament that is virtually a wedding song, so densely is it packed with wedding themes—a wedding song that has become a lament.

APPENDIX: A BASIC ANALYSIS OF ERINNA'S DIALECT

West Greek/Doric Features of Wide Distribution

inherited long -α is preserved

genitive pl. of α-stems in -ᾱν (λευκᾶν [15])

α + ε contract into η (ἐφοίτη [26])

second person pronoun τύ (e.g., 18)

thematic infinitives in -ην (ἰδῆν [33])

ποτί as opposed to πρός (ποτ' ὄρθρον [22])

first pl. active primary ending -μες as opposed to -μεν (ἀθύρομες [20])

τόκα as opposed to τότε (25)

Doric Features of Restricted Distribution

compensatory lengthening after the loss of digamma: κώρα < κόρϝα (3)

pronoun τῆνος as opposed to ἐκεῖνος, κῆνος (e.g., 24)

Aeolic (Lesbian) Features

diphthongization of vowel before secondary -ns: feminine participles in -οισα, -εισα (e.g., κατακλαίοισα [31], στονάχεισα [18])

geminate -νν from -σν (σελάννα [6, 12], χελύννα [5, 7, 16])

athematic conjugation of the contract verbs (γόημι [18])

Epic-Ionic Features

ν-movable (e.g., ποσσίν [16])

ἄσσα (29)

Epic Archaisms

"long" datives (e.g., θαλάμοισιν [21], χαίταισιν [34])

omission of the augment (ἄκουσας [29], ἄϋσα [16])

ACKNOWLEDGMENTS

The initial version of this chapter was presented at the "Displaced Dialects" conference at the University of Washington in 2003. I am grateful to the participants for their comments, and to the Department of Classics and The Simpson Center for the Humanities for funding and helping to organize the conference. Versions of the paper were also presented at the APA in 2004, and at the University of Victoria, Canada, in 2005. Thanks to both audiences for their feedback. Thanks also to Ann Suter for her editorial work on the final version.

NOTES

1. On Erinna's date, see Donado 1973. The Suda and *AP* 9.190.3 report the number of lines; the latter also declares the verses to be ἴσοι Ὁμήρῳ and concludes with a comparison to Sappho. The Suda makes Erinna a companion and contemporary of Sappho, no doubt on the strength of their poetic similarities. Cervelli 1952 argues that Erinna was in fact from Lesbos. Rauk 1989 offers an extensive comparison of the *Distaff* to Sappho 94.

2. Athenaios 7.283D; *PSI* 1090; Stobaios 4.51.4; West 1977.

3. An early, detailed analysis of the *Distaff* as a lament is Bowra 1936. See also Skinner 1982 for a comparison of Erinna, Briseis, and the *Trojan Women*.

4. On γόος as a more highly individualized type of lament than θρῆνος, see Alexiou 1974, 11–12, 102–103. For a useful synthesis of the typical elements in a γόος (praise for the dead, antithesis between the mourner and the deceased, tripartite structure, antiphony, etc.), see Tsagalis 2004, 15.

5. Arthur 1980, 65.

6. Rauk argues that Erinna's poem belongs to the same genre as Sappho 94 and that "both are examples of farewells addressed to female companions who leave to be married" (1989, 101). I agree with Rauk on many points but have misgivings about his overall reconstruction of the poem. It seems that he envisages an Erinna who recollects Baukis's wedding (and their farewells) in one part of the poem and bewails the death of her friend in another. This, however, leaves the relationship between the supposed "wedding lament" (compared to Sappho 94) and the funeral lament unclear.

7. In this argument, I align myself with other essays in this collection that seek to enlarge our understanding of how lament functions on a variety of occasions. See, for example, Suter on male lament, Rutherford and Bachvarova on lament as important for civic order, and Bachvarova on laments for propitiating tutelary deities.

8. E.g., Alexiou 1974, 120–122; Alexiou and Dronke 1971; Danforth and Tsiaras 1982, esp. 74–85; Herzfeld 1981; Saunier 1999, 287–291.

9. Danforth and Tsiaras 1982, 80.

10. This text is provided solely as an aid to the reader and is not a papyrological publication. I have tried to represent, approximately, the layout of the papyrus but have not attempted to reflect accurately the size of every lacuna or to mark uncertain readings. The text is based on West 1977 and Lloyd-Jones and Parsons 1983 and includes some of the most uncontroversial supplements suggested by West.

11. Nagy 1994, 14; Todorov [1978] 1990, 20.

12. Nagy 1994, 13.

13. For a discussion of the epigrams, see Luck 1954; Scholtz 1973. The authenticity of all three epigrams ascribed to Erinna (*AP* 6.352, 7.710, 7.712), two related and one unrelated to the *Distaff*, has been questioned; see Latte [1953] 1968, 522; West 1977, 114; cf. Cameron and Cameron 1969, 285. The question of authenticity makes no difference for my argument.

14. *AP* 7.710.5: χὤτι με νύμφαν εὖσαν ἔχει τάφος; *AP* 7.712.1: Νύμφας Βαυκίδος εἰμί. Translations are mine throughout, unless otherwise indicated.

15. Bibliography on the subject is imposing. See Rehm 1994 for a book-length study of the coincidence of death and marriage in Athenian tragedy, and

Seaford 1987 on perverted wedding in tragedy, which often involves coincidence with death. See also Alexiou 1983, 88–90, and 2002, 105–109, 120–122, 152–157, 178, 195–196, 230 n. 64; Danforth and Tsiaras 1982; Giannakis 1998; Saunier 1968; Tsagalis 2004, 85, n. 256. For Romanian evidence, see Kligman 1988. I am grateful to Christos Tsagalis for some of these references.

16. See, e.g., Sophocles *Trachiniae* 144–149 (cited below); Seaford 1986. Petropoulos 2003, 62–73, gathers documentation, in addition to Alexiou's and Seaford's, of the youth as flower, plant, or fruit motif. See esp. Petropoulos 2003, 64–69, on the topos of youth plucked as a flower or fruit before its time, in both funerary and nuptial contexts.

17. Sourvinou-Inwood 1988, 121–122 (with references), 127–134. Saffron garments also occurred in the context of wedding (see below). Cunningham 1984 argues that the bridal veil was of saffron color and that it is referred to as κρόκου βάφας in *Agamemnon* 239. The color of the wedding dress is not certain, but it might have been purple (Oakley and Sinos 1993, 16).

18. See Garland 1990, 210–213. It seems that the marriageable age for a woman extended in Athens from about thirteen to twenty-five, while in Sparta eighteen to twenty was usual. The desirable age for marriage for the male seems to have been later, around thirty.

19. *Works and Days* 695–700.

20. Plato, *Republic* 460e1–5; Aristotle, *Politics* 1334b28–30.

21. In this sense, one might call the *Distaff* a proleptic self-lament. Cf. Suter, this volume, on male self-lament, which may permit the living and the dead to share their grief. See also Tsagalis 2004, 143–149, esp. 147, for a discussion of Achilles' lament for Patroklos in *Iliad* 18 as a proleptic self-lament.

22. Bowra 1936, 328.

23. Pomeroy 1978 and Arthur 1980 are prime examples of works that discuss the thematic significance of the tortoise game.

24. Plutarch, *Conjugal Precepts* 142D.

25. Plutarch, *Isis and Osiris* 381D.

26. Nagy [1973] 1990b, esp. 227–234. The relevance of the white rock theme for Erinna is noted by Arthur (1980, 61) and Stehle (2001, 188–189).

27. Menander F 258K.

28. Bowra 1936, 325, 328; West 1977, 98.

29. Nagy [1973] 1990b, 223–225.

30. *Scholia in Pindarum BDEGQ* 246a1, 246b1.

31. Calame 1997, 184.

32. On the Leukippides and Leukippoi, see Calame 1997, 176–177, 185–191. On Leukippos (or, rather, various Leukippoi) as a hero of initiation, see Dowden 1989, 49–70.

33. Calame 1997, 189–191. For Tyndaridai as λευκόπωλοι or λευκίπποι, e.g., see Pindar, *Pythian* 1.66; Euripides, *Helen* 638, *Phoenissae* 606; Hesykhios, *s.v.* Διόσκουροι.

34. Bakkhylides, Fr. dub. 61 M. On the marriage of the Leukippides and Tyndaridai, see Calame 1997, 188, with references; Larson 1995, 64–65.

35. On the game as "childish" see, e.g., Arthur 1980, 60–62; Snyder 1989, 92; Stehle 2001, 190; West 1977, 102–105.

36. Magrini 1975.

37. West 1977, 103.

38. Bremer 1987.

39. The scholiast (*Scholia in Pindarum*) adds that such nights were selected for weddings (κατὰ ταύτας γὰρ ἐποίουν τοὺς γάμους).

40. For more on this passage, see below.

41. Cf. Dutsch, this volume, on Roman *neniae* (both "laments" and "children's chants") as repetitive incantations that ease transitions, including those from life to death and those dramatized in games. See below on repetitions in the *Distaff.*

42. West 1977, 104–105.

43. Neri 1998a.

44. *Scholia in Theocritum* UEA 2.110.

45. *AP* 9.190.5–6.

46. This is called "a wedding text" by Austin (1991, 221). The idea of marriage is always in the background and often in the foreground of the narrative from the moment when Odysseus encounters Nausikaa until he departs from Scheria. Lattimore's 1969 analysis of the episode is very illuminating on this point (I am grateful to one of the anonymous reviewers of this chapter for this helpful reference).

47. For *Distaff*, this is suggested by West (1977, 105–106).

48. Cf. Anacreon *PMG* 358.1–4. On the ball in connection with Persephone, see Sourvinou-Inwood 1991, 147–180, esp. 159–163. Sourvinou-Inwood concludes that "the ball belongs to the sphere of marriage and prenuptial rites and also to the funerary realm" (1991, 163).

49. West 1977, 104.

50. Rauk 1989.

51. Nicander, fr. 16 Gow/Scholfield = Athenaios 7.282.

52. Apollonios Rhodios, *Founding of Naucratis* fr. 8 Powell = Athenaios 7.283d–f.

53. Rauk 1989, 105.

54. Seaford 1987, 119, 124–125.

55. Ibid., 119. Euploia is also a cult title of Aphrodite on Knidos, according to Pausanias (1.1.3).

56. Scholtz 1973, 26–27.

57. Stehle 2001, 193. Mormo frightens children, for example, in Theokritos 15.40 and in Callimachus *Hymn to Artemis* 70–71. On her function as a childhood bogey in the *Distaff*, see Bowra 1936, 332–333; West 1977, 107. On Mormo as a "negative pole of the maternal imago," see Arthur 1980, 64–65.

58. On this translation of βοτρυχώδεος, see Mastronarde 1994, 562.

59. Cf. Kassandra's words in Aeschylus *Agamemnon* 1178–1181.

60. The expression χεῖρ' ἐπὶ καρπῷ, which occurs in Homer (*Iliad* 24.671; *Odyssey* 18.258), corresponds to the groom's gesture, which was a distinct part of the wedding (at least in Athens), the grasping of the bride's wrist (or hand, on some vases). On this gesture, see Jenkins 1983, 138; Neumann 1965, 59; Oakley and Sinos 1993, 32; Sourvinou-Inwood 1987, 139–141; Sutton 1989, 345.

61. See Collard 1975, 370–371, on metrical and consequent textual difficulties in Euripides' *Suppliants* 1022. Cf. also *AP* 5.128 regarding Theokritos 2.140.

62. Crusius (*RE* 6.456) suspected that the title was a later invention (which, however, would not solve the question). This idea is opposed by Levin (1962, 199–200) and Cameron and Cameron (1969).

63. See Cameron and Cameron 1969.

64. Cf. *Odyssey* 5.27–28. Nausikaa is expected to take with her in marriage some of the clothes she washes.

65. Cf. Hagesikhora and Aigido in Alkman's *Partheneion* as discussed by Nagy (1990a, 345–370).

66. On Adonis and Adonaia, see Alexiou 1974, 55–57; Atallah 1966; Detienne 1972, 188–215; Nagy 1985, 60–63; Reed 1995; Winkler 1990, 188–193.

67. See Masson 1990, 179–182.

68. There are similar definitions in *Etymologicum Magnum* 192.18; Hesykhios *Glossae rhetoricae*; and Photios, *s.v.* βαυκίδες.

69. Cf. Sappho 39: πόδας δὲ/ποίκιλος μάσλης ἐκάλυπτε/Λύδιον κάλον ἔργον.

70. Nagy 1990a, 263–313, esp. 263–264 and 281–286.

71. Cf. Reed 1995, 337, on Adonis and the hunt. Reed tentatively suggests that Adonis's hunt may "assimilate him to a paradigm—not an antitype—of the successful passage from boyhood to manhood" while also considering the possibility that "Adonis' boar hunt might brand him as a pathetic antithesis of all a boy must do to become a man" (1995, 337).

72. On the gardens of Adonis, see Burkert 1979, 107; Detienne 1972, 187–226, esp. 192–200; Nagy 1985, 62; Stehle 1996, 200–201; Winkler 1990, 192. Cf. Reed 1995.

73. On laments, see Alexiou 1974, 146–160. On antiphonal wedding song, see Tsagalis 2004, 82–85, esp. 84 n. 254, with references. On antiphonal question and answer, anaphora, and refrain in wedding song, see Petropoulos 2003, 25–29.

74. Suda includes a note on dialect (both Doric and Aeolic) in its entry on Erinna. Cf. Antiphanes *AP* 11.322, on the Alexandrian "bookworms" who labor over Erinna.

75. Buck 1955, 49, 101. Lengthening after the loss of postconsonantal digamma is characteristic of the Argolic and Doric dialects of Crete, Thera, Cos, Rhodes, and colonies. The use of τῆνος is attested in Delphian, Heraclean, Argolic of Aegina, Megarian, and Sicilian Doric writers (Theokritos, Sophron, Epikharmos).

76. For a basic overview of Erinna's dialect, see the appendix. For a discussion of the dialect, see Donado 1972.

77. Arthur 1980, 57; Levin 1962, 194–196; West 1977, 117; cf. Pomeroy 1978, 19–20 (on Teos).

78. West 1977, 117.

79. Dialect generally correlates with genre in poetry before Erinna's time. For example, elegiacs tend to be in Ionic, whereas choral poetry is predominantly Doric; tragic choruses have Doric features, which are lacking in spoken dialogue. See Buck 1955, 14–16.

80. Cf. also Sappho 104 Voigt.

81. Sacerd. gramm. 6.517.4 K (codd. AB): *hymenaicum dimetrum dactylicum Sapphicum monoschematistum est: semper enim duobus dactylis constat.*

82. Hesykhios, *s.v.* ἀδώνιον.

83. Strunk 1961.

84. Pausanias 4.33.2.

85. Wachter 2001, 341.

86. See ibid., 61.

BIBLIOGRAPHY

Alexiou, M. 1974. *The Ritual Lament in Greek Tradition*. Cambridge.

——. 1983. Sons, Wives and Mothers. Reality and Fantasy in Some Modern Greek Ballads. *Journal of Modern Greek Studies* 1: 73–112.

——. 2002. *The Ritual Lament in Greek Tradition*. Rev. D. Yatromanolakis and P. Roilos. Lanham, Md.

Alexiou, M., and P. Dronke. 1971. The Lament of Jephtha's Daughter: Themes, Traditions, Originality. *Studi Medievali* 12: 819–863.

Arthur, M. 1980. The Tortoise and the Mirror: Erinna *PSI* 1090. *Classical World* 74: 53–65.

Atallah, W. 1966. *Adonis dans la littérature et l'art grecs.* Paris.

Austin, N. 1991. The Wedding Text in Homer's *Odyssey. Arion* 1 (2): 221–243.

Barnard, S. 1978. Hellenistic Women Poets. *Classical Journal* 73: 204–213.

Blümel, W. 1982. *Die Aiolischen Dialekte. Phonologie und Morphologie der inschriftlichen Texte aus generativer Sicht.* Göttingen.

Bowie, A. 1981. *The Poetic Dialect of Sappho and Alcaeus.* Salem, Mass.

Bowra, C. 1936. Erinna's Lament for Baucis. In *Greek Poetry and Life: Essays Presented to Gilbert Murray on His Seventieth Birthday, January 2, 1936,* 325–342. Oxford.

Bremer, J. 1987. Full Moon and Marriage in Apollonius' *Argonautica. Classical Quarterly* 37: 423–426.

Buck, C. 1955. *The Greek Dialects.* Chicago.

Burkert, W. 1979. *Structure and History in Greek Mythology and Ritual.* Berkeley.

Calame, C. 1997. *Choruses of Young Women in Ancient Greece: Their Morphology, Religious Role, and Social Function.* Trans. D. Collins and J. Orion. Lanham, Md.

Cameron, A. 1969. Erinna's *Distaff. Classical Quarterly* 19: 285–288.

Cervelli, M. 1952. Erinna e l'età che fu sua. *Annali di Istituto Superiore di Scienze e Lettere, S. Chiara di Napoli* 4: 195–246.

Collard, C. 1975. *Euripides* Supplices. *Edited with Introduction and Commentary.* Groningen.

Cunningham, M. 1984. Aeschylus, *Agamemnon* 231–247. *Bulletin of the Institute of Classical Studies* 31: 9–12.

Danforth, L., and A. Tsiaras. 1982. *The Death Rituals of Rural Greece.* Princeton.

Detienne, M. 1972. *Les Jardins d'Adonis.* Paris.

Donado, J. 1972. Notas Sobre Erina. *Estudios Clásicos* 16: 67–86.

———. 1973. Cronologia de Erinna. *Emerita* 41: 349–376.

Dowden, K. 1989. *Death and the Maiden: Girls' Initiation Rites in Greek Mythology.* London.

Garland, R. 1990. *The Greek Way of Life from Conception to Old Age.* London.

Giangrande, G. 1969. An Epigram of Erinna. *Classical Review* 19: 1–3.

Giannakis, G. 1998. Τὸ ποιητικὸ μοτίβο Γάμος-Θάνατος στὴν αρχαία ελληνικὴ καὶ στὴν ινδοευρωπαϊκή. Δωδώνη [Dodoni] 27 (2): 98–113.

Herzfeld, M. 1981. Performative Categories and Symbols of Passage in Rural Greece. *Journal of American Folklore* 94: 44–57.

Hooker, J. 1977. *The Language and Text of the Lesbian Poets.* Innsbruck.

Householder, F., and G. Nagy. 1972. *Greek: A Survey of Recent Work.* The Hague.

Jenkins, I. 1983. Is There Life After Marriage: A Study of the Abduction Motif in Vase Paintings of the Athenian Wedding Ceremony. *Bulletin of the Institute of Classical Studies* 30: 137–145.

Johnston, S. 1999. *Restless Dead: Encounters Between the Living and the Dead in Ancient Greece.* Berkeley.

Kligman, G. 1988. *The Wedding of the Dead. Ritual, Poetics, and Popular Culture in Transylvania.* Berkeley.

Larson, J. 1995. *Greek Heroine Cults.* Madison, Wisc.

Latte, K. [1953] 1968. *Erinna.* Göttingen. Reprint, in *Kleine Schriften zu Religion, Recht, Literatur und Sprache der Griechen und Römer,* ed. O. Gigon, W. Buchwald, and W. Kunkel, 508–525. Munich.

Lattimore, R. 1969. Nausikaa's Suitors. *Illinois Studies in Language and Literature* 58: 88–102.

Levin, D. 1962. Quaestiones Erinneanae. *Harvard Studies in Classical Philology* 66: 193–204.

Lloyd-Jones, H., and P. Parsons, eds. 1983. *Supplementum Hellenisticum*. Berlin.

Luck, G. 1954. Die Dichterinnen der griechischen Anthologie. *Museum Helveticum* 11: 170–187.

Magrini, M. 1975. Una nuova linea interpretative della Conocchia di Erinna. *Prometheus* 1: 225–236.

Masson, O. 1990. *Onomastica graeca selecta*. Paris.

Mastronarde, D. 1994. *Euripides* Phoenissae. *Edited with Introduction and Commentary.* Cambridge.

Mickey, K. 1981. Dialect Consciousness and Literary Language: An Example from Ancient Greek. *Transactions of the Philological Society* 1981: 35–66.

Nagy, G. 1973. Phaethon, Sapphic's Phaon, and the White Rock of Leukas. *Harvard Studies in Classical Philology* 77: 137–178.

———. 1979. *The Best of the Achaeans: Concepts of the Hero in Archaic Greek Poetry.* Baltimore.

———. 1985. Theognis and Megara: A Poet's Vision of His City. In *Theognis of Megara: Poetry and the Polis,* ed. T. Figueira and G. Nagy, 22–81. Baltimore.

———. 1990a. *Greek Mythology and Poetics.* Ithaca, N.Y.

———. 1990b *Pindar's Homer. The Lyric Possession of an Epic Past.* Baltimore.

———. 1994. Genre and Occasion. *Metis* 9–10: 11–25.

Neri, C. 1977. Erinna a Ossirinco. *Zeitschrift für Papyrologie und Epigraphik* 115: 57–72.

———. 1996. *Studi sulle Testimonianze di Erinna.* Bologna.

———. 1998a. Baucide e le Bambole. (Erinna: *SH* 401, 1–4, 19–22). *Athenaeum* 86: 165–178.

———. 1998b. Cambio di ritmo: Erinna, *SH* 401.14 SGG. e Carm. Pop. Fr.30(C). *Prometheus* 24: 19–24.

Neumann, G. 1965. *Gesten und Gebären in der griechischen Kunst.* Berlin.

Oakley, J., and R. Sinos. 1993. *The Wedding in Ancient Athens.* Madison, Wisc.

Page, D. 1953. *Corinna.* London.

Palmer, L. 1980. *The Greek Language.* Atlantic Highlands, N.J.

Pardini, A. 1991. Problemi dialettali Greci ed interpretazioni antiche e moderne: P.S.I. 1090 (Erinna); P.Oxy 8 (Anonimo); P. Antinoe S.N. (Teocrito). *Zeitschrift für Papyrologie und Epigraphik* 85: 1–7.

Petropoulos, J. 2003. *Eroticism in Ancient and Medieval Greek Poetry.* London.

Pomeroy, S. 1978. Supplementary Notes on Erinna. *Zeitschrift für Papyrologie und Epigraphik* 32: 17–21.

Rauk, J. 1989. Erinna's *Distaff* and Sappho Fr. 94. *Greek, Roman and Byzantine Studies* 30: 101–116.

Reed, J. 1995. The Sexuality of Adonis. *Classical Antiquity* 14: 317–347.

Rehm, R. 1994. *Marriage to Death: The Conflation of Wedding and Funeral Rituals in Greek Tragedy.* Princeton.

Rix, H. 1976. *Historische Grammatik des Griechischen.* Darmstadt.

Saunier, G. 1968. Les chansons de noces à thèmes funèbres. Recherches sur la famille et la société grecques. Unpublished Ph.D. dissertation, University of Paris.

———. 1999. *Ελληνικὰ Δημοτικὰ Τραγούδια. Τὰ Μοιρολόγια.* Athens.

Scholtz, U. 1973. Erinna. *Antike und Abendland* 18: 21–29.

Seaford, R. 1986. Wedding Ritual and Textual Criticism in Sophocles' *Women of Trachis*. *Hermes* 114: 50–59.

——. 1987. The Tragic Wedding. *Journal of Hellenic Studies* 107: 106–130.

Skinner, M. 1982. Briseis, the *Trojan Women*, and Erinna. *Classical World* 75: 265–269.

Snyder, J. 1989. *The Woman and the Lyre. Women Writers in Classical Greece and Rome*. Carbondale, Ill.

Sourvinou-Inwood, C. 1987. A Series of Erotic Pursuits: Images and Meanings. *Journal of Hellenic Studies* 107: 131–153.

——. 1988. *Studies in Girls' Transitions. Aspects of the* Arkteia *and Age Representations in Attic Iconography*. Athens.

——. 1991. *Reading Greek Culture. Texts and Images, Rituals and Myths*. Oxford.

Stehle, E. 1996. Sappho's Gaze: Fantasies of a Goddess and a Young Man. In *Reading Sappho. Contemporary Approaches*, ed. E. Greene, 193–225. Berkeley.

——. 2001. The Good Daughter: Mother's Tutelage in Erinna's *Distaff* and Fourth-Century Epitaphs. In *Making Silence Speak: Women's Voices in Greek Literature and Society*, ed. André Lardinois and Laura McClure, 179–200. Princeton.

Strunk, K. 1961. Der böotische Imperativ δίδοι. *Glotta* 39: 114–123.

Sutton, R. 1989. On the Classical Athenian Wedding: Two Red-Figure *Loutrophoroi* in Boston. In *Daidalikon: Studies in Memory of Raymond V. Schoder, S.J.*, ed. R. Sutton, 331–360. Wauconda, Ill.

Todorov, Tz. [1978] 1990. *Genres in Discourse*. Trans. C. Porter. Cambridge.

Tsagalis, C. 2004. *Epic Grief. Personal Laments in Homer's Iliad*. Berlin.

Wachter, R. 2001. *Non-Attic Greek Vase Inscriptions*. New York.

Watkins, C. 1976. Syntax and Metrics in the Dipylon Vase Inscription. In *Studies in Greek, Italian and Indo-European Linguistics, Offered to Leonard R. Palmer on the Occasion of His 70th Birthday*, ed. A. Morpurgo Davies and W. Meid, 431–442. Innsbruck.

West, M. 1977. Erinna. *Zeitschrift für Papyrologie und Epigraphik* 25: 95–119.

Winkler, J. 1990. *The Constraints of Desire*. New York.

11

LAMENT IN LUCAN'S
BELLVM CIVILE

ALISON KEITH

L ament in Classical antiquity has been studied extensively in Greek
ritual and literature, primarily from the perspectives of anthropology,
feminism, and literary criticism.[1] Roman codes and conventions of funerary lamentation, however, have received far less attention, although Vergil's *Aeneid* has been the focus of some discussion.[2] In this study I explore
the literary representation of lament in Classical Rome but press the
investigation beyond Vergil to Lucan, beyond female lamentation to
male, and beyond public lament to private lament.[3] In a stimulating article
surveying lament in the growth and eclipse of Roman epic, Elaine Fantham has suggested that "[c]ommunal public lament is...used by
Lucan...to anticipate the catastrophe of Pompey's death" throughout
his epic.[4] My study complements her discussion of public lament by
focusing on the private personal laments for Pompey of his wife Cornelia
and of his quaestor Cordus in conjunction with Cato's public eulogy of
Pompey. In the course of my discussion I shall consider what thematic
functions lament plays in the poem; what intertextual relationships can be
traced between Lucan's depiction of lament and laments in Vergil's *Aeneid*
and other epic poems, both Greek and Latin; and finally, to what extent
lament can be characterized as a gendered or class-marked genre in Lucan's
epic (i.e., what social hierarchies lament enacts in the poem) and how Lucan's
representation of lament reflects attitudes toward lament in Roman society.
I shall suggest that Lucan plays on his audience's expectation of lamentation
as a female genre, and, more specifically, a wifely obligation, throughout the
poem.[5] At the climactic moment of Pompey's death, however, we shall see

233

that lament is not only an obligation owed the dead husband by his wife but also an obligation owed the *patronus* by his social inferiors, male and female.[6]

Fantham suggests that "for Lucan public mourning is so powerful a symbol that he marks the outbreak of civil war in his second book with all the symptoms of official and unofficial mourning."[7] Indeed Lucan explicitly compares the advent of public mourning at Rome to a Roman matron's private response to death in the household (2.16–28):

[E]rgo, ubi concipiunt quantis sit cladibus orbi
constatura fides superum, ferale per urbem
iustitium; latuit plebeio tectus amictu
omnis honos, nullos comitata est purpura fasces.
tum questus tenuere suos magnusque per omnis
errauit sine uoce dolor. sic funere primo
attonitae tacuere domus, cum corpora nondum
conclamata iacent nec mater crine soluto
exigit ad saeuos famularum bracchia planctus,
sed cum membra premit fugiente rigentia uita
uoltusque exanimes oculosque in morte minaces,
necdum est ille dolor nec iam metus: incubat amens
miraturque malum.

And so, when they perceived what great disasters the faith
of the gods would cost the world, public business ceased
throughout the city, and funeral mourning prevailed; every
public rank was concealed, covered in the dress of the common
people. The purple accompanied no rods and axes. Then they
held back their laments, and great grief wandered among all
citizens without a word. Thus, at the first moment of death, the
household is stunned and silent, when the corpse lies as yet
unlamented nor has the mother unbound her hair and driven the
maidservants' arms to savage blows, but still embraces her child's
limbs, growing stiff with the loss of life, his lifeless face and eyes,
menacing in death; her emotion is not yet grief, but nor does fear
remain: out of her mind, she hangs over his bed amazed at her loss.[8]

Lucan here focuses on the citizens' "great voiceless grief," comparing it with the moment of stunned loss when a Roman matron recognizes that her child is dead, even before lamentation begins. This moment of silence and delay—in both city and household, narrative and simile—reflects the poet's own paradoxical desire *not* to narrate the civil war, *not* to reach the end of the Republic, *not* to give voice to the lamentation that is his narrative's due.[9] Thus in the midst of Pharsalia, for example, Lucan initially refuses to tell how Caesar's forces conquered Pompey's: "[H]anc fuge, mens, partem belli tenebrisque relinque . . . a potius pereant lacrimae pereantque querellae:/quidquid in hac acie gessisti, Roma tacebo" (Shun this part of the war, spirit, and leave it in shadows ... ah, rather let tears and plaints perish: I shall pass over in silence, Rome, whatever you did in this conflict; 7.552, 555–556).[10] The poet's promise of silence, however, is immediately followed by forty lines of impassioned denunciation of the very battle narrative he has just forsworn.[11]

In book 2 as well, the simile emphasizing the pervasive silence before lamentation is immediately followed by a moving description of the Roman matrons congregating in the city's shrines to fill the city with laments: "[C]rebris feriunt ululatibus aures" (They strike the god's ears with their constant cries of lamentation; 2.33). Lucan even records the lament of one of the matrons, as she anticipates the disasters that civil war will bring (2.36–42):

> [Q]uarum una madentis
> scissa genas, planctu liuentis atra lacertos,
> "nunc" ait "o miserae, contundite pectora, matres,
> nunc laniate comas neue hunc differte dolorem
> et summis seruate malis. Nunc flere potestas
> dum pendet fortuna ducum: cum uicerit alter
> gaudendum est."

> One of their number, whose cheeks were torn and bloody,
> her shoulders black and bruised from blows, said, "Now, o
> wretched mothers, now tear your hair, don't postpone this
> grief and save it for the height of evils. Now we can weep,
> while the destiny of the generals hangs in the balance: when
> one of the two has won, we shall be required to rejoice."

Despite the violence of the matrons' mourning here, the poet offers no criticism of their actions as socially disruptive.[12] His purpose, rather, seems to be to emphasize the desperate plight of the Republic at the outbreak of civil war, on the verge of the loss of *libertas*: only at this juncture can Rome give free rein to her mourning. Indeed the sorrowing matron pronounces the impossibility of public mourning once a victor has emerged from civil war (cum uicerit alter/gaudendum est [2.41–42]).

Elsewhere in the poem, however, Lucan associates public mourning with the death of Pompey.[13] In book 7, for example, before the battle of Pharsalia, he lingers over a description of the sleeping Pompey, who is unaware that the coming day will doom both him and the Republic (7.7–44). The poet wrings particular pathos from the counterfactual picture of the funeral rites Rome would have performed for her favorite had he died there (7.37–39, 43–44):

> [T]e mixto flesset luctu iuuenisque senexque
> iniussusque puer; lacerasset crine soluto
> pectora femineum ceu Bruti funere uolgus.
>   . . .

o miseri, quorum gemitus edere dolorem,
qui te non plen pariter planxere theatro.

Youths and old men, their laments blended, would have
wept for you, Magnus, and boys too, unbidden; the crowd
of women would have unbound their hair and beaten their
breasts, just as at Brutus's funeral. . . . Wretches! Their
groans brought forth grief, though they could not lament
you in the thronged theater.

Public lament, Lucan imagines, would have prominently included men
(iuuenisque senexque / . . . puer) in addition to the expected crowd of
women (femineum . . . uolgus). Such scenes of public lament for Pompey,
however, are eclipsed in number, extent, and intensity by Lucan's obsessive
elaboration of Cornelia's obligation to observe the traditional rites of mourning not only after Pompey dies but also before and even during his death.[14]

In two speeches before Pompey's death, Cornelia rehearses the substance of the lamentation she will actually pronounce when she witnesses
her husband's murder in Egypt (8.637–662). At her first appearance in the
poem, she responds to her husband's decision to send her from the
battlefield with a plaintive speech (5.759–815) that implicitly likens their
parting to the final parting of death. Pompey determines to conceal her on
Lesbos in order that his destiny may not overwhelm her too (5.754–759):

[T]utior interea populis et tutior omni
rege late, positamque procul fortuna mariti
non tota te mole premat. si numina nostras
inpulerint acies, maneat pars optima Magni,
sitque mihi, si fata prement uictorque cruentus,
quo fugisse uelim.

Meanwhile you must be concealed, safer than peoples and
every king; the fate of your husband may not crush you, placed
far away, with its whole mass. If destiny should have impelled
our battle lines to defeat, Magnus's best part would remain, and
I would have a place where I would wish to flee, if destiny and
a cruel victor pursue me.

Pompey's suggestion that with his wife hidden on Lesbos his best part
will remain (5.757) implicitly canvasses the possibility of his demise in civil
war, and, in response, Cornelia collapses in an overwhelming access of
grief (5.759–760): "uix tantum infirma dolorem/cepit, et attonito cesser-
unt pectore sensus" (scarcely did she sustain such great grief in her
weakness, and her senses fled from her stricken breast). Swooning is the
conventional female response to both the anticipation and the discovery of
a loved one's death in Classical epic, and Cornelia's collapse here evokes
the long epic tradition of female lament—from the famous scene in *Iliad*

22 where Andromache learns of Hector's death (Hom. *Il.* 22.447–448); through the scene in which the mother of Euryalus, following Andromache's model, swoons and drops her wool work when she hears the news of her son's death (Verg. *Aen.* 9.473–476); to an equally famous scene in Ovid's *Metamorphoses* where Alcyone learns of her husband Ceyx's intention to consult the oracle of Apollo on Delos and immediately imagines his death (Ov. *Met.* 11.416–420). Moreover, the plaintive words Cornelia utters when she recovers from her swoon contribute further to her implicit characterization as a lamenting widow ("tandem vox maestas potuit proferre querellas" [at last she was able to utter her sad plaints; 5.761]; cf. Luc. 7.555, quoted above), for the Augustan elegists had made the term *querella* a quasi-technical term for elegiac lament in their emphasis on that genre's association with death and derivation from funerary lament.[15]

Yet Cornelia's opening words seem to deny the funerary implications of Pompey's speech: "[N]ostros non rumpit funus amores/nec diri fax summa rogi, sed sorte frequenti/plebeiaque nimis careo dimissa marito" (Death does not break our love nor the final torch of the dread pyre, but, dismissed with a common and all too familiar lot, I lose my husband [i.e., by divorce]; 5.763–765). Her description of her dismissal by Pompey as divorce implies her rejection of his ill-omened allusion to his own death. As her speech progresses, however, she is unable to sustain the analogy with divorce and reverts to the imagery of their parting as death. She imagines first her death alone ("[S]ecura uidetur/sors tibi, cum facias etiamnunc uota, perisse?" [Does it seem a happy lot to you, when you are even now making your prayers, that I should have perished {i.e., by separation from my husband}?]; 5.771–772) and then their joint death ("[U]t nolim seruire malis sed morte parata/te sequar ad manes" [Suppose that I were unwilling to wait on these evils, and by preparing my own death I followed you to the underworld]; 5.773–774). In thus picturing her death as the result of his, Cornelia returns full circle to Pompey's anticipation of his imminent death, and she concludes by accepting her widowhood: "[F]eriat dum maesta remotas/fama procul terras, uiuam tibi nempe superstes" (Until the sad report strikes those faraway lands, I will surely live, surviving you; 5.774–775).

Despite her initial attempt to disavow the suggestion of her husband's death, then, Cornelia's first speech in the poem is marked as a lament as much by the poet's designation of her words as *querellae* as by her speech's content and form—including rhetorical questions and reproaches, expressions of contrast between her life of mourning and his in the shadow of death, and her wish for a better outcome, all of which are hallmarks of the genre of lament.[16] Lucan thus casts her speech as an anticipatory lament, and the scene ends as it began, with Cornelia swooning at the prospect of Pompey's death ("[L]abitur infelix manibusque excepta suorum/fertur ad aequorea . . . harenas" [The unhappy woman swooned and, taken up in the hands of her attendants, is carried to the seashore]; 5.799–800). Lucan explicitly characterizes her departure for Lesbos, without Pompey, as widowhood (5.804–810):

[F]ida comes Magni uadit duce sola relicto
Pompeiumque fugit. quae nox tibi proxima uenit,   (805)
insomnis; uiduo tum primum frigida lecto
atque insueta quies uni, nudumque marito
non haerente latus. somno quam saepe grauata
deceptis uacuum minibus conplexa cubile est
atque oblita fugae quaesiuit nocte maritum!   (810)

Magnus's faithful companion goes alone, her master left
behind, and flees Pompey. The night that came next brought
you no sleep; then for the first time in a widowed bed rest
was cold for you, unused to being alone, without a husband's
naked flank pressing near. Weighed down in sleep how often
she embraced the empty couch with her deceived hands and
forgetful of her flight sought her husband in the night!

Two books later, Lucan depicts Cornelia waiting for Pompey on
Lesbos in the same state of crushing grief (8.40–49):

[C]onscia curarum secretae in litora Lesbi   (40)
flectere uela iubet, qua tunc tellure latebas
maestior, in mediis quam si, Cornelia, campis
Emathiae stares. tristes praesagia curas
exagitant, trepida quatitur formidine somnus,
Thessaliam nox omnis habet; tenebrisque remotis   (45)
rupis in abruptae scopulos extremaque curris
litora; prospiciens fluctus nutantia longe
semper prima uides uenientis uela carinae,
quaerere nec quidquam de fato coniugis audes.

Pompey bids them set sail for Lesbos's shores, entrusted
with his beloved Cornelia, where then you were concealed,
Cornelia, sadder than if you stood in the midst of Emathia's
fields. Forebodings harass her sad cares, her sleep is interrupted
by anxious fear, every night brings the Thessalian battlefield
before her; in the morning you run to the rocks over the sheer
cliff at the edge of the shore; looking out over the waves you
are always the first to see the sails of a coming craft nodding
from afar, nor do you dare to ask anything about your husband's fate.

Cornelia already lives a life of quasi mourning in anticipation of Pompey's
death, and with the arrival of her defeated husband the poet urges her to
give full rein to lament: "[V]ictus adest coniunx. quid perdis tempora
luctus?/cum possis iam flere, times" (Your conquered husband is here.
Why do you lose the opportunity for mourning? Though you could weep,
you fear; 8.53–54). Lucan's address to his character draws attention to the
fact that lamentation is Cornelia's perpetual mode throughout the poem.

Pompey disembarks as a figure of mourning himself, in imitation of the social death that he experiences as a result of his defeat at Pharsalus (8.54–57):

> ...[T]um puppe propinqua
> prosiluit crimenque deum crudele notauit,
> deformem pallore ducem uoltusque prementem
> canitiem atque atro squalentes puluere uestes.

> Then as the ship neared, Cornelia jumped up and
> marked the god's wicked crime, the commander
> ghastly with pallor, the white hair around his face and
> his clothing dark with black dust.

His pallor and clothing dark with dust are the conventional symbols in antiquity of death and mourning (as an imitation of death).[17] Cornelia responds to the anticipatory vision of his death by swooning once again, in a passage that illustrates the reciprocal relationship between death and mourning in Roman thought (8.58–67):

> [O]buia nox miserae caelum lucemque tenebris
> abstulit, atque animam clausit dolor; omnia neruis
> membra relicta labant, riguerunt corda, diuque   (60)
> spe mortis decepta iacet. Iam fune ligato
> litoribus lustrat uacuas Pompeius harenas.
> quem postquam propius famulae uidere fideles,
> non ultra gemitus tacitos incessere fatum
> permisere sibi, frustraque attollere terra   (65)
> semianimem conantur eram; quam pectore Magnus
> ambit et astrictos refouet conplexibus artus.

> Night came over the poor wretch, covering sky and light
> in shadows, and grief stopped her breath; abandoned by
> her muscles her limbs collapsed, her heart stood still, and
> for a long time she lay deceived by the hope of death. Now
> with the ship tied up on shore Pompey walked over the
> empty strand, and after her faithful attendants saw him approach
> they did not allow themselves to reproach destiny beyond uttering
> stifled groans, and they tried in vain to raise their half-dead
> mistress from the ground; Magnus folded her in his arms and
> warmed her rigid limbs by his embrace.

Cornelia's physical response to the sight of her defeated husband also mimics death. But Pompey reproves her for succumbing to grief while he still lives (8.78–83):

> ...[N]unc sum tibi gloria maior
> a me quod fasces et quod pia turba senatus

tantaque discessit regum manus: incipe Magnum
sola sequi. deformis adhuc uiuente marito
summus et augeri uetitus dolor: ultima debet
esse fides lugere uirum.

I am now a greater source of glory for you because the
magistrates, the devoted crowd of senators, and so great
a band of kings, have abandoned me: begin to be
Magnus's sole follower. The highest grief, grief that is
forbidden to be increased, is unbecoming while your
husband still lives: to mourn your husband ought to be
the final mark of loyalty.

In response to his rebuke, however, Cornelia continues to give voice to her grief, rehearsing several of the most prominent themes of the genre of lamentation in her pervasive self-reproaches and expressions of desire for death.

She opens with a conventional feature of lamentation in her wish that Pompey's victorious enemy had suffered his fate (8.88–89): "[O] utinam in thalamos inuisi Caesaris issem/infelix coniunx et nulli laeta marito!" (O would that I had married hated Caesar, ill-fated wife that I am and fortunate for no husband!). This wish is really a curse, for she has brought disaster to both her husbands (8.90–97):

[B]is nocui mundo: me pronuba ducit Erinys   (90)
Crassorumque umbrae, deuotaque manibus illis
Assyrios in castra tuli ciuilia casus,
praecipitesque dedi populos cunctosque fugaui
a causa meliore deos. o maxime coniunx,
o thalamis indigne meis, hoc iuris habebat   (95)
in tantum fortuna caput? cur inpia nupsi,
si miserum factura fui?

Twice I have harmed the world: a Fury presided
as matron of honor over my wedding, and the shades
of the Crassi, and I, devoted to their shades, brought
the Assyrian disaster into the camp of civil war, hurled
nations headlong to their destruction, and drove all the
gods in flight from the better cause. O greatest husband,
unworthy of marriage with me, did chance hold this law
over so great a life? Why did I impiously marry you, if I
was going to make you wretched?

As a mourner who holds herself responsible for the death she laments, she observes a perpetual state of lamentation throughout the poem and repeatedly expresses her desire to die (8.97–102):

... [N]unc accipe poenas,
sed quas sponte luam: quo sit tibi mollies aequor,
certa fides regum totusque paratior orbis,
sparge mari comitem. mallem felicibus armis
dependisse caput: nunc clades denique lustra,
Magne, tuas.

Now pay the penalty, but a penalty that I shall willingly
pay: that the deep may be smoother for you, the loyalty
of kings certain, and the whole world readier to serve you,
scatter your companion over the sea. I would rather have
laid down my life in exchange for your victorious arms:
now finally expiate your disaster, Magnus.

Yet her closing words also reveal what Sheila Murnaghan has characterized as "a normally hidden world of competition among women, centered on the validating attention of men" (8.102–105):[18]

... [U]bicumque iaces ciuilibus armis
nostros ulta toros, ades huc atque exige poenas,
Iulia crudelis, placataque paelice caesa
Magno parce tuo.

Wherever you lie, cruel Julia, avenge our marriage with
civil war, come here, exact the penalty, and spare your
Magnus, sated by the death of your rival.

Cornelia's jibe at Julia recasts the murderous confrontation of Roman strongmen in a civil war over the spoils of empire as a catfight between two women competing for Pompey's marital attention. Her words recall Julia's apparition as a ghost to Pompey at the opening of book 3, when she predicts disaster at the start of his voyage (Luc. 3.20–23) and calls his new wife a sexual rival (*paelex* [3.23]). Here Cornelia accepts Julia's accusation in an effort to placate her ghost and preserve her husband.[19] Her efforts, however, cannot succeed in preserving the bonds of community in the midst of the civil war and serve only to disrupt them.

Georgia Nugent and Sheila Murnaghan, among others, have observed that women's lamentation may pose a threat to the masculine ideal of heroic glory espoused in epic poetry by emphasizing the pain and suffering this ideal causes the wider community.[20] And this dynamic animates the reunion of Pompey and Cornelia, for her proleptic lament provokes her listeners to tears (8.105–108):

... [S]ic fata iterumque refusa
coniugis in gremium cunctorum lumina soluit
in lacrimas. duri flectuntur pectora Magni,
siccaque Thessalia confudit lumina Lesbos.

So saying she collapsed again in her husband's embrace
and melted the eyes of all to tears. The breast of hard
Magnus is broken, and Lesbos flooded the eyes that were
dry at Pharsalia.

Even Pompey, who was able to witness the battle of Pharsalia with dry
eyes, is stricken by her lamentation, silenced by the power of her grief.
    He decisively rejects the Lesbians' invitation, however, to make their
island his base and insists on departing immediately with Cornelia, a sight
to which the Lesbians respond with further lamentation (8.146–158):

> . . . [D]ixit maestamque carinae
> inposuit comitem. cunctos mutare putares
> tellurem patriaeque solum: sic litore toto
> plangitur, infestae tenduntur in aethera dextrae.
> Pompeiumque minus, cuius fortuna dolorem   (150)
> mouerat, ast illam, quam toto tempore belli
> ut ciuem uidere suam, discedere cernens
> ingemuit populus; quam uix, si castra mariti
> uictoris peteret, siccis dimittere matres
> iam poterant oculis: tanto deuinxit amore   (155)
> hos pudor, hos probitas castique modestia uoltus,
> quod summissa animis, nulli grauis hospita turbae,
> stantis adhuc fati uixit quasi coniuge uicto.

He spoke and placed his sad companion aboard ship.
You would think all were exchanging their land, the
ground of their fatherland: so the whole shore rang with
lament, and hostile hands strained against heaven. They
felt less for Pompey, whose fate indeed roused their grief,
but watching her leave, whom they'd seen during the whole
period of war as their fellow citizen, the people groaned
aloud; if she had sought the camp of a victorious husband,
scarcely could the matrons have sent her away with dry eyes;
with such love had her modesty bound the people to her,
along with her goodness and the diffidence of her chaste
demeanor, because humble of spirit and troublesome in her
visit to none, she lived as if her husband had been defeated
when his fortune still stood firm.

Lucan implicitly compares the Lesbians' lamentations at the departure of
Cornelia and the defeated Pompey to a lament for the fall of a city (8.147–
149), thus apparently assimilating Pompey's defeat to the conquest of
Lesbos.[21] Singled out in this general scene of lamentation are the Lesbian
matrons (*matres* [8.154]), the female representatives of the community of
Lesbos (cf. *cunctos* [8.147], *populus* [8.153]) that has sheltered both

Cornelia and her defeated husband. In marking lamentation as an essentially female genre, Lucan follows both Classical epic convention (e.g., Hector's mourners, Hecuba, Helen, and Andromache in *Iliad* 24; and the Trojan women mourning Anchises on the Sicilian strand in *Aeneid* 5) and Roman social custom, which not only prescribed mourning for female family members but also made provision for hiring paid female mourners (*praeficae*).[22] It is striking, however, that the Lesbian matrons in this scene reflect not on the glorious epic achievements of Pompey but on the sorrows of his wife.[23] Pompey's defeat is viewed in this passage primarily through the lens of Cornelia's personal grief, but her private lamentation provokes further (public) lamentation in the throng, with the poet privileging her private loss at the prospect of Pompey's death over his public calamity in the defeat at Pharsalus.

In the two speeches we have considered thus far, Cornelia rehearses the substance of the lamentation she will actually pronounce when she witnesses her husband's murder at the hands of Ptolemy's minions later in the book (8.637–662).[24] As in her first appearance in the poem, she tries to prevent Pompey from abandoning her when he leaves his flagship on the invitation of the Egyptian king's ministers to enter their small craft, though on this occasion she fears not her husband's death but his disgrace in submitting to alien authority (8.577–595). Pompey ignores her pleas, however, and leaves her to watch his murder at the hands of a Roman soldier on the orders of Ptolemy. As in her earlier laments, Cornelia here reproaches herself as the cause of Pompey's death (8.639–642, 647–650):

> [O] coniunx, ego te scelerata peremi:
> letiferae tibi causa morae fuit auia Lesbos,
> et prior in Nili peruenit litora Caesar;
> nam cui ius alii sceleris?
> ... haud ego culpa
> libera bellorum, quae matrum sola per undas
> et per castra comes nullis absterrita fatis
> uictum, quod reges etiam timuere, recepi.

> O husband, I have wickedly destroyed you: the cause
> of your deadly delay was inaccessible Lesbos, and Caesar
> reached the shores of the Nile earlier; for who else has the
> prerogative of the crime? ... By no means am I free from
> blame for the wars; for I was the only one of the matrons who
> followed him on sea and in camp, deterred by no misfortunes,
> and received him defeated, which even kings feared to do.

Interspersed with these self-reproaches are expressions of Cornelia's determination to die (8.653–658), which recall her expressions of desire for death in the earlier speeches. Other conventional themes of lament, moreover, appear for the first time here, such as the questions she addresses to her dead husband (8.651–653): "[H]oc merui, coniunx, in tuta puppe relinqui?/perfide, parcebas? Te fata extrema petente/uita digna fui?" (Did I deserve, husband, to be abandoned to the safety of the ship? Were you trying to spare me, faithless one? Was I worthy of life when you were seeking the limits of your destiny?). Yet the highly rhetorical presentation of her questions and their location in the middle of her speech differentiate them strikingly from mourners' traditional expressions of anxiety in the form of hesitant questions at the beginning of a lament, even in the aftermath of violent death, as here.[25] Similarly, the contrast she draws between Pompey's disdain for his own death and his anxiety about hers plays on a traditional theme of lament, the contrast between the mourner's condition and that of the dead, but again in a series of highly mannered *sententiae* more typical of Lucan's epigrammatic style than of earlier laments in the Classical epic tradition (8.642–647):

> ...[S]ed, quisquis in istud
> a superis inmisse caput uel Caesaris irae
> uel tibi prospiciens, nescis, crudelis, ubi ipsa
> uiscera sint Magni; properas atque ingeris ictus,
> qua uotum est uicto. poenas non morte minores
> pendat et ante meum uideat caput.

> But whoever you are (*sc.* who is attacking Pompey), sent
> by the gods against that life, either attending to Caesar's
> anger or your own, you do not know, cruel man, where
> Magnus's very vitals are; you hasten to heap on the blows
> where the defeated man wishes. Let him pay the penalty
> no less than death and see my head fall first.

Cornelia concludes with her determination to die now, for in the aftermath of Pompey's death she will be enslaved to Caesar (8.653–661):

> ...[M]oriar, nec munere regis.
> aut mihi praecipitem, nautae, permittite saltum,
> aut laqueum collo tortosque aptare rudentes,
> aut aliquis Magno dignus comes exigat ensem;
> Pompeio praestare potest, quod Caesaris armis
> inputet. o saeui, properantem in fata tenetis?
> uiuis adhuc, coniunx, et iam Cornelia non est
> iuris, Magne, sui: prohibent accerser mortem;
> seruor uictori.

> I shall die, nor by the gift of the king. Allow me, sailors,
> either to leap headlong or to fit a noose of twisted rope
> around my neck; or let some friend of Pompey prove worthy
> of him by driving home his sword in my body. He can do for
> Pompey's sake what he can claim as a service to Caesar's

arms. Cruel men, do you restrain me in my haste to die? You
are still alive, husband, yet already Cornelia has ceased to be
independent, Magnus: they prevent me from summoning death;
I am saved for the victor.

Here Cornelia alludes to another conventional theme of lamentation, the
contrast of the mourner's former freedom and social prominence with her
future slavery. The wish for death expresses her recognition of the social
death she suffers when she loses the man through whom her social position is defined. This speech, like the earlier ones, concludes with her mini-
death in a swoon as she is led away by attendants (8.661–662): "[S]ic fata
interque suorum / lapsa manus rapitur trepida fugiente carina" (So saying
she swooned among friendly hands and is snatched away trembling as the
ship flees).

Since Pompey's flagship flees the scene of his death, however, the laying
out of the corpse and ritual lament over it are conducted by his *cliens*, the
quaestor Cordus (8.712–822). Nonetheless, Lucan shows Cordus explicitly
acknowledging the Roman social expectation of the wife's performance of
these duties (8.739–742): "[S]it satis, o superi, quod non Cornelia fuso/
crine iacet subicique facem conplexa maritum/imperat, extremo sed abest a
munere busti/infelix coniunx nec adhuc a litore longe est" (Be content with
this, o gods, that Cornelia does not lie prostrate with disheveled hair—does
not embrace her husband and bid the torch be applied; that his unhappy
wife, though still not far distant from the shore, is not here to pay her last
tribute to the dead). In Cornelia's absence, Cordus must retrieve Pompey's
body from the sea (8.715–726), and he also pronounces a lament over the
corpse. He begins by reproaching Fortuna for her abandonment of a former
favorite (8.726–738):

> ... [P]ostquam sicco iam litore sedit,
> incubuit Magno lacrimasque effudit in omne
> uolnus, et ad superos obscuraque sidera fatur:
> "non pretiosa petit cumulato ture sepulchra
> Pompeius, Fortuna, tuus, non pinguis ad astra
> ut ferat e membris Eoos fumus odores,
> ut Romana suum gestent pia colla parentem,
> praeferat ut veteres feralis pompa triumphos,
> ut resonant tristi cantu fora, totus ut ignes
> proiectis maerens exercitus ambiat armis.
> da vilem Magno plebei funeris arcam,
> quae lacerum corpus siccos effundat in ignes;
> robora non desint misero nec sordidus ustor."

When Pompey's body came to rest on dry land, he cast
himself upon Magnus, pouring tears into every wound;
and thus he addressed Heaven and the dim stars: "No costly

pyre with heaped-up incense does your favorite, Pompey, ask
of you, Fortune; he does not ask that the rich smoke should
carry to the stars Eastern perfumes from his limbs; that
devoted Romans should bear on their shoulders the dear father
of their country; that the funeral procession should display his
former trophies; that the Forum should be filled with mournful
music; or that a whole army, with dropped arms, should march
mourning round the burning pile. But grant to Magnus the paltry
bier of a pauper's burial, to let down the mutilated body on the
unfed fires; let not the hapless corpse lack wood or a humble
hand to kindle it."

Of particular interest here is Cordus's contrast between the grand
public funeral so prominent a general should receive (8.729–735) and
the mean private funeral he can actually offer Pompey (8.736–738). The
contrast Cordus draws here between the funeral Pompey deserves and the
funeral he actually receives is itself another topos of lament (we may
compare Catullus 101). This contrast is conventionally drawn in Greek
lament too, but Lucan Romanizes it by representing the grand public
funeral Pompey should have had as the ceremony of the *funus publicum*,
"a special kind of *funus indictiuum*, to which all citizens were invited . . .
decreed to a benefactor of the State and paid for by the State treasury."[26]
Instead, Pompey receives a pauper's funeral without even the services of a
professional *ustor* (who was employed to burn dead bodies). Moreover
Cordus has to rob the funeral pyre belonging to another corpse in order
to kindle a poor one for Pompey, thereby acting as *ustor* himself
(8.752–758).[27]

Cordus does his best, however, to supply the full obsequies to Pompey's corpse, and he accordingly utters a lament over Pompey's corpse
(8.759–775):

> [I]lle sedens iuxta flammas "o maxime" dixit
> "ductor et Hesperii maiestas nominis una,   (760)
> si tibi iactatu pelagi, si funere nullo
> tristior iste rogus, manes animamque potentem
> officiis auerte meis: iniuria fati
> hoc fas esse iubet; ne ponti belua quidquam,
> ne fera, ne uolucres, ne saeui Caesaris ira   (765)
> audeat, exiguam, quantum potes, accipe flammam,
> Romana succense manu. fortuna recursus
> si det in Hesperiam, non hac in sede quiescent
> tam sacri cineres, sed te Cornelia, Magne,
> accipiet nostraque manu transfundet in urnam.   (770)
> interea paruo signemus litora saxo,
> ut nota sit busti; si quis placare peremptum
> forte uolet plenos et reddere mortis honores,

inveniat trunci cineres et norit harenas,
ad quas, Magne, tuum referat caput."   (775)

Sitting by the flames, Cordus said: "O greatest general
and sole grandeur of Hesperian name, if this pyre is more
bitter for you than to be tossed by the sea, or than no
burial at all, then turn away your shade and mighty spirit
from my services; the injury of Fate bids this be lawful;
that no monster of the deep nor beast nor bird nor rage of
cruel Caesar may dare, receive the flame, all that you can
(receive), kindled by a Roman hand. If Fortune should grant
a return to Italy, such sacred ashes as these will not rest here,
but Cornelia will receive you, Magnus, and will transfer
them from my hand to an urn. Meanwhile, let me mark the
shore with a small stone to be the mark of your grave; if
perhaps anyone wishes to appease your shade and return
death's full dignities to you, let him find the ashes of your
body and recognize the sands to which he must restore your head."

We find here the traditional themes of the ritual lament, especially in the contrasts between Pompey's glory in life and ignominy in death and between Cordus's makeshift grave for Pompey and Cornelia's permanent memorial for her husband. An innovation in the epic tradition of lament is struck here, however, in the contrast Lucan implies between Pompey's patronage of Cordus in life as his commanding officer (*ductor* [8.760]) and Cordus's burial of Pompey in death, depicted as his duty (*officiis... meis* [8.763]) to his erstwhile commander. Throughout the passage Lucan emphasizes the social obligation that motivates Cordus's piety toward his patron. In addition to Cordus's reference to the services owed to his commander that he performs, he closes the burial rites at the approach of daybreak with the observation that *pietas* compels him to bring his service to an end by gathering up the half-burned bones and burying them and quenching the fire (8.785–789):

> ... [C]ogit pietas inponere finem
> officio. semusta rapit resolutaque nondum
> ossa satis neruis et inustis plena medullis
> aequorea restinguit aqua congestaque in unum
> parua clausit humo.

> *Pietas* compels him to bring to an end his service. He
> snatched up the half-burned remains, the bones not yet
> sufficiently released from the tissue, and he extinguished
> them with sea-water, heaped them together, and enclosed
> them in a bit of earth.

Cordus's disposal of Magnus's corpse is ritually correct, inasmuch as he kindles the corpse on the pyre, drenches the remains, and collects the ashes for safekeeping until Cornelia can transfer them to an urn (8.786–793).[28] He has thus discharged the duties of the relatives and dependents toward the deceased insofar as he can. Lucan, however, emphasizes the pathos of his solitary lament and burial of Pompey's corpse through his performance of these rituals alone, on a hostile foreign shore, and especially, as Cordus himself reiterates in his lament, in the absence of Pompey's wife, Cornelia, who should perform the ritual herself.[29]

In the following book, Lucan represents Cornelia discharging her wifely obligation to the dead Pompey when she delivers a formal lament for him off the shore of Egypt in sight of his pyre (9.55–108). She begins by reproaching Fortune at some length for preventing her from performing the funerary rites Cordus has furnished (9.55–72), before turning to lament proper with a direct address to her dead husband (9.73–75; cf. 9.98, 9.104) that draws a contrast between his former good fortune ("elapsus felix de pectore Magnus" [the Magnus of prosperous days has slipped from my heart]; 9.81) and his ignominious death and burial in Egypt ("hunc volumus, quem Nilus habet" [I want this man, whom the Nile holds]; 9.82). Cornelia's lament opens and closes with the self-reproaches with which we are familiar, but its central message is addressed to Pompey's sons, and thence to Cato and Pompey's followers, urging them in Pompey's name to avenge his death by continuing to prosecute the war against Caesar (9.84–97):

> [T]u pete bellorum casus et signa per orbem,
> Sexte, paterna moue; namque haec mandata reliquit   (85)
> Pompeius uobis in nostra condita cura:
> "me cum fatalis leto damnauerit hora,
> excipite, o nati, bellum ciuile, nec umquam,
> dum terris aliquis nostra de stirpe manebit,
> Caesaribus regnare uacet. uel sceptra uel urbes   (90)
> libertate sua ualidas inpellite fama
> nominis: has uobis partes, haec arma relinquo.
> inueniet classes, quisquis Pompeius in undas
> uenerit, et noster nullis non gentibus heres
> bella dabit: tantum indomitos memoresque paterni   (95)
> iuris habete animos. uni parere decebit,
> si faciet partes pro libertate, Catoni."

> You, Sextus, seek the hazards of war and raise your father's
> standards throughout the world; for Pompey left for you, his
> sons, these instructions stored in my care: "When the destined
> hour has condemned me to death, take over the civil war, my
> sons, and never, while any offshoot of our line remains on
> earth, grant Caesars the chance to rule. Stir up kings or states
> strong in their own freedom by the fame of our name; I leave
> you this role and these arms. Any Pompey who goes to sea

will find fleets, and our successor will bring war to many nations;
only keep your spirits unconquered and mindful of your father's
power. Cato alone it is fitting to obey, if he rallies a party for freedom."

Cornelia's call to renewed aggression invites comparison with what Helene
Foley has characterized as the "ethics of vendetta" that informs such
laments as Electra's in Sophocles' tragedy of the same name.[30] Indeed,
Cornelia's incitement of Pompey's sons to further military action, whether
on their own authority or under the command of Cato, inspires the
narrative action of the rest of the epic.

Yet the comparison of Cornelia's laments to an "ethics of vendetta"
must not be pressed too far because Rome employed judicial and political
mechanisms (including the senatorial sanction of military force) in place of
feuds or vendettas. Lucan is careful to distinguish the private setting of
Cornelia's lament at the beginning of book 9—delivered as a reproach to
Fortune aboard Pompey's flagship, her only audience Pompey's son Sextus—from the public context of military and political action. And just as her
earlier speeches rehearsing the themes of lamentation ended in her fainting
and removal by devoted attendants, so her final lament concludes with her
veiling and retreat to the innermost recesses of the ship (9.109–116):

[S]ic ubi fata, caput ferali obduxit amictu
decreuitque pati tenebras puppisque cauernis   (110)
delituit, saeuumque arte conplexa dolorem
perfruitur lacrimis et amat pro coniuge luctum.
illam non fluctus stridensque rudentibus Eurus
mouit et exsurgens ad summa pericula clamor,
uotaque sollicitis faciens contraria nautis   (115)
conposita in mortem iacuit fauitque procellis.

So saying, she covered her head with a mourning veil; she
determined to endure the shadows and withdrew to the ship's
hold; and hugging her savage grief closely, she enjoys her
tears and loves her grief in place of her husband. She is unmoved
by the waves, the howling of the east wind in the rigging, and the
shouts that rose at the greatest dangers, and uttering prayers
opposed to those of the harassed sailors, she lay disposed in the
attitude of death and favored the storms.

Cornelia's voluntary removal from the sailors' view recalls, and respects,
the gendered separation of lamenting women from the public gatherings
of men in Vergil's *Aeneid* (books 5 and 9).[31]

When Pompey's flagship arrives at Cato's camp in Libya where the
army is already in mourning, however, Cornelia emerges from her self-
imposed seclusion and prompts the people to lamentation by her example
(9.167–181):

[I]nterea totis audito funere Magni
litoribus sonuit percussus planctibus aether,
exemploque carens et nulli cognitus aeuo
luctus erat, mortem populos deflere potentis.   (170)
sed magis, ut uisa est lacrimis exhausta, solutas
in uoltus effusa comas, Cornelia puppe
egrediens, rursus geminato uerbere plangunt.
ut primum in sociae peruenit litora terrae,
collegit uestes miserique insignia Magni   (175)
armaque et inpressas auro, quas gesserat olim,
exuuias pictasque togas, uelamina summo
ter conspecta Ioui, funestoque intulit igni.
ille fuit miserae Magni cinis. accipit omnis
exemplum pietas, et toto litore busta   (180)
surgunt Thessalicis reddentia manibus ignem.

Meanwhile when Magnus's death was reported the air rang
with the sound of mourning along the whole shore, and
unexampled and unknown to any age, there was general
grief, and the people lamented the death of their leader. But
more, when Cornelia was glimpsed, worn out by weeping
and with her loosened hair spread over her face, leaving the
ship, they renewed their lamentation with redoubled blows.
As soon as she reached the shores of the allied land, she gathered
the clothing and insignia of poor Magnus, his arms and the robes
embroidered with gold, which he had once worn, his colored
togas and the triumphal toga that he had thrice worn in Jupiter's
sight, and put them on a funeral pyre. They constituted wretched
Magnus's ashes. All devotion to duty followed her example, and
on the whole shore funeral pyres arise, returning fire to the
Thessalian dead.

By collecting the garments and military insignia of her dead husband to
throw on the funeral pyre she erects for him here (9.174–179), Cornelia
shows exemplary devotion (*pietas*) to her dead husband, and her example
is contagious. She inspires individual soldiers in the army to imitation, as
they erect pyres for their dead up and down the shore (9.179–181). The
army's mimetic response to the sight of Cornelia intensifies their earlier
spontaneous mourning at the death of Pompey, which Lucan singles out as
unparalleled in Roman history (9.167–170). Whether or not that was the
case historically, such grief for a dead commander is not without parallel in
the poem itself, as we have seen already in Cordus's discharge of Roman
funerary ritual over Pompey's corpse. Indeed, we may link Cordus's
mourning for his dead commander with the army's collective lament for
their leader, in their shared capacity as his military subordinates and
dependents. The juxtaposition of these successive scenes thus illustrates

both the gender affiliations and the class lines of lamentation: lament is not
only an obligation owed the dead man by his wife but also an obligation
owed the *patronus* by his social inferiors.[32]

The gendered and class-marked contrast that distinguishes this kind of
spontaneous private lamentation from organized public commemoration
is decisively illuminated in the dead Pompey's eulogy by Cato soon after
Cornelia's shipboard lament (9.190–214):

"[C]iuis obit" inquit "multum maioribus inpar   (190)
nosse modum iuris, sed in hoc tamen utilis aeuo,
cui non ulla fuit iusti reuerentia; salua
libertate potens, et solus plebe parata
priuatus seruire sibi, rectorque senatus,
sed regnantis, erat. nil belli iure poposcit,   (195)
quaeque dari uoluit uoluit sibi posse negari.
inmodicas possedit opes, sed plura retentis
intulit. inuasit ferrum, sed ponere norat.
praetulit arma togae, sed pacem armatus amauit.
iuuit sumpta ducem, iuuit dimissa potestas.   (200)
casta domus luxuque carens corruptaque numquam
fortuna domini. clarum et uenerabile nomen
gentibus et multum nostrae quod proderat urbi.
olim uera fides Sulla Marioque receptis
libertatis obit; Pompeio rebus adempto   (205)
nunc et ficta perit. non iam regnare pudebit,
nec color imperii nec frons erit ulla senatus.
o felix, cui summa dies fuit obuia uicto
et cui quaerendos Pharium scelus obtulit enses.
forsitan in soceri potuisses uiuere regno.   (210)
scire mori sors prima uiris, sed proxima cogi.
et mihi, si fatis aliena in iura uenimus,
fac talem, Fortuna, Iubam; non deprecor hosti
seruari, dum me seruet ceruice recisa."

"A citizen has died," he said, "much inferior to our ancestors
in acknowledging the limit of the law, but useful nonetheless
in this day and age, which has no reverence for what is right;
he was powerful while freedom was safe and alone remained
a private citizen though the people were ready to serve him;
he was the ruler of the Senate, but the Senate ruled. He
demanded nothing by right of war, and what he wanted to be
given he wanted to be able to be denied him. He possessed
boundless wealth, but he brought in more than he held back.
He seized upon the sword, but he knew how to lay it down.
He preferred arms to the toga, but, though armed, he loved
peace. Assuming power pleased our general, but so did laying

it down. His household was pure and lacking in extravagance,
never corrupted by the fortune of its master. His name is famous
and revered among all peoples and benefited our city greatly.
True faith in freedom perished long since, with the reception of
Sulla and Marius within the city; now even the pretence of
freedom has perished with Pompey's loss to the state. Now there
will be no shame in ruling, nor will there be any pretence of
possessing military authority legally conferred, nor will the Senate
be any screen. Happy the man whose last day followed closely on
his defeat and whom the Egyptian crime offered the sword he
should have sought. Perhaps, Pompey, you could have lived
under your father-in-law's tyranny. Men's happiest lot is to know
how to die, but the next is to be compelled. And if we are fated to
come into the power of another, make Juba such for me, Destiny;
I do not disdain to be saved for my enemy, provided that he saves
me by cutting off my head."

Before the army Cato pronounces a funerary eulogy that offers public
testimony to Pompey's allegiance to the legal conventions of Roman
warfare and politics (9.215–217) and celebrates Pompey wholly as a public
citizen—*ciuis* is the opening word of his speech (9.190)—and one,
moreover, who had always acted within the parameters of Roman law
(9.195–196). While deprecating Pompey's ambition, Cato praises him
for respecting the forms of Republican government and lending his
name to the Republican cause.[33]

Cato's eulogy of Pompey functions as an expression of Roman order
and hierarchy in its appeal to the political values of the community.[34] It is
designed to inspire in Pompey's soldiers a renewed commitment to Republican government and, therefore, to the continuation of the war
against Caesar. Yet, although Lucan praises Cato's speech as a greater
honor to Pompey than a funerary eulogy delivered from the speaker's
rostra in the forum (9.215–217), the soldiers, impervious to Cato's appeal, turn mutinous (9.217–220): "[F]remit interea discordia uolgi,/
castrorum bellique piget post funera Magni;/cum Tarcondimotus lin-
quendi signa Catonis/sustulit..." (Meanwhile mutiny raged in the
crowd, and after Pompey's funeral, the camp tired of war; when Tarcondimotus raised the signal for deserting Cato...). In this crisis, Cato taunts
the soldiers that in abandoning the Republican cause at this juncture they
are implicitly aiding the tyrannical cause of Caesar by turning over to him
both Cornelia and Pompey's sons (9.276–278): "[R]apiatur in undas/
infelix coniunx Magni prolesque Metelli,/ducite Pompeios, Ptolemaei
uincite munus" (Let Pompey's unhappy wife, Metellus's daughter, be
seized and carried over the sea, lead Pompey's sons, and outdo Ptolemy's
gift to Caesar).

In the context of the epic's narrative it is Cato's public argument here,
rather than Cornelia's private call for vengeance earlier, that ultimately

carries the day, as he appropriates the themes of Cornelia's lament and adapts them to political ends and finally persuades the army to fight a legitimate war against Caesar (9.292–293): "[S]ic uoce Catonis/inculcata uiris iusti patientia Martis" (In this way by Cato's speech was the endurance of lawful warfare inculcated in his men).[35] In undertaking to prosecute the war against Caesar, Cato confers political legitimacy on the personal pleas for vengeance and curses enunciated in Cornelia's laments, thereby underlining the public and political aspects of her laments and pleas for vengeance. But for the audience of Lucan's epic (as opposed to the characters in it), this conclusion must be complicated by the power of Cornelia's laments and their continuing impact on the narrative impetus of the poem.[36] For as we have seen, within the narrative economy of the epic, the determination to continue to prosecute the war with Caesar after Pompey's death is first sounded by Cornelia, in her final lament in the company of Pompey's son Sextus. By giving voice to Cornelia's series of impassioned lamentations and by following in the closing books of his epic the narrative course proposed in her final lament, Lucan affirms the power of women's lamentation in ancient Rome and the central role of Cornelia in the commemoration of Pompey.

NOTES

1. Alexiou 1974, 2002; Derderian 2001; Dué 2002, 2006; Foley 2001; Holst-Warhaft 1992, 2000; Loraux 1990; Seremetakis 1991.

2. On Roman funerary ritual, see Bodel 1999; Corbeill 2004, with full bibliography; Hopkins 1983; Toynbee 1971. For women's lament in Roman funerary ritual, see Richlin 2001; Dutsch, this volume. On lament in Vergil's *Aeneid*, see Fantham 1999, 223–226; Nugent 1992; Perkell 1997; Wiltshire 1989. Recent scholarship has also analyzed the many scenes of female lament in Statius's *Thebaid* from literary, feminist, and sociohistorical perspectives: see Dietrich 1999; Fantham 1999; Lovatt 1999; Pagán 2000.

3. I was unable to consult Behr 2007 while drafting this chapter. For discussion of male lament, albeit in a Greek context, see Suter, this volume. Richlin (2001) argues that at Rome male lament was a conventional feature of the law courts.

4. Fantham 1999, 222–223.

5. On the gendered expectations of public lament in Rome, see Dutsch, this volume.

6. Treggiari 1993, 484–498, esp. 493–495; Richlin 2001. On the function of class distinctions in Roman lament, see Richlin 2001, 241–245.

7. Fantham 1999, 223.

8. I quote the text from Housman's *Lucan* (1958); unless otherwise stated, all translations are my own.

9. Masters (1992, 3–10) brilliantly sketches Lucan's thematization of delay as a means of registering an anti-Caesarian ("Pompeian") reluctance to renarrate the civil war in his *Bellum Ciuile*; the simile (2.21–28) stands as yet another instance of this thematization.

10. Cf. Masters 1992, 5: "Lucan is always on the sidelines, so to speak; often entering into the poem in his own person, he shouts encouragement or cries out in

dismay," as here. For this Lucanian reflex, see the bibliography collected in Masters 1992, 5 n. 14.

11. Cf. ibid., 10: "The poem is a civil war. Lucan is Caesarian in his ambition, but Pompeian in his remorse; the Pompeian in him condemns Caesar, but the Caesarian in him condemns—kills—Pompey."

12. Cf. Fantham 1999, 223. Corbeill notes of mourning ritual in classical antiquity that "the woman's function tends to concentrate on ensuring the destiny of the individual corpse, while men use grieving to maintain the continuity of the community and the status of families within the community" (2004, 69). This statement encapsulates the gender ideology of lament in ancient Rome, where women's laments—with the exception of the *nenia*, on which see Dutsch, this volume—were ideally restricted to the private sphere. For this reason, excessive (i.e., public) lament, particularly by women, was restricted by senatorial legislation at Rome: see Corbeill 2004, 75–77. Livy 22.55.3–8 records the Senate's public decree confining women to their homes and forbidding them to lament publicly in the aftermath of Cannae. This gender division contrasts strongly with the Greek tradition, where women's public lamentation was used to showcase the families' status. The results were similar however: repeated legislative efforts to limit women's public lament; see Alexiou 1974, 14–23; Loraux 1990, 19–48. For a comparison between Greek and Roman conventions of lament, see Loraux 1990, 49–56.

13. Fantham 1999, 223.

14. On the Roman association of women with excessive emotion, especially in the context of grief and mourning, see Richlin 2001, 231–235.

15. See Papanghelis 1987; Saylor 1967; cf. Hor. *C.* 2.9.9, Domitius Marsus fr. 7 Courtney; and Ov. *Am.* 3.9.1–4. Classical literary criticism had long associated the genre of elegy with mourning, and this association was the subject of renewed elaboration in the elegiac and lyric poetry of the Augustan period: see Hinds 1987, 103–104; cf. Hor. *C.* 1.33.2, 2.9.9, *AP* 75–78; Prop. 1.22; and Cat. 65.12.

16. On the conventional themes and formulas of lament, based on Greek culture but mutatis mutandis applicable to ancient Rome, see Alexiou 1974, 161–184; Derderian 2001, 35–40. Perkell (this volume) questions the normative value of the laments in *Iliad* 24, and her literary critical reading of these laments persuasively demonstrates both their individual force and their closural propriety within the epic. By Lucan's day, the cultural authority of the Homeric epics had lent these laments a "canonical" status—whether for emulation, transgression, or problematization.

17. Murnaghan 1987, 27 n. 12. Richlin (2001, 240–243) argues—in dialogue with Stears (this volume)—that this attire is an indicator of low social status.

18. See Murnaghan 1987, 209.

19. Cf. Mayer 1981, 99.

20. See Nugent 1992, on Verg. *Aen.* 9.477–502; Murnaghan 1999. Cf. Derderian 2001, 15–62. See also Perkell, this volume, with more bibliography, for Homer's manipulation of this function of lamentation.

21. On city laments, a very ancient pan-Mediterranean genre, see Bachvarova, this volume; Alexiou 1974, 83–101.

22. See Corbeill 2004, 77; Toynbee 1971; Dutsch, this volume.

23. Cf. Perkell, this volume, on the Iliadic focus on "bitterness and pain" in female lament and the lamenting woman's expression of an alternative range of moral and human value, unrelated to martial glory.

24. Lucan's portrait of Cornelia is reminiscent of the Iliadic Helen. See Martin (this volume), who analyzes her speeches and finds them so full of lament characteristics (in, e.g., diction and imagery) that he argues that she is portrayed as a lamenter long before her lament for Hector in *Iliad* 24.

25. Cf. Alexiou 1974, 161–165.

26. Toynbee 1971, 55. Cf. Alexiou 1974, 178–181, esp. 179, where she notes the frequency of this conventional topos of lament in Latin epigraphy. The funeral of Sulla, described by Appian in his *Civil Wars* (*BC* 1.105–106), was a particularly magnificent example of the kind, as Toynbee notes: "His corpse was carried on a golden litter and was accompanied by more than two thousand golden crowns and by axes and other symbols of the offices held by him in life. In the procession were trumpeters and pipers, Vestal Virgins, the senators and magistrates, and vast crowds of soldiers, horse and foot, as well as of citizens" (1971, 55).

27. Lucan writes:

[S]ic fatus plenusque sinus ardente fauilla
peruolat ad truncum, qui fluctu paene relatus
litore pendebat. summas dimouit harenas
et collecta procul lacerae fragmentea carinae
exigua trepidus posuit scrobe. nobile corpus
robora nulla premunt, nulla strue membra recumbent:
admotus Magnum, non subditus, accipit ignis. (8.752–758)

So saying he filled his pockets with the burning embers
and rushed back to the body, which, as it hung upon the
shore, had nearly been carried back by a wave. He scraped
away the surface of the sand, and hastily laid in a narrow
trench the pieces of a broken boat which he had gathered
at a distance. No wood supports that famous corpse, on no
pile are the limbs laid; the fire that receives Magnus is not
laid beneath him but beside him.

28. Toynbee 1971, 50.

29. Corbeill (2004, 77–84) adduces visual and textual evidence to show that men and women performed some of the same mourning gestures in the domestic funerary context but that certain gestures (such as bare feet) were gender specific to women, as was the more excessive wailing. See also Suter, this volume, for similar evidence in the Greek materials.

30. Foley 2001, 151, with bibliography on modern Greek comparanda.

31. Cf. Nugent 1992.

32. Corbeill (2004, 83) comments that the performance of private mourning ritual is commonly gender specific to women but notes the performance of such ritual by clients of the deceased, slaves and freedmen, on a relief from the tomb of the Haterii. For reliefs that show women taking the lead in the expression of grief in ancient Roman funerary ritual, see Corbeill 2004, figs. 8 and 13.

33. The antitheses of Cato's speech are typical of Greek lament; cf. Alexiou 1974, 131–160.

34. Cf. Corbeill 2004, 68–82. On the conventions of the Roman *laudatio funebris*, see Kierdorf 1980; for the manipulation of aristocratic funerals for political ends, see Flower 1996, 91–127.

35. Male co-option of women's laments is a recurrent theme of the contributions to this volume, especially those by Bachvarova, Rutherford, Perkell, and Stears.
36. Cf. the conclusions of Perkell 1997 and her chapter in this volume.

BIBLIOGRAPHY

Alexiou, Margaret. 1974. *The Ritual Lament in Greek Tradition*. Cambridge.
———. 2002. *The Ritual Lament in Greek Tradition*. 2nd ed. Rev. D. Yatromanolakis and P. Roilos. Lanham, Md.
Behr, F. D. 2007. *Feeling History: Lucan, Stoicism, and the Poetics of Passion*. Columbus, Ohio.
Bodel, J. 1999. Death on Display: Looking at Roman Funerals. In *The Art of Ancient Spectacle*, ed. B. Bergmann and C. Kondoleon, 259–281. Studies in the History of Art 56. Washington, D.C.
Corbeill, A. 2004. *Nature Embodied. Gesture in Ancient Rome*. Princeton.
Derderian, K. 2001. *Leaving Words to Remember: Greek Mourning and the Advent of Literacy*. Leiden.
Dietrich, J. S. 1999. *Thebaid*'s Feminine Ending. *Ramus* 28: 40–52.
Dué, C. 2002. *Homeric Variations on a Lament by Briseis*. Lanham, Md.
———. 2006. *The Captive Woman's Lament in Greek Tragedy*. Austin.
Fantham, R. E. 1999. The Role of Lament in the Growth and Eclipse of Roman Epic. In *Epic Traditions in the Contemporary World*, ed. M. Beissinger, J. Tylus, and S. Wofford, 221–235. Berkeley.
———, ed. 1992. *Lucan, De Bello Civili Book II*. Cambridge.
Flower, H. 1996. *Ancestor Masks and Aristocratic Power in Roman Culture*. Oxford.
Foley, H. 2001. *Female Acts in Greek Tragedy*. Princeton.
Hinds, S. 1987. *The Metamorphosis of Persephone*. Cambridge.
Holst-Warhaft, G. 1992. *Dangerous Voices: Women's Laments and Greek Literature*. London.
———. 2000. *The Cue for Passion: Grief and Its Political Uses*. Cambridge, Mass.
Hopkins, K. 1983. *Death and Renewal. Sociological Studies in Roman History 2*. Cambridge.
Housman, A. E., ed. 1958. *Lucan, Belli Civilis Libri Decem*. Rev. ed. Oxford.
Kierdorf, W. 1980. Laudatio funebris: *Interpretationen und Untersuchungen zur Entwicklung der römischen Leichenrede*. Meisenheim am Glan, Germany.
Loraux, N. 1990. *Les mères en deuil*. Paris.
Lovatt, H. 1999. Competing Endings: Re-reading the End of the *Thebaid* Through Lucan. *Ramus* 28: 126–151.
Masters, J. 1992. *Poetry and Civil War in Lucan's* "Bellvm Civile." Cambridge.
Mayer, R., ed. 1981. *Lucan, Civil War VIII*. Warminster, U.K.
Murnaghan, S. 1987. *Disguise and Recognition in the* Odyssey. Princeton.
———. 1999. The Poetics of Loss in Greek Epic. In *Epic Traditions in the Contemporary World*, ed. M. Beissinger, J. Tylus, and S. Wofford, 203–220. Berkeley.
Nugent, S. G. 1992. Vergil's "Voice of the Women" in *Aeneid* V. *Arethusa* 25: 255–292.
Pagán, V. E. 2000. The Mourning After: Statius' *Thebaid* 12. *American Journal of Philology* 121: 423–452.
Papanghelis, T. 1987. *Propertius: A Hellenistic Poet on Love and Death*. Cambridge.
Perkell, C. 1997. The Lament of Juturna: Pathos and Interpretation in the *Aeneid*. *Transactions of the American Philological Association* 127: 257–286.

Richlin, A. 2001. Emotional Work: Lamenting the Roman Dead. In *Essays in Honor of Gordon Williams: Twenty-five Years at Yale*, ed. E. Tywalsky and C. Weiss, 229–248. New Haven.

Saylor, C. 1967. *Querelae*: Propertius' Distinctive, Technical Name for His Elegy. *Agon* 1: 142–149.

Seremetakis, C. N. 1991. *The Last Word: Women, Death, and Divination in the Inner Mani*. Chicago.

Toynbee, J. M. C. 1971. *Death and Burial in the Roman World*. Ithaca, N.Y.

Treggiari, S. 1993. *Roman Marriage. Iusti Coniuges from the Time of Cicero to the Time of Ulpian*. Oxford.

Wiltshire, S. F. 1989. *Private and Public in Virgil's* Aeneid. Amherst, Mass.

12

NENIA: GENDER, GENRE, AND LAMENT IN ANCIENT ROME

Dorota Dutsch

Two discourses were involved in the Roman funeral. One, the official *laudatio funebris*, a speech commemorating members of the upper class, was the domain of male relatives of the deceased. The other, a chant called *nenia*, was entrusted to female professionals and could thus offer us a rare example of Roman women's poetic skills.[1] But while the *laudatio* is relatively well documented, the *nenia* remains an enigma.[2] We have no script of a genuine lament sung at a Roman funeral, and what evidence we do have is baffling.[3] The word *nenia* itself, in addition to meaning "funeral chant," could denote a nursery rhyme, a load of rubbish, or a magical incantation, and it even—according to one late source—had some obscure connection with the extremity of the intestine.[4] Finally, a goddess with this name, apparently worshipped in a small shrine outside the Porta Viminalis (*Fest.* 163M), was believed to look after those living out their final days.[5]

In the hope of exposing the strange twist of imagination that brought together the meanings of "dirge" and "rubbish" (not to mention a section of the digestive tract) into a single Latin word, this essay will try to assemble the scattered evidence regarding various types of the *nenia*. Through a detailed examination of this evidence, I will attempt to recover some of the rules and cultural connotations of this lost genre practiced by women from the grove of the goddess Libitina.

THE CROSSING

The *nenia* was embedded in an elaborate sequence of rites that accompanied the ultimate transition, the one between life and death. The Romans, it can be argued, conceptualized physical death as only the initial phase of a larger transformation, as the deceased person remained a member of the clan, either one of the friendly *di manes* or one of the hostile *lemures*, demanding annual propitiation. The funeral ritual thus involved the delicate task of driving the deceased away from the living without antagonizing him or her. It was a matter to be handled with extreme care, and all members of the community, both male and female, had their particular roles to play in this ritual.[6]

The journey from life to death officially began when the relatives summoned the deceased by name (*conclamatio*); no reply was taken as a proof of death not only for obvious biological reasons but also because of the belief that a living person would respond to his or her name even while asleep.[7] The women then had the ritually unclean job of washing the body in cold water and dressing it before the laying out (*collocatio*) that all attended.[8] Next both men and women marched in the grand procession (*pompa*) that formed after a few days of the *collocatio* to accompany the deceased to the place of burial, and, although both genders expressed grief, only the female relatives were expected to engage in moaning and self-mutilation.[9] Affluent families would also hire professional mourners, called *praeficae*, who not only conducted the ritual wailing but also sang the *nenia* to the accompaniment of pipe music.[10] Music was so essential to the execution of the dirge that Ovid was able to assert that, during a legendary exile of the flute players from Rome, "no *nenia* led the recently dead on their ultimate journey" (*Fasti* 6.668), stressing the importance of the music and intimating at the same time that both the music and the dirge were meant to have an effect on the deceased.[11]

A relief from Amiternum, believed to depict a typical nonaristocratic *pompa* from the late Republic or early Empire, gives the impression that, crowded and noisy though the procession, with its musicians and professional wailers, must have been, the participants walked in set formation. The relief shows the musicians with their instruments and the *praeficae* tearing their hair in front of the catafalque, while the surviving members of the *gens* (both male and female) follow the bier.[12] Did this arrangement—musicians and *praeficae* at the head of the procession, the relatives at the end, and the bier in between—have any symbolic connotations? The evidence from aristocratic funerals, which, in addition to musicians and *praeficae*, employed actors to impersonate the dead man and his distinguished ancestors, suggests that it did.[13] According to the testimony of Diodorus of Sicily (60–30 B.C.E.), the impersonators of the dead walked at the head of the procession with the musicians and hired mourners.[14] The funeral procession would thus have portrayed the family on a continuum from past to present:

first the impersonated ancestors, then the liminal figure of the recently dead member, and finally, the living. In this symbolic configuration, the *praeficae* walking at the head of the procession would then have been associated with the afterlife. It is tempting to conjecture that the role of the ritual performers (the *praeficae*, the musicians, and the impersonators of the dead) might have been to lure the spirits of the newly deceased by song and music, enticing them to abandon the company of the living and cross over to the realm of the dead. Emanating from the side of the bier that represented the afterlife, the sound of the *nenia* would have thus been well suited to guide "the recently dead on their ultimate journey" (Ovid *F.* 6.668). The assumption that the paid mourners led the deceased to the underworld, where he or she would henceforth belong, sheds new light on the role of the *praeficae* and, consequently, on the character of the *nenia*.

THE SINGER AND HER SONG

Praefica, the title given to each of the professional mourners, is usually taken to signify "the one in charge."[15] Her function was comparable to that of the leading lamenters in Greek epic.[16] However, the Roman *praeficae*, or ritual performers enacting grief, were not related to the deceased and in this respect more closely resemble the specialized *taptara* wailers who appear in Hittite texts.[17] According to Varro (*L.* 7.70), even Aristotle, in a lost treatise on barbarian customs, commented on the Roman habit of hiring "a woman from the sacred grove [of Libitina] to sing praises in front of the house of the deceased" and might have reflected on the benefits of hiring strangers to perform such an intimate task as praising the individual achievements of the dead.[18]

A rationale for this custom can be found in Servius's comment on line 484 in book 9 of the *Aeneid*, where his manuscript reads *funera mater*.[19] Proposing that the word *funera* is a contraction for *funerea*, the commentator offers an otherwise unattested piece of information: "[N]am apud maiores funereas dicebant eas ad quas funus pertinet, ut sororem, matrem: nam praeficae, ut et supra diximus, sunt planctus principes, non doloris" (Our ancestors called the women concerned with the funeral, such as a mother or a sister, *funereae*; for the *praeficae*, as we said above, stand out in mourning but not in pain). The credibility of Servius's reading of *funera* is less relevant than his final statement drawing a sharp distinction between the ritual gestures of lament and real pain. Indeed, as will be discussed later, this split between prescribed mourning and grief is vital to an understanding of the Roman funerary custom—the duty of the *praeficae* was not to feel genuine grief but to enact it.

In addition to the gestures of mourning and the *nenia*, the *praefica* appears to have performed a eulogy at some earlier stages. One of the oldest descriptions of the *praefica* is an account that can be reconstructed from Nonius's quotations from Varro (116–127 B.C.E.) hinting that the meaning of the name *praefica* had undergone some changes in the recent past:

[I]bi a muliere, quae optuma uoce esset, perquam laudari; dein
neniam cantari solitam ad tibias et fides . . . ; haec mulier
uocitata olim praefica usque ad Poenicum bellum.
(Serv. Dan. *A*.727, Non. 145 Met 67M z 101)[20]

There praise was uttered by a woman whose voice was best; then
usually the *nenia* was performed to the accompaniment of the flute
and a stringed instrument. . . . This woman used to be called
praefica until the Punic War.

According to this account, a woman with an exquisite voice "praised" the
deceased before singing the *nenia* to the accompaniment of both the flute
and a stringed instrument (*fides*), and in earlier times this performer of
praise and lament would have been called a *praefica*, whereas later this title
was presumably also used for all hired mourners.[21] Although the nature of
this eulogy remains unclear, the reference to the quality of the performer's
voice suggests that, unlike the *laudatio funebris*, her eulogy was sung
rather than spoken. The *nenia* itself seems to have been a musical piece
as well.[22] Varro's juxtaposition of *laudari* and *neniam cantari*, however,
invites the reader to think of the two genres as distinct and intimates that
(originally at least) the *nenia* would have had a function apart from
praising the dead. The two might have also been performed at different
times and in different venues. Whereas the eulogy apparently would have
been sung in front of the house (Varro *L*. 7.70), the *nenia*, along with the
fletus and *planctus*, belonged to the funeral procession.

In *De legibus*, Cicero testifies to yet another style of funeral, in which
the *nenia* complemented a *laudatio funebris* in the assembly rather than
the eulogy performed by the chief wailer:

Reliqua sunt in more: funus ut indicatur, si quid ludorum;
dom<in>usque funeris utatur accenso atque lictoribus
honoratorum uirorum laudes in contione memorentur,
easque etiam cantus ad tibicinem prosequatur, cui nomen
neniae. (2.61–62)

The remaining [funeral arrangements] depend on custom:
that there must be a funeral and perhaps some games; that
he who is in charge of a funeral should be granted torches
and lictors, that the praiseworthy acts of distinguished men
should be commemorated in the assembly, and that this should
also be followed by a song performed to pipe music, which
is called *nenia*.[23]

Cicero clearly distinguishes between "praises in the assembly" and the
nenia, stressing once again that the *nenia* is quite distinct from the
praises in the assembly, and that it was the very last element of the funeral
ritual.[24]

THE SINGER AND HER TEARS

According to Servius (*ad Aen.* 6.216), lamentations did not end until the body was burned, the ashes were collected, and the last word, *ilicet*, "you may go," was pronounced. Only then were the people standing around and responding to the lamentations (*fletibus*) of the *praefica* free to go. Because it was executed by the mourners, the *nenia* was associated with the traditional sounds and gestures of grief. Just such a perception of the *nenia* as closely linked to the other elements of the mourner's performance informs Horace's (65–8 B.C.E.) famous claim to immortality, where we find *neniae* listed along with the appearance of mourning (*luctus*), lamentations (*quaerimoniae*), and wailing (*clamor*) as customary tokens of grief.[25] As noted above, these tokens were not reserved for the *praeficae*, who seem rather to have acted as leaders showing others the ritual way to mourn. According to Claudius (*Gram.* 80), the name *praefica* meant that she "was to instruct the slave-women on how to lament."[26] Servius (*ad Aen.* 6.216) explains that she was the "leader of lamentations" (*princeps planctuum*), and Festus (223.16, Lindsay 250) confirms that such "leaders" were hired to lament the dead and to direct the chest beating.[27]

The exact meaning of the ritual actions of mourners (directed by the *praeficae*) was deemed obscure even before Cicero's time (106–43 B.C.E.). In *De legibus* (2.59–64), he quotes injunctions against excessive spending from the laws of the Twelve Tables. In the laws targeting luxury was a clause specifically forbidding excessive lamentation (*nimiam lamentationem*):

"[M]ulieres genas ne radunto neue lessum funeris ergo habento."
Hoc ueteres interpretes, Sex. Aelius, L. Acilius, non satis se
intellegere dixerunt, sed suspicari uestimenti aliquod genus
funebris, L. Aelius "lessum" quasi lugubrem eiulationem, ut uox
ipsa significat.

"Let the women not scratch their cheeks or have a *lessus* on
account of the funeral." Ancient commentators, Sex. Aelius and
L. Acilius, said that they did not quite understand the meaning
of the latter [*lessus*] but suspect that it was some kind of
funerary attire. L. Aelius said that *lessus*, as the name itself suggests,
was some sort of funerary ululation.

Given the context—laws against excessive spending—we may speculate that this injunction of the Twelve Tables pinpoints the use of the *praeficae* who charged for their services. This reference to mourning in the context of spending is disturbing precisely because it calls attention to the fact that these women were selling rather intimate merchandise—their own blood and tears.

Servius reports that, according to Varro, the display of blood had a quite specific ritual function—"to make amends to those in the nether-land."[28]

He goes on to explain that while some men consider this custom a substitute for human sacrifice, others maintain that the blood is offered not only as a spectacle but also as a make-believe feast for the spirits of the dead, "so that they may seem (*ut videantur*) to obtain what they had lost."[29] In light of Servius's comments, the "sacrifice" of the *praeficae* appears to have been meant to offer a semblance and only a semblance (it is not desirable to fortify the dead excessively) of nourishment for the dead expected to lure them in the direction of the funeral conduct.

There is, as Corbeill has demonstrated in a recent monograph on the cultural functions of gesture in Rome, ample evidence that certain rituals of the Roman obsequies mirrored the rituals surrounding birth.[30] Given this evidence, it seems legitimate to correlate the role of the women in the funeral rites with the role they played in the ceremonies associated with birth. Indeed, in discussing the female mourners, Corbeill draws attention to an offering other than blood and tears that they would surely have provided when exposing and beating their breasts—milk. In support of his thesis, he quotes a remark by Servius, which states that the shadows of the dead sustain themselves on blood and milk, the beaten breast supplying the latter: "[U]mbrae autem sanguine et lacte satiantur: unde feminae quae mortuos prosequuntur ubera tundunt, ut lac exprimant" (The shadows satisfy their appetite on blood and milk; this is why the women who accompany the dead beat their breasts in order to press out milk; Serv. *ad Aen.* 5.78).[31]

This interpretation, as Corbeill observes, has linguistic support: the literary sources refer several times to breasts exposed at funerals as *ubera* (usually meaning "lactating breasts") rather than the more neutral *pectora*. The comment of Servius implies, therefore, that the weeping and bleeding mourners might also have acted as macabre wet nurses of sorts, guiding their charges in the direction of the tomb. Certainly, as women in charge of the nurturing of the "new-dead," the *praeficae* would have performed duties reminiscent of those of nurses. Similar female figures linked to both death and birth appear in Hittite documents wherein "the midwife" was possibly a stock figure played by ritual actors during funerals and the day of one's death was known as "the day of the mother."[32] It is not entirely surprising, then, that the song of the Roman *praeficae* leading the dead on their final journey bore the same name as a nursery rhyme.

THE SINGER AND HER STATUS

To be sure, selling praises and tears must not have been a highly respected occupation in Roman society. A monody sung by the soldier Stratophanes in Plautus's (241–153 B.C.E.) *Truculentus* insinuates that this capacity to praise anyone is coextensive with a lack of personal virtue. When the (not so) brave warrior desires to put down "those who wield sharp tongues at home" (490–494), he suggests that such a man could easily replace a *praefica* at his funeral: [A]rgutum civem mihi habeam pro praefica,/quae alios conlaudat, eapse sese vero non potest ("I could have a shrill-voiced man instead of a *praefica* who praises others but cannot in fact praise herself"; 495–496). Thus, by the third to second century B.C.E., the *praefica* was construed as a giver of praise, but only such praise as could be dismissed as worthless babble, and the worthlessness was thought to derive from the reputation of the *praefica* herself.[33]

The satirist Lucilius (ca. 180–103 B.C.E.) would seem to concur with just such a view; he alludes to the actions of the *praeficae* as metonymic of insincere praise, the very kind of praise he refuses to bestow on his own friends. When describing the hired mourners, he stresses their status as paid performers and the fact that their feigned emotional engagement involves not only their words but also their bodies (953–955):"[M]ercede quae conductae flent alieno in funere/praeficae, multo et capillos scindunt et clamant magi" (The *praeficae* hired for money weep at a stranger's funeral, tear their hair, and shriek loudly; 955).[34] Based on the premise that the ritual performer mourns but does not grieve, the satirical remarks found in Plautus and Lucilius exploit the traditional split between mourning and pain so poignantly identified by Servius. The rationale for the mockery may, however, entail more than mistrust toward a performer whose feigned grief was liable to become symbolic of hypocrisy. The price for scratches and cuts implied in the Twelve Tables laws against spending reminds us that the mourners were paid for producing blood and tears, that is, secretions from their own bodies. Not unlike wet nurses and prostitutes, the women from the grove of Libitina were selling more than their words.

THE OTHER PRAISE

The evidence for a basic text of the *nenia* is so scarce that we must begin our discussion of what the genre might have been by specifying what it was not. It was not a *laudatio funebris*. The best-attested and most exhaustively studied aspect of the Roman funeral, the *laudatio* was a hallmark of distinction reserved for members of the upper classes, both male and female, and often sanctioned by the state.[35] In the case of particularly influential individuals, the *laudatio* was delivered in the forum (instead of the place of burial) and followed by the procession of *imagines*.[36] Praising the ancestors of the dead and his or her commendable achievements was entrusted to a male, often to the youngest and least experienced of the *gens*, because the task was considered an easy one.[37] By setting grief in a larger moral, social, and historical context, the *laudatio* thus encouraged the acceptance of loss and almost always featured a consolatory portion addressed to the living.[38]

The *laudatio funebris* portrayed the deceased aristocrat as someone who had obtained gifts from the community (its cultural heritage, education, and tokens of recognition) and had in turn served this community in various capacities. The *laudatio* represented the final transaction between the individual and his or her society: in exchange for acknowledging the special contribution of the deceased aristocrat, the community garnered for itself an edifying example. Polybius (200–118 B.C.E.), in stressing this latter aspect of the public *laudatio*, describes the solemn and static spectacle: praises were uttered in the forum in front of a standing audience, with the body of the dead placed in the upright position at the rostra while the actors impersonating the ancestors were seated nearby (6.53.1).

The performance context of the *nenia* would have been quite different from the stationary and controlled character of the *laudatio*, whether uttered at the burial place or *in foro*. All sources agree in stressing that the dirge was chanted after the *laudatio*, that is, when the procession regrouped with the musicians, the actors (representing at this point both the dead and the ancestors), and the *praeficae* at its head.[39] Far from a staid prose speech, the *nenia* was most likely a chant performed in procession (cf. Sen. *Ap.* 12.3) amid ritual shrieks. The difference between the *nenia* and the prose *laudatio* is apparent in Appian's reference to Caesar, who "in the midst of mournful songs seemed to speak in person," uses the word *threnos*, the best Greek approximation for the word *nenia*, also suggesting that the comments uttered by the impersonators of the dead might have occasionally interfered with the lamentations and offering us a glimpse into this strange atmosphere wherein the deceased person had the opportunity to comment on his or her own death.[40]

PARODIES

These scattered allusions to the circumstances under which the *nenia* was performed still leave us without specific information regarding its content; for this we must turn to literary imitations. Just one longer poem in our entire Latin corpus is labeled a *nenia*, a parody appearing in Seneca's *Apocolocyntosis*, beginning at 12.3. The lines linking the dirge to the main narrative offer an interesting testimony to first-century perceptions about the *nenia*'s function and the reactions expected from its addressee. In accordance with Appian's information that the dead were envisioned as listening and, at times, even responding to their own dirges, Claudius is shown as a consumer satisfied with his funeral and his *nenia*, both of which are said to have played a crucial role in his posthumous experience (12.3): "Claudius ut vidit funus suum, intellexit se mortuum esse. Ingenti enim μεγαλῷ χορικῷ naenia cantabatur anapaestis" (Upon seeing his own funeral, Claudius understood that he was dead. For a *naenia* in anapests was being chanted by a huge *grand choeur*).

This comment, though meant to highlight Claudius's purportedly abysmal stupidity, sums up the function of the *nenia* and the funeral procession as a performance to convince the dead that they are no longer alive. This assumption that the dirge is ultimately addressed to the deceased and meant to please them also informs the intervention by Seneca that ends the *nenia* (13.1): "Delectabatur laudibus suis Claudius, et

cupiebat diutius spectare" (Claudius found delight in his own praises and
wanted to look at his funeral some more).

The *nenia* that so pleased its addressee is performed by a chorus
during the funeral procession and (being a song performed in procession)
is appropriately set in anapests:

> Fundite fletus, edite planctus, resonet tristi clamore forum:
> cecidit pulchre cordatus homo
> quo non alius fuit in toto
> fortior orbe.
> Ille citato vincere cursu   (5)
> poterat celeres, ille rebelles
> fundere Parthos levibusque sequi
> Persida telis, certaque manu
> tendere nervum, qui praecipites
> vulnere parvo figeret hostes,   (10)
> pictaque Medi terga fugacis.
> Ille Britannos ultra noti litora ponti
> et caeruleos scuta Brigantas
> dare Romuleis colla catenis
> iussit et ipsum nova Romanae   (15)
> iura securis tremere Oceanum.
> Deflete virum, quo non alius
> potuit citius discere causas,
> una tantum parte audita,
> saepe neutra. Quis nunc iudex   (20)
> toto lites audiet anno?
> Tibi iam cedet sede relicta,
> qui dat populo iura silenti,
> Cretaea tenens oppida centum.
> Caedite maestis pectora palmis,   (25)
> O causidici, venale genus.
> Vosque poetae lugete novi,
> vosque in primis qui concusso
> magna parastis lucra fritillo."[41]

Pour out tears, utter laments, let the forum resound with sorrowful clamor:
Dead is a man with the heart of a hero.
No one was a match for his strength
all the world wide.
This was a man who had been able to outrun the swiftest in hasty race, to crush
the rebellious Parthians, to pursue the Persians with light arrows, and
to strain the
bow with steady hand to deal a tiny wound
to the fleeing enemy right in the painted back of cowardly Medes.

He commanded the Britons who live beyond the shores of the known sea
and the blue-painted Brigantes
to yield their necks to the Roman yoke and
Ocean himself [he made] tremble before the new laws of the Roman
hatchet.
Bewail the man who faster than anyone
could dispense justice,
having heard only one of the two parties
and sometimes neither. Which judge will now listen to litigations all
year long?
On your behalf, he who gives the dead their laws and rules the
hundred cities of
Crete resigns his seat.
Batter your chests with baleful hands,
O you lawyers, you mercenary race.
Mourn, you modernist poets,
and, more than anyone, you who have made big money shaking
the dice box.

Seneca's *nenia* incorporates elements of a eulogy and has a tripartite structure consisting of calls to mourning, declarations of death, and eulogies.
There are three calls to mourning, each expressed in the imperative mood
(1, 19, 27) and followed by a unit that in itself is tripartite. The first and
longest (5–17) includes two mock-heroic lists, each naming three military
achievements. On land, Claudius excelled at the three skills characteristic of
a coward: running fast, attacking the Parthians, and even using a coward's
weapons of choice (bow and arrows) to attack the Persians and Medes.[42]
The catalog of his (alleged) naval triumphs is tripartite as well (the Britons,
the Brigantes, and Ocean himself). The second call to mourning (19) is
followed by a mock praise of his civic virtues that forms a thesis, antithesis,
and synthesis triad: Claudius was the fastest judge; Claudius was the slowest
judge (that is, he was consummately unpredictable); Minos was preparing to
yield his seat to the worst of judges (18–25).[43] Yet a third call to mourning
(*caedite pectora* [27]) naming three groups of people who have the most
reason to deplore Claudius's death—lawyers, poets, and gamblers—concludes the poem. In addition, this masterpiece of triplicity is composed of
three types of utterances:

Refrains summoning the onlookers to perform gestures of mourning
      (1, 19, 27–29)

Proclamations of death, either direct (2) or implied by an image (21)

Eulogies of Claudius's military (3–17) and civic (18–25) achievements

Eden in his commentary on the *Apocolocyntosis* asserts that the material of Seneca's poem "follows in essence the pattern of arrangement of a

laudatio funebris."[44] Because this would imply that the dirge for Claudius offers us no information about the *nenia*, we must examine this statement closely, comparing Seneca's mock *nenia* with Kierdorf's outline of the later *laudatio*:

> Preface and Epilogue;
>
> The praise of the deceased;
>
> Family and ancestors
>
> Education and Private life
>
> *Honores*
>
> *Res gestae* and *virtutes*
>
> Address to the listeners;
>
> Consolation for the bereft.[45]

Although the eulogy portion of Seneca's *nenia* with its emphasis on *honores* and *res gestae* does indeed resemble the funeral speech, the poem as a whole conspicuously lacks several structural elements characteristic of the *laudatio*. Granted that references to family and ancestors (whom Claudius shared with Nero) might have been suppressed for political reasons, the absence of any reference to education, private life, and, most of all, a consolatory paragraph would still constitute a marked departure from the basic rhetorical pattern. Moreover, the elements present in the mock *nenia* that are not typical of the *laudatio*—calls to mourning and declarations of death—further imply that the peculiarities of Seneca's poem might have been derived from a different model of funerary discourse.

In fact, these same features are found in an earlier "funerary" poem, namely, Catullus's mock lament for Lesbia's *passer* (Poem 3):

> Lugete, o Veneres Cupidinesque,
> et quantum est hominum venustiorum:
> passer mortuus est meae puellae,
> passer, deliciae meae puellae,
> quem plus illa oculis suis amabat—
> nam mellitus erat suamque norat
> ipsam tam bene quam puella matrem,
> nec sese a gremio illius movebat,
> sed circumsiliens modo huc modo illuc
> ad solam dominam usque pipiabat.
> qui nunc it per iter tenebricosum
> illuc, unde negant redire quemquam.
> at vobis male sit, malae tenebrae
> Orci, quae omnia bella devoratis:
> tam bellum mihi passerem abstulistis.

o factum male! o miselle passer!
tua nunc opera meae puellae
flendo turgiduli rubent ocelli.[46]

Lament, O Venuses and Cupids
and all of you, rather charming gentlemen:
the finch is dead, my girl's finch,
my girl's pet;
she loved him more than her own eyes,
for he was a darling and knew his
mistress as well as a girl knows her mother;
he would never leave her lap,
but hopping around here and there
he would chirp just for his mistress.
Now he travels the path of shadows
to that place whence no one, they say, returns.
Damn you, you damned shadows
of death who swallow all things beautiful!
You took away from me such a sweet little bird!
What have you done? Poor little birdie!
Because of you, my girl's lovely eyes
are a bit puffy and red from tears.

Like the mock *nenia* for Claudius, Catullus's *passer* poem begins with a call to mourning immediately followed by an announcement of death (without naming the deceased).[47] Moreover, Catullus's list of three groups of mourners (*Veneres Cupidinesque et quantum est hominum venustiorum*) corresponds to a similar catalog in the final summons of Seneca's *nenia*.[48] In both cases the laudatory portion begins with the relative pronoun and has a similar grammatical structure, mainly clauses introduced by *qui* or *ille*. In both poems, this laudatory portion ends with an image depicting the deceased in the underworld (the *passer* is walking toward Orcus; Claudius is told that Minos is ready to hand in his resignation). Both parodies lack the consolatory element and conclude with a complaint.[49] Both introduce a direct address to the deceased toward the end, and finally, both have a similarly repetitive structure often associated with the oldest Latin *carmina*.[50]

These correspondences suggest that the Roman *nenia* (after having absorbed the *laudatio praeficae*) possibly included the following:

1. Repeated calls to mourning specifying the various gestures (e.g., *caedite pectora*) and sounds (*fletus, planctus*) the *praeficae* were about to make and utter (possibly instructions for the mourners);
2. Repeated announcements of death using a simple formula (cf. Cat. 3.3–4: *passer mortuus est*; and Sen. 3: *cecidit homo*);
3. Lists of the achievements introduced by *qui/quae* or *ille/illa*; and

4. References to groups of people (both our examples have groups of
   three) who are most likely to mourn.

While both our *neniae* contain elements of the *laudatio*—possibly related to the sung *laudatio* of the *praefica* as much as to the spoken
laudatio funebris—the structural and stylistic features of the two poems
fit the ritual function and the performance context conjectured above for
the funeral *nenia*. Specific references to the ritual acts of mourning (cries
and self-mutilation) correspond to the ritual actions performed and
directed by the *praeficae*; the absence of proper names would, in the
actual performance context, be complemented by the ritual *conclamatio*.
Finally, repeated declarations of death correspond to the function of the
nenia—that of guiding the dead away from the house and the surviving
family. Hence, the aesthetic that informs these two mock *neniae* clearly
depends on inner correspondences and repetitions, the latter being especially appropriate for a song performed in procession, that is,
one designed to deliver the same message at various times to different
audiences.

CHILDREN'S *NENIAE*

The only excerpt from an authentic *nenia* that has come down to us is a
portion of a children's poem. The following half a line is reported by
Horace (*Ep.* 1.1.59–63): "Rex eris...si recte facies ("You will be the
ruler...if you follow the rule").[51] Because, as the poet tells us, this line
had been recited (*decantata*) by generations of Curii and Camilli, we can
assume that it came from a *nenia puerorum* of considerable antiquity.[52]
This Latin rhyme apparently belonged to that moment of suspense at the
end of a game just before the results were announced.[53] Moreover, Porphyry (*ad Ep.* 1.1.626) implies that the same *nenia* was still sung in his
times (*pueri lusu cantare solent*) and quotes the second half of this line,
giving us a sample of the stylistic features of a *nenia* outside the funerary
context: "Rex erit qui recte faciet, qui non faciet, non erit."

(a) Ruler will be—who will act by the rule, (b)
(b) Who will not act—will not be. (a)

This juvenile *nenia* reveals a chiastic and highly repetitive structure.
All the words are used twice, with the exception of *rex* and *recte*, which are
nonetheless connected through the root *reg-*. Like the word *nenia* itself,
Porphyry's reconstruction of Horace's jingle relies heavily on duplication.
Two lines of two clauses each, expressed in repeating words, form an even
more radically patterned text than what we have been able to conjecture
for the funerary *nenia*. This highly repetitive language is, moreover,
inscribed in a grammatical pattern consisting of two conditionals typical
of oracular responses and magical formulas.[54]

MARSIAN *NENIA*

The formal similarities between the *nenia* and magical incantation are hardly surprising, given that *nenia* is one of numerous terms the Romans used to denote a text endowed with magical power.[55] A *nenia* of this type was strongly associated with the Marsi, a people of central Italy famed as snake charmers (snakes, it is useful to recall, sometimes represented ancestral spirits; cf. *Aen.* 5.84–93), and the imagery used by the Augustan poets to illustrate how the Marsian song worked relies consistently on images of splitting apart or opening. Horace, for example, reports two folk beliefs, one that the *Marsa nenia* (*Ep.* 17.29) was capable of splitting open a victim's head (*caput dissilire*), and the other that "Marsian voices" could gain control over a person's mind (*Ep.* 5.75–76).[56] It would seem that by the second century B.C.E. the Marsi were already well known for their magical abilities: a fragment of Lucilius containing a description of a glutton invites the reader/listener to picture a man "about to split apart in the middle, just like when the Marsian splits snakes apart with his song" (20.575–576).[57] Furthermore, Marsian chants could lull to sleep vicious hissing snakes and soothe the wounds from their bites. These soothing and sedative effects of the Marsian song are underscored in Vergil's description of Umbro, the leader of the Marsi and a renowned snake charmer:

[V]ipereo generi et graviter spirantibus hydris
spargere qui somnos cantuque manuque solebat
mulcebatque iras et morsus arte levabat.
Sed non Dardaniae medicari cuspidis ictum
evaluit, neque eum iuvere in volnera cantus
somniferi et Marsis quaesitae montibus herbae. (*Aen.* 7.753–758)

With his song and his hand he could shower sleep on the race of vipers and furiously hissing snakes; with his art, he could calm their anger and appease their bites. But he was not strong enough to alleviate the blow of the lance of the descendant of Dardanus. Nor did his sleep-bringing chants nor the herbs gathered in the Marsian mountains.

Together, then, Umbro's healing *cantus* and the head-splitting *Marsa nenia* epitomize the dual nature of the *nenia* as magically endowed with a *pharmakon*-like power to heal as well as harm and to close as well as to open wounds.[58]

According to a strange tale reported by Ovid, the Marsian *nenia* could also cause harm in a more roundabout way by transforming "old women" into strange birds known as *striges* (*Fast.* 6.142–147), which uttered piercing cries and fed on the innards (*intestina*) of newborn babies (an interesting parallel for the newly dead).[59] Ovid tells us that if a nurse happened to enter the infant's room after a visit from these vampire birds, on the baby's pale cheeks she would find the claw marks through which the vampires drew blood (146–147).[60] This blood from the marks on the child's cheeks bears an uncanny resemblance to the blood oozing from the scratches on the cheeks of the mourners, which was an offering to otherworldly creatures. Plautus relates a similar superstition in the *Pseudolus* when he defines *striges* as creatures that "eat up the innards (*intestina*) of the living" (820).[61] Such beliefs associating the *nenia* with loss of the *intestina* (meaning blood and inner strength) through puncture wounds might account for Festus's rather odd comment linking *nenia* to *extrema intestina* (see n. 4).

CONCLUSION

Outside the funeral context, the *nenia* belonged to a discourse associated with the crossing of boundaries. The piercing sound of the *nenia* is itself evoked through various images of penetrating or breaking through, which seem to emphasize the moment at which the vitality leaks through the body's compromised boundaries. Because the Roman dirge has the same name as this splitting song believed to rob the living of their strength, it is reasonable to conjecture that it may similarly have aimed to rob the dead of their remaining strength. As the deceased being escorted to the place of burial were believed to be still vacillating between life and death, loss of vitality would have been an aim of the song that assisted them in crossing to the other side of life.

In light of the magical uses of the *nenia*, its role at the funeral—a ceremony during which a recently deceased person was gradually transformed into an ancestral spirit—becomes clearer. The hired mourners who performed the dirge flattered and appeased the dead and lured them in the direction of the procession. The funerary *nenia* would thus seem to have been a subgenre of a particular discourse used in other types of social performance that involved boundary crossing. The dirge was performed by women who acted as caregivers for the dead, liminal figures of nurses or midwives assisting them in their transition to the other side. Like the incantation of the Marsi, the dirge was associated with breaking through barriers—in the case of the *nenia*, the barrier between life and death.[62] The women from the grove of Libitina would seem to have had the task of helping to effect the split between the living members of the clan and their recently dead relative. Indeed, the extant literary echoes of the *nenia* suggest that a peculiar and highly patterned language, one informed by the aesthetics of repetition, was needed for such a passage. Porphyry's *nenia*, marked by an obsessive concern for patterns, offers a striking example of such discourse. The funeral *nenia* would thus have shared with other subgenres, such as magical incantations and nursery rhymes, both its purpose—to ease transitions—and its aesthetics, exploring patterns within and beyond the symbolic meaning of words.

ACKNOWLEDGMENTS

I am grateful to Ann Suter for her comments on earlier versions of this chapter and to Chris Maisto for her editorial help. I also benefited from the useful advice of several friends and colleagues (Stephen Evans, Frances Hahn, Carolyn Jones, Jo-Ann Shelton, and Benjamin Victor) at various stages of research and writing.

NOTES

1. On gender roles in Roman obsequies, see Corbeill 2004, 68–88; Van Sickle 1987, 44–45. Richlin (2001, 231–233) draws attention to the figure of man in mourning but argues that the task of dealing with pollution was preferably assigned to lower-class women (2001, 241–243). This contrast is reminiscent of that between lament and ἐπιτάφιος λόγος in the Greek tradition; see Derderian 2001, 188; Holst-Warhaft 1992, 4–5. Alexiou ([1974] 2002, 107–108) proposes a broader analysis of the various genres of funerary poetry and prose, dividing them into those based on the ritual act of lamentation performed by women and accompanied by music (θρῆνος, γόος, and κομμός) and those based on the literary activities of men (epigram, ἔλεγος, and ἐπιτάφιος λόγος). Just like the Roman distinction (as argued in Richlin 2001), the Greek needs to be nuanced. As Ann Suter (this volume) argues, male lament probably played a more important role in Greek ritual than previously thought. On the perception of male grief (as distinguished from ritual lamentation), see Treggiari 1998, 19–22.

2. Two monographs, Kierdorf's (1980) and Ochs's (1993), are entirely devoted to the *laudatio*.

3. Heller (1943) collects all ancient passages using the word *nenia*.

4. The dubious spelling *naenia* is found in Plautus (*Ps.* 1278). The link between *nenia* and intestine is suggested in Paul. *Fest.* 163M—*Quidam aiunt neniae ductum nomen ab extremi intestini uocabulo*—and could be derived from *Bac.* 889. On that passage, see Dutsch 2006. Gowers (1992, 108) points out that, etymological accuracy notwithstanding, the association of the *nenia* with offal and rubbish is a valid reflection of ancient perceptions of the Roman dirge.

5. Cf. Aug. *Civ.* 6.9 (Varro *Ant. Div.* 14 fr. 65 Agahd); Arnob. *Nat.* 4.7. On the possible etymologies of *nenia*, see Ernout and Meillet 1967, 437. Grimal (1986, 231) views Nenia as one of the *di indigetes* that accompanied human beings from birth to death.

6. For succinct accounts of the Roman funeral, see, for example, Hopkins 1983, 217–219; Latte 1960, 101; Toynbee 1971, 44–45.

7. For a late testimony to such beliefs, see Apuleius *Met.* 2.30 and his account of how, when the witches called on the dead Thelyphron, he slowly answered their call, obliged by the power of the name, but was preceded by the guardian of his corpse, who happened to bear the same name and who responded to the call faster and thus unwittingly submitted to the mutilation in place of the corpse.

8. Servius (*ad Aen.* 6.218) reports, on Pliny's authority, that both the *conclamatio* and the water temperature were methods of verifying if death had indeed taken place. By the time of Martial, *collocatio* could last up to seven days; cf. Martial *Epigr.* 10.97.3.

9. See the references in Treggiari 1993, 489, 490 n. 47. In the famous tale about the widow of Ephesus, Petronius (*Sat.* 111.2) describes escorting the body with loose hair and beating the naked breast as "the common custom" (*vulgari more funus passis prosequi crinibus aut nudatum pectus in conspectu frequentiae plangere*). Nevertheless, the satirical context implies that this may well be hyperbole: the widow's initial behavior can be expected to surpass an already exaggerated "norm" of wifely duties. Treggiari's (1993, 489–490) cautious assessment that such disfigurement might have been common only in some circles might be preferable to Corbeill's (2004, 82–84) view that mutilation and breast-beating were the norm.

10. Lucilius, fr. 956. Cf. Seneca *Apoc.* 12.3; if there was a *laudatio funebris*, the *nenia* followed it; Cic. *Leg.* 2.61–62. These male musicians, however, acquired a special status that distinguished them from other men, for they were, like actors, considered unfit to bear arms; cf. Jory 1970, 232–233.

11. *Ducit supremos nenia nulla toros*; see also Livy 9.30.5–10. All translations are mine.

12. On the relief of Amiternum, see Toynbee 1971, 46–47, and, more recently, Holliday 2002, 143–144; Hughes 2005. On the meaning of *praefica*, 'the one in charge', see note 15 below.

13. The notion of impersonating the dead is reminiscent of the phenomenon of the "ventriloquism" of the Delian maidens described by Martin (2003, 120–121) and reprinted in this volume.

14. This is part of his description of the funeral of L. Aemilius Paulus (31.25.2), who would have died in 160 B.C.E. See also Sumi 2002, 559–560. If we can trust the testimony of Pliny the Elder (first century C.E.), in the past, when actors were not employed, ancestral wax masks were carried instead (*N.H.* 35.2.6).

15. *OLD*; cf. Ernout and Meillet 1967, 212, under *praeficio*: *qui dirigait*.

16. E.g., *Il.* 18.51, 22.430. Cf. Lizzi 1995, 52–53.

17. On the wailers and other elements of the (especially royal) funerary ritual, see Haase 1994, 219–229; Rutherford, this volume.

18. Asconius Pedianus in his comment on Cicero's *Pro Milone* 29.10 mentions Lucus Libitinae as a place where fasces were kept.

19. Mynors 1969, 9.486, reads: *te tua funere mater.*

20. See also Nonius Marcellus (62 M, Lindsay 92): *praeficae dicebantur apud veteres quae adhiberi solent funeri, mercede conductae, ut flerent et fortia facta laudarent.*

21. See Kierdorf 1980, 97–98.

22. Later descriptions of the *nenia* usually use *carmen* and *cantus*, both of which can refer to magical incantation as well as to singing. Cf., e.g., Quint. *Inst.* 8.2.8: *carmen funebre proprie "nenia"*; and Cic. *De legibus* 2.62.1. Porph. defines *nenia* as *carmen lugubre* (Hor. *Car.* 2.1.37–38) or as *cantus funerum* (*ad Od.* 2. 20 L21). Conversely, the earliest testimony to the *nenia* in Plautus (254–184 B.C.E.) refers to "speaking the *naenia*" (*Truc.* 213: *dicere naeniam*).

23. The text continues to provide a rather confusing piece of information: *quo uocabulo etiam [<apud>] Graecos cantus lugubres nominantur.* Nenia is not attested for us in Greek except for *neniaton*, meaning a Phrygian chant (cf. Ernout and Meillet 1967, 437), and for one reference in a Greek Armenian dictionary to Galen probably written in the sixth century C.E. (Greppin 1987, 489).

24. *De vita populi romani* fr. 110 suggests that by the first century B.C.E., the *nenia* may thus have incorporated the *laudatio praeficae* mentioned by Varro; cf. Kierdorf 1980, 96; Leo 1965, 255; Prieur 1986, 21; Toynbee 1971, 45–47.

25. Cf. Nisbet and Hubbard 1978, 347, on 2.20.2.

26. *Quae praeficeretur ancillis, quemadmodum lamentarentur, praefica est dicta* (Varro *De Lingua* 7.70).

27. Festus 223.16, Lindsay 250: *Praeficae dicuntur mulieres ad lamentandum mortuum conductae quae dant ceteris modum plangendi, quasi in hoc ipsum praefectae.*

28. Quoted in Servius *ad Aen.* 3.67: *ut sanguine ostenso inferis satisfaciant.*

29. Ibid.: *ut id quod amiserunt videantur accipere.*

30. Corbeill (2004, 89–106) assembles such evidence and shows that it supports his hypothesis that Roman funerary ritual can be analyzed as a double birth.

31. Ibid., 86 n. 84.

32. Haase (1994, 216, 233) mentions this euphemism for the day of death along with other ones referring to parents. For a discussion of the meaning of the *hasawas*, "old/wise woman," as "midwife," see Gurney 1977; on the role of these women in magical ritual and in funerals, see Gurney 1977, 45–46, 59–63. Rutherford's (this volume) analysis of the ritual of the *summanza*-cord suggests that it might be symbolic of the umbilical cord.

33. See also Plautus fr. 7.1 *Frivolaria* in Non. 66M: *superaboque omnis argutando praeficas,* "And I shall surpass all the *praeficae* in babbling," where the *praefica* is again used as a byword for a producer of empty words.

34. See Gellius *Noctes* 18.7.3: mourners' voices become the very synonym for emptiness—*philosophi mera estis, ut M. Cato ait, "mortualia"; glosaria namque colligitis et lexidia, res taetras et inanes et friuolas tamquam mulierum uoces praeficarum.*

35. Varro, *De Vita Populi Romani* fr. 110. Cf. Kierdorf 1980, 96; Leo 1965, 255; Prieur 1986, 21; Toynbee 1971, 45–47. Plutarch observed that, unlike the Greek ἐπιτάφιος λόγος, which was reserved for men who died in battle, the Roman *laudatio funebris* could be granted to any man whom the state desired to honor (cf. Ochs 1993, 105). References to prose *laudationes* performed by men to honor prominent political figures in Roman historians imply that such speeches were performed at least as early as the fifth century B.C.E. Livy (2.47.11) mentions speeches by M. F. Vibulanus; see Kierdorf 1980, 95, for more references to other early *laudationes.*

36. Cf. Flower 1996, 115–118.

37. See Van Sickle's emphatic statement about the differences between the *nenia* and the *laudatio*: "The special language of funerals falls into two domains, one male and the other female" (1987, 44). As Ochs points out, commenting on Cic. *De Orat.* 2.10.44–45: "Cicero . . . comes close to removing the funeral speech from the compass of rhetoric. His near dismissal is significant in that he recognizes the unique constraints that praising the dead imposes" (1993, 105). But cf. Ochs 1993, 107.

38. *Laudatio Turiae* is an exception (cf. Kierdorf 1980, 116).

39. Non. 67.8 (quoting Varro *De Vita* 4): *laudari . . . dein neniam cantari;* Cic. *Leg.* 2.62: *at laudes . . . ut cantus . . . prosequatur;* Diom. *GLK* 1.484.22–485.8: *carmen . . . extremum atque ultimum.*

40. Appian *BC* 2.146.611; Horace in *Carm.* 2.1.38 refers to the genre practiced by Simonides of Keos, Θρῆνος, as *nenia.* See also Sumi's (2002, 566–567) analysis of the Suet. *Iul.* 84.2 in support of such an interpretation of Appian's reference to Caesar (that is, his impersonator) speaking on his funeral.

41. There are numerous metrical similarities between the *nenia* and the lament sections in Seneca's tragedies; see Weinreich 1923, 113–114.

42. These are false in Claudius's case; for detailed explanations, see Athanassakis 1973, 115, 117, 119.

43. The first clause introduced by the ablative of *qui* is followed by a rhetorical question introduced by the interrogative *quis*.

44. Eden 1984, 131.

45. Kierdorf 1980, 59.

46. See Quinn 1959, 96, on reading Cat. 3 as a *nenia*; this interpretation lends additional credibility to A. Pomeroy's (2003) reading of *deliciae* as possibly referring to a child slave.

47. This is also significant in the case of Catullus's *passer*, given that Roman pets were given names; Toynbee (1973, 121, 400 n. 315) lists some popular dog names and quotes Fronto's (4.6.2) affectionate reference to his own *passercula minuscula*, named Gratia.

48. Though the apostrophe to those most aggrieved appears to be typical of the *nenia*, the motif existed in Hellenistic literature and is attested in the refrain of Moschus's third ode to Bion, in which the Sicilian Muses are ordered to mourn (3.8, 3.13, 3.19, etc.), as well as in Lucian's *De Luctu*; cf. Alexiou [1974] 2002, 131–140.

49. Three other poems by Catullus (96, 68, and 101) express sorrow at someone's death. Poem 96 is an epigram (cf. *A. P.* 7, 474) ending with the strange and paradoxical consolation that Calvus's love would probably have impressed the deceased girl more than her own death. Poem 68a uses grief to justify a *recusatio*. Poem 101, which addresses Catullus's deceased brother, is a dirge: the poem's only theme is bereavement, and it uses the whole range of vocabulary associated with mourning (*fletus, miser, luctus*) to describe his emotions. However, even this poem differs from our proposed paradigm for the *nenia* by representing the subject (Catullus) as able to put an end to his mourning. The emphatic closure—*atque in perpetuum, frater, ave atque vale*—gives the poem a different flavor from the typically inconsolable tone of the *nenia* (cf. Hor. *Carm.* 2. 20.21).

50. See, e.g., Conte 1994, 20–21, 28, with a bibliographical note. To define a *nenia* Roman writers tend to use the nouns *carmen* or *cantus*. Quintilian (*Inst.* 8.2.8) defines the *nenia* as *carmen funebre*, Cicero (*De Legibus* 2.62.1) calls it a *cantus*, and Porphyry glosses it as *carmen lugubre* (on *Od.* 2.20 L21) or *cantus funerum* (on *Od.* 2.20 L21). Varro's note on the *praefica* quoted above likewise refers to the chanting of the *nenia* (*neniam cantari*); Serv. Dan. *A.* 727, Non. 145.24 *Met* 67M z 101.

51. Nonius (145.24–27), my source for the definition of *nenia* as a song performed during funerals, also describes it (once again on Varro's authority) as "silly and unrefined" (*ineptum et inconditum carmen*), indicating that the funeral *nenia* and the *nenia* of childish rhymes may have been quite close in form.

52. This collocation of lament and childish playfulness is not unparalleled: recall the quotations from the "torty-tortoise" game in Erinna's *Distaff*; see Levianiouk, this volume.

53. See Kiessling and Heinze 1984, 13, on *Ep.* 1.1.59–63, quoting scholia to Pl. *Theat.* 146a.

54. Grottanelli (1996) compares Porphyry's *nenia* with the couplets mocking Caesar (Cassius Dio 43.20), oracular responses noted by Gellius (3.3.7–8), and a magical tablet from Fiesole, dated to the third century B.C.E.; see esp. his (1996, 243) formal analysis. Horace also knew of a *nenia* chanted at the end of the day (*Carm.* 3.28.9–16), possibly as a sort of lullaby meant to calm the listener. According to the testimony of the fifth-century antiquarian Martianus Capella,

similar calming effects could have been ascribed to the funerary *nenia*: Capella has a personified Harmony claim that with her help people have successfully used the *nenia* to appease (*sedaverunt*) the angry spirits of the underworld (9.925).

55. Burris 1936, 143. Similar connections exist between the Greek γόος and γόης; cf. Richlin 2001, 243; and see Bachvarova, this volume.

56. Cf. Porph. *ad Ep.* 17.28.2: *Ipsis, inquit, malis adductus sum, ut credam Sabell<i>s carminibus defigi mentes humanas. Sabella autem carmina pro Marsis posuit, et neniam pro incantatione*; *Ep.* 5.75–76: *Nec vocata mens tua/Marsis redibit vocibus.*

57. Propertius's textually problematic 3.6.28 ascribes a magical power of attraction to bones taken out from gutted snakes: *et lecta exsectis anguibus ossa trahunt*. In light of our argument, the manuscript reading could then hold.

58. Kiessling and Heinze 1984.

59. See also *Ars* 2.102, where, combined with other magical sounds, the Marsian chant is said to assist Medea. In fact, the *strix*, though usually glossed as "bird" (cf. *OLD*), is likely to be a bat; see Oliphant 1913.

60. On the *striges*' habit of drinking blood, see also Prop. 4.5.17. For the fullest account of the witches' habits of transforming themselves into small animals (birds, dogs, mice, and flies are mentioned) in order to enter the room where a dead body is kept and feast on the corpse, see Ap. *M.* 2.23–30.

61. Thus, *uiuis ... intestina quae exedint.*

62. The children's song we hear about, a chant apparently sung before the announcement of results, would also seem linked to a moment of transition. The *Rex erit* chant can be said to have eased the transition between being unaware and aware of the results of a competition, and the lullaby would have helped the transition between being awake and asleep. On funerary ritual as a form of "rite of passage," see Davies 1997, 17–19.

BIBLIOGRAPHY

Alexiou, Margaret. [1974] 2002. *The Ritual Lament in Greek Tradition.* Cambridge. Reprint, New York.

Athanassakis, Apostolos. 1973. *Seneca:* Apocolocyntosis. Lawrence, Kans.

Burris, E. E. 1936. The Terminology of Witchcraft. *Classical Philology* 31 (2): 137–145.

Conte, G. B. 1994. *Latin Literature: A History.* Baltimore.

Corbeill, Anthony. 2004. *Nature Embodied: Gesture in Ancient Rome.* Princeton.

Davies, Douglas, J. 1997. *Death, Ritual, and Belief: The Rhetoric of Funerary Rites.* London.

Derderian, Katherine. 2001. *Leaving Words to Remember: Greek Mourning and the Advent of Literacy.* Leiden.

Dutsch, Dorota. 2006. On Mice and Vampires: Plautus *Bacchides*, 884–9. *Mnemosyne* 59 (3): 421–425.

Eden, P. T. 1984. *Seneca:* Apocolocyntosis. Cambridge.

Ernout, A., and A. Meillet. 1967. *Dictionnaire étymologique de la langue latine.* 4th ed. Paris.

Flower, H. I. 1996. *Ancestor Masks and Aristocratic Power in Roman Culture.* Oxford.

Gowers, Emily. 1992. *The Loaded Table: Representations of Food in Roman Literature.* Oxford.

Greppin, J. A. C. 1987. Latin *Nenia* and the Armenian Galen Dictionary. *American Journal of Philology* 108 (3): 487–490.

Grimal, Pierre. 1986. *The Dictionary of Classical Mythology.* Oxford.

Grottanelli, Cristiano. 1996. Il gioco e la sorte: Sulla filastrocca del re in Roma antica. *Studi e materiali di storia delle religioni* 20 (1–2): 237–246.

Gurney, O. R. 1977. *Some Aspects of Hittite Religion.* Oxford.

Haase, Volkert. 1994. *Geschichte der hethitischen Religion.* Leiden.

Heller, J. L. 1943. Nenia παιγνίον. *Transactions of the American Philological Association* 74: 215–268.

Holliday, Peter. 2002. *The Origins of Roman Historical Commemoration in the Visual Arts.* Cambridge.

Holst-Warhaft, Gail. 1992. *Dangerous Voices: Women's Laments and Greek Literature.* London.

Hopkins, Keith. 1983. *Death and Renewal.* Cambridge.

Hughes, L. A. 2005. Centurions at Amiternum: Notes on the Apisius Family. *Phoenix* 59: 77–91.

Jory, E. J. 1970. Associations of Actors in Rome. *Hermes* 98: 224–253.

Kierdorf, Wilhelm. 1980. Laudatio funebris. *Interpretationen und Untersuchungen zur Entwicklung der römischen Leichenrede.* Meisenheim am Glan, Germany.

Kiessling, Adolf, and Richard Heinze. 1984. *Q. Horatius Flaccus: Oden und Epoden.* 14th ed. Berlin.

Latte, Kurt. 1960. *Römische Religionsgeschichte.* Munich.

Leo, Friedrich. 1965. *Die griechisch-römische Biographie nach ihrer literatischen Form.* Hildesheim.

Lizzi, Rita. 1995. Il sesso e i morti. In *La mort au quotidien dans le monde romain: Actes du colloque organisé par l'Université de Paris IV (Paris-Sorbonne, 7–9 October 1993)*, ed. François Hinard and Marie-Françoise Lambert, 49–68. Paris.

Martin, Richard P. 2003. Keens from the Absent Chorus: Troy to Ulster. *Western Folklore* 62 (2003): 119–142.

Mynors, R. A. B. 1969. *P. Vergili Maronis Opera.* Oxford.

Nisbet, R. G. M., and Margaret Hubbard. 1978. *A Commentary on Horace:* Odes Book II. Oxford.

Ochs, D. J. 1993. *Consolatory Rhetoric: Grief, Symbol, and Ritual in the Greco-Roman Era.* Columbia, S.C.

Oliphant, S. G. 1913. The Story of the *Strix*: Ancient. *Transactions of the American Philological Association* 44: 133–149.

Pomeroy, A. J. 2003. Heavy Petting in Catullus. *Arethusa* 36: 49–60.

Prieur, Jean. 1986. *La mort dans l'antiquité romaine.* Rennes.

Quinn, Kenneth. 1971. *The Catullan Revolution.* Ann Arbor, Mich.

Richlin, Amy. 2001. Emotional Work: Lamenting the Dead. In *Essays in Honor of Gordon Williams: Twenty-five Years at Yale*, ed. Elizabeth Tylawsky and Charles Weiss, 229–248. New Haven.

Smyth, G. R. 1970. *Thesaurus Criticus ad Sexti Propertii Textum.* Leiden.

Sumi, G. S. 2002. Impersonating the Dead: Mimes at Roman Funerals. *American Journal of Philology* 123 (4): 559–585.

Toynbee, J. M. C. 1971. *Death and Burial in the Roman World.* Ithaca, N.Y.

———. 1973. *Animals in Roman Life and Art.* Ithaca, N.Y.

Treggiari, S. 1993. *Roman Marriage:* Iusti Coniuges *from the Time of Cicero to the Time of Ulpian.* Oxford.

——. 1998. Home and Forum: Cicero Between Public and Private. *Transactions of the American Philological Association* 128: 1–23.

Van Sickle, John. 1987. The *Elogia* of the Cornelii Scipiones. *American Journal of Philology* 108: 41–55.

Weinreich, Otto. 1923. *Senecas* Apocolocyntosis; *die Satire auf Tod, Himmel- und höllenfahrt des Kaisers Claudius.* Berlin.

INDEX

281